Implementing Distributed Systems with Java and CORBA

T0237939

Markus Aleksy · Axel Korthaus
Martin Schader

Implementing Distributed Systems with Java and CORBA

With 27 Figures and 13 Tables

 Springer

Dr. Markus Aleksy
Dr. Axel Korthaus
Professor Dr. Martin Schader

University of Mannheim
Schloss
68131 Mannheim
Germany

markus.aleksy@uni-mannheim.de
axel.korthaus@uni-mannheim.de
martin.schader@uni-mannheim.de

Cataloging-in-Publication Data

ISBN 978-3-642-06334-3   e-ISBN 978-3-540-28047-7

Springer is a part of Springer Science+Business Media

springeronline.com

© Springer Berlin · Heidelberg 2010
Printed in Germany

Hardcover-Design: Erich Kirchner, Heidelberg

Preface

This book addresses readers interested in the design and development of distributed software systems with Java and CORBA. The programming language Java, first introduced by Sun Microsystems in 1995 in an attempt to remedy some of the deficiencies of C++, has meanwhile pervaded all fields of software development. CORBA, the Common Object Request Broker Architecture, is an industry standard that enables the platform- and programming language-independent implementation of distributed object-oriented systems.

When developing and testing the examples and exercises for this book, we used three different Object Request Broker products (ORBs) that are available free of charge. The first is JacORB 2.2, a Java object request broker originated in the CS department at Freie Universität Berlin, see http://www.jacorb.org ™ 2
Platform Standard Edition 5.0 Development Kit (JDK), see http://java.sun.com
The third ORB is OpenORB 1.3.1 developed by the Community OpenORB Project, see http://openorb.sf.net. Detailed information on downloading, installing, and customizing these ORBs can be found in Appendix E and at the book's website http://www. The second one is part of Sun's Java wifo.uni-mannheim.de/CORBA in subdirectory ORB.

Under this URL, one also has the possibility to give feedback, send in corrections, or submit any other suggestions for improvement. In subdirectory Examples all the book's examples are provided; in subdirectory Exercises, one finds our solutions to the exercises compiled at the end of the chapters. In the examples, we concentrated on the respective CORBA concept to be explained and did not extend and elaborate them to simulate development of real-world applications.

We would like to thank Lisa Köblitz and Michael Schneider for testing the example programs. Lisa also helped us create the figures and illustrations included throughout the book. Colleen Litschke carefully read and reread the text and corrected earlier versions; many thanks for improving our English. Finally, special thanks to Dr. Martina Bihn of Springer-Verlag and her team for the reliable successful cooperation, which we meanwhile have experienced for many years. Financial help from the University of Mannheim's Prechel-Stiftung e.V., who supported us in multiple ways, is gratefully acknowledged.

Markus Aleksy, Axel Korthaus, Martin Schader

Malibu, Mannheim, Paris   June 2005

Contents

1 Preliminaries

This book addresses readers that are interested in the design and development of distributed software systems relying on the *Common Object Request Broker Architecture* (CORBA). CORBA is an industry standard that has considerably changed the way that modern information systems are developed. It enables the platform- and programming language-independent implementation of distributed object-oriented systems and supports the migration of legacy systems into modern architectures as well. This book is intended in particular for students of computer science and management information systems in their graduate studies as well as for practitioners and professional software developers looking for fast access to CORBA technology and wanting to profit from meaningful code examples. We expect our readers to be equipped with some basic knowledge on distributed systems and to be well versed in object-oriented programming in Java since a detailed introduction into these topics is beyond the scope of this book. In order to visualize static and dynamic system aspects, we employ the *Unified Modeling Language* (UML), which, in its version 2.0, represents the current industry standard for object-oriented modeling languages.

1.1 Organization of the Book

The book is divided into eighteen chapters. Chapter 1 is dedicated to the present preliminary remarks that are intended to provide our readers with some general hints concerning working with the book. Chapter 2 provides some fundamental key concepts—it briefly recapitulates the object-oriented paradigm as well as some basic knowledge on distributed systems. Subsequently, in Chapter 3, we discuss the most important concepts of the CORBA standard that lay the foundation for understanding the CORBA-based development of distributed, object-oriented systems. The central focus of Chapter 4 is the *Interface Definition Language* (IDL)—this is the CORBA-specific language for the description of interfaces, which enables us to define CORBA objects independently of platform and programming language. Chapter 5 provides the link to implementations of distributed systems in a concrete programming language. Here, we focus on the explanation of IDL's binding to the Java programming language. In Chapter 6, we introduce a rather technical part of the CORBA specification, namely the elements of the ORB runtime system, which include the *Object Request Broker* (ORB) itself, the *Portable Object Adapter* (POA), the *Dynamic Invocation Interface* (DII), the *Dynamic Skeleton Interface* (DSI), and others.

In Chapter 7, we start our "hands on" work with CORBA by presenting a first example and describing how it can be deployed and run using the three different ORB products we employ throughout the book. Each of the subsequent chapters contains one or more practical examples that can be executed and tested by our readers. In Chapter 8, we demonstrate how to create remote objects in a distributed system by using an implementation of the well-known "Factory" design pattern. Different design alternatives to be considered in the process of specifying an IDL interface are the special focus of Chapter 9. In Chapter 10, we provide a closer look at the powerful object-oriented principles of inheritance and polymorphism in the context of CORBA and show how to use the so-called inheritance approach as well as the so-called delegation approach. Distributed Callbacks, the focus of Chapter 11, are a technique that can be very useful if clients and servers have to change their roles temporarily. In Chapter 12, we present an example that makes use of the CORBA concept of value types, which allows passing data type instances to remote objects using "by-value" instead of "by-reference" semantics. An enormous degree of flexibility in the development of CORBA applications stems from the `DynamicAny` API and the Dynamic Invocation and Dynamic Skeleton Interfaces, which free CORBA developers from static type restrictions and are illustrated by examples in Chapters 13 through 15. Working with different configurations of the Portable Object Adapter is the topic of Chapter 16. The last two chapters, Chapter 17 and 18, are dedicated to two CORBA services that enhance the basic functionality offered by the ORB runtime system. While the first service, CORBA's *Naming Service* (NS), is fundamental and is required in almost any real-world CORBA application, the second, CORBA's *Event Service* (ES), can be used to realize an event-based, decoupled and asynchronous communication between the elements in a distributed system.

Due to the enormous scope of the CORBA specification, we have attempted to avoid repetition and redundancy in this book wherever possible. Consequently, the best way to gain a thorough understanding of the book's topic is through a sequential study approach from the beginning to the end. Since chapter subjects are cumulative, basics that were already introduced are prerequisites for understanding the discussions in later parts of the book. Possible solutions to the exercises can be found on the *World Wide Web* (WWW) on the book's home page (see the following section).

At the end of each central chapter, we have compiled a number of exercises that enable readers to examine their learning success independently and to develop and test further ideas related to the covered subjects.

1.2   Additional Material

The central reference for the explanations in this book is the CORBA specification version 3.0.3 of the *Object Management Group* (OMG), which can be downloaded free of charge from the OMG's website at `http://www.omg.org`. The source code for the example programs, as well as further information and updated material for this book, can be found at the book's website `http://www.wifo.uni-mannheim.de/CORBA`. Under this URL, one also has the possibility to give feedback, send in corrections, or submit any other suggestions for improvement.

To supply interested readers with a comfortable possibility to compile and run the example programs on their own, we tested each of the examples with three different Object Request Broker products available free of charge. The first one is the ORB that is part of the *Java Development Kit* (JDK). The second one is the *OpenORB* product and number three is the product *JacORB*. Detailed information on the possibilities for downloading, installing, and customizing the software can be found in Appendix E.

1.3   Conventions Used in This Book

At this point, we want to briefly mention the fonts we use in the book and explain their meanings. These font conventions are simple and also used by numerous other authors. In addition to the "normal" Times New Roman font, we use other font types that have special semantics. For the examples and for code fragments, we use the `Courier` font. *Technical terms* or *specific identifiers* are printed in *Times New Roman* italics. This, however, only holds for the complete terms, not for their abbreviations.

Very often, we encounter misunderstandings with respect to the usage of the terms *operation* and *method*. Therefore, already at this early stage, we want to discuss their differing semantics. The Object Management Group, originator of the CORBA standard, uses the term operation in the context of the specification of interfaces with the help of the Interface Definition Language in order to describe the *behavioral aspects* of an object. In the Java community, on the other hand, the term *method* is used for the member of a class declaration that, typically, implies the existence of a concrete implementation of such a behavior in the form of Java statements. We strictly adhere to these definitions, attempting to make it immediately clear to our readers whether the respective reflection takes place on CORBA's IDL level or on the level of the Java programming language.

1.4   How to Read This Book

It is not necessary to read this book from front to back. One might want to start writing first test applications very soon. In that case, it is recommended to read the introduction and the overview of CORBA's concepts in Chapters 2 and 3, have a glance at the Interface Definition Language basics in Chapter 4, and then begin concrete CORBA development with the examples in Chapter 7. The nature of Chapters 5 and 6 is more that of a technical specification. They may be consulted occasionally during program development while working through the examples in Chapters 7 through 18.

2 Introduction

Today, the construction of distributed systems based on objects is the most dominant approach in the area of software development, especially when it comes to enterprise information systems. In principle, various fundamentally different base technologies can be employed in this context in order to enable communication in distributed systems—due to their infrastructural function, they are denoted as *middleware*. In most cases, however, technologies prevail that rely on the object-oriented paradigm as their basis and that represent an extensive further development of the traditional concept of the so-called *Remote Procedure Calls* (RPCs). Meanwhile, modern programming languages like Java, the language that we concentrate on throughout this book, offer built-in language constructs for distributing objects. But, normally, these cannot comply with the complexities of systems designed for large-scale enterprise distributed applications. Among the current highly successful and most advanced technologies in the area of middleware, we want to mention in particular

- Microsoft's vendor-specific .NET-Standards, e.g., the *Distributed Component Object Model* (DCOM) or the *Component Object Model Plus* (COM+), respectively,
- language-specific standards like the specifications of the *Java 2 Platform, Enterprise Edition* (J2EE) that are based on Sun Microsystems' *Remote Method Invocation* (RMI), and
- above all, the vendor- and platform-independent architecture for distributed objects that the *Object Management Group* (OMG) describes in its *Common Object Request Broker Architecture* (CORBA) standard.

The purpose of this book is to provide a well-founded introduction into the CORBA architecture and to demonstrate the numerous advantages of CORBA. One characteristic feature is, for example, that CORBA enables us to integrate distributed objects to an application system that is implemented on different hardware architectures and operating systems, uses different ORB products, and defines its objects in different programming languages. If modern middleware technology is utilized, these objects can be distributed worldwide, opening up new dimensions of software development where objects are designed and tested spatially separate from each other and then are executed on remote nodes in a computer network.

Before we go into the concepts of the CORBA standard in more detail in Chapter 3, we want to summarize briefly some basic concepts of the object-oriented paradigm that are essential for the work of the OMG. Due to its wide acceptance and distribution, we refrain from giving full details and assume that readers are fundamentally acquainted with object-oriented principles. If this should not be the case, preparatory study of an introductory textbook on this subject is recommended. The same holds true for the topic of distributed software systems, the main characteristics of which are examined more closely in Section 2.2. Supplied with these foundations, readers should be well prepared for the subsequent examination of the fundamentals of CORBA technology.

2.1   Object-Oriented Paradigm

At the beginning of this section, we briefly but concisely present the most relevant basic concepts of the object-oriented approach. Although the roots of object orientation can be traced as far back as 1967 when SIMULA 67, a language for system design and simulation, was created, the concept did not become successful in the area of programming languages before the 1980s with Smalltalk and C++. It was not until the end of the 80s and the beginning of the 90s that object orientation began its advance in the early phases of the software lifecycle, namely analysis and design. Since then, object technology has even been applied to modeling purposes within the scope of business engineering tasks and, in the 1990s, became the dominating paradigm for system modeling and software development. The continuing success of Java as a programming language and UML as a modeling language are evidence of its infiltration into the mainstream. The UML standard, for example, serves as the foundation of several up-to-date model-driven software development approaches, such as OMG's *Model Driven Architecture*. Also, component technology, which is quite popular at the moment, is conceptually still built upon the ideas and technologies of object orientation.

Object technology is based on the assumption that human cognition relies on the perception of reality in the form of objects—objects that have characteristic properties and show specific behavior, that are related to each other, and that can interact amongst themselves. From an object-oriented software development perspective, an *object* is the IT-suitable representation of a real-world object obtained by applying the principle of *abstraction*. It need not necessarily exist physically but may also be of a conceptual nature. Technically seen, the object encapsulates a number of *attributes* in the form of variables whose set of values determine the actual *state* of the object as well as a number of *operations* or *methods* that describe the dynamic *behavior* of the object and supply its functionality in the form of executable statements.

To the outside, the object makes its functionality available via a public interface containing the signatures (operation names and parameter types) and the return types of the operations that may be invoked through other objects. This principle is central for the approach chosen by CORBA's designers and is discussed in detail later. The functionality of the entire object-oriented system is realized through the cooperation of the objects the system encompasses. To that end, the objects communicate by exchanging *messages*. A message from a sender object to a receiver object results in the invocation of one of the receiver's methods. This exchange of messages requires that at least the sender object "knows" the receiver object. To do so, the objects can, for example, be connected through an *association* or they can be related in an *aggregation* where one object is part of the other object, the so-called *whole*.

Objects that are characterized by the same properties and the same behavior are grouped into *classes*. A class is a description of an object type. It serves as a template for the generation of *instances* of that type; objects are instantiated from the class. For all its objects, the class specifies the attributes that the objects contain and defines the operations that can be invoked on these object data.

Encapsulation of semantically related data and functions in objects is a feature that markedly distinguishes the object-oriented approach from the classical structured software development technologies. It encourages principles like *modularization*, *information hiding*, and *programming by contract*. With the last two principles, the separation of interface and implementation is addressed. An object can only be accessed via its precisely defined public interface, visible from outside the object in such a way that no knowledge on the implementation of the object's attributes and operations by internally encapsulated data structures and algorithms is needed and the inner structure of the object is hidden to the outside world. In that sense, the interface serves as a contract between the object and its environment concerning the object's functionality. If that contract is observed, the data structures and the methods, i.e., the implementation of the operations, can be modified without any side-effects or influences on other parts of the system or on the users of objects of the respective class.

A core concept of the object-oriented approach is the *generalization principle*. With its application, we can build more general *superclasses* from existing classes that are now called *subclasses*. Conversely, we generate more specialized classes from existing classes through *specialization*. A subclass *inherits* all the properties and the behavior of its superclasses and can specify additional characteristics. According to the *substitution principle*, every object of a subclass is also an object of its superclasses. This implies, in particular, that a subclass object can be used in any context where a superclass object is expected. On the programming language level, the principle of generalization or specialization is implemented via the concept of *inheritance*, where a subclass inherits the interfaces and the concrete implementations of its superclasses. But, in addition, it is allowed to *redefine* inherited methods in subclasses as long as their interface remains unchanged. If a class is provided with more than one direct superclass—direct meaning "immediately above it in the class hierarchy"—the term *multiple inheritance* is used. Otherwise, we speak of *single inheritance*. The most central advantages of generalization/specialization or inheritance, respectively, are avoidance of redundancies and reduction of complexity.

Polymorphism is one of the most powerful mechanisms of object orientation. It allows that sending a message in order to invoke a certain operation results in the execution of different methods, depending on the class type of the receiver object. The executed methods, however, must all implement the respective operations. It is mandatory that the class of the receiver object is part of a class hierarchy and that, during specification of the message, an object of one of the superclasses was expected as receiver. Recall that the receiver object can be used in any invocation on a superclass object and note that all the possibly executed methods must implement the respective operation of the superclass. By so-called late *binding*, the assignment of the message to a concrete method is deferred until run-time of the system.

In the past, the aspect of *reusability* was very often mentioned as a central objective of the object-oriented approach and as one of the main arguments for its application. It is assumed that the basic principles of the object-oriented paradigm, such as encapsulation, information hiding, and inheritance, are especially favorable to software reuse. Classes can be organized in class libraries and can be repeatedly imported into the development of applications in two different ways. One possibility would be *black box reuse*, where a class is employed solely through accessing its public interface. On the other hand, with *white box reuse*, a new class is defined through the inheritance of not only the interface but also the implementation details from an existing class.

From a technical point of view, the development of distributed object systems poses a considerably higher challenge in comparison to the development of a monolithic object-oriented program executed in a single address space on a single host. Having recalled the basic principles of object orientation, we can now take a closer look at the specific challenges connected with the development of distributed systems and the specific features that characterize them. On this basis, it is then easier to comprehend CORBA's dedicated object model and understand the technical concepts that are chosen in the standard. Both are introduced and discussed in Chapter 3. We see that, in comparison to the object model described in this section, CORBA's object model is partially reduced and somewhat modified in order to adapt it to the special requirements of a distributed system world as CORBA sees it.

2.2   Distributed Systems

Generally speaking, a *distributed system* consists of a number of software components that are more or less autonomous and reside and can be executed on separate computers (*hosts*) that are linked by a computer network. The overall system functionality is realized through the integrated interaction of the individual components. Typically, the distributed components do not share a common storage space and their cooperation is coordinated by decentral administration software.

According to Linnhoff-Popien [Linn98], the top three layers of the well-known ISO OSI reference model have the highest relevance to the implementation of distributed systems. In her view, general reasons for distributed system developments were historical circumstances such as

- the performance explosion of processors,
- the development of faster networks,
- the advances of software technology, and
- the renunciation of hierarchical system structures.

More specifically, Emmerich [Emme00] sees the existence of typical global, non-functional requirements as the most frequent reason for the decision to construct a distributed system instead of implementing a centrally organized system. Examples of such requirements are

- scalability,
- openness,
- heterogeneity, and
- fault tolerance.

Scalability denotes the ability of a system to adapt its performance flexibly to increased demands that exceed the processing power of a single computer. To reach that goal, it is necessary to partition the system into different components that reside on separate hosts in the network and that are able to communicate with each other. It is crucial to ensure that the overall performance remains acceptable when the number of components is drastically increased.

Openness of a system is indispensable if it is embedded in a higher-level system or in an environment and has to interact with components from this environment. These components from the system's environment are often administrated by remotely located autonomous organizational units, making the distributed system approach necessary, as, for example, in the computer support of a supply chain between manufacturers and retailers within the scope of *Supply Chain Management*. In a narrow sense, by an open distributed system, we mean a set of autonomous subsystems whose specifications (interfaces) have been disclosed so that they can cooperate in coordination to work on a joint task. To that end, these subsystems are connected via some communication network.

Closely related to openness is the problem of *heterogeneity*, i.e., the presence of different hardware and software environments that have to be integrated. Especially in the IT domain, technology changes in very short cycles and, due to cost and time restrictions, it is rarely possible or even sensible to re-implement existing and working system components repeatedly with the help of the most recent technologies. Instead, we have to design a distributed system in such a way that legacy systems can remain on their accustomed hard- and software platform but that it is nevertheless possible to integrate them with new components.

In special cases, the need may arise to increase the *fault tolerance* of the system by installing critical system components redundantly on more than one computer. Then, even if one component fails, some other component of the distributed system can take over the task and the system's service is still provided.

One additional desirable goal during the design of distributed systems is hiding the distribution aspects from the system users so that they perceive the distributed system as one entity and cannot distinguish it from a single, integrated computing facility. It is equally desirable that application programmers developing problem-specific system components should not be bothered with the complexity resulting from the system's distribution so that they can, for the most part, proceed as they do during implementation of one monolithic application. These aspirations resulted in the introduction of a dedicated software layer in distributed systems for which the term middleware, previously mentioned, has been coined. The middleware layer is inserted between the network operating system and the application components. Its tasks are, in particular, encapsulating distribution and heterogeneity aspects. There are several different types of middleware:

- classical, transaction-oriented middleware that enables distributed transactions—with typical products such as IBM CICS or BEA Tuxedo,
- *Message-Oriented Middleware* (MOM) that mainly enables asynchronous message passing in distributed systems—with typical products such as IBM MQSeries or DEC MessageQueue,
- specialized middleware approaches, for example, to support mobile agents, or
- RPC-based approaches and the related object-oriented middleware that enables remote procedure calls or invocations of operations on remote objects. Products in this category implement the above-mentioned technologies RMI/J2EE, DCOM/COM+, and CORBA.

Due to their special relevance for the development of today's middleware technologies, we briefly discuss the basic principles of *Remote Procedure Calls* (RPCs), which were introduced in the 1980s and were widely used. Important representatives of that technology were,

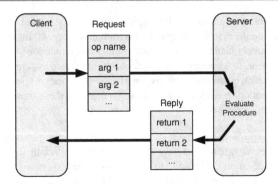

Figure 1: Execution of a RPC ([Bolt02], p. 7)

e.g., SUN RPCs as well as *Distributed Computing Environment* (DCE) RPCs. For the application, an RPC appears like a local function call, which, however, in reality is not executed
locally. Instead, the values of the procedure's parameters are sent via the network to a remote
application, the so-called *server*, which executes the procedure. If the procedure generates return values, they are sent via the network back to the calling application, the so-called *client*.
When a client performs a RPC, the parameter values of the call are packaged into a *request*
package by a process called *marshaling*. They are then sent on the transport layer of the network to the server, typically with the help of the *User Datagram Protocol* (UDP) or the
Transmission Control Protocol (TCP). Marshaling brings the parameters into a format suitable for transportation over the network. The request (the remote call) itself consists of a
RPC message that contains the name of the remote procedure and the list of parameters; it is
transported embedded in a UDP or TCP package. After the arrival of the request on the
server side, an *unmarshaling* takes place, which unpacks the parameters, and, consecutively,
the procedure is executed. As soon as the execution is terminated, the return values—if
any—are marshaled into a *reply* package that is then sent back to the client. RPC uses synchronous communication; therefore, the client is blocked and waits until the remote procedure returns. The reply is, again, a RPC message, which, in addition to a number of return
values, can also contain an error status. Figure 1 schematically demonstrates the course of a
basic RPC. In the end, RPCs represent the basic principle also employed during CORBA
communication. However, there, the RPC principles are performed in an object-oriented
manner and they are implemented with considerable extensions. At this point, it should be
noted that CORBA supports not only synchronous but also asynchronous communication between clients and servers.

In the context of middleware's role for distributed systems, Emmerich identifies eight different forms of *transparency*, layered on top of each other, that a distributed system should ideally possess:

- *access transparency* and *location transparency* as the basis,
- *migration transparency, replication transparency*, and *concurrency transparency* on
  the next level, and
- *scaling transparency, performance transparency*, and *failure transparency* on the
  highest level of the layered transparency model.

One of the most basic forms of transparency of distributed systems is *access transparency*. This term expresses the objective that the interfaces for service requests are identical in the local as well as in the remote case so that the system's services are perceived indistinguishably. Regardless of whether or not a server component resides on the same host as the client component or is installed on a remote host in the network, the client component uses the same interface to access services of the server component.

Access transparency is complemented by *location transparency*. This characteristic says that the physical location of server components need not be known to the client components. Programmers of service requesting components do not have to be concerned with where the service providing components are installed on the network since the identification and discovery of these components is suitably supported by the middleware in use.

On the basis of the first two dimensions of transparency, one can achieve the so-called *migration transparency*. It allows the movement of a service-providing component from one host to another host within the system without needing to inform the service-requesting component of this or even modifying its implementation. Access transparency and location transparency are essential for this type of transparency since transparent migration may not change the server interface as the client sees it nor may the physical location of the server components be of any relevance.

One technique to increase reliability and optimize performance of the system and to enable scalability and fault tolerance is the replication of components—the generation of component replicas whose states are synchronized with that of their originals. In order to conceal this technical measure, the so-called *replication transparency* is the aim. In the case of its realization, clients or client programmers need not know whether a requested service is provided by the original server component or by a replica of the server. Again, access transparency and location transparency are preconditions for this type of transparency.

A third form of transparency, based on access and location transparency, is *concurrency transparency*. It is defined as the concealment of the possibility that several clients concurrently request services of a component from users and application programmers. How the middleware employed controls concurrency and ensures integrity of the commonly used components has no relevance for the user or the application programmer.

On the highest level of the layered transparency model, we find *scaling transparency* and *performance transparency*. Both forms are rather similar. The first implies that users or programmers need not know how scalability of the system as a whole is reached through insertion or removal of components; it is allowed to expand or to shrink in scale without changes being expected from them. The second form is related to single requests and hides the details of possible reactions and reconfigurations of the system in order to guarantee high system performance as loads vary. *Failure transparency* is also defined on the highest transparency level. It is a system characteristic that hides failure of components from users and programmers and lets them complete their tasks or developments. The last three transparency forms are supported by, or are even only possible through, concurrency transparency and replication transparency.

3 Concepts of the CORBA Standard

3.1 Object Management Group

At the beginning of this chapter, we discuss and classify the CORBA standard and introduce the Object Management Group, which is the originator of the CORBA standard. The OMG is a consortium of hardware manufacturers, software developers, network operators, and software end-users. In 1989, it was founded by eight companies (3Com, American Airlines, Canon, Data General, Hewlett-Packard, Philips Telecommunications, Sun Microsystems, and Unisys); but, after a few months, it became an independent international organization, opening membership to other firms and institutions. At the moment, the OMG has approx. 470 members: software and hardware vendors, companies from various industries, information system users, consulting firms, and research laboratories. The core of OMG's work is the definition of an architecture for the distribution and cooperation of object-oriented software components in heterogeneous, distributed environments. The OMG promotes modular software development, i.e., the separation of an application into components, sets of objects that collaboratively accomplish a specific task. As opposed to most other standards organizations (for example, the *Open Software Foundation* (OSF)), the OMG does not produce software. On the contrary, standards (guidelines, specifications, and architectural models) are defined that encompass basic requirements concerning applications and their components to which all standard-compliant software products must adhere. Compliance with the specifications assures that—without any modifications of program code—applications can be ported to different hardware architectures and operating systems. Moreover, programs developed independently of each other, written in different programming languages, and run on different hardware platforms in different locations can interoperate and exchange messages.

3.2 Object Management Architecture

In the *Object Management Architecture* (OMA) *Guide*, OMG's first published central document, aims and procedures of the OMG as well as its basic object management architecture are recorded. On that basis, the *Core Object Model* is described; it is OMG's object model specifying the conceptual requirements any system has to adhere to if it is to be standard-compliant. One central aspect of the OMA is the definition of interfaces, the externally visible functional properties of objects. For that purpose, the OMG provides its own *Interface Definition Language* (IDL), which is used in order to describe those properties in a standardized and implementation-independent way. Various programming languages (e.g., C++ and Smalltalk but also non-object-oriented languages such as COBOL) can be employed to implement an object. For those languages, the OMG defines *language mappings*, which specify how the interfaces and data structures declared in IDL are to be converted into constructs of the respective programming language. The core of the Object Management Architecture is the *Object Request Broker* (ORB), which the CORBA standard defines. It is the communication component responsible for locating and initializing objects as well as for managing communication between client and server. Objects use the ORB to communicate with other objects in a distributed environment. Like a mail distributor, it enables message passing to a destination host and, from there, to the receiver object. In addition to the ORB, four categories of application components are described by OMA. They are differentiated with respect to the way the services they provide are suitable to support a specific application profile (see Figure 2):

- *CORBAservices*™ (a.k.a. CORBA Services): These are general-purpose, system-related extensions of the core functionality of an ORB that are relevant to the basic operation of a distributed application. If required, application programmers can fall back on these services, for example, if the application needs additional functionality such as transactions, security, or persistence.

- *CORBAfacilities*™ (a.k.a. Horizontal CORBA Facilities): This notion encompasses advanced, more application-specific functionality affecting essential parts of an application, for example, user interfaces, document processing, or print services. In comparison to CORBA Services objects, these objects reside at a higher level of abstraction.

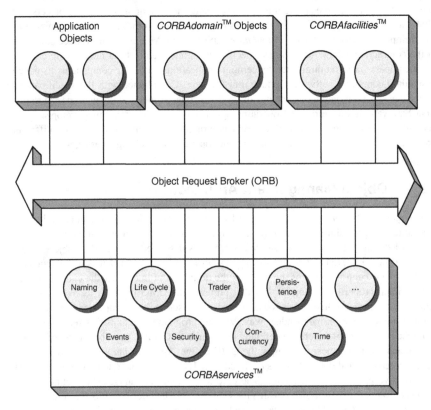

Figure 2: The Object Management Architecture

- *CORBAdomain™* **Objects** (a.k.a. Domain CORBA Facilities): They denote partial solutions for specific application domains or industries that are standardized with respect to their basic construction principle. Examples are domain interfaces in finance or telecommunication.

- **Application Objects:** The actual applications, concrete software products that are not standardized by the OMG (for example, a web server, a text processor, or a CAD program), fall into this category. Also, all the objects in the example programs that we discuss later are application objects.

In separate standards, the OMG describes the functionality of the components in these classes and defines the interfaces of their objects. Concrete implementations are left to application programmers. However, in some cases, standard solutions are available off-the-shelf.

3.3 Common Object Request Broker Architecture

The Common Object Request Broker Architecture is the quintessence of the specifications of OMG's Object Management Architecture. It is a technical communication infrastructure for applications built upon distributed objects. Based upon the Object Request Broker, the CORBA architecture provides the fundamental framework enabling object-oriented Remote Procedure Calls in order to support communication and cooperation of the objects distributed in a system. In the following, the principal elements of CORBA are discussed in more detail.

3.4 Elements of the CORBA Standard

It is the aim of the following sections to present in turn the constituent parts of the CORBA standard and to briefly discuss their scope of functions.

3.4.1 Object Request Broker

The Common Object Request Broker Architecture specifies the basic services for object communication. We have already mentioned that the main features of the mechanism rely on Remote Procedure Calls. In addition to the static interface descriptions that are also used by RPC, a highly flexible *Dynamic Invocation Interface* (DII) is provided that even enables binding to new servers at run-time. The Object Request Broker constitutes the architecture's communication component and is sometimes denoted as the "object bus" (in the style of a PC bus with its slots) or, somewhat simplistically, "mail distributor". In no way does the standard determine how a concrete ORB implementation should be realized nor does it give any recommendations. Conceivable approaches would be a realization of the ORB by means of runtime libraries or of daemon processes, with the help of a central server, as a part of the operating system, or by combinations of these options. The most widely-used approaches that we know of combine runtime libraries with daemon processes.

Basically, it is the task of the ORB to establish *client/server* relationships between objects. Here, a client is an object that intends to invoke an operation on another object. The implementation of an object—in OMG's terminology also called *servant*—is a batch of program code that, among other things, determines which actions are to be executed when an object operation is invoked, i.e., it defines the corresponding object method. Normally, several object implementations are integrated into one executable program, which then acts as a server. A client can invoke a method of a server object residing on the same machine or installed on another host somewhere on the network. The ORB accepts the invocation call and is then responsible for finding the object that offers the corresponding method, delivering the call's parameters to the respective object implementation, and returning potential invocation results. Should client and server employ differing data formats, the ORB also has to take over the conversion of data. The client need not have any knowledge of the location where the invoked object is stored, the programming language in which it is implemented, the operating system or the hardware of its host, or any other aspects not directly part of the object's interface. Thus, CORBA-based applications are able to communicate with each other across the boundaries of the utilized computer architecture and the available software products. This ability, however, implies that at least one CORBA-compliant product exists for each involved platform.

It does not mean, though, that an application could, for example, be developed under Unix and that the generated binary code could be executed on different platforms, i.e., computer architectures and/or operating systems. Platform independence has to be understood from a "distributed perspective", meaning that the entire application may be composed of distributed components implemented in different languages and executed on different platforms. In that case, it is irrelevant which CORBA-compliant products were utilized to develop the individual components.

This type of independence requires that

- for each participating computer architecture and its operating system, a CORBA-compliant product exists,
- for the programming language used, an IDL mapping is defined, and
- the employed product is at least CORBA 2.0-compliant since CORBA 2.0 was the version that introduced *Interoperable Object References* (IOR) as well as the *Internet Inter-ORB Protocol* (IIOP) into the standard. Both are necessary conditions for the interoperability discussed above; they are dealt with in more detail in Section 3.7.

3.4.2   Object Adapter

Technically seen, an object adapter is the connecting link between the ORB and the proper object implementations. From a logical perspective, it connects CORBA objects that are specified by means of IDL to their implementations, which were written in a certain programming language. When the ORB receives a client request, it routes this request out to the ORB on the server side. Subsequently, the server-side ORB transmits the request to an object adapter. The object adapter then has to determine to which object implementation the request has to be forwarded. During the concrete implementation of a distributed object, one has to decide on a certain object adapter. Since its interface to the ORB core depends on the core, problem-free porting of objects from one ORB to another requires that the same object adapter exists on the new core.

Within the framework of the CORBA specification, up to now, two object adapters were standardized:

- the *Basic Object Adapter* (BOA) and
- the *Portable Object Adapter* (POA).

The Basic Object Adapter was the first object adapter specified by the OMG. But this specification was heavily criticized. Due to the BOA's partially imprecise specification, problems concerning porting of existing applications to other ORBs often occurred. Additional complications arose because the specified functionality seemed not extensive enough to cover all potential application purposes, so each vendor supplied his own additional functionality. This was the motivation for replacing the BOA specification in CORBA 2.2 with the Portable Object Adapter, which should avoid and solve portability problems. Further, more specialized object adapters can exist alongside the POA. They are required if an external system wants to administer its objects by itself but, on the other hand, wants to admit other systems access to these objects. An object-oriented database system may serve as an example of such an external system.

With the specification of POAs, the OMG has established a fine-grained taxonomy that for the first time provides more precise definitions of, among others, the notions of *client*, *server*, *CORBA object*, *servant*, *object identity* (object ID), and *object reference*. In short, these terms can be characterized in the following way:

- **Client**
  A *computational context* that invokes (remote) operations on an object and, for that purpose, accesses an object reference for that object.

- **Server**
  A *computational context* in which the implementation of a CORBA object exists. On the operating system level, it is usually realized as a separate process.

- **CORBA Object**
  A CORBA object is a virtual entity supplied with an identity, an interface, and the corresponding implementation. From a client's view, a CORBA object can be identified via an object reference containing, among other things, the object's identity. The server's view of the object's identity is managed by the POA and is implemented by means of a servant.

- **Servant**
  A servant *is* a *programming language entity* that exists in the context of a server and implements the IDL interface for one or more CORBA object. A servant is responsible for handling the requests of a client.

- **Object Identity**
  In the context of the POA, the notion object identity is used to identify a certain CORBA object. Object identities are normally managed by the POA. It is also possible that they are specified during implementation of a server application. Object IDs are hidden from clients, encapsulated by object references.

- **Object Reference**
  An object reference is the link between clients and servers. It contains all the information needed to invoke an operation on a remote object. Thus, a client must have an

object reference to make invocations on a CORBA object because the object reference encapsulates the location details of that object. The Interoperable Object Reference includes the *Internet Protocol* (IP) address, the port number as well as a multitude of additional details, e.g., on the object ID or the POA's identity.

The distinction between clients and servers is a consequence of the roles that the different components adopt. "Pure" client applications only use the functionality provided by other components and do not offer any functionality on their own. "Pure" server applications make various services available without having to rely on the functionality of other components. Hybrid components can act as clients and as servers at the same time. That is, on the one hand, they provide certain services that may be used by other components. And, on the other, they are dependent on the functionality of other components. All CORBA applications that offer services over their interfaces and that simultaneously use services of the standardized CORBA infrastructure automatically fall into the category of "hybrid" applications.

3.4.3 Interface Definition Language

For the development of flexible distributed applications, especially for heterogeneous platforms, a strict separation between interface and implementation of objects is needed. First of all, objects are therefore defined in a dedicated language, the Interface Definition Language, which is also specified by the Object Management Group. The IDL is used to define the interfaces of objects. For the specification of object interfaces, only the externally accessible attributes and operations are of central interest—similar to the `public` declarations in a Java or C++ class. Attributes or methods that are merely destined for internal usage may not be part of an IDL definition. Using a programming language- and platform-specific IDL compiler, the IDL interfaces have to be translated as we describe in Section 3.5. The implementation of the interface's operations can later be carried through, as usual, in the selected programming language. In the following sections, we utilize the IDL notation for the specification of types, exceptions, and operations. A more detailed description of IDL is given in Chapter 4.

3.4.4 Interface Repository

The *Interface Repository* (IR) has to perform the task of storing the interface definitions of CORBA objects. The metadata stored within the IR can be accessed at run-time in order to generate dynamic invocations using the Dynamic Invocation Interface and/or the Dynamic Skeleton Interface. The IR is itself a CORBA server that has to be activated separately from the client and server processes and can be located anywhere in the network. The IR is described by a set of IDL interfaces determining how the IR can be accessed remotely.

Putting an IDL file into the IR leads to a decomposition process that inserts the elements contained in the IDL file into a parse tree. The different constructs, like modules, interfaces, operations, etc., are reflected by corresponding interfaces defined in the IR specification. In order to explore the metadata information, a client might need to traverse the parse tree using dedicated operations for this purpose.

In order to keep track of the different named IDL data types, the IR uses *Repository Identities* (repository IDs), which are unique type identifier strings. However, repository IDs are also generated if no IR is used because the IDL compiler generates them as it produces the stub and skeleton code for a CORBA application (cf. Section 3.5).

In principle, different ways of obtaining initial access to an Interface Repository exist. Irrespective of the chosen type of access, it is always the purpose to determine how a CORBA object is structured. For example, if a client has obtained an object reference to a CORBA object but has no information on the operations or attributes supported by that object, it can acquire that information at run-time. By calling the respective operation, the client obtains the description of the interface belonging to the reference passed to the call. Subsequently, the client can analyze that result in more detail, e.g., by inquiring which arguments a certain operation expects, what their respective types have to be, or whether a return value is to be expected. Thereafter, the client can make use of the Dynamic Invocation Interface in order to send a request to the object.

Note that the IR is usually realized as a stand-alone component and not all available ORB products provide this component. Anyway, for many CORBA applications an IR implementation is not needed at all.

3.4.5   Dynamic Invocation Interface

There are two ways that a client can invoke server operations: static or dynamic. In both cases, the client has to know the object reference of the corresponding CORBA object. The server cannot distinguish a static from a dynamic invocation. While the static interface is automatically generated by the IDL compiler, programmers have to generate a dynamic method invocation by themselves via the Dynamic Invocation Interface. Should the IDL interface not be available, programmers have to rely on the interface definition stored in the Interface Repository.

Compared to dynamic invocations, we strictly prefer static invocations since they are

- faster,
- more manageable (due to the known IDL definition),
- more robust (due to better type-checking abilities), and
- easier to implement.

At run-time, the Dynamic Invocation Interface enables the client to generate invocations that are subsequently transmitted to the server. The DII supports synchronous (default), deferred-synchronous, and asynchronous communication modes. Synchronous communication is initiated by means of the operation invoke(). In order to communicate in deferred-synchronous mode, the operations send and get_response() (or poll_response(), respectively) have to be invoked. Since both statements can appear at any place in a program (where, obviously, send must be executed prior to get_response()), the results of an invocation already carried out can be retrieved and evaluated later. The third alternative is the invocation of the operation send_oneway(). With that operation, asynchronous invocations are enabled. A detailed description of the DII is provided in Section 6.6 and Chapter 14 contains implementation examples in Java.

3.4.6   Dynamic Skeleton Interface

The Dynamic Skeleton Interface was introduced in CORBA 2.0. Analogous to the DII, it provides a run-time mechanism for server-side management of components whose IDL definitions are not known during implementation and compilation of the server. The DSI provides an interface that can handle a certain class of requests at run-time. It analyzes the incoming messages with respect to target object and method and tries to determine the receiver of the message. With the help of the DSI, a server can execute the request of a client dynamically such that the client is unable to notice any difference in comparison to static execution. In order to do so, the server uses a *skeleton*—an ORB component that assists its object adapter in directing the invocation to the right operation of a servant (cf. Section 3.5). A detailed description of the DSI is provided in Section 6.7 and Chapter 15 contains an implementation example in Java.

3.4.7   Implementation Repository

One component of CORBA repeatedly mentioned in the standard but not specified in detail is the Implementation Repository. Its task is to administrate different server implementations. Should, at the start of a client, the corresponding server implementation not be active, then it is automatically started by the Implementation Repository, provided that the server has been registered there beforehand. Exceptions are the so-called persistent servers that, as a rule, have to be started manually and that, afterwards, can permanently wait for client requests. Since the OMG has so far abstained from formally specifying the Implementation Repository, it is the vendor's decision whether and how this repository is implemented. This is a severe disadvantage for the design of interoperable CORBA applications as developers cannot act on the assumption that an Implementation Repository is actually available and that they can start the needed server implementations automatically if required. As one consequence, they themselves have to be concerned about detecting and solving the problem of a crashed server.

Following, Figure 3 provides an overview of the single components of CORBA-based applications.

3.5   Procedural Steps in Developing a CORBA-Based Application

The development of a CORBA-based application normally begins with the creation of an IDL interface. This interface definition is then compiled by means of an IDL compiler. The IDL compiler used is product-specific and tied to a specific platform—hardware and operating system—as well as programming language. Therefore, the type and number of files generated by the compiler varies. In principle, two sets of files are generated: *stub* file(s) and *skeleton* file(s).

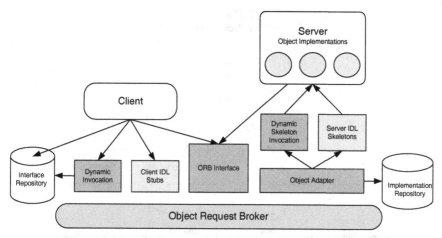

Figure 3: Central Components of CORBA-Based Applications

The stub files are later needed by the client. A stub is created in constructs of the client's programming language; therefore, a remote object in a C++ program is locally represented by a C++ object even if its remote implementation within the server may be written in Java. For each object it accesses on the server side, a client needs the corresponding stub. The classes generated in the stub file(s) are so-called *proxy* classes. They undertake the task of accepting a client's request and passing this message via the ORB to the appropriate object implementation. If parameters have to be passed with the message, the stub also translates, or marshals, the client-language data types into a format suitable for transmission over the ORB. Should the invocation produce a return value, it is transmitted on the network to the proxy, which unmarshals and forwards it to the client. Here, it is irrelevant whether the actual object implementation resides on the same host, meaning that no physical network exists between the components, or whether it resides on a remote host somewhere on the Internet. The developer of a client application has to implement the application logic from the view of the end-user (*client code*); whereby, the IDL operations realized on the server side are utilized as services.

The skeleton files are needed by the object implementations that are later instantiated in the server application and that actually implement the interfaces and types defined in the IDL interface (*server code*). In Java, the classes generated in the skeleton file(s) can, for example, serve as superclasses for the implementations and have to be extended in order to supply the required application logic. Subsequently, both parts of the application, client and server, have to be linked to the ORB runtime library. The complete procedure is demonstrated in Figure 4 below.

3.6   Remote Invocations

One of the central principles of object-orientation is encapsulation, the separation of interface and implementation. As discussed in Section 2.2, for distributed object-oriented systems, ad-

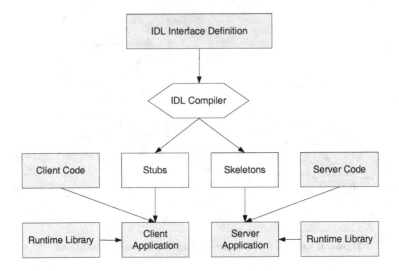

Figure 4: Procedural Steps in Developing a CORBA-Based Application

ditional aspects of encapsulation concerning transparency requirements come into play, for example, *location transparency*, which denotes hiding the location where a software object resides. It is not possible to infer the host where an object resides by analyzing the object's interface. If that principle is followed, a user can formulate a method invocation identically, irrespective of whether the object is local or remote. This is realized by the proxy objects mentioned above. They have the same interface as the proper object; however, they reside locally on the caller's machine. The caller transmits its request to the proxy object, which forwards it to the remote server object. The caller, therefore, only "sees" the proxy object. Invocations between distributed objects always result from intermediation of the ORB. And, as briefly discussed above, there are two types of client-side calls: static calls, employing the *client stubs* containing the respective proxy objects; and dynamic calls via the Dynamic Invocation Interface that need the aid of an Interface Repository. Together with the object adapter, the ORB is responsible for localizing the corresponding implementation, possibly starting the server program, provided that a suitable daemon or agent and an Implementation Repository are available, delivering the request, and returning the result if there is any. On the server side, both types of calls are either handled by a static interface using *server skeletons* or by the Dynamic Skeleton Interface. For the server it is indistinguishable whether an operation was invoked statically or dynamically. In the same way, a client also cannot discriminate between static or dynamic execution of its request. In Figure 5, the principle of separating client and server-side object implementation as well as the different invocation types are demonstrated.

3.7   Interoperability in the CORBA Standard

The functionality provided by the ORB is already sufficient to act as a communication medium and to provide the basic requirements for interoperability between applications—

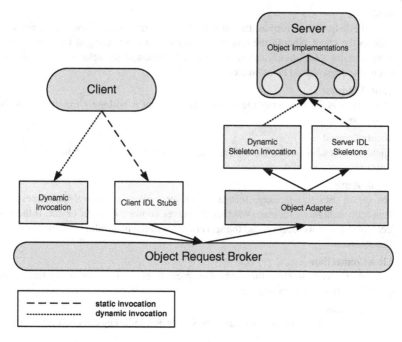

**Figure 5: Separation of Client and Object Implementation
and Different Types of Invocation**

independent of the employed programming languages and platforms. However, as soon as ORB products of different vendors are used, advanced concepts are needed. The interoperability between different ORB implementations defined by the OMG is based on two elements:

- definition of a communication protocol as well as
- introduction of a unique object reference.

In the following subsections, we briefly go into these two significant elements.

3.7.1   Protocols Defined by CORBA

In CORBA version 2.0, a protocol to enable communication between ORBs of different vendors was introduced for the first time. The *General Inter-ORB Protocol* (GIOP) specifies a standardized transmission syntax, the *Common Data Representation* (CDR), together with several message formats. One important characteristic of CDR is that it provides a complete binding of all data types defined in IDL and also supports different byte orderings and memory alignments. The GIOP definition incorporates the following message formats:

- **Request**
  This format enables a client's access to the object implementation.

- **Reply**
  With the help of this format, the output and/or return values of the server are sent back to the client. Should the object implementation have changed its location, the reply contains a *LocationForward* message and the new object reference to which the original request should be redirected.

- **CancelRequest**
  This format is used to notify the server that the client is no longer expecting a reply for its request.

- **LocateRequest**
  Clients can send a *LocateRequest* message to determine whether or not a particular object reference is valid.

- **LocateReply**
  The server uses this message format to answer a client's *LocateRequest* message. This reply contains a message whether the server knows the object or not. If the object has changed its location and the server knows it, the new valid object reference is also returned.

- **CloseConnection**
  If a server intends to close the connection prematurely and not serve any further requests, this format has to be used.

- **MessageError**
  This format is used by the client and the server and indicates communication problems.

In version 2.1 of the CORBA standard, the GIOP message formats were extended by the *Fragment* message. With this format, large data sets sent or returned with requests or replies can be broken into smaller packages (fragments). These fragments contain an identifier indicating whether additional fragment messages are to be expected or the final fragment was received. The evaluation of a request or reply is postponed until the last fragment was received. Additionally, several of the data structures used internally by the ORB were modified in CORBA 2.1. However, these changes do not affect application programmers; they are only relevant to developers of ORBs or bridges from one protocol version to another. In addition to the single-direction protocol where a client's ORB initiates a connection, GIOP also provides a *bidirectional* variant that allows clients as well as servers to act as originators of a message.

GIOP is an abstract protocol. The actual communication is handled through the Internet Inter ORB Protocol. The IIOP specifies how GIOP messages can be exchanged over *Transmission Control Protocol/Internet Protocol* (TCP/IP) connections. ORB manufacturers can also implement additional, so-called *Environment-Specific Inter-ORB Protocols* (ESIOP) as long as the basic requirements for ORB-to-ORB communication are met.

3.7.2 Interoperable Object Reference

The introduction of the Interoperable Object Reference in CORBA 2.0 enabled the worldwide unambiguous referencing of objects for the first time. The IOR is a dedicated object reference that consists of a type identifier and a number of *Interoperability Profiles* (IOP).

With the help of the IOR, it is possible to uniquely identify objects across systems and their environments (in particular, their address spaces). Profiles contain an Internet address, a port number and an object identifier (denoted as *object key* in the standard) that the ORB generates and uses internally. The actual content of this key is transparent to application developers (*opaque*). Only the ORB that generated the IOR knows the exact meaning of its content.

An IOR can be *transient* or *persistent*. The latter does not imply that the corresponding CORBA object is also persistent. Should a server application be terminated and later restated, then all transient IORs are invalidated. This is not the case with persistent IORs. A persistent IOR has the advantage that it has to be delivered to the client application only once. But, this assumes that, each time the server is restarted, the Internet address of the server host was unmodified and its port number is still free since both values are part of the IOR.

4 Introduction to the Interface Definition Language

In order to describe the interfaces of objects offering services, the OMG introduced the Interface Definition Language (IDL). IDL is a purely declarative language, meaning that, with its help, the needed data types and interfaces—with their attributes, operation signatures, and exceptions—are described. The actual algorithmic implementation of operations, however, is not provided. The IDL provides the basis for programming language independence since only an IDL compiler translates the IDL specifications into a certain programming language. In addition to the *language mapping* from IDL to Java covered in this book, several other mappings to programming languages such as Ada, C, C++, COBOL, Lisp, PL/1, Python, and Smalltalk were defined by the OMG. Furthermore, non-standardized mappings exist that are available in proprietary ORBs, e.g., IDL to Eiffel, Objective-C, and Perl.

4.1 Lexical Elements of IDL

The smallest units that an IDL specification consists of are called *lexical elements* (or *tokens*). In IDL, there are five classes of lexical elements:

- white space,
- identifiers,
- keywords,
- literals, and
- operators and separators.

White space characters are blanks, horizontal and vertical tabulators, form feeds, newlines, and comments; they are ignored by the IDL compiler.

Identifiers, *keywords*, and *literals* are separated by white space. We also use white space to improve readability of our specifications by uniformly formatting them.

4.1.1 Comments

Comments are developer explanations and remarks used for documentation purposes and are not to be considered by the IDL compiler. A *line comment* starts with the characters // and terminates at the end of this line. A *block comment* is started by the characters /* and is terminated with the characters */. Block comments can extend across several lines; they do not nest. A line comment has no special meaning within a block comment. And, similarly, a block comment has no special meaning within a line comment.

4.1.2   Identifiers

The names that developers assign to the modules, interfaces, data types, constants, or operations they define are called identifiers. An IDL identifier is made up of an arbitrarily long sequence of characters; by "character", we mean the ASCII alphabetic characters, the digits from 0 to 9, and the *underscore* character ('_'). The first character of an identifier must be an ASCII alphabetic character or an underscore. Upper- and lower-case letters are treated as the same letter. However, once one has decided in favor of a certain notation, e.g., `Publisher`, this must be consistently retained. Any differences in the spelling of the same name, for example, `publisher`, neither references the element previously named `Publisher`, nor is it acceptable as a new identifier for another element.

Identifiers starting with an underscore constitute a special case—they are called *escaped identifiers*. Escaped identifiers should only be used in exceptional cases. It should be noted that the underscore is virtually ignored by the IDL compiler so that, e.g., the identifiers `Publisher` and `_Publisher` are treated equivalently. The reason for the OMG to introduce this concept is that IDL is constantly evolving, resulting in the definition of new IDL keywords, and therefore collisions with existing programs might occur. The result of employing the underscore now is that, on the one hand, the identifier cannot collide with a new IDL keyword. And, on the other, in the code generated by the IDL compiler, the original identifier is used. As an example, the character sequence `_factory` would not be treated as the IDL keyword `factory` but would be admissible as an identifier. The OMG recommends using escaped identifiers only for legacy interfaces or for mechanically generated IDL.

When selecting identifiers during interface definition, one should bear in mind that the interface can be translated into a multitude of programming languages. Therefore, one should refrain from identifiers like `class`, `for`, `if`, `PERFORM`, etc.

4.1.2.1   Excursion: Style Guidelines for IDL Identifiers

It is highly recommended certain conventions be followed when selecting IDL identifiers. Syntactically, these are not compulsory; but, they provide other readers of IDL interfaces with helpful information and simplify their orientation concerning the different types of elements in an IDL specification. In the OMG IDL Style Guide, the OMG recommends employing upper-case and lower-case letters as well as underscores according to the following rules:

1. Identifiers for modules, interfaces, value types, type definitions, constructed types (`struct`, `union`, and `enum`), and exceptions are written in mixed upper- and lower-case letters. No underscores appear in an identifier; all words begin with an upper-case letter with the remaining letters being lower-case.

   Examples: `DatabaseAdapter`, `Product`, `CosEventChannelAdmin`

2. Identifiers for operations, attributes, parameters, and members of structures are written in lower-case letters. Underscores are used to separate words in multi-word identifiers.

   Examples: `register_consumer`, `age`, `production_date`

3. Identifiers for values of enumeration types and constants are written in upper-case letters. Underscores are used to separate different words (see above).

   Examples: MAX_NUMBER_OF_USERS, MONDAY, VAT_RATE

4.1.2.2   Excursion: Additional Formatting Rules

In addition to the conventions for the creation of IDL identifiers, there are several rules concerning the usage of braces and the indentation of text that should be followed consistently in order to increase the readability of the resulting IDL code. With respect to the placement of braces, the OMG IDL Style Guide proposes two different alternatives:

- the opening brace '{' is placed in a new line following the line containing the beginning keyword with the same indentation as the keyword or
- the opening brace '{' is on the same line as its beginning keyword.

For both variants, it is recommended that the closing brace '}' be placed alone on a new line at the same level as the keyword. Code enclosed in between the braces should be indented one additional level.

Concerning indentation, it is generally accepted that the first IDL specification begins flush left without leading white space (blanks, tabulators, etc.). If a single definition has to be continued on another line, it should be indented to the next level—even more if this helps to clarify the coherence of the different components. Ideally, one horizontal tabulator is used per indentation level.

Example for variant 1:

```
interface Count
{
    readonly attribute long value;
    void increment();
    void reset();
};
```

Example for variant 2:

```
interface Count {
    readonly attribute long value;
    void increment();
    void reset();
};
```

4.1.3   Keywords

The identifiers listed in Table 1 are reserved as IDL *keywords*; they may not be used otherwise (e.g., as user-defined identifiers).

Table 1: IDL Keywords

abstract	*emits*	inout	*provides*	truncatable
any	enum	interface	public	typedef
attribute	*eventtype*	local	*publishes*	typeid
boolean	exception	long	raises	typeprefix
case	factory	module	readonly	unsigned
char	FALSE	*multiple*	setraises	union
component	*finder*	native	sequence	*uses*
const	fixed	Object	short	ValueBase
consumes	float	octet	string	valuetype
context	getraises	oneway	struct	void
custom	*home*	out	supports	wchar
default	import	*primarykey*	switch	wstring
double	in	private	TRUE	

The IDL keywords written in italics are only of interest in the context of the *CORBA Component Model* (CCM), which does not fall within the scope of this book. Therefore, they are not discussed in the following chapters.

Keywords must be written exactly as shown in the list above. For example, module is a valid IDL keyword; usage of Module or MODULE, respectively, is an error.

4.1.4   Punctuation Characters

In addition to its keywords, IDL applies so-called *punctuation characters* that act as, among other things, operators or are employed for grouping or terminating definitions. The list below displays all valid IDL punctuation characters.

```
;    {    }    :    ,    =    +    –    (    )    <    >
[    ]    '    "    \    |    ^    &    *    /    %    –
```

Further IDL elements of special meaning are the following characters or character sequences. They are of relevance since the IDL preprocessor is activated before the actual translation of IDL source files begins.

```
#    ##    !    ||    &&
```

4.1.5   Preprocessor Directives

A #include directive instructs the compiler to read an additional IDL file before translating the specification at hand. This enables reuse of data types and interfaces that are defined in a different source file without having to input them once again.

The #pragma directive is a means of determining, among other things, the type identification (repository ID) of an object for distributed applications and, especially, the Interface Repository. This allows for several objects with the same interface, implementation, and functionality but with different type identifications generated by the *pragma* directive to be active at the same time.

Three forms of pragma directives are detailed in the standard:

- #pragma prefix *string*, which is used to add the specified prefix to the repository ID,
- #pragma version *name major.minor*, which is used to modify the version number of an object, and
- #pragma *name id*, which is used to determine the repository ID, for example, for access via DCE.

It should be noted that the IDL interfaces published by the OMG contain the directive #pragma prefix "omg.org" but the corresponding classes of Java-ORB are elements of the package org.omg; an example is org.omg.CosNaming.

Furthermore, with CORBA version 3.0, a new IDL keyword typeprefix was introduced. It replaces the former use of the preprocessor directive #pragma prefix. Therefore, more recent specifications use the new keyword while older, but still valid, specifications remain unchanged.

4.1.6   Syntax Notation

Not every sequence of lexical elements is a correct IDL specification. The IDL grammar determines which sequence of symbols is valid and can be translated by the IDL compiler and which is not. To define IDL grammar, we employ *syntax rules*, whose notations are formulated in the well-known *Extended Backus-Naur Form* (EBNF). The complete set of IDL syntax rules is given in Appendix A. Table 2 explains the symbols that IDL-EBNF utilizes and describes their meanings.

Table 2: IDL EBNF Symbols

Symbol	Description
::=	is defined as
|	alternative
<text>	non-terminal syntactical element
"text"	literal

*	zero or more occurrences of the preceding syntactical element
+	one or more occurrences of the preceding syntactical element
{ }	the enclosed syntactical elements are grouped into a single syntactical element
[]	the enclosed syntactical element is optional (zero or one occurrences)

As an example, we analyze the first two rules of the OMG IDL grammar provided in Appendix A.

```
(1) <specification> ::= <import>* <definition>.+
(2) <definition> ::= <type_dcl> ";"
                    | <const_dcl> ";"
                    | <except_dcl> ";"
                    | <interface> ";"
                    | <module> ";"
                    | <value> ";"
                    | <type_id_dcl> ";"
                    | <type_prefix_dcl> ";"
                    | <event> ";"
                    | <component> ";"
                    | <home_dcl> ";"
```

The rules illustrate the basic composition of an IDL file. One can see that it consists of a (non-empty) sequence of definitions, which, in turn, specify types, constants, exceptions, interfaces, modules, values, etc. Additionally, this sequence is terminated by a ";" punctuation character. It may be initiated by several import declarations, the composition of which is specified in different syntax rules.

4.2 IDL Types

After having treated the lexical elements that constitute an IDL specification in the preceding sections, we examine, in the following, in which way types, constants, exceptions, interfaces, modules, and values are defined in IDL. All the code fragments shown in the next sections are valid IDL and, thus, can be translated with an IDL compiler. In order to do this, they have to be stored in a file named with the extension ".idl".

The constants, the attributes, the operation parameters, and the return results, which we define in an IDL specification, all have a *data type* that the IDL compiler maps to the corresponding type in the chosen implementation language.

The data types provided by IDL can be differentiated into *basic types*, *constructed types*, *template types*, *arrays*, *native types*, *interfaces*, and *value types* (see Figure 6). The basic types are built into IDL and can be used without further preparation; all the other types have to be declared by developers to be suitable for their particular application.

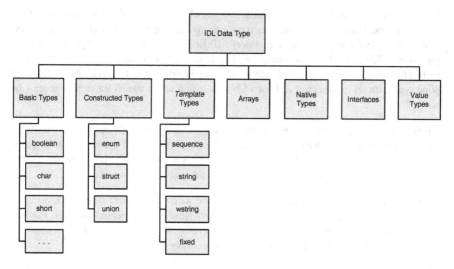

Figure 6: IDL Data Types

4.2.1 Basic Types

The *basic types* provided by IDL are suitable for storing simple values like, e.g., integer numbers, floating-point numbers, or characters. They are further classified into *arithmetic types*, *character types*, and *boolean types* as well as the data types octet and any. In addition, a type void is declared, which is used as a return type for operations that do not return a result.

The *arithmetic types* are, again, broken down into *integer types* and *floating-point types*. IDL's integer types are short, unsigned short, long, unsigned long, long long, and unsigned long long; they represent integer values in the ranges indicated in Table 3 given below.

Table 3: Ranges of Integer Data Types

Data Type	Range
short	-2^{15} to $2^{15} - 1$
unsigned short	0 to $2^{16} - 1$
long	-2^{31} to $2^{31} - 1$
unsigned long	0 to $2^{32} - 1$
long long	-2^{63} to $2^{63} - 1$
unsigned long long	0 to $2^{64} - 1$

The basic types float, double, and long double are provided for storing floating-point numbers. The ranges of these data types comply with the standards defined by the *Institute of Electrical and Electronics Engineers* (IEEE). The type float represents single-precision (Č 32 bit) floating-point numbers. The double type represents double-precision (Č 64 bit) floating-point numbers; and, long double is a double-extended (Č 79 bit) floating-point type with an exponent of at least 15 bits in length and a signed fraction of at least 64 bits.

Application developers should employ the long double type with caution since that type was introduced after CORBA 2.0 and is not yet supported by all programming language mappings. For example, no IDL to Java mapping exists for long doubles and developers of interoperable applications should, at the present time, abstain from using them.

OMG IDL supports two character types, char and wchar. The data type char occupies one byte (8 bit) and can encode arbitrary characters from a byte-oriented code set. Furthermore, the type wchar (*wide char*) can encode characters from any code set such as *Unicode*, for example. The size of wchar is implementation-dependent.

The basic type boolean is used to denote logical (*boolean*) values. Its range consists of the two values FALSE and TRUE.

In order to transmit 8-bit values that may not undergo any conversion during message communication, the basic type octet can be utilized.

The last but most powerful data type in IDL is type any. An any can store arbitrary OMG IDL types: basic or constructed types, template types, arrays, interface, etc., as well as user-defined types.

4.2.2   Constructed Types

The *constructed data types* are IDL types that developers compose from other types and that they label with a name. In that group belong *structures* (struct), *enumeration types* (enum), and *discriminated unions* (union), discussed below successively.

4.2.2.1   Structures

A *structure* aggregates a number of data elements that belong together and assigns a name to the emerging new type. The individual members of a structure each have their own type and name; the types may be unequal. The definition of a structure begins with the keyword struct, followed by an identifier—the name of the structure—and the list of members, which is enclosed in '{' and '}' and terminated by ';'. A member is defined by its type and its name; each definition is terminated by ';'. A structure can contain an arbitrary number of members of all valid IDL types. Nesting of structures is also allowed (see syntax rules (69)–(71) in Appendix A).

For example:

```
// simple structure

struct Product
{
  unsigned long product_number;
  string name;
  double price;
  float vat_rate;
};

// nested structure

struct OrderItem
{
  unsigned long quantity;
  struct Product
  {
    unsigned long product_number;
    string name;
    double price;
    float vat_rate;
  } item;
};
```

Structures define a new scope. All the identifiers of the members of a structure must be unique. However, if structures are nested, the identifiers of members from the enclosing structure can be reused in an embedded structure to name members of that inner structure.

Nested structures can also evolve if we use the name of a structure defined beforehand as the type of the member of a newly defined structure. The example below demonstrates this issue:

```
// structure

struct AlphanumericDate
{
  string date;
};

// structure

struct NumericDate
{
  unsigned short day;
  unsigned short month;
  unsigned short year;
};

// outer structure

struct Date
{
  // inner structures
```

```
    AlphanumericDate a_date;
    NumericDate n_date;
};
```

As a result of the name scoping rules, it is possible to name the string-member in Al-phanumericDate by date and, again, to choose the name Date for the last structure in the example. In Section 4.8, we discuss the IDL scoping rules in more detail.

4.2.2.2   Enumerations

An *enumerated type* defines a list of maximum 2^{32} named values, the so-called *enumerators*, which establish the range of that type. The type itself obtains a name (see syntax rules (78), (79)). IDL guarantees that an enumerated type is mapped to a data type that consists of at least 32 bits and, therefore, can represent all enumerator values. Differing from other programming languages like, e.g., C or C++, no assumptions on the actual values of enumerators can be made. In the example below, it is not allowed for MO to be assigned the value 0. The only certainty that developers can rely on is that the order in which the identifiers appear in the specification of an enumeration defines the relative order of their values. In the example, the value of MO is less than that of TU.

Example of an enumerated type:

```
enum DaysOfTheWeek
{
   MO, TU, WE, TH, FR, SA, SU
};
```

Enumerated types do not define a new scope. Therefore, the identifiers in an enumeration may not collide with identifiers introduced previously. In the example below, the second definition would be an error since APRIL is used twice:

```
enum Month
{
   JANUARY, FEBRUARY, MARCH, APRIL, MAY, JUNE, JULY,
   AUGUST, SEPTEMBER, OCTOBER, NOVEMBER, DECEMBER
};

enum User
{
   APRIL, CHRIS, TOM, MARTIN, AXEL, MARCUS
};
```

Note that, in the context of an enum specification, a typedef declaration (see Section 4.2.3) is redundant and should not be utilized.

4.2.2.3   Unions

An IDL *union* (sometimes called *variant*) is a cross between the union and switch-statement known from C and C++, respectively. Therefore, a union can, at any given time, contain an element of a type that is specified by the case-labels in the switch. A union consists of one or more case-labels, each followed by a combination of data type and corresponding identifier (see syntax rules (72)–(77)). Differing from a structure, a union can hold only a single value of one of its members. The value of the *discriminator*, whose type is specified in the switch, decides which union member is used. The discriminator must be type boolean or char, an integer type, or a previously defined enumerated type. The members of the union can be of any IDL type.

Example of a union type:

```
union Date switch(short)
{
  case 1:
    long numeric;
  case 2:
    string alphanumeric;
  default:
    any two_formats;
};
```

As far as possible, the IDL compiler checks the plausibility of the definition of a union provided by a developer and tries to eliminate errors. For example, since a boolean can only hold the values TRUE or FALSE, the following union definitions are correct:

```
union Date1 switch(boolean)
{
  case TRUE: string alphanumeric;
  default: long numeric;
};

union Date2 switch(boolean)
{
  case FALSE: long numeric;
  default: string alphanumeric;
};

union Date3 switch(boolean)
{
  case TRUE: string alphanumeric;
  case FALSE: long numeric;
};
```

However, the definition below is an error since the default-label can never be reached:

```
union Date4 switch(boolean)
{
  case TRUE: string alphanumeric;
  case FALSE: long numeric;
  default: any two_formats;
};
```

From the view of object orientation, unions are antiquated language constructs that are hard to understand, error-prone, and have little relation to the principles of object-oriented software development. In the following, we do without them.

4.2.3   Excursion: Named Data Types

In IDL, it is possible to introduce new names for any data type. This is done with the
`typedef` keyword. One should capitalize on that possibility in order to declare speaking
names for complex or self-defined types. For example:

```
typedef short SmallInt;
typedef long MidInt;
typedef long long BigInt;
```

On the other hand, `typedef`-names are mandatory when attributes or operations are defined
since direct specifications of new structures, enumerated types, sequences, unions, or fixed
types are not feasible there.

`typedef`s are also mandatory when fixed types (see Section 4.2.4.1), sequences (see Section 4.2.4.3), or arrays (see Section 4.2.5) are defined.

Newly defined types should not be redefined under an additional name as in the code fragment below:

```
typedef long Key;
typedef Key PublicKey;    // unconvincing
```

4.2.4   Template Types

Three *template types* are provided by IDL: *fixed types*, *string types*, and *sequences*. One
common characteristic of these types is that they require or offer the opportunity to specify
additional information when they are declared. With this specification, the size of the type
and, in the case of a sequence, the type of its elements is indicated.

4.2.4.1   Fixed Types

With the help of the `fixed` keyword, new numeric data types that are able to represent
fixed-point decimal numbers of up to 31 significant digits can be defined. When specifying
such a type, the total number of significant digits, as well as the scale (that is the number of
digits following the decimal point), have to be given in the form `fixed<n, m>`. The scale
must be a positive number less than the total number; 0 is a valid scale value. For example,
`fixed<10, 2>` is a fixed type with the range -99,999,999.99 to 99,999,999.99 and an ac-
curacy of 0.01. Fixed types can only be specified in the context of a `typedef` declaration.

From the syntax rules concerned here ((42)–(47), and (96)), we see that the general syntax is

```
typedef fixed<total_number, scale> identifier;
```

The result of the IDL definition `typedef fixed<6, 2> Count;` is the specification of
a new type named `Count`, which can store decimal fractions with four digits before and two
digits following the decimal point (six digits in total). The range of this newly defined type
therefore is -9,999.99 to 9,999.99.

The keyword fixed was only introduced after CORBA version 2.0, meaning that it is not supported by older ORBs. For that reason, during development of interoperable applications intended to run on different ORBs, fixed types should only be employed when it can be ensured that all involved platforms support them.

Additional example of a valid fixed type:

```
typedef fixed<31, 0> BigInt;
```

4.2.4.2   String Types

A *string* consists of all possible 8-bit characters included in the ISO Latin-1 (8859.1) character set; only null, the bit sequence 00000000 is excluded. As in a sequence (see Section 4.2.4.3 below), the maximum number of elements can be specified (bounded string) or unspecified (unbounded string). An unbounded string can contain an arbitrary number of characters; it is declared with the keyword string. A bounded string is declared in the form string<*n*>, where *n* is a positive integer constant that determines the string's maximum size.

The data type wstring (*wide string*) is similar to the string type; the only difference is that it supports Unicode characters (*wide character*; see Section 4.3.1.4). wstrings can also be declared bounded. In that case, the form wstring<*n*> is used.

Examples of strings:

```
// unbounded strings

typedef string CharacterString;
typedef wstring WideCharacterString;

// bounded strings

typedef string<20> CharacterString20;
typedef wstring<10> WideCharacterString10;
```

(See syntax rules (42)–(47), (81), and (82).) Since the wstring data type was introduced after CORBA version 2.0, it is not supported by older ORBs and should be employed with caution when interoperable applications intended to run on different platforms are implemented.

4.2.4.3   Sequences

A *sequence* is a one-dimensional array of values of the same type. Any valid IDL type is feasible for the elements of a sequence. The maximum number of elements in a sequence can be specified (bounded sequence) or unspecified (unbounded sequence). An unbounded sequence can contain an arbitrary number of elements. Its actual size is only restricted by the amount of memory available at run-time. For a bounded sequence, the maximum size of its elements is indicated in the type declaration and fixed at compile-time; it must be a positive integer constant. This fixed size is to be interpreted as an upper bound; the actual number of elements (also called length) can be less than or even zero.

Sequence types can only be specified in the context of a `typedef` declaration (see syntax rules (42)–(47), (80)). The elements of a sequence can be of a sequence type.

Examples of sequences:

```
typedef sequence<long> Vector;        // unbounded
typedef sequence<long, 10> Vector10;  // bounded

// sequence with structure

typedef Product Article; // from section 4.2.2.1
typedef sequence<Article> ProductCatalog;

// nested sequences

typedef sequence<float> Row;
typedef sequence<Row> Matrix;
```

Sequences are similar to arrays, which we discuss in the next section, Section 4.2.5. However, while the size of an array must be specified during its definition, this is optional for sequences. Thus, sequences offer more flexibility since they can store a large amount of data not known during the definition of the IDL interface and which is only determined at runtime. Conversely, marshaling and passing the values of arrays during a method invocation is often faster since the array's size is known.

4.2.5   Arrays

Arrays consist of a number of values of the same type. An array is defined with the keyword `typedef` followed by any IDL type, an identifier, and the array size, which is enclosed in brackets, '[' and ']'. It is not possible to define an array without specifying its size. The size must be a positive integer constant. Multi-dimensional arrays are defined by appending additional bracketed size specifications. For example:

```
// one-dimensional arrays

typedef string TermsAndConditions[100];
typedef long Array10[10];

// multi-dimensional arrays

typedef long Matrix2D[10][20];        // two-dimensional
typedef float Matrix3D[10][20][10]; // three-dimensional
```

4.2.6   Native Types

The keyword `native` provides a declaration of new basic data types for use by an object adapter. These are considered *opaque* and resemble the basic IDL types. The mapping of such a type depends on the programming language. Therefore, its usage should be reserved to ORB developers. Application developers should not employ native types in their programs and we do not go into a detailed explanation of their specifics here.

4.2.7   Interfaces

The *interface* is the fundamental and most important IDL type. It describes the services offered by a CORBA object residing on the server. In an interface, the behavior of an object is declared by specifying its *operations* and its state is declared by specifying its *attributes*. This data type is covered in detail in Section 4.5.

4.2.8   Value Types

Value Types were introduced in the CORBA specification 2.3. By declaring value types, it is possible not only to send references to objects from one host to the other but also to transmit copies of objects. The definition and the main application areas of value types are discussed more precisely in Section 4.6.

4.3   IDL Constants

4.3.1   Literal Constants

At the beginning of this chapter, we mentioned that the sequence of lexical elements making up an IDL specification could also contain literals. These denote a value that the IDL compiler can determine directly and that it then incorporates into the code it generates. Since their notation already expresses their value, such constants are also named *literal constants* (or *literals*). IDL distinguishes between the following literals:

- integer literals,
- floating-point literals,
- fixed-point literals,
- character literals,
- string literals, and
- boolean literals.

4.3.1.1   Integer Literals

Integer literals can be denoted decimal (base ten), octal (base eight), or hexadecimal (base sixteen).

In decimal notation, an integer literal is the digit 0 or it is a sequence of digits that begins with 1–9.

In octal notation, an integer literal starts with the digit 0, which is followed by a (non-empty) sequence of octal digits (0–7).

In hexadecimal notation, an integer literal starts with the sequence 0x or 0X, which is followed by a (non-empty) sequence of hexadecimal digits (0–9, A–F, or a–f).

Some examples of integer literals are 0 (decimal), 11 (decimal), 011 (octal, decimal value is 9), 0x11 (hexadecimal, decimal value is 17).

The standard does not specify the type (short, unsigned short, long, etc.) of an integer literal.

4.3.1.2   Floating-point Literals

Floating-point literals consist of a sequence of decimal digits (*integer part*), a decimal point, a sequence of decimal digits (*fraction part*), the letter e or E, an optional sign, and a further sequence of decimal digits (*exponent*). The e or E stands for "times 10 to the power of".

Several abbreviated forms are admissible:

- either the integer part or the fraction part, but not both, can be omitted and
- either the decimal point or the letter e (or E) and the exponent, but not both, can be omitted.

Some examples of floating-point literals are 10., .10, 10.10, 10E2, .10e2, 10.0E-10.

The standard does not specify the type (float, double, or long double) of a floating-point literal.

4.3.1.3   Fixed-point Literals

A *fixed-point literal* consists of a sequence of decimal digits (*integer part*), a decimal point, a sequence of decimal digits (*fraction part*), and the letter d or D. If an abbreviated notation is used,

- either the integer part or the fraction part, but not both, can be omitted and
- the decimal point, but not the letter d (or D), can be omitted.

The type of a fixed-point literal is determined by the number of its digits—leading or trailing zeros are not considered here. For example, 123.45d is of type fixed<5, 2>.

4.3.1.4   Character Literals

A *character literal* is a sequence of one or more characters enclosed in single quotation marks ('). Character literals are of type char. A character's size is 8 bits; it can have any numerical value between 0 and 255. The ISO Latin-1 (8859.1) standard defines all admissible characters and their values. In addition to the ASCII characters, this character set provides other characters, e.g., French accents or German umlauts.

Non-graphic characters (such as white space characters) and the characters ', ", and \ can be represented via *escape sequences*.

Table 4 below shows all the escape sequences valid in IDL.

Table 4: Escape Sequences in IDL

Escape Sequence	Description
\n	newline
\t	horizontal tabulator
\v	vertical tabulator
\b	backspace
\r	carriage return
\f	form feed
\a	alert
\?	question mark
\'	single quotation mark
\"	double quotation mark
\\	backslash
\ooo	octal number
\xhh	hexadecimal number
\uhhhh	Unicode character

The escape sequence \ooo consists of a \, followed by one, two, or three octal digits. \xhh consists of \x, followed by one or two hexadecimal digits.

Some examples of char literals that all represent the letter A are 'A', '\x41', and '\101'.

Literals of the type wchar are specified completely analogous; the only difference is that they require the prefix L, as in, e.g., L'a'. For wchar literals, the additional escape sequence \uhhhh is admissible. With its help, any Unicode character can be represented. Here, \uhhhh stands for \u, followed by one, two, three, or four hexadecimal digits. Some examples are L'\u00c4' (Ä), L'\u00e4' (ä), L'\u010c' (Č), L'\u010d' (č), L'\u0141' (Ł), L'\u0142' (ł), L'\u00c5' (Å), and L'\u00e5' (å).

Here, again, problems might arise from the fact that not all of today's IDL compilers accept the prefix L. Moreover, since the data type wchar was only introduced in CORBA version 2.0, interoperability problems with older ORBs that do not support that type might result.

The attempt to initialize a char constant with a wchar literal, or vice versa, a wchar constant with a char literal, may yield a warning or an error message from the IDL compiler and should be avoided.

4.3.1.5   String Literals

A *string literal* is a sequence of characters enclosed by double quotation marks ("). All characters mentioned in Section 4.3.1.4 are admissible with the exception of '\0', the character with numeric value 0. A string literal is of type string<*n*>, where *n* is the number of characters enclosed in the quotation marks. Characters in strings adjacent in an IDL specification are concatenated to a single string.

Some examples of string literals are "AbC", "Ab" "C" (also equals "AbC"), and "string3".

Wide string literals, literals of type wstring<*n*>, are specified analogously; they simply have to begin with an L prefix and, differing from string literals, they may also contain Unicode characters.

The same caution that was advisable concerning the employment of wchar literals is also indicated in the case of wide string literals.

Initialization of a string constant with a wide string literal, or vice versa, a wide string constant with a string literal, may yield a warning or an error message from the IDL compiler and should be avoided.

4.3.1.6   Boolean Literals

There are two *boolean literals*: TRUE and FALSE.

4.3.2   Declaration of Symbolic Constants

In addition to the literal constants that we addressed in Section 4.3.1, the IDL also knows *symbolic constants*, which are specified with a type, an identifier (the "symbol"), and a value. From syntax rules (27)–(38) (see Appendix A), one can see that the following types are admissible for symbolic constants:

- all integer types (short, long, ..., unsigned long long),
- all floating-point types (float, double, long double),
- all fixed-point types (here, the number of digits and the scale are determined from the constant's value),
- the character types char and wchar,
- the string types string and wstring (bounded as well as unbounded),
- the boolean type, and
- the type octet.

Furthermore, any type that is named by a typedef declaration and belongs to the list above or is enumerated is also admissible.

In its simplest form, the value of a symbolic constant is specified by means of a literal constant. The examples below demonstrate how this works for all types of literals discussed in Section 4.3.1.

Declaration of integer symbolic constants:

```
const short S1 = 0;      // decimal
const short S2 = 11;     // decimal
const short S3 = 011;    // octal, decimal value is 9
const short S4 = 0x11;   // hexadecimal, decimal value is 17
```

Declaration of symbolic floating-point constants:

```
const double D1 = 10.;
const double D2 = .10;
const double D3 = 10.10;
const double D4 = 10E2;
const double D5 = .10E2;
const double D6 = 10.0e-10;
```

Declaration of a symbolic fixed-point constant:

```
const fixed F = 123.45d; // the type is fixed<5, 2>
```

Declaration of symbolic character constants:

```
const char C1 = 'A';
const char C2 = '\n'; // newline
const char C3 = 'ß';
const char C4 = '\x41'; // 'A'
const char C5 = '\101'; // 'A'
const wchar WC1 = L'a';
const wchar WC2 = L'\u00c4'; // 'Ä'
const wchar WC3 = L'\u00e4'; // 'ä'
const wchar WC4 = L'\u010c'; // 'Č'
const wchar WC5 = L'\u010d'; // 'č'
const wchar WC6 = L'\u0141'; // 'Ł'
const wchar WC7 = L'\u0142'; // 'ł'
const wchar WC8 = L'\u00c5'; // 'Å'
const wchar WC8 = L'\u00e5'; // 'å'
```

Declaration of symbolic string constants:

```
const string TEXT1 = "AbC";
const string TEXT2 = "Ab" "C"; // equals "AbC"
const string TEXT3 = "\xA" "b";
```

The last example declares a string that contains the two characters '\xA' and 'b' and not the single character with the hexadecimal value '\xAb'.

```
const wstring WS = L"\u00dcber"; // equals "Über"
```

It is also possible to provide the value of a symbolic constant with the specification of a *constant expression*. This is a simple expression, the value of which can be determined at compile-time by the IDL compiler.

Only literals and identifiers of previously defined symbolic constants are allowed as operands in a constant expression.

As operators, all IDL operators identified in Section 4.3.2.1 can be applied. Their operation is comparable to that of the operators known from C++ and Java. Below, we give diverse examples for the usage of operators in constant declarations.

4.3.2.1   Operators

The IDL provides the following operators:

$$+ \quad - \quad * \quad / \quad \% \quad << \quad >> \quad \& \quad | \quad \char94 \quad \sim$$

The unary operators + and − are applicable to floating-point and fixed-point operands; the binary operators *, /, +, and − can operate on two floating-point or on two fixed-point operands.

The unary operators +, −, and ~ and the binary operators *, /, %, +, −, <<, >>, &, |, and ^ can operate on integer operands.

Unary + and − determine the operand's sign. The unary negation operator provides the bit-complement of its operand.

The binary operators +, −, *, and / yield the result of addition, subtraction, multiplication, and division of their operands, respectively. Operator % yields the remainder from the division of the first operand by the second. For b≠0, (a/b)*b + a%b equals a. For b=0, the result is undefined.

The operators << and >> shift the left operand left and right, respectively; the number of bits is specified by the right operand. Vacated bits are filled with 0. In both cases, the value of the right operand must be Č0 and < 64.

The operators &, ^, and | generate logical bitwise AND, Exclusive-OR, and Inclusive-OR combinations of their operands. The results are indicated in the following Table 5:

Table 5: Results of the Bit-Operators

bit 1	bit 2	bit 1 & bit 2	bit 1 | bit 2	bit 1 ^ bit 2
0	0	0	0	0
0	1	0	1	1
1	0	0	1	1
1	1	1	1	0

Examples for applying operators in constant expressions:

```
// unary operators with integer operands

const long LO1 = +1;
const long LO2 = -1;
const long  LO3 = ~0x00ff; // decimal value is -256
const short SO1 = ~0x00ff; // as above
const unsigned long LO4 = ~0x00ff; // result 4294967040

// shift operators

const short SO2 = 0x0001 << 2; // result 4
const unsigned short SO3 = 0x0010 >> 1; // result 8

// bit operators
// INCLUSIVE OR

const short SO4 = 0x00f0 | 0x000f; // 0x00ff
const short SO5 = 0x00f0 | 0x00ff; // 0x00ff

// AND

const short SO6 = 0x00f0 & 0x000f; // 0x0000
const short SO7 = 0x00f0 & 0x00ff; // 0x00f0

// EXCLUSIVE OR

const short SO8 = 0x00f0 ^ 0x000f; // 0x00ff
const short SO9 = 0x00f0 ^ 0x00ff; // 0x000f

// unary operators with floating-point operands

const float FO1 = +1.;
const float FO2 = -.1;

// binary operators

const float FO3 = 1.0;
const float FO4 = FO3 + 2. - 1.; // 2.0
const float FO5 = 2. * FO1; // 2.0
const float FO6 = FO3 / FO4; // 1.0
const long LO5 = 7;
const long LO6 = 3;
const long LO7 = LO5 / LO6; // 2
const long LO8 = LO5 % LO6; // 1
```

4.4   Exceptions

With the help of *exceptions*, developers can determine the reaction of their applications on the occurrence of a situation where it is not possible to proceed normally through the code of an operation's implementation. Potential reasons might be, e.g., that a non-existing file has to be opened, that an element in a list has to be accessed but is not found, or that the connection to another object was interrupted.

In IDL, it is possible to define *simple exceptions*, containing no additional information except for their type name, and *constructed exceptions* that can provide additional information on the exceptional condition that has occurred during execution of the request. In the second case, they widely resemble a structure; an exception can also contain an arbitrary number of members of different IDL types (see syntax rule (86)). While a structure can itself be a member of a sequence, a union, or an enclosing structure and can also appear as an attribute in an interface, exceptions can only be utilized in the context of an operation declaration. For example:

```
// simple exception

exception Error { };

// exception with additional details

exception ErrorReport
{
  string error_message;
  short  error_code;
  string date;
};
```

4.5   Interface Declarations

The structure and purpose of an *IDL interface* are similar to those of a Java interface or an abstract C++ class. The aim is to determine the externally visible (in Java or C++ specified `public`) attributes and operations of an object. Constants, further types, and exceptions can also be defined in an interface (see syntax rules (4)–(11)). We see that, in its simplest form, an interface starts with the keyword `interface`, continues with the interface name, and then provides the attributes, operations, and other elements of the interface, which are enclosed in braces '{' and '}' delimiting the interface *body*. As usual, the declaration is terminated by ';'. An interface defines a new scope of its own; all identifiers introduced in an interface declaration must be unique unless they are defined in an embedded scope, for example, a structure. The interface is the central IDL type. Without interfaces, no CORBA application with distributed, cooperating objects would be possible. Supertype for all interfaces— with the exception of abstract and local interfaces, described below—is the interface `CORBA::Object`.

Example for an interface declaration:

```
interface ShopServer
{
  const unsigned long MAX = 100;
  // terms and conditions
  typedef sequence<string, MAX> TaC;
  exception Error { };
  readonly attribute TaC terms_and_conditions;
  readonly attribute unsigned long minimum_turnover;
  boolean order(in string product) raises(Error);
};
```

If an interface B refers to an interface A and if, reciprocally, B is needed in the declaration of A, then a *forward declaration* of A is necessary. This declares that A is the name of an interface type without defining the internal composition of A. The example below demonstrates how the problem can be solved that, in the declaration of B, operation returns a reference to an A-object, while A's declaration follows that of B. Without the possibility to forward declare an interface name, the problem could not be solved. Simply rearranging the two interfaces would pose the problem reciprocally—B would be referenced before being declared.

```
interface A; // forward declaration of A

interface B
{
  A get_a();
};

interface A // definition of A
{
  B get_b();
};
```

An interface can be *derived* from one or several other interfaces, which are then called *base* interfaces or *superinterfaces*. In that case, the derived interface, or *subinterface*, inherits all elements (types, constants, exceptions, attributes, and operations) of the superinterfaces and can use them as if they were its own elements. Inheritance is specified by inserting the list of superinterfaces behind the name of the derived interface, separated from that by a ':'. A derived interface may redefine any name of the types, constants, and exceptions that have been inherited.

A difference from inheritance in C++ and Java is that in IDL neither overloading nor overriding of operations is admissible. For example:

```
interface X
{
  short opa(in short i);
  short opa(in short i, in long l); // error: overloading
};

interface Y : X
{
  short opa(in short i); // error: overriding
};
```

One further difference from C++ and Java is that an interface cannot contain embedded interface declarations.

An interface declaration can begin with the keyword abstract. The interface is then *abstract* and need not be implemented in a concrete programming language. Nevertheless, it can serve as superinterface for other interfaces. Unless they are themselves abstract, interfaces derived from an abstract interface have to implement all inherited definitions. Abstract interfaces may only inherit from other abstract interfaces. Supertype for all abstract interfaces is the interface CORBA::AbstractBase.

An interface declaration can also begin with the keyword local, declaring a *local* interface. Note that an interface cannot be declared local and abstract at the same time. Objects implementing a local interface are *local objects*, which have to reside in the same address space as their callers. Supertype for all local interfaces is the interface CORBA::LocalObject.

Several special restrictions apply to local interfaces and their utilization. For example, they may not appear

- as parameter, return, attribute, or exception types in the context of the declaration of an operation in a non-local interface or
- as type of the state member of a value type.

A local interface may inherit from other interfaces; but, again, several restrictions have to be noted. Table 6 gives an overview on admissible inheritance relationships.

Table 6: Inheritance Rules for Interfaces

Superinterface / Subinterface	abstract	local	neither abstract nor local
abstract	✓	—	—
local	✓	✓	✓
neither abstract nor local	✓	—	✓

The following example demonstrates how an inheritance hierarchy of interfaces may be defined. Besides single inheritance, multiple inheritance, where an interface derives from more than one superinterface, is shown. An abstract interface File is declared, with derived subinterfaces ReadOnlyFile and WriteOnlyFile each declaring an additional specific operation. Finally, the interface ReadAndWriteFile is declared, which, for its part, inherits from both interfaces ReadOnlyFile and WriteOnlyFile (see Figure 7).

```
abstract interface File
{
  void open();
  void close();
};

interface ReadOnlyFile : File
{
  string read_line();
};

interface WriteOnlyFile : File
{
  void write_line(in string data);
};
```

```
interface ReadAndWriteFile : ReadOnlyFile, WriteOnlyFile
{
  void change_mode();
};
```

If an interface multiply inherits from several supertypes, as `ReadAndWriteFile` in the example above, ambiguities concerning the names of the inherited elements (attributes, operations, etc.) might arise. In Section 4.8 we briefly describe how such name conflicts can be resolved.

4.5.1   Attribute Declarations

The data elements defined in an interface body are called *attributes* (see syntax rules (9), (85), and (104)–(111)). The state of an object is described by the values of its attributes. In any implementation language, an attribute is mapped to two methods for reading and writing its attribute value, the so-called *accessor* functions (also *getter* and *setter* functions). An attribute can be specified `readonly`; in that case, only the method to retrieve its value is generated.

Examples for attributes:

```
typedef fixed<6, 2> Thousand;
attribute Thousand amount;
readonly attribute long product_id;
attribute ProductCatalog product_catalog;
  // see section 4.2.4.3
attribute Product article; // see section 4.2.2.1
```

Even attributes can raise exceptions in CORBA. This is a consequence of their implementation through accessor functions and can be enabled with the IDL keywords `getraises` for the corresponding getter and `setraises` for the corresponding setter method, respectively. We do not go into details regarding these possibilities since not all known ORBs support that functionality at the moment.

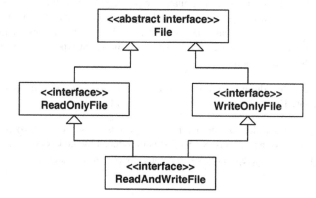

Figure 7: Example of Inheritance of Interfaces

4.5.2   Operation Declarations

On the interface level, *operations* specify, in principle, the behavior of objects to be implemented later in a concrete programming language. In IDL, an operation declaration consists of the type of the operation's *return result*, an identifier that determines the operation's *name*, and a *parameter list*, which is enclosed in parentheses, ' (' and ') ', and specifies zero or more parameters as well as an optional *list of exceptions* that can be raised during execution of the operation and is also enclosed in parentheses (see syntax rules (87)–(95)). An operation declaration may begin with the keyword `oneway`, which influences its invocation semantics (see below). It may end with a *context* expression, which provides a list of properties of the caller's environment that need to be supplied to the server—this powerful concept must be handled with care if platform-independency is an objective. It is not covered in our book.

Operations that do not return a result must specify the result type as being `void`. For each parameter in the parameter list, the type and the name have to be given. In addition, each parameter specifies information on the direction in which its value is to be passed between client and server. This information is provided by a *directional attribute* that precedes the parameter's type. IDL offers three directional attributes:

- `in`, the parameter value is passed from client to server,
- `out`, the parameter value is passed from server to client, and
- `inout`, the parameter value is passed in both directions.

It should be noted that parameters not of an interface type (in other words, that are not to be represented by CORBA objects in the application) are always *passed by value*. For objects, however, the value of their IOR is passed, i.e., the object's state itself is not copied. This standard approach can be modified by making use of value types that support passing of objects by value and is discussed in Section 4.6. (Details on parameter passing are given in Section 5.17.)

When an operation is declared with the keyword `oneway`, invocations of that operation carry best-effort semantics. This does not guarantee delivery of the call but implies that the operation is to be invoked at most once. The caller gets an immediate return and does not know whether the request has actually been executed by the server. For these reasons, only `in` parameters are admissible for `oneway` operations, the result type must be `void`, and there must be no list of exceptions.

All the ORBs we studied during our work showed the same behavior towards realization of `oneway` operations. The calls were asynchronous and non-blocking.

If an operation specifies which exceptions may be raised as a result of its invocation, it declares a non-empty list of exceptions. Such a list is introduced by the keyword `raises` and contains the names of the exception types, separated by commas, and enclosed in parentheses.

Examples for operation declarations:

```
interface Calculator
{
    exception DivisionByZero { };
    // operation with result
    long add(in long op1, in long op2);
    // operation with result and exception
    double divide(in long dividend, in long divisor)
        raises(DivisionByZero);
    // oneway operation
    typedef sequence<long> Values;
    oneway void sum(in Values v);
    long get_result();
    // operation without result
    // (but note the inout parameter)
    void scalar_mult(in long s, inout Values v);
};
```

4.6   Value Types

Since version 2.3 of the CORBA standard, it is possible to pass objects by value rather than by reference in an operation. For this, one uses a *value type*—which can declare the same elements as an interface, thus, types, constants, exceptions, attributes, and operations. Moreover, a value type can provide a *state definition* and *initializers* that determine its initial state. A number of different kinds of value types exist: *regular*, *boxed*, and *abstract*. Therefore, the syntax rules for value type are numerous ((13)–(26)).

A regular value type's state members are defined via specific attributes differing from the definition of the attributes in an interface declaration in two aspects. On the one hand, they are not defined with the usage of the keyword `attribute` (and also without `readonly`). On the other hand, they must be declared `public` or `private`. Access to the value of `private` state members is restricted to the marshaling code and the implementation code of the value type's operations; they are not transmitted to the server. Both sender and receiver must provide an implementation of every transmitted value type so that invocations of the value types' operations are always local and not remote. (However, the implementation code of a value type operation may contain remote invocations.)

Initializers can be defined for regular value types. With regard to their function, these initializers resemble the constructors in object-oriented programming languages although there is no such thing as a default "initializer". Syntactically, they are largely similar to operations where the operation's return type is substituted by the keyword `factory` and only `in` parameters are used. An example for a regular value type:

```
valuetype Time
{
    // private state members
    private unsigned short hours;
    private unsigned short minutes;
    private unsigned short seconds;
```

```
    // initializer
    factory init(in unsigned short hours,
       in unsigned short minutes,
       in unsigned short seconds);
    // local operations
    unsigned short get_hours();
    unsigned short get_minutes();
    unsigned short get_seconds();
    boolean equals(in Time another_time);
};
```

If an initializer is not provided for every state member, there is no portable way for clients to create an instance of this type and to transmit it to the server.

The example below demonstrates how a newly defined value type Amount is employed as parameter type as well as result type in the declaration of an operation convert(), which is an element of an interface CurrencyConverter.

```
valuetype Amount
{
    // initializer
    factory create(in double v, in string c);
    // local operation
    boolean compare(in Amount another_amount);
    // state members
    public double value;
    public string currency;
};

interface CurrencyConverter
{
    Amount convert(in Amount a, in string currency);
};
```

As noted above, the IDL distinguishes two further categories of value types, namely, boxed and abstract value types. Boxed value types cannot inherit from other types, have no operations, and define only one single unnamed state member (see syntax rule (15)). They are typically used as simple containers that can be easily represented in IDL. For example:

```
interface Subscriber
{
    void receive(in string message);
};

valuetype SubscriberSeq sequence<Subscriber>;
```

Value types can also be declared abstract. This means that they may not be instantiated. No state members or initializers may be defined for abstract value types; only operation declarations are admissible.

Value types may inherit from other value types, an interface, and any number of abstract interfaces. As in the case of interface inheritance, a colon, ':', is used between subtype and supertypes. By means of the keyword `supports`, it is indicated that the value type also provides the functionality specified in an interface. For example:

```
abstract interface OutputFormatter
{
  string print();
};

interface Product : OutputFormatter
{
  attribute unsigned long product_id;
  attribute string name;
  attribute double price;
  attribute float vat_rate;
};

valuetype Amount supports OutputFormatter
{
  ... as above
};

interface Display
{
  void show(in OutputFormatter formatter);
};
```

The abstract interface `OutputFormatter` specifies an operation `print()`. This operation can, for example, be invoked in order to convert an object into a suitable `string` representation. To similarly enable this for objects relying on an interface definition as well as for values, an interface (in the example: `Product`) can inherit from `OutputFormatter` and a value type (in the example: `Amount`) can support the interface `OutputFormatter`. Now, the `Display` operation `show()` can be invoked for instances of both types.

With the exception of boxed value types, a value type may be subtype of one or many other value types, provided that these supertypes are themselves not boxed. Also, regular as well as abstract value types may support at most one interface. Should a value type be subtype of another value type that already supports an interface, that subtype may not support an additional interface. Therefore, the following example is an error:

```
interface IfaceExmpl1
{
  ...
};
interface IfaceExmpl2
{
  ...
};
valuetype VTExmpl1 supports IfaceExmpl1
{
  ...
};
```

```
// error
valuetype VTExmpl2 : VTExmpl1 supports IfaceExmpl2
{
   ...
};
```

Here, value type VTExmpl2, as a subtype of VTExmpl1, must support IfaceExmpl1; and, it is also declared to support the IfaceExmpl2 interface, which is not allowed by IDL.

In Table 7, the inheritance relationships between value types and interfaces, respectively, are summarized.

Table 7: Value Types, Interfaces, and Inheritance

supertype / subtype	interface	abstract interface	abstract value type	regular value type	boxed value type
interface	multiple	multiple	not admissible	not admissible	not admissible
abstract interface	not admissible	multiple	not admissible	not admissible	not admissible
abstract value type	single (supports)	multiple (supports)	multiple	not admissible	not admissible
regular value type	single (supports)	multiple (supports)	multiple	single	not admissible
boxed value type	not admissible	not admissible	not admissible	not admissible	not admissible

4.7   Module Declarations

IDL *modules* provide a means of preventing name conflicts. A module constructs a new scope so that identifiers that were already defined in another module can be reused. All names of constants, interfaces, exceptions, etc., from the CORBA specification are contained in the module CORBA.

A module definition begins with the keyword module and, subsequently, the module name. Then, the definitions of the module's constants, types, exceptions, interfaces, and values follow; they are enclosed in '{' and '}'. Nested modules are admissible (see syntax rules (3)).

Typically, an IDL specification has the following structure (which is, with respect to correct IDL grammar, somewhat abbreviated):

```
module identifier
{
   constant declaration; ...
   type declaration; ...
```

```
    exception declaration; ...
    interface identifier [: superinterface]
    {
        constant declaration; ...
        type declaration; ...
        exception declaration; ...
        attribute declaration; ...
        operation declaration; ...
    }; ...
};
```

For example:

```
module eShop
{
    interface ShopServer
    {
        // constant
        const short MAX = 100;
        // types
        typedef sequence<string, MAX> TaC;
        typedef sequence<string> ProductCatalog;
        // exception
        exception ProductOutOfStock { };
        // attributes
        readonly attribute TaC terms_and_conditions;
        readonly attribute long minimum_turnover;
        // operations
        void order(in string product, in long quantity)
            raises(ProductOutOfStock);
        ProductCatalog get_product_range();
        double get_price(in string product);
    };
};
```

4.8   Scoping

The *scope* of an identifier is the IDL code where its name can be used. IDL provides multiple nested levels of scope. At the highest level, each IDL file constitutes a scope. Within a file, the modules, interfaces, value types, structures, unions, operations, and exceptions each define their own smaller scope. For operations, scope is delimited by the parentheses, '(' and ')'; otherwise, '{' and '}' embrace the scope. An identifier's scope begins immediately following its declaration and extends until the end of the respective module, interface, value type, structure, union, operation, or exception declaration. It ends immediately preceding the closing '}' or ')'. Irrespective of case, an identifier can only be defined once in a scope. However, scopes may be nested and identifiers can be redefined in nested scopes.

The specifications of an entire IDL file, together with the contents of any files included by a #include directive, form the *global scope*. Identifiers from a surrounding scope are valid in an inner scope. They can also be redefined in the inner scope in order to name a different entity. For example:

```
module M
{
   typedef short M; // error: redefinition in same scope

   typedef fixed<6, 2> T;
   interface I
   {
      attribute T x;
      void m(); // correct: redefinition in inner scope
   };
};
```

Identifiers from other scopes may be used—once they are defined—if they are fully *qualified* with the name of their module, interface, value type, structure, union, and exception, respectively. The qualified name is constructed by prefixing the identifier with the module, interface, ..., exception name and a ": :". For example:

```
module Currencies
{
   enum Currency
   {
      EUR, GBP, JPY, USD
   };
   typedef fixed<10, 6> ExchangeRate;
   exception InvalidCurrency { };
   interface CurrencyServer
   {
      ExchangeRate get_exchange_rate(in Currency c)
         raises(InvalidCurrency);
   };
};

module BankApplication
{
   typedef fixed<10, 2> Amount;
   interface CurrencyConverter
   {
      // parameter types qualified
      // since declared in another module
      Amount convert(in Amount a,
         in Currencies::Currency source,
         in Currencies::Currency target)
         raises(Currencies::InvalidCurrency);
   };
};
```

In this example, module Currencies contains the declarations of the numeric type ExchangeRate, different abbreviated currency names (Currency), and an exception (InvalidCurrency) as well as the interface CurrencyServer. Some of these declarations, e.g., the data type Currency, might be useful for other applications. Even if such an application is specified in a different module, it can use these declarations by qualifying their names with the module name, e.g., Currencies::Currency.

Had we defined the exception `InvalidCurrency` not in the scope of module `Curren-cies` but in the scope of the interfaces `CurrencyServer`, then, the `raises` expression of the `BankApplication`'s operation `convert()` would need further qualification and use `Currencies::CurrencyServer::InvalidCurrency` as an exception name.

Identifiers from the global scope can be accessed when their names are prefixed with a simple "`::`". For example, the following would be correct IDL code:

```
exception E
{
  long l;
};

module M
{
  interface E
  {
    void m() raises(::E);
  };
};
```

However, such unnecessarily confusing code should be avoided in one's own applications. The OMG style guide recommends the use of file scope notation only in situations when no other scope resolution exists. The style guide also recommends that file-level definitions not be used; rather interface declarations and other definitions should always be embedded in modules instead.

Qualification of names may be helpful in order to prevent ambiguities that might otherwise arise from multiple inheritance, as in the example below:

```
interface A
{
  typedef long X;
};

interface B
{
  typedef short X;
};

interface C : A, B
{
  typedef X Y; // error: X ambiguous
  typedef A::X Y; // ok
};
```

Again, there must be good reasons, e.g., IDL code from a library that has to be reused, for employing such a construction.

4.9   Concluding Remarks

In the following sections, we provide some general comments concerning the development of CORBA-based programs that are mainly intended for practical application.

4.9.1   Interoperability

If the CORBA standard is selected to be employed as the basis for developing multi-layered distributed applications, it may happen that decisions concerning the application's design are made requiring different platforms or programming languages on the client and on the server side. These decisions might further have as a consequence that, during development of the business logic server, a different ORB has to be used as on the client side. This, in turn, implies interoperability of the involved ORBs. Since CORBA 2.0 provided the framework of interoperability for the collaboration of various ORBs, no principal problems should be expected here.

However, when ORBs of different vendors are employed that are, in addition, based on differing versions of the CORBA specification, certain problems might arise. In that case, developers first should determine to what extent the available products actually support all the elements defined by IDL. Only thereafter, can definition of the interfaces and development of the application commence. Especially in the case of multi-department or multi-company projects based on diverse products, it has to be ensured that IDL types or keywords not supported by all of them are not used. This aspect is also of central importance with regard to *Enterprise Application Integration* and *Supply Chain Management* since, in that context, different ORB products relying on differing versions of the standard, in particular, come into operation and have to be integrated.

The ORB products available on today's market support the CORBA standard's different versions more or less completely. Due to the mentioned reasons, the basis for CORBA applications where interoperability aspects are essential should always be CORBA version 2.0. Furthermore, keywords and data types introduced in higher versions of the standard such as, e.g., `abstract`, `fixed`, `local`, `long double`, `supports`, `truncatable`, `valuetype`, `wchar`, and `wstring` should not be used; or, at a minimum, they should not be employed without an initial exploration determining whether or not all involved ORBs support them to the required extent.

4.9.2   Using Anonymous Types

In a number of places, the IDL syntax rules permit developers to define anonymous types. In the current specification of the CORBA standard, such definitions are deprecated since they caused problems for some language mappings. For example, it is allowed but deprecated to define an anonymous sequence as in the example below:

```
typedef sequence<sequence<float> > matrix;
```

Note that, in order to prevent them from being translated as operator ">>", white space has to separate the two '>' characters.

Such a construction should now be realized as follows:

```
typedef sequence<float> columns;
typedef sequence<columns> matrix;
```

The new rule also affects other parts of the IDL. The following valid IDL definitions,

```
const string<5> SYSTEM = "CORBA";

interface I
{
  readonly attribute wstring<3> INSTITUTION = "OMG";
  sequence<long, 5> become_member();
};
```

should now be replaced by

```
typedef const string<5> SystemType;
const SystemType SYSTEM = "CORBA";

interface I
{
  typedef wstring<3> InstitutionType;
  readonly attribute InstitutionType INSTITUTION = "OMG";
  typedef sequence<long, 5> Result;
  Result become_member();
};
```

4.10 Exercises

1. IDL conformity

   a) Find out whether your IDL compiler accepts identifiers that only differ with respect to upper- and lower-case.
   b) What is the effect of including a line comment within a block comment?
   c) Which characters are contained in the following string constant: const string s = "\xf" "f" "\010" "10";
   d) How can the character " be inserted into a string constant?
   e) Find out whether your IDL compiler accepts the prefix L for literals of types wchar and wstring.

2. Nesting

   a) Is it admissible to define a module within another module definition?
   b) Is it admissible to define an interface within another interface definition?
   c) Is it admissible to define a structure within another structure definition?

3. Inheritance

   a) Can an interface inherit from multiple other interfaces?
   b) Can an abstract interface be supertype of a non-abstract interface?

   c) Can an abstract interface be subtype of a non-abstract interface?

   d) Can a value type inherit from multiple other value types?

   e) Can a value type support multiple interfaces?

4. Is it possible to pass a CORBA object as well as the instance of a value type as an argument to an operation that has an interface type as parameter?

5. Find all errors in the following module declaration. How would a correct solution look?

```
module Applications
{
  module ECommerce
  {
    typedef String Text;
    interface ShopServer
    {
      struct Product
      {
        int product_no;
        Text name;
        double price;
        float vat_rate;
      };
      typedef sequence<Product> ProductCatalog;
      void order(in Product, in int quantity);
      ProductCatalog get_product_catalog();
    };

    interface DatabaseAdapter
    {
      typedef sequence<Text> ResultSeq;
      exception Disconnected { };
      void connect();
      ResultSeq query(Text sql)
        throws Disconnected();
      void disconnect();
    };
  }
}
```

6. Determine the value of the two symbolic constants.

```
const short S = 0x0010>>1;
const long long L = ~0x00ff;
```

7. When the IDL compiler translates the definition of an interface, it replaces symbolic constants by their values. What does this imply for the parameter of the operation f(), which C inherits from A?

```
const long L = 3;
interface A
{
  typedef float Par[L];
```

```
    void f(in Par x);
};

interface B
{
    const long L = 30;
};

interface C : B, A
{
};
```

8. Use qualified names to produce clarity in interface D.

```
module A
{
    interface B
    {
        typedef string<100> Text;
    };
};

interface C
{
    typedef string<1000> Text;
};

interface D : A::B, C
{
    attribute Text small;
    attribute Text big;
};
```

9. Use qualified names to produce clarity in this IDL file.

```
enum Color
{
    RED, ORANGE, GREEN, YELLOW
};

module M
{
    enum Color
    {
        RED, GREEN, BLUE
    };
    const ::Color c = ORANGE;
};

const Color c = M::RED;
```

5   IDL to Java Mapping

We have already discussed that CORBA's independence of programming languages is based primarily on the fact that only an IDL compiler translates the interface definition into a specific language. In order to standardize this process, the OMG has specified language mappings for Ada, C, C++, COBOL, Lisp, PL/1, Python, and Smalltalk. In this chapter, we address the "OMG IDL to Java Language Mapping" [OMG02].

5.1   Introductory Remarks

All Java classes and interfaces, which constitute the essential specification of the CORBA standard, are to be found in the Java package `org.omg` and in packages on a lower level in the hierarchy such as `org.omg.CORBA`. The package `org.omg` also contains several classes needed to access diverse CORBA Services. For example, Java classes and interfaces related to OMG's Naming Service are located in the package `org.omg.CosNaming` while those pertaining to the *Event Service* are members of the packages `org.omg.CosEvent-Comm` and `org.omg.CosEventChannelAdmin`. All other Java implementations of elements defined in the CORBA specification or in the CORBA Services framework also adhere to this packaging scheme.

If a new type is introduced in an IDL definition, the IDL to Java compiler generates several files, each containing a Java class declaration related to that type, from this type's IDL specification. Thus, for each newly defined IDL type, a `<type>Holder` as well as a `<type>Helper` file, where `<type>` stands for the type name, are created. These are studied in more detail in Sections 5.4 and 5.5, respectively. Depending on the IDL type, additional files and classes are created; they are discussed at the appropriate place in the following sections.

5.2   Names

In general, IDL identifiers are mapped to Java identifiers with no change. However, there are some exceptions to this rule. These were introduced in order to avoid name collisions with Java keywords, Java constants, and methods from class `java.lang.Object`. In such cases, the respective identifier is appended with the prefix '_'. The basis for such "reserved" names is the *Java Language Specification 1.0, First Edition, Section 3.9* [GJS96], where the following Java keywords are listed:

abstract	default	if	private	throw
boolean	do	implements	protected	throws
break	double	import	public	transient
byte	else	instanceof	return	try
case	extends	int	short	void

catch	final	interface	static	volatile
char	finally	long	super	while
class	float	native	switch	
const	for	new	synchronized	
continue	goto	package	this	

The additional Java constants that might collide with an IDL identifier are true, false, and null.

Also, the methods of class java.lang.Object (see the *Java Language Specification 1.0, First Edition, Section 20.1* [GJS96]) belong to the reserved names whose collision with IDL identifiers has to be excluded. They are given below:

clone	equals	finalize	getClass	hashCode
notify	notifyAll	toString	wait	

These method names might cause problems since the class java.lang.Object serves as superclass of all Java classes and, thus, also of all Java implementations of interfaces defined in IDL. Should such an IDL interface define an operation that has a correspondingly named method counterpart in java.lang.Object (e.g., wait()), then directly adopting this name in the Java implementation would result in overriding the inherited method, which would, in most cases, not be intended or even recognized and would lead to undesirable side-effects. The IDL compiler would, therefore, map the valid IDL identifier wait to the Java identifier _wait, normally without indicating this intervention.

5.3   Mapping for Basic Data Types

Following Table 8 shows the mapping of IDL's basic types to Java.

Table 8: Mapping for Basic Types

IDL Type	Java Type	Exceptions
boolean	boolean	
char	char	CORBA::DATA_CONVERSION
wchar	char	CORBA::DATA_CONVERSION
octet	byte	
string	java.lang.String	CORBA::MARSHAL CORBA::DATA_CONVERSION
wstring	java.lang.String	CORBA::MARSHAL CORBA::DATA_CONVERSION
short	short	
unsigned short	short	
long	int	

unsigned long	int	
long long	long	
unsigned long long	long	
float	float	
double	double	
long double	*not defined yet*	
fixed	java.math.BigDecimal	CORBA::DATA_CONVERSION
any	org.omg.CORBA.Any	

The exceptions listed in the last column may be raised at run-time because the Java type is larger than IDL and, therefore, can contain inadmissible values.

Note that the unsigned IDL types unsigned short, unsigned long, and unsigned long long are mapped to Java's signed types short, int, and long. For developers, this means that they are responsible for ensuring that the values of such a type do not become negative. Furthermore, the IDL type long is mapped to int in Java. The reason is that the range of the latter is sufficient to hold all admissible values of the IDL type. The IDL type long double is not yet supported by the Java mapping.

5.4 Holder Classes

In order to pass parameters that have been defined inout or out, so-called *holder classes* are generated. For the basic IDL data types such as long or any, corresponding classes are already available in package org.omg.CORBA, for example, org.omg.CORBA.Long-Holder and org.omg.CORBA.AnyHolder.

If an IDL interface provides new user-defined types, then, during translation of the IDL file, the IDL compiler automatically generates the appropriate holder classes. Naming of these compiler-generated classes always follows the same schema, where

<type> becomes <type>Holder in Java.

Thus, for a user-defined IDL type T, the holder class THolder is generated. The example below shows the general layout of a holder class THolder, where it is irrelevant whether T is a basic IDL type already supported by a holder class included in the runtime library or a user-defined type for which the IDL compiler still has to generate the holder class.

```
// THolder.java

public final class THolder implements
  org.omg.CORBA.portable.Streamable {

  public T value;

  public THolder () { }
  public THolder (T initial) {
```

```
        value = initial;
    }
    public org.omg.CORBA.TypeCode _type () {
        ...
    }
    public void _read(
        org.omg.CORBA.portable.InputStream is) {
        ...
    }
    public void _write(
        org.omg.CORBA.portable.OutputStream os) {
        ...
    }
}
```

In addition to an instance variable value, the holder class declares two constructors. The first is a default constructor that initializes this variable to its default value—false for booleans, 0 for arithmetic types, null for reference types. The second constructor, an argument of the (Java) type T, must be passed and is used to initialize the variable value. The holder class also declares the methods _read() and _write(), which are needed for marshaling, as well as a method _type(), which returns the type (more precisely, the *TypeCode* of the type) of the stored value.

In the following, Table 9, the holder classes already defined in package omg.org.CORBA are compiled.

Table 9: Pre-defined Holder Classes

IDL Type	Holder Class
boolean	BooleanHolder
char	CharHolder
wchar	CharHolder
octet	ByteHolder
string	StringHolder
wstring	StringHolder
short	ShortHolder
unsigned short	ShortHolder
long	IntHolder
unsigned long	IntHolder
long long	LongHolder
unsigned long long	LongHolder
float	FloatHolder
double	DoubleHolder
fixed	BigDecimalHolder
long double	–
Object	ObjectHolder
any	AnyHolder

5.5   Helper Classes

Helper classes are relevant in the context of user-defined IDL types. They are helpful for determining and manipulating type information, enable insertion and extraction of instances of the newly defined type into or from an `Any` (IDL any), and provide methods to read from an input stream or write to an output stream. Like the holder classes described above, helper classes are automatically generated by the IDL compiler for each user-defined IDL type. Naming of the compiler-generated holder classes follows a schema, where

`<type>` becomes `<type>Helper` in Java.

Thus, for an interface `T`, a helper class `THelper` is generated. The following example shows parts of the helper class `THelper` with the most relevant methods:

```
// THelper.java

public final class THelper {
    public static T narrow(org.omg.CORBA.Object obj) {
      ...
    }
    public static void insert(org.omg.CORBA.Any any, T s) {
      ...
    }
    public static T extract(org.omg.CORBA.Any any) {
      ...
    }
    public static org.omg.CORBA.TypeCode type() {
      ...
    }
    public static String id() {
      return "IDL:T:1.0";
    }
    public static T read(
      org.omg.CORBA.portable.InputStream is){
        ...
    }
    public static void write(
      org.omg.CORBA.portable.OutputStream os, T s) {
        ...
    }
}
```

The method `narrow()` can be used for down-casts of server-side object references. A down-cast is a typecast that converts a type `K` to a type `L`, where `K` is a supertype of type `L`. The methods `id()` and `type()` provide useful information on the type. While method `id()` returns the type as a string, the result of calling `type()` is a `TypeCode` (see Section 6.5 for details). The methods `insert()` and `extract()`, respectively, define functionality to store an instance of the newly defined type in an instance of a container of type `Any` or, reciprocally, to extract a `T` object from the container. The methods `read()` and `write()`—which are also called by the holder's `_read()` and `_write()`—are necessary for marshaling and not directly called by application programmers. There are no helper

classes for the pre-defined basic IDL types. Their functionality is directly accomplished by
the ORB's runtime library.

5.6   Mapping for Modules

IDL modules, which are defined with the introductory keyword module, are mapped by the
IDL compiler to a Java package with the same name. The module's type declarations are
mapped to corresponding Java class declarations or interface declarations and become part of
the generated package.

For example, the result of the IDL definition of this module,

```
module Demo
{
  ...
};
```

is the Java declaration

```
package Demo;
```

In the case of nested modules, for example,

```
module Outer
{
  ...
  module Inner
  {
    ...
  };
};
```

the Java code, which is generated in order to realize the declarations contained in module
Inner, begins with the package declaration

```
package Outer.Inner;
```

For that reason, Java programs intending to use elements declared in package Outer as well
as elements from package Outer.Inner without each time fully qualifying their names
with the package names have to import both packages separately. Since Java does not include lower-level packages, the following two statements would have to be included in the
corresponding Java files:

```
import Outer.*;
import Outer.Inner.*;
```

5.7   Mapping for Constants

The Java mapping of constants depends on the scope in which they are introduced. If the constant is defined as an element of an interface, then it is mapped to an instance variable of the same name in the Java interface called *<interface>*Operations generated by the IDL compiler. *<interface>* stands for the interface's name here. For example, the IDL interface

```
module M
{
  interface I
  {
    const long L = -1;
  };
};
```

results in, among others, a file IOperations.java containing the code

```
package M;

public interface IOperations {
  int L = (int)(-1L);
}
```

If the constant, however, is not declared within an IDL interface, then the IDL compiler generates a public Java interface of the same name. This interface has an instance variable named value, which is initialized with the constant's value. For example, the IDL specification

```
module M
{
  const double D = 1.0;
};
```

is mapped to the Java interface

```
package M;

public interface D {
  double value = 1.0;
}
```

Some IDL compilers, e.g., the IDL compiler which is part of Sun's JDK, augment the code, which is prescribed logically by the standard, by attaching additional Java modifiers so that the result could look like this:

```
package M;

public interface D {
  public static final double value = (double)(1.0);
}
```

Note that in the above examples, as well as in all future examples, we follow OMG's style guide and embed all IDL definitions within a module.

5.8   Mapping for `typedefs`

We have already discussed that the `typedef` can be used in order to associate an identifier with a data type and that this is in some cases mandatory (fixed, string, sequence, and array types). Since Java does not support such constructs, for all types newly introduced via `typedef`, a new helper class is generated.

5.9   Mapping for `structs`

An IDL type defined as a `struct` results in the generation of a Java class with the same name, which is specified `public` and `final`. The corresponding holder and helper classes are generated as well. The generated Java classes are stored in their own Java package. The name of the package depends upon whether the structure was defined in the scope of an IDL module or within an interface definition. In the first case, the package name is the name of the module. In the second, the package name *<interface>*`Package` is used. For example:

```
module M
{
  struct s1
  {
    unsigned long ul;
  };

  interface I
  {
    struct s2
    {
      double d;
    };
  };
};
```

Here, the Java class `s1` is stored in package `M` while class `s2` is allocated to the package `M.IPackage`. For applications that want to refer to class `s1` by its simple name, this implies that they have included the import statement `import M.*;`. Applications referring to `s2`, similarly, need an `import M.IPackage.*;` or they have to use qualified names. If both structures are needed, both `import` statements are necessary.

For all members of a `struct` definition, `public` instance variables are inserted into the code of the generated Java class. Also, two `public` constructors are generated. The first is a default constructor; the second is a constructor that needs arguments with initializers for all members of the structure in the ordering of their IDL specification.

For example, the code clipping from an interface definition

```
struct Date
{
  unsigned short day;
  unsigned short month;
  unsigned short year;
};
...
```

would generate this Java class:

```
public final class Date
  implements org.omg.CORBA.portable.IDLEntity {

  public short day;
  public short month;
  public short year;

  public Date() { }

  public Date(short day, short month, short year) {
    this.day = day;
    this.month = month;
    this.year = year;
  }
}
...
```

If a typedef declaration is used to introduce a new name for a data type previously declared, this has no influence on the generated Java code. For example, the fragment from an interface definition

```
struct Date
{
  unsigned short day;
  unsigned short month;
  unsigned short year;
};

typedef Date Birthday;

Birthday get_birthday(in string name, in string surname);
...
```

would have the result that a Java method get_birthday() with the "original" return type is generated:

```
Date get_birthday(String name, String surname);
```

This not only holds for return values of operations but also for other possible usage of type identifiers declared via typedef such as, e.g., as a parameter in an operation's signature, as a name of an attribute, etc.

5.10   Mapping for enums

An enumerated type specified in IDL is mapped to a Java class with the same name, which is declared `public` and `final`. The corresponding holder and helper classes are generated as well. The generated Java classes are stored in their own Java package. The name of the package is determined following the same rules as discussed above in Section 5.9 on the mapping of structures.

The individual enumerators from the IDL definition of an enumerated type are mapped to `public` `final` class variables. Furthermore, two methods, `value()` and `from_int()`, are generated. The first is declared `public` and may be used to retrieve the numeric value (of Java type `int`) associated with an enumerator. Values are assigned sequentially starting with 0. The second is a `public` class method, which, reciprocally, returns an instance of the enumerated type from its numerical value. If the specified value is out of range, an exception of type `org.omg.CORBA.BAD_PARAM` is raised. A fragment of the Java class for the enumerated type

```
enum Weekday { MON, TUE, WED, THU, FRI, SAT, SUN };
```

is shown below:

```
public final class Weekday
    implements org.omg.CORBA.portable.IDLEntity {

    private int value = -1;
    public static final int _MON = 0;
    public static final Weekday MON = new Weekday(_MON);
    public static final int _TUE = 1;
    public static final Weekday TUE = new Weekday(_TUE);
    public static final int _WED = 2;
    public static final Weekday WED = new Weekday(_WED);
    public static final int _THU = 3;
    public static final Weekday THU = new Weekday(_THU);
    public static final int _FRI = 4;
    public static final Weekday FRI = new Weekday(_FRI);
    public static final int _SAT = 5;
    public static final Weekday SAT = new Weekday(_SAT);
    public static final int _SUN = 6;
    public static final Weekday SUN = new Weekday(_SUN);

    public int value() {
      return value;
    }

    public static Weekday from_int(int value) {
      switch (value) {
        case _MON: return MON;
        case _TUE: return TUE;
        case _WED: return WED;
        case _THU: return THU;
        case _FRI: return FRI;
        case _SAT: return SAT;
        case _SUN: return SUN;
```

```
        default: throw new org.omg.CORBA.BAD_PARAM();
      }
    }
    ...
  }
```

If a new enumerated type is defined via a `typedef` declaration, this does not generate an additional class with the new name. This case is handled in the same way as in the example above at the end of Section 5.9.

5.11 Mapping for Sequences

IDL sequences are mapped to Java arrays with the same name, irrespective of whether they are bounded or unbounded in IDL. For bounded sequences, however, bounds checking is carried out at run-time when they are marshaled as parameters during an operation invocation. If the index for the corresponding Java array is out of bounds, an `org.omg.CORBA.MAR-SHAL` exception is raised. Since a sequence is directly mapped to a convenient self-contained Java construct, no dedicated class has to be generated. Instead, the IDL compiler inserts the Java array into the code wherever the sequence type is needed. Nevertheless, the complementary holder and helper classes are necessary. The two IDL definitions,

```
typedef sequence<long> UnboundedLongSequence;
```

and

```
typedef sequence<long,10> BoundedLongSequence;
```

therefore result in generating four classes: `UnboundedLongSequenceHolder`, `UnboundedLongSequenceHelper`, `BoundedLongSequenceHolder`, and `BoundedLongSequenceHelper`.

5.12 Mapping for Arrays

The mapping of IDL arrays is the same as that of bounded IDL sequences. They are also mapped to Java arrays and bounds are checked at run-time. Only the respective holder and helper classes are generated and, everywhere the IDL array type is needed, the Java array is directly inserted in the generated code. Java's subscripting operator " [ ] " is applied to access the elements of the array.

5.13 Mapping for Exceptions

In CORBA, there are two kinds of exceptions: *CORBA system exceptions*, which may be raised through the CORBA runtime, and *user exceptions*, which application developers can define on the IDL level. In Java, exceptions from the first category are implemented as subclasses of the class `java.lang.RuntimeException`, which, for its part, inherits from the class `java.lang.Exception`. User-defined exceptions, however, are implemented as subclasses of the class `org.omg.CORBA.UserException`, which inherits from the class `java.lang.Exception` and implements the Java interface `org.omg.COR-BA.portable.IDLEntity`.

Figure 8 shows the class diagram for the exception class hierarchy of CORBA's exception classes as implemented in Java.

To a large extent, the mapping of IDL exceptions corresponds to that of `structs`. For each IDL exception, a `public final` Java class with the same name is declared. Also, the corresponding holder and helper classes are generated and all these classes are stored in a Java package that, depending on whether the exception is defined on a module or an interface level, is named according to the rules discussed above in Section 5.9 on the mapping of structures.

The Java class implementing an IDL exception has two or three constructors, depending on whether it is a simple exception or a constructed exception that provides information specific to the exceptional condition (see Section 4.4). In the case of a simple exception, a default constructor and a constructor with a parameter of type `String` are generated. The latter can be passed a description of the reason for the exception.

In the case of a constructed exception, two constructors are generated in addition to the default constructor. The first needs initial values for all members of the exception; the second also expects a first string reason argument.

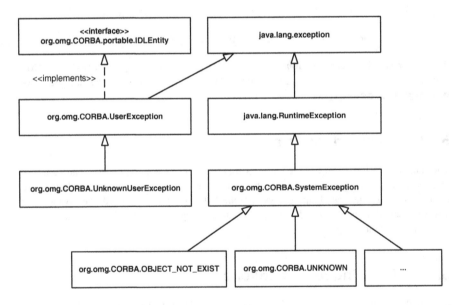

Figure 8: Exception Classes of the Java Mapping

The IDL code snippet below,

```
module Example
{
  exception Error { };

  exception ErrorReport
  {
    string error_message;
    short  error_code;
    string date;
  };
};
```

thus results in the following Java code:

```
// Error.java

package Example;

public final class Error
   extends org.omg.CORBA.UserException {

   public Error() {
     ...
   }
   public Error(String reason) {
     ...
   }
}

// ErrorReport.java

package Example;

public final class ErrorReport
   extends org.omg.CORBA.UserException {

   public String error_message;
   public short error_code;
   public String date;
   public ErrorReport() {
     ...
   }
   public ErrorReport(String error_message,
     short error_code, String date) {
     ...
   }
   public ErrorReport(String reason,
     String error_message, short error_code,
     String date) {
     ...
   }
}
```

5.14   Mapping for Interfaces

Here, three cases have to be distinguished that were already introduced in Section 4.5 and
that differ with regard to their IDL to Java mapping:

- non-local, non-abstract interfaces ("regular" interfaces),
- local interfaces, and
- abstract interfaces.

In the following subsections, these three interface types are treated individually.

5.14.1   Regular IDL Interfaces

Non-local, non-abstract IDL interfaces, so-called *regular* interfaces, are mapped to two public Java interfaces by the IDL compiler:

- the *operations interface*, and
- the *signature interface*.

The operations interface has a name that is composed from the identifier of the original IDL
interface and the suffix `Operations`, which is appended at the end. It contains the mappings of all the operations of the IDL interface, including the accessors for the interface's attributes. If an operation of the IDL interface raises an IDL exception, the corresponding Java
method must throw the corresponding Java exception (see the list of IDL and Java exceptions in Appendix B). On the server side, the operations interface is implemented through the
generated skeleton code and the servant class created by the programmer.

The signature interface has the same name as the IDL interface; it extends the corresponding
operations interface and also the Java interfaces `org.omg.CORBA.Object` as well as
`org.omg.CORBA.portable.IDLEntity`. On the client side, it is implemented by the
generated stub code and used as signature type in method declarations when interfaces of the
specified type are used in other interfaces. Moreover, clients use references to objects implementing that interface so that one could informally call it an "accessor interface".

In addition to these two Java interfaces, once again, helper and holder classes are generated
for each IDL interface type.

Furthermore, the classes `<interface>POA`, `<interface>POATie`, and `_<inter-
face>Stub` are created, where `<interface>` stands for the name of the interface. These
classes are needed for executing a remote operation invocation.

The simple IDL interface definition

```
interface I
{
};
```

thus, has the result that the following `java` files are generated:

- I,
- IOperations,
- IPOA,
- IPOATie,
- _IStub,
- IHolder, and
- IHelper.

The class IPOA is relevant for the *inheritance approach*, which is most commonly used and is discussed below in this section. There, class IPOA serves as superclass for the implementation of the Java interface I that developers have to carry through. In OMG terminology that implementation is named *servant*. IPOA is an abstract class, which extends org.omg. PortableServer.Servant and implements the Java interfaces IOperations (generated by the IDL compiler) as well as org.omg.CORBA.portable.InvokeHandler (from the ORB runtime library). Since no implementation of the operations in the operations interface IOperations is provided by IPOA, users subclassing IPOA (and thus writing the servant) must develop implementations for the methods in IOperations.

The class IPOATie is not generated by all IDL compilers. It is relevant for the *delegation approach*, which is also discussed below. IPOATie is a subclass of class IPOA.

The public Java class _IStub is used on the client side to implement the client stub. As usual, the IDL compiler-generated class IHolder is employed to transmit instances of the data type I during invocations of operations with signatures specifying inout or out parameters of type I. The class IHelper supplies the already known helper methods.

It is always recommended to either start reading the operation declarations in the generated operations interface whenever one is not sure how the IDL interface is mapped to Java or to copy these declarations for one's implementation of the servant.

We noted above that there are two possible approaches in CORBA that can be followed when implementing the IDL interfaces of a CORBA-based application: the inheritance approach, which is also called the *POA approach*, and the delegation approach, which is also called the *tie approach*. A programmer implementing the inheritance approach has to write a servant class, which inherits from the superclass named <interface>POA, that the IDL compiler generates. Since the POA class implements the operations interface, all functionality of the IDL interface is then available. It should be noted that—in the case of programming languages not supporting multiple inheritance—a disadvantage of this approach is that the servant class obtains a superclass and, thus, has used up its possibilities to inherit from direct superclasses.

When programmers follow the delegation approach, they make use of the <interface>POATie class as a *delegator* class. This class adopts the role of the servant; however, it does not execute the corresponding methods but simply delegates each operation invocation to a class that implements the methods declared in the Java interface <interface>Operations with their intended functionality. Now, this class is not involved in an inheritance relationship with the other IDL compiler-generated classes and is free to inherit from any user-defined class. A disadvantage of the delegation approach is that it introduces one additional level of indirection, which reduces the application's performance. For an overview of the dependencies between the compiler-generated classes or interfaces and the respective implementation class additionally required in each approach, have a look at Figure 12, provided in the context of the `Counter` example in Chapter 7.

5.14.2   Local IDL Interfaces

As is the case for regular interfaces, discussed above in Section 5.14.1, operations and signature interfaces as well as holder and helper classes are generated for local IDL interfaces. The signature interface is somewhat modified and declared in this manner:

```
interface <interface>
  extends <interface>Operations,
  org.omg.CORBA.LocalInterface,
  org.omg.CORBA.portable.IDLEntity {
    ...
}
```

Note that, in comparison to the mapping for regular interfaces, the generated signature interface features an added inheritance relationship to the Java interface `org.omg.COR-BA.LocalInterface` while it does not extend `org.omg.CORBA.Object` any longer. The classes `<interface>POA`, `<interface>POATie`, and `_<interface>Stub` are no longer needed and, therefore, the compiler does not generate them. In this case of a local interface, the IDL compiler-generated superclass `<interface>LocalBase` establishes the basis for the implementation of the servant class by the programmer. These requirements of the standard are, at present, implemented with varying conformity by current IDL compiler products. Starting from merely non-conformant naming of the generated classes up to completely missing support for local interfaces.

5.14.3   Abstract IDL Interfaces

The mapping of abstract IDL interfaces exhibits the particularity that their signature and operations interfaces are quasi merged so that only one single `public` Java interface is generated. This interface receives the same name as the IDL interface and is constructed following similar mapping rules as the operations interface of a non-abstract IDL interface. However, it is new that this interface takes on the role of the signature interfaces and, therefore, inherits from `org.omg.CORBA.portable.IDLEntity`. As usual, the corresponding holder and helper classes are generated as well following the known schemes of the IDL compiler. It finally should be noted that the interface `CORBA::AbstractBase`, which is the IDL supertype for all abstract interfaces, is mapped to the class `java.lang.Object` in Java.

5.15   Mapping for Value Types

IDL value types' mappings to Java differ depending on their definitions. Therefore, we have to differentiate three characteristics:

- regular value types,
- abstract value types, and
- boxed value types

(see Section 4.6). In the following subsections, we consider these three cases consecutively.

5.15.1   Regular Value Types

A regular value type is mapped to an abstract Java class of the same name, which, for each `public` state member of the value type, declares a corresponding `public` instance variable and, analogically, for `private` state members, declares corresponding `protected` instance variables. Normally, the class implements the interface `org.omg.CORBA.portable.StreamableValue`. But, if it was determined that the value type should resort to user-defined marshaling routines, then the Java class instead has to implement the interface `org.omg.CORBA.portable.CustomValue`. Both interface types are subinterfaces of the interface `org.omg.CORBA.portable.ValueBase` so that the sole method that it declares is, in any case, a member of the abstract Java class, which the IDL compiler generates. The `ValueBase` superinterface is defined as follows:

```
package org.omg.CORBA.portable;

public interface ValueBase extends IDLEntity {
  String[] _truncatable_ids();
}
```

In Section 4.6, we introduced the type `Time` as an example of a value type:

```
valuetype Time
{
  // private state members
  private unsigned short hours;
  private unsigned short minutes;
  private unsigned short seconds;
  // initializer
  factory init(in unsigned short hours,
    in unsigned short minutes,
    in unsigned short seconds);
  // local operations
  unsigned short get_hours();
  unsigned short get_minutes();
  unsigned short get_seconds();
  boolean equals(in Time another_time);
};
```

According to the procedure depicted above, this IDL definition is mapped to the Java class `Time` below:

```
public abstract class Time
    implements org.omg.CORBA.portable.StreamableValue {

  private String[] _truncatable_ids = {"IDL:Time:1.0"};
```

```
protected short hours;
protected short minutes;
protected short seconds;

public abstract short get_hours();
public abstract short get_minutes();
public abstract short get_seconds();
public abstract boolean _equals(X.Time another_time);

public void _write(
  org.omg.CORBA.portable.OutputStream os) {
  ...
}
public void _read(
  org.omg.CORBA.portable.InputStream os) {
  ...
}
public String[] _truncatable_ids() {
  return _truncatable_ids;
}
public org.omg.CORBA.TypeCode _type() {
  return TimeHelper.type();
}
}
```

In addition to this abstract Java class, the IDL compiler generates the well-known helper and holder classes for regular value types. Furthermore, in the case where, by means of the `factory` keyword, the value type specifies at least one initializer operation, a *value factory* interface is also generated. This interface extends the interface `org.omg.CORBA.portable.ValueFactory` and provides a method for each initializer declared in the IDL value type. In the above example, this Java code would likewise be generated:

```
public interface TimeValueFactory
  extends org.omg.CORBA.portable.ValueFactory {
  Time init(short hours, short minutes, short seconds);
}
```

Developers now have to provide an adequate implementation of this value factory interface and register it with the ORB so that it is accessible at run-time.

5.15.2 Abstract Value Types

According to OMG's IDL to Java specification, an abstract value type is mapped to a Java interface, which, in turn, extends the interface `org.omg.CORBA.portable.ValueBase`. Recall that it is not possible to construct instances of an abstract value type. They are, rather, designated to be used solely as supertypes for regular value types, which can then be instantiated, or as supertypes for other abstract value types. The operations and attributes of an abstract value type are included in the Java interface using the normal rules. And, again, helper and holder classes are generated by the IDL compiler.

5.15.3 Boxed Value Types

There are two general cases to consider concerning the mapping of boxed value types: value types that are mapped to Java's primitive types and those that are mapped to Java classes.

If the type contained in a boxed value type can be mapped to a primitive Java type (which concerns, e.g., the IDL types `float`, `long`, `wchar`, `boolean`, and `octet`), then, a Java class with the same name is created for this value type. This class declares a `public` instance variable named `value`, which has the Java type determined by the rules given in Section 5.3. Moreover, the class implements the already known interface `org.omg.COR-BA.portable.ValueBase`. An example:

```
valuetype FloatValue float;

interface DisplayFloatValue
{
  void display(in FloatValue fv);
};
```

For that example, the IDL compiler generates the files `FloatValue.java`, `Float-ValueHelper.java`, and `FloatValueHolder.java` in order to map the boxed value type as well as several files to map the IDL interface declaration according to the rules discussed in Section 5.14. We take a closer look at the files `FloatValue.java` and `DisplayFloatValueOperations.java`, in order to further exemplify some of the mapping details.

```
// FloatValue.java

public class FloatValue
    implements org.omg.CORBA.portable.ValueBase {

  public float value;
  private static String[] _ids = {FloatValueHelper.id()};

  public FloatValue(float initial) {
    value = initial;
  }
  public String[] _truncatable_ids() {
    return _ids;
  }
}

// DisplayFloatValueOperations.java

public interface DisplayFloatValueOperations {
  void display(FloatValue fv);
}
```

The example shows how a Java class is generated that adopts the name `FloatValue` from the value type and is employed wherever the value type was utilized as a data type on the IDL level. The IDL operation `display()` of interface `DisplayFloatValue` has, for example, a parameter `fv` of value type `FloatValue` and, from the listing of file `DisplayFloatValueOperations.java`, one can see that the corresponding Java method `display()` accordingly declares a parameter of the respective Java reference type `Float-Value`.

If, in contrast to the case just considered above, the data type managed by the boxed value type is an IDL type that has to be mapped to a Java class (e.g., in case of a `string`, `enum`, `struct`, `sequence`, `any`, or `interface`), then value type as such is mapped to this class. Any further Java class with the name of the boxed value type is not generated. The rules for mapping an IDL type to a Java class were already discussed in the previous sections of this chapter.

One additional example shall demonstrate the difference from the first case:

```
valuetype FloatValueSeq sequence<float>;

interface DisplayFloatValueSeq
{
  void display(in FloatValueSeq fvs);
};
```

For this modified example, the IDL compiler now only generates the files `FloatValue-SeqHelper.java` and `FloatValueSeqHolder.java` for the `FloatValueSeq` type. For the interface, again, the known set of files is generated; here, we only single out the file `DisplayFloatValueSeqOperations.java` in order to demonstrate how the `FloatValueSeq` parameter of IDL operation `display()` is mapped:

```
// DisplayFloatValueSeqOperations.java

public interface DisplayFloatValueSeqOperations {
  void display(float[] fvs);
}
```

It becomes clear that the IDL type `sequence<float>` contained in the boxed value type determines the simple mapping of the `FloatValueSeq` type to the Java type `float[]` (see the mapping rules for sequences in Section 5.11).

As mentioned previously, it holds for all boxed value types, irrespective of the type they contain, that the holder and helper classes are created as usual.

5.16   Mapping for anys

The data type any, which is the most flexible and powerful IDL type, is mapped to the Java class `org.omg.CORBA.Any`. This class implements the Java interface `org.omg.COR-BA.portable.IDLEntity` and provides all the methods needed to insert instances of all Java counterparts of the pre-defined IDL types into an Any object (`insert_<type>()`) as well as to extract them from an Any object (`extract_<type>()`). For unsigned integer types, instead of the complete IDL keyword `unsigned`, only the letter u is prefixed. Table 10 below shows part of the methods declared in class `Any`. Should a conversion error occur during extraction (e.g., a `short` is inserted and an attempt is made later to extract a `boolean`) an exception of type `org.omg.CORBA.BAD_OPERATION` is thrown.

In order to insert instances of the Java counterparts of user-defined IDL type into an Any object and to extract them from an Any object, respectively, the insert() and extract() methods of the helper classes are used (see Section 5.5).

Table 10: Insert and Extract Methods for Pre-defined IDL Types

IDL Type	Any Methods
short	short extract_short(); void insert_short(short);
unsigned short	short extract_ushort(); void insert_ushort(short);
long	int extract_long(); void insert_long(int);
unsigned long	int extract_ulong(); void insert_ulong(int);
long long	long extract_longlong(); void insert_longlong(long);
unsigned long long	long extract_ulonglong(); void insert_ulonglong(long);
float	float extract_float(); void insert_float(float);
double	double extract_double(); void insert_double(double);
boolean	boolean extract_boolean(); void insert_boolean(boolean);
octet	byte extract_octet(); void insert_octet(byte);
char	char extract_char(); void insert_char(char);
wchar	char extract_wchar(); void insert_wchar(char);
string	String extract_string(); void insert_string(String);
wstring	String extract_wstring(); void insert_wstring(String);
fixed	java.math.BigDecimal extract_fixed(); void insert_fixed(java.math.BigDecimal);
any	org.omg.CORBA.Any extract_any(); void insert_any(org.omg.CORBA.Any);
valuetype	java.io.Serializable extract_Value(); void insert_Value(java.io.Serializable);
Object	org.omg.CORBA.Object extract_Object(); void insert_Object(org.omg.CORBA.Object);

Objects of class Any can be obtained from the ORB, which is described in detail in Section 6.2, by invoking its method create_any().

5.17   Mapping for in, inout, and out Parameters

The parameter passing semantics of IDL in parameters are *call-by-value*. Normal Java parameters are generated; the same holds for the return result of an IDL operation. Java's usual parameter passing mechanism is employed and the result of a Java method is returned as a result of the corresponding IDL operation. As long as the type of the in parameter is not a value type, for the Java side, it holds that during run-time the Java object to be passed is generated and owned by the caller. In the method itself, the argument may not be modified and the receiver may not retain a reference to the argument beyond the duration of the call. Violation of this rule may lead to unexpected system behavior. For in parameters of a value type, conversely, a true copy of the Java object generated by the caller is created on the receiver's side; thus, the receiver can by all means modify that copy or store a reference to it beyond the call's duration.

IDL out and inout parameters define a *call-by-result* and combined *call-by-value/result* semantics, respectively. They cannot be passed directly with the standard Java mechanism. In these cases, the holder classes must be used instead (see Section 5.4). Suitable holder classes for pre-defined IDL data types are already supplied by the ORB's runtime library. In the case of new, user-defined IDL types, the necessary holder classes are automatically generated by the IDL compiler. In order to pass parameters, the client provides an instance of the respective holder class for each out and inout parameter, which is then passed (*by value*). The content of the holder class object—the instance variable called value—can be modified during the call. After the invocation, the client then can further process the possibly modified content.

Java objects that are used as arguments for an out parameter or that are returned as an invocation result are generated and owned by the receiver of the call. Once the call is completed, ownership of these objects migrates to the caller and the receiver may no longer utilize a reference to these objects. Otherwise, unexpected system behavior may result. For inout parameters, rules corresponding to those discussed for pure in parameters combined with those for out parameters apply in combination.

It should be noted that the rules identified above do not apply to primitive Java types or immutable Java objects of type java.lang.String.

5.18   Mapping for Attributes

As already mentioned in Section 4.5.1, attributes are mapped via accessor methods for getting and setting the attribute value; in the case of readonly attributes, only the get method is generated. The mapping of the attribute's type follows the rules already discussed above. For the two IDL attribute definitions

```
attribute unsigned long id;
```

and

```
readonly attribute string name;
```

the IDL compiler generates three Java methods:

```
int id() {
   // get method
};
void id(int i) {
   // set method
};
String name() {
   // get method only
};
```

5.19   Mapping for Operations

The mapping of an operation specified in IDL is the result of combining the diverse mapping rules for the single parts constituting the operation and were already addressed above. The operation name is built according to the mapping rules for identifiers (see Section 5.2). Return type and in parameters of the operation are mapped according to the rules for mapping data types (see Sections 5.3, 5.9–5.16). For inout and out parameters, the appropriate holder classes are utilized.

The example below may, once more, exemplify this procedure:

```
long notify(in string message,
   out unsigned long how_many);
```

The Java method that is generated is

```
int _notify(String message, IntHolder how_many) {
   ...
};
```

Since the operation name notify is a reserved Java identifier, it is prefixed with an underscore. The return type long and the in parameter's type string are mapped to the Java types int and String, respectively (see Table 8). The out parameter of IDL type unsigned long is mapped according to Table 9 and becomes an IntHolder.

5.20   Exercises

1. What is the purpose of helper classes?

2. What is the purpose of holder classes?

3. Does an IDL compiler also create AnyHelper and AnyHolder classes?

4. Which of the files generated by an IDL compiler are needed by the client and which are needed by the server?

5. Determine the mapping of the following Java interface:

```
interface Exercise
{
  attribute char c;
  readonly double d;
  void f(in string s);
  long g(in unsigned long ul);
  void h(inout short s1, out short s2);
};
```

6. Given module M:

```
module M
{
  interface I { attribute long l; };
  struct S { long l; };
  interface Test
  {
    void op(...);
  };
};
```

Insert the following definitions of operation op() and inspect what the IDL compiler generates from M; analyze the operations interface TestOperations.

    a) `void op(in long x);`

    b) `void op(in S x);`

    c) `void op(in I x);`

    d) `void op(out long x);`

    e) `void op(out S x);`

    f) `void op(out I x);`

    g) `void op(inout long x);`

    h) `void op(inout S x);`

    i) `void op(inout I x);`

6 Important Elements of the ORB Runtime

The CORBA standard specifies a number of so-called *pseudo objects* that represent the ORB runtime. Its core consists of the pseudo objects ORB, Object, and POA. Additional pseudo objects support, e.g., the Dynamic Invocation Interface, the Dynamic Skeleton Interface, the generation of TypeCodes, etc. The prefix "pseudo" indicates that pseudo objects should not normally be regarded as conventional CORBA objects. They cannot be passed or returned as arguments or return values of operation invocations and they do not inherit from CORBA:: Object like all regular CORBA objects.

Typically, the code for such pseudo objects is provided in the form of (class) libraries. Here, the difficulty for the developers of the CORBA standard concerned the necessity of specifying highly platform-related components of the CORBA system in a way suitable for different programming languages. In order to avoid the need to define the core repeatedly for each language, once again, one fell back on the idea of a language-independent specification by means of an Interface Definition Language. However, in this context, the so-called *Pseudo IDL* (PIDL), a variant of the well-known CORBA IDL, was employed.

In contrast to IDL, PIDL interfaces do not specify normal CORBA objects but, as a rule, define local objects for which invocations are executed differently, typically in the form of usual function calls. Also, the rules for mapping an operation or an attribute to a specific programming language may differ from the IDL rules and may even be adjusted depending on the context. With the help of PIDL, CORBA's pseudo objects are specified through pseudo interfaces discussed subsequently. Instead of specifying PIDL interfaces, the OMG recently has begun to describe "locality-constrained" objects, such as POA, with the help of IDL. Here, the keyword local is employed.

In the following, we introduce the most important pseudo interfaces with which CORBA programmers are again and again confronted. In addition, we explain the mapping of these pseudo interfaces to the Java programming language. It should be noted that the pseudo interface implementations of some ORB products provide vendor-specific extensions. These supplementary methods are not standard-conformant; seen from the portability perspective, they should not be used and we, therefore, do not discuss them here.

6.1 Initializing a CORBA Application

In order to be able to make use of the CORBA environment as middleware, i.e., to invoke the operations of interface CORBA::ORB, an application first has to obtain a reference to an ORB pseudo object. This is carried out by initializing the ORB environment with the help of an invocation of operation ORB_init(), which is discussed in Section 6.1.1 below. In a pure client application, it is then already possible to obtain references to service providing CORBA objects, e.g., by means of the CORBA Naming Service, and to subsequently invoke operations on these objects. If, on the other hand, a server application provides these objects, after the ORB's initialization, a reference to an object adapter must be obtained. This adapter, typically the *root POA*, serves as a connecting link between the ORB and the servants. It registers and activates servants (see Section 6.3.1 below). The corresponding functionality is provided by the ORB pseudo object, found by invoking ORB_init(). This pseudo object implements the ORB pseudo interface; the most important ORB operations are dealt with in Section 6.2.

6.1.1 Operation ORB_init()

An invocation of operation ORB_init() initializes the ORB and, thus, constitutes the first step in setting up the CORBA environment for a CORBA application. According to the standard, this operation is *not* regarded as belonging to the proper ORB pseudo interface, defined by the operations explained below in Section 6.2. The following fragment from the PIDL specification of the module CORBA illustrates the definition of this operation:

```
// PIDL

module CORBA
{
  typedef string ORBid;
  typedef sequence<string> arg_list;
  ORB ORB_init(inout arg_list argv,
    in ORBid orb_identifier);
  ...
};
```

The first argument the operation expects is of type arg_list, which denotes a sequence of strings. This sequence can provide information that has to be passed to the ORB. The second argument is of type ORBid (an alias for type string introduced for reasons of type safety); it is employed to identify the ORB used.

The mapping of operation ORB_init() to the Java programming language is not covered until the end of Section 6.2; this method is mapped to three Java class methods that are part of the public abstract class ORB from package org.omg.CORBA. We therefore decided to discuss them in connection with the mapping of the pseudo interface CORBA::ORB.

6.2 Pseudo Interface CORBA::ORB

As described above, the ORB is responsible for managing all communication, in its entirety, in a distributed CORBA application. It plays the role of a communication bus whose main task consists of transmitting client requests to the appropriate server. The ORB's functionality is described in the pseudo interface CORBA::ORB. This includes operations that determine initial references, e.g., a reference to the root POA, needed in order to make objects accessible to operation invocations. In addition, operations to convert an object reference to a string representation and vice versa are provided. Furthermore, a number of operations concerning the Dynamic Invocation Interface, the Dynamic Skeleton Interface, or the generation of TypeCodes are provided and numerous additional operations are defined that we cannot discuss here due to reasons of space.

6.2.1 Operation `list_initial_services()`

This operation is typically invoked at the start time of an application. It determines and lists the available CORBA Services. The syntax is

```
typedef string ObjectId;
typedef sequence<ObjectId> ObjectIdList;
ObjectIdList list_initial_services();
```

The return result of this invocation is a sequence of `strings` containing the names of the available services. In order to obtain a reference to one or more of these services, the operation `resolve_initial_references()` may be invoked.

6.2.2 Operation `resolve_initial_references()`

To allow an application to determine at start time which objects have references available, the operation `list_initial_services()` is provided. Very often, in a distributed application, it is first of all necessary to obtain an object reference to the Naming Service. With the help of this basic service, the application can then find further object references in a standardized way in order to communicate with other objects distributed in the network and to request their services. In order to obtain a reference to the Naming Service, the operation `resolve_initial_references()` is invoked and the string "NameService" is passed as an argument. Here, it should be noted that such an invocation does not guarantee that the ORB actually returns the respective object reference. Reasons for failure might be that the Naming Service had not yet been started or that, although active, it is not known to the ORB. Should a Naming Service be active, its reference must be communicated to the ORB; otherwise, the service is not available to applications. Various solutions to solve that problem exist, e.g., the passing of command-line parameters, the creation of configuration files, or the setting of environment variables. In the case of an ORB that disposes of a dedicated daemon or agent and an Implementation Repository, programmers can assume that the reference to the Naming Service is actually found and returned. The specific, non-standardized components of such a proprietary solution would see to it that the service, should it be inactive at the time of the invocation, is automatically started so that the expected object reference can be returned.

The PIDL notation of operation `resolve_initial_references()` is

```
typedef string ObjectId; // repeated for clarity
exception InvalidName {};
Object resolve_initial_references(
   in ObjectId identifier) raises(InvalidName);
```

Table 11 indicates the `strings` that may be passed at present as arguments to this operation together with the types of the return results. The non-availability of a particular reference is indicated by throwing an `InvalidName` exception.

Table 11: Admissible Arguments and Corresponding Return Types
for `resolve_initial_references()`

ObjectId (alias string)	Return Type
`"RootPOA"`	PortableServer::POA
`"POACurrent"`	PortableServer::Current
`"InterfaceRepository"`	CORBA::Repository or CORBA::ComponentIR::Repository
`"NameService"`	CosNaming::NamingContext
`"TradingService"`	CosTrading::Lookup
`"SecurityCurrent"`	SecurityLevel1::Current or SecurityLevel2::Current
`"TransactionCurrent"`	CosTransaction::Current
`"DynAnyFactory"`	DynamicAny::DynAnyFactory
`"ORBPolicyManager"`	CORBA::PolicyManager
`"PolicyCurrent"`	CORBA::PolicyCurrent
`"NotificationService"`	CosNotifyChannelAdmin:: EventChannelFactory
`"TypedNotificationService"`	CosNotifyChannelAdmin:: TypedEventChannelFactory
`"CodecFactory"`	IOP::CodecFactory
`"PICurrent"`	PortableInterceptors::Current
`"ComponentHomeFinder"`	Components::HomeFinder
`"PSS"`	CosPersistentState:: ConnectorRegistry

6.2.3 Operations `object_to_string()` and `string_to_object()`

The ORB interface contains definitions of two conversion operations. The first operation, `object_to_string()`, may be invoked in order to convert a CORBA object reference into its corresponding string representation. Following its conversion, the reference can, for example, be stored in a file or a database. This operation is typically employed when different ORBs are used on the server and on the client side or when CORBA Services of a vendor differing from the ORB provider are to be used on the server or on the client side. The second operation, `string_to_object()`, is the counterpart of the just described operation `object_to_string()`. It is invoked whenever the reference to a CORBA object has to be reconstructed from its string representation.

The concrete syntax of both operations:

```
string object_to_string(in Object obj);
Object string_to_object(in string str);
```

6.2.4 Thread-Related ORB Operations

To support single-threaded ORBs as well as multi-threaded ORBs, several operations are specified in the ORB interface:

- `boolean work_pending();`
  This operation returns an indication of whether or not the ORB needs the main thread in order to perform its work. If the result is TRUE, the main thread is needed; a result of FALSE indicates the opposite.

- `void perform_work();`
  If this operation is invoked by the application's main thread, it instructs the ORB to perform its task (e.g., to accept client requests). Should there be no tasks to complete, the invocation does nothing and the main thread is not blocked.

- `void run();`
  Application developers primarily utilize operation `run()`. An invocation of this operation has the result that the ORB is enabled to accept client requests at all. This operation is blocking; after its invocation, the main thread of the server application is suspended and the control flow is passed to the server-side ORB, which loops and waits for client requests. The operation blocks until an invocation of operation `shutdown()` is performed by some other thread.

- `void shutdown(in boolean wait_for_completion);`
  The operation `shutdown()` serves to release all resources obtained by the ORB and to instruct it to shut down. The invocation also causes all object adapters to be destroyed. With the argument of type `boolean`, one can affect whether the operation blocks until the ORB finishes processing all actual requests and actually shuts down (TRUE) or not (FALSE). If the value is FALSE, the operation invocation returns immediately, even if the shutdown is not yet complete.

- `void destroy();`
  An invocation of this operation destroys the ORB so that its resources can be reclaimed by the application. Normally, it is not invoked until a `shutdown()` was performed. If `shutdown()` was not invoked, the shutdown process is started first. In that case, the operation blocks during shutdown and subsequently destroys the ORB.

6.2.5 Java Mapping of Pseudo Interface CORBA::ORB

In Java, the PIDL-specified pseudo interface ORB is mapped to a public abstract class ORB:

```
package org.omg.CORBA;

public abstract class ORB { ... }
```

Let us first have a look at the mapping of operation `ORB_init()`, discussed in Section 6.1.1. There, we saw that `ORB_init()` is not part of the pseudo interface `CORBA::ORB`. Since Java does not allow global methods, the mapping had to assign this operation to some class, which, due to obvious reasons, was the `ORB` class. To satisfy Java's language-specific requirements and possibilities, the operation `ORB_init()` is not mapped to one single method but to three `public` class methods, all members of class `ORB` and named with the (overloaded) identifier `init()`. It has to be distinguished whether ORB initialization is performed by a stand-alone Java application or by a Java applet, which is restricted by its more rigorous security restrictions.

The first of these three mappings defines a simple default initialization method that returns a reference to a severely limited singleton `ORB` object, which can solely be used to create `Any`s or provide a factory for `TypeCode`s:

```
public static ORB init();
```

If called multiple times, this method always returns the same Java object. If that object is used for other than the intended factory purposes, a system exception is thrown.

The second alternative of the `init()` method is specifically dedicated for stand-alone Java application usage:

```
public static ORB init(String[] args, Properties props);
```

It is passed an array of strings that are the command-line arguments and a list of Java properties (see below).

A list of Java properties can also be passed to the third alternative of the method `init()`. Since this method should be used by an applet, the first argument should be a reference to that applet:

```
public static ORB init(Applet app, Properties props);
```

There are two properties that every ORB must be able to interpret but that may be complemented by additional, product-specific properties.

- `org.omg.CORBA.ORBClass`: This property object can provide the name of an ORB implementation class.
- `org.omg.CORBA.ORBSingletonClass`: This property object can provide the name of a singleton ORB implementation class that can only be used as a `TypeCode` factory.

Setting these two properties is normally indispensable for the following reasons. Since version 1.2, Sun's Java Development Kit (JDK) itself includes classes and interfaces that implement the CORBA runtime and that are by default loaded and employed. Often, however, one intends to work with an independent ORB product; therefore, it is necessary to set both properties in order to make the product-specific classes and interfaces available and to hide the JDK's built-in implementation.

In principle, we have three options for setting the Java properties `org.omg.CORBA.ORB-Class` and `org.omg.CORBA.ORBSingletonClass`:

- using the class `java.util.Properties`,
- using the file `orb.properties`, or
- using command-line arguments when invoking the Java interpreter.

If it is admissible to hard code the necessary information directly into the source code, then the first option is most suitable. The respective Java program must contain the following code fragment:

```
Properties props = System.getProperties();
props.put("org.omg.CORBA.ORBClass",
  "YourORBClass");
props.put("org.omg.CORBA.ORBSingletonClass",
  "YourORBSingletonClass");
System.setProperties(props);
```

In this code example, the entries *YourORBClass* and *YourORBSingletonClass* should only be seen as placeholders. In the first complete example in Section 7.6, we give the concrete values that need to be set when working with the ORB products JacORB and OpenORB, respectively. Subsequent to setting the properties, each of the two variants of the `ORB.init()` method that expect a `Properties` argument may be invoked in order to initialize the ORB runtime.

The second option is about specifying the classes to be loaded in a dedicated configuration file for the JDK, the file `orb.properties`. In this simple text file, at least the two following lines have to be inserted:

```
org.omg.CORBA.ORBClass=YourORBClass
org.omg.CORBA.ORBSingletonClass=YourORBSingletonClass
```

To enable the Java runtime to find that information, this properties file has to be copied into the directory `JDK_DIR\jre\lib`; here, `JDK_DIR` is a placeholder for the installation directory of one's Java distribution; a typical value might be `c:\jdk1.5.0`. Obviously, this option is not advisable for a multi-user system where different users might have differing preferences concerning the ORBs they want to utilize.

The third option provides the relevant information in the form of command-line arguments. When invoking the Java interpreter, these have to be specified as follows:

```
java -Dorg.omg.CORBA.ORBClass=YourORBClass
  -Dorg.omg.CORBA.ORBSingletonClass=YourORBSingletonClass
    YourApplication
```

Note that property names and values have to follow immediately after the `-D` flags without any white space and that the above invocation must be stated on one single command line. *YourApplication* denotes the client or server application to be started. The disadvantages of this option are that the invocation is complex and error-prone and that one can easily forget the property names and their specification. One should at least provide a batch or script file for program start in that case.

We now turn to the central operations that we already described above and that are in fact part of the pseudo interface CORBA::ORB. First, we have the operation `list_initial_services()`, discussed in Section 6.2.1. It lists the CORBA services available at the start time of an application. As expected, it is represented in Java by the method

```
public abstract String[] list_initial_services();
```

More interesting is the mapping of the operation `resolve_initial_references()`, which we addressed in Section 6.2.2. With its help, we obtain object references to the services available at the start time. The Java mapping has this form:

```
public abstract org.omg.CORBA.Object
  resolve_initial_references(String object_name)
    throws org.omg.CORBA.ORBPackage.InvalidName;
```

With the `String` argument, we provide the method with the name of the service that is needed. In Table 11, the names of the services that every ORB implementation must understand are listed. If the name argument is unknown, an `InvalidName` exception is thrown. In the concrete examples in the second part of the book, we use this method very often to obtain a reference to the root POA by invoking it with the string `"RootPOA"` (in this example, it is assumed that orb references a correctly initialized ORB pseudo object):

```
org.omg.CORBA.Object obj =
  orb.resolve_initial_references("RootPOA");
```

From Table 11, we can see that the IDL return type of this invocation is `PortableServer::POA` and, therefore, `org.omg.PortableServer.POA` on the Java level. To continue with the above example, the variable `obj` must be converted to the correct Java type. For that conversion, the `narrow()` method from class `POAHelper`, which we described in Section 5.5 should be used:

```
org.omg.PortableServer.POA rootPOA =
  org.omg.PortableServer.POAHelper.narrow(obj);
```

In principle, this corresponds to a Java downcast such as

```
org.omg.PortableServer.POA rootPOA =
  (org.omg.PortableServer.POA)obj;
```

This, however, would be an improper approach because on the Java level nothing is known about the IDL inheritance hierarchy so that a type-check whether this downcast is admissible could not be carried out here.

In addition to the just described "bootstrap" operations, we introduced two conversion operations in Section 6.2.3, `object_to_string()` and `string_to_object()`, which may be invoked to transform an object reference (IOR) into a string and vice versa for storage or transmission purposes.

The Java representations of these operations are

```
public abstract String object_to_string(
    org.omg.CORBA.Object obj);
```

and

```
public abstract org.omg.CORBA.Object string_to_object(
    String str);
```

It is guaranteed that an IOR converted into its string representation via an invocation of ob-ject_to_string() can be regained by a subsequent string_to_object() invocation and still references the same object, irrespective of whether the operations were carried out through different ORBs. However, it should be observed that the return type of string_to_object() is the generic type CORBA::Object (and, therefore, on the Java level, the type org.omg.CORBA.Object) so that the resulting object reference has to be converted to the expected object type through an invocation of the narrow() method of the appropriate helper class (see Section 5.5).

In Section 6.2.4, we introduced several thread-related operations. These operations were a-dopted after standardization of the first version of the IDL to Java Language mapping. For reasons of binary compatibility, they were not mapped to abstract methods as usual but instead to concrete methods that may throw a single Java run-time exception of type org.omg.CORBA.NO_IMPLEMENT. As is the case with abstract methods, vendors of ORB products have to override these methods by suitable implementations in the subclasses they provide. The Java declarations of these operations are simply as follows:

```
public boolean work_pending() {
    throw new org.omg.CORBA.NO_IMPLEMENT();
}
public void perform_work() {
    throw new org.omg.CORBA.NO_IMPLEMENT();
}
public void run() {
    throw new org.omg.CORBA.NO_IMPLEMENT();
}
public void shutdown(boolean wait_for_completion) {
    throw new org.omg.CORBA.NO_IMPLEMENT();
}
public void destroy() {
    throw new org.omg.CORBA.NO_IMPLEMENT();
}
```

6.3   Portable Object Adapter

The Portable Object Adapter is OMG's standard object adapter. As already described in Section 3.4.2, an object adapter is the link between the ORB and the proper object implementations. The OMG followed several objectives when specifying the POA. To the greatest possible extent, the specification should cover all application areas; moreover, the typical OMG criteria, portability, scalability, and flexibility, had to be met. The interfaces provided by the

POA can be classified into several categories according to their functionality. There are interfaces with operations managing association of object references with servants that implement the business logic defined by an IDL interface. The second category of operations concerns transparent activation of CORBA objects. Operations for setting specific strategies (*policies*) when associating CORBA objects with servants form the third category and allow concurrent support of CORBA objects with different properties.

The association of a CORBA object with a servant is called *incarnation*. Transferring a CORBA object into a state where it can process client requests is called *activation*. Incarnation of an object is thus a necessary condition for its activation.

6.3.1   POA Policies

The standard supports numerous different policies that are specified when a POA is created and that govern its behavior.

- Thread Policy
  The POA supports three different threading models: the *ORB-Controlled Model*, where the ORB is responsible for assigning requests (ORB_CTRL_MODEL); the *Single Thread Model*, where requests are processed sequentially (SINGLE_THREAD_MODEL); and the *Main Thread Model*, where the POA only uses the main thread to process requests sequentially (MAIN_THREAD_MODEL).

- Lifespan Policy
  The lifespan of the objects managed by the POA can be specified either TRANSIENT or PERSISTENT. Transient objects cannot outlive the POA instance in which they were created. Requests received afterwards cause an OBJECT_NOT_EXIST exception to be thrown. This restriction is abolished for persistent objects.

- ID Assignment Policy
  The assignment of IDs to objects can be carried out automatically by the POA (SYSTEM_ID) or by the application (USER_ID).

- ID Uniqueness Policy
  This policy determines whether servants can support one single object ID (UNIQUE_ID) or one or more IDs (MULTIPLE_ID).

- Servant Retention Policy
  With this policy, it is specified whether the POA stores a mapping of object IDs and servants in an *Active Object Map* (RETAIN) or not (NON_RETAIN). The decision has several consequences concerning the usage of the request processing models discussed below. The RETAIN strategy may be combined with the USE_ACTIVE_MAP_ONLY strategy, the USE_DEFAULT_SERVANT strategy, or the USE_SERVANT_MANAGER strategy; whereas, due to the missing Active Object Map, the NON_RETAIN strategy can only be combined with the remaining two request processing models.

- Request Processing Policy
  This policy determines in which way client requests are passed to the respective servants. Three cases are distinguishable. First, it is possible to dispatch requests *exclusively* via the Active Object Map (USE_ACTIVE_MAP_ONLY). The second possibility is to process the request by a default servant (USE_DEFAULT_SERVANT). A de-

fault servant accepts all requests that do not concern objects in the Active Object Map (if existent). The last alternative is the utilization of a servant manager (USE_SERV-ANT_MANAGER). Instances of that type are objects that adopt the task of managing servants. According to their functionality, two different subtypes may be distinguished: *servant activator* and *servant locator*. Servant activators are used by POA instances created with the RETAIN policy. Their task is to carry out incarnation of servants for use in later requests. Servant locators are used by POA instances created with the NON_RETAIN policy. They provide servants that may be used for processing of one single request.

- Implicit Activation Policy
When the server application attempts to obtain a reference for a servant that is not already active (that is, not associated with an object ID), the POA may implicitly activate an object (IMPLICIT_ACTIVATION policy). *Implicit activation* requires that the POA is configured with servant retention policy RETAIN and assignment policy SYSTEM_ID. If the NO_IMPLICIT_ACTIVATION policy is chosen, the POA does not support implicit activation of servants.

Any server application must generate at least one POA instance, the root POA. The root POA is a pre-defined object adapter configured as shown below.

- Thread Policy: ORB_CTRL_MODEL
- Lifespan Policy: TRANSIENT
- ID Assignment Policy: SYSTEM_ID
- ID Uniqueness Policy: UNIQUE_ID
- Servant Retention Policy: RETAIN
- Request Processing Policy: USE_ACTIVE_OBJECT_MAP_ONLY
- Implicit Activation Policy: IMPLICIT_ACTIVATION

Furthermore, a server application can generate and utilize additional, differently configured POA instances as direct or indirect child POAs inherited from the root POA.

6.3.2   Overview on POA Functionality

The locality-constrained interface of the POA is defined in the module PortableServer:

```
module PortableServer
{
  local interface POA
  {
    ...
  };
  ...
};
```

As noted above, the operations provided by the POA specification may be classified into different categories according to their functionality. The first kind is related to the POA itself and comprises two operations.

- void POA create_POA(in string adapter_name,
     in POAManager a_POAManager,
     in CORBA::PolicyList policies)
     raises(AdapterAlreadyExists, InvalidPolicy);

  This operation creates a new POA instance. The new POA is generated as a child of the target POA on which the operation is invoked. The specified adapter_name identifies the new POA with respect to other POAs with the same parent. If the parent POA already has a child with that name, an exception of type AdapterAlreadyExists is raised. If the value of the POAManager argument is null, a new POAManager instance is created and associated with the new POA.

- void POA find_POA(in string adapter_name,
     in boolean activate_it)
     raises(AdapterNonExistent);

  This operation may be invoked to find a specific instance of a child POA. If the target POA has a child with the specified name, that child is returned. If a child with the specified name does not exist and the value of the boolean argument is TRUE, activation of the child POA is attempted. If successful, that child is returned; otherwise, the exception is raised.

The second class of functionality deals with generating object references. The POA specification provides two operations for that purpose.

- Object create_reference(in CORBA::RepositoryId intf)
     raises(WrongPolicy);

  In order to invoke this operation successfully, the target POA instance must have been configured with the ID assignment policy SYSTEM_ID; otherwise, the WrongPolicy exception is raised. The specified repository ID determines the type of the generated object reference.

- Object create_reference_with_id(in ObjectId oid,
     in CORBA::RepositoryId intf)
     raises(WrongPolicy);

  This operation generates an object reference with the specified object ID and type. If it is invoked on a POA instance that was configured with the SYSTEM_ID policy and the passed object ID value was not generated by the system or this POA, a WrongPolicy exception is raised.

The next category concerns the detection and specification of *servant manager* objects. Two operations are provided for this.

- ServantManager get_servant_manager()
     raises(WrongPolicy);

In order to invoke this operation properly, the target POA instance must have been configured with the USE_SERVANT_MANAGER policy; otherwise, a Wrong-Policy exception is raised. The invocation returns a reference to the Servant-Manager object associated with the POA. If no servant manager has been associated with the POA, a null reference is returned.

* `void set_servant_manager(in ServantManager imgr)`
  `raises(WrongPolicy);`

  This is the counterpart of the above get operation. Again, the USE_SERVANT_MA-NAGER policy is required. The invocation sets the default servant manager associated with the POA. It may only be invoked once after the POA was created; otherwise, a system exception is raised.

The fourth type of operations deals with getting and setting servant objects. Two operations are available.

* `Servant get_servant()`
  `raises(NoServant, WrongPolicy);`

  This operation requires that the target POA instance is configured with the request processing policy USE_DEFAULT_SERVANT; if not, a WrongPolicy exception is raised. The invocation returns a reference to the *default servant* object. If no servant has been associated with the POA, an exception of type NoServant is raised.

* `void set_servant(in Servant p_servant)`
  `raises(WrongPolicy);`

  This is the counterpart of the above get operation. The USE_DEFAULT_SERVANT policy is also required. The operation registers the specified servant as the target's default servant.

The fifth function category comprises activation, deactivation, and destruction of CORBA objects. Four operations are available.

* `ObjectId activate_object(in Servant p_servant)`
  `raises(ServantAlreadyActive, WrongPolicy);`

  Proper invocation of this operation requires that the target POA instance is configured with the SYSTEM_ID and RETAIN policies. Otherwise, a WrongPolicy exception is raised. If the POA uses the UNIQUE_ID policy and the servant specified as argument is already in the Active Object Map, a ServantAlreadyActive exception is raised. Otherwise, the operation generates an object ID, enters it together with the specified servant in the Active Object Map, and returns the object ID.

- void activate_object_with_id(in ObjectId oid,
    in Servant p_servant)
    raises(ObjectAlreadyActive, ServantAlreadyActive,
    WrongPolicy);

This operation requires that the target POA instance is configured with the RETAIN policy. Otherwise, a WrongPolicy exception is raised. In the conditions stated above, a ServantAlreadyActive exception is raised. If the object denoted by the oid is already active, an ObjectAlreadyActive exception is raised. Otherwise, the invocation enters the corresponding entry in the Active Object Map.

- void deactivate_object(in ObjectId oid)
    raises(ObjectNotActive, WrongPolicy);

The target POA instance must be configured with the RETAIN policy; otherwise, a WrongPolicy exception is raised. The invocation causes the object ID passed as oid value to be deactivated and removed from the Active Object Map of this POA. Before the ID is removed from the Active Object Map, all active requests to the corresponding object are completed. After the operation has returned, no further requests to the object are accepted.

- void destroy(in boolean etherealize_objects,
    in boolean wait_for_completion);

This operation destroys the POA instance for which it is invoked. All child POAs, as well as their descendants, are also destroyed. The name of the destroyed POA may be reused in the same process to create a new POA. The technical details of the destruction process of a POA can be found in the CORBA specification [OMG04c].

In a further category of operations, we find various conversion routines.

- ObjectId servant_to_id(in Servant p_servant)
    raises(ServantNotActive, WrongPolicy);

With this operation, the object ID of the specified servant, if active, is determined and returned.

- Servant id_to_servant(in ObjectId oid)
    raises(ObjectNotActive, WrongPolicy);

The counterpart of the preceding operation, the servant associated to the object ID in the Active Object Map, is returned.

- Object servant_to_reference(in Servant p_servant)
    raises(ServantNotActive, WrongPolicy);

If the specified servant is active, the invocation determines and returns the servant's object reference.

- `Servant reference_to_servant(in Object reference)`
  `raises(ObjectNotActive, WrongAdapter, WrongPolicy);`

The counterpart of the preceding operation; if the specified object is present in the Active Object Map, the servant associated with that object is returned.

- `Object id_to_reference(in ObjectId oid)`
  `raises(ObjectNotActive, WrongPolicy);`

If an object with the specified ID is currently active, this operation returns the object's reference.

- `ObjectId reference_to_id(in Object reference)`
  `raises(WrongAdapter, WrongPolicy);`

The counterpart of the preceding operation, the object ID corresponding to the specified object reference is returned.

All the above operations require certain policy settings for the target POA in order to complete their invocation without raising an exception such as, e.g., `WrongPolicy`. The number of possible configurations is so extensive that we do not go into details here. However, we come back to the operations and their requirements during discussion of the examples in the following chapters.

The last category of POA functionality concerns policy creation operations. These operations return a policy object with the specified value.

- `ThreadPolicy create_thread_policy(`
  `in ThreadPolicyValue value);`
- `LifespanPolicy create_lifespan_policy(`
  `in LifespanPolicyValue value);`
- `IdUniquenessPolicy create_id_uniqueness_policy(`
  `in IdUniquenessPolicyValue value);`
- `IdAssignmentPolicy create_id_assignment_policy(`
  `in IdAssignmentPolicyValue value);`
- `ImplicitActivationPolicy`
  `create_implicit_activation_policy(`
  `in ImplicitActivationPolicyValue value);`
- `ServantRetentionPolicy create_servant_retention_policy(`
  `in ServantRetentionPolicyValue value);`
- `RequestProcessingPolicy create_request_processing_policy(`
  `in RequestProcessingPolicyValue value);`

In the POA interface, a number of `readonly` attributes are defined that allow us to determine some of the current state values. For example:

- `readonly attribute CORBA::OctetSeq id;`
  This attribute stores the POA's unique ID.
- `readonly attribute string the_name;`
  This attribute stores the name assigned to the POA when it was created.
- `readonly attribute POA the_parent;`
  This attribute identifies the parent of the POA. The parent of the root POA is null.
- `readonly attribute POAList the_children;`
  This attribute identifies the set of all direct child POAs of the POA.
- `readonly attribute POAManager the_POAManager;`
  This attribute identifies the `POAManager` instance associated with the POA.
- `readonly attribute POAManagerFactory`
  `the_POAManagerFactory;`
  This attribute identifies the `POAManagerFactory` that created the POA.

In the following, we briefly discuss a number of interfaces from the POA specification; some of which were already mentioned above.

6.3.3   POA Manager

Each POA object has an associated *POA manager*. The task of this `POAManager` object is to encapsulate the state of the POAs with which it is associated. A POA manager may be associated with one or more POAs. It can assume four different states: *active*, *inactive*, *holding*, or *discarding*. In Figure 9 below, the state diagram for the processing states of a `POAManager` is shown.

The `POAManager` interface contains the following operations:

- `void activate() raises(AdapterInactive);`
  This operation changes the state of the POA manager to *active*. In that state, the POAs it manages are enabled to process requests. The `AdapterInactive` is raised if the operation is invoked while the manager is in the inactive state. All the operations below that define a `raises(AdapterInactive)` clause behave in that way (see the above state diagram).
- `void hold_requests(in boolean wait_for_completion)`
  `raises(AdapterInactive);`
  This operation may be invoked to change the POA manager's state to *holding*. Entering the holding state causes the managed POAs to queue incoming requests. If the value of the `wait_for_completion` argument is `FALSE`, the operation returns immediately after changing the state.

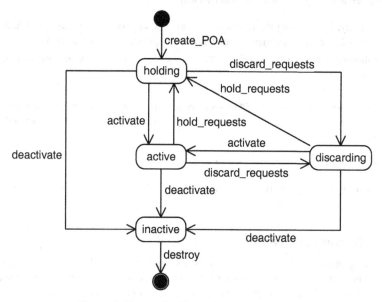

Figure 9: Processing States of a POAManager

- void discard_requests(in boolean wait_for_completion)
  raises(AdapterInactive);
  This operation changes the state of the POA manager to *discarding*. As a consequence, the POAs it manages are caused to discard incoming requests. In addition, any requests that have been queued but have not started executing are also discarded. The
  value provided for wait_for_completion has the same consequence as above.

- void deactivate(in boolean etherealize_objects,
  in boolean wait_for_completion)
  raises(AdapterInactive);
  This operation changes the state of the POA manager to *inactive*. In that state, the
  POAs it manages reject requests that have not begun to be executed as well as any
  new requests. If etherealize_objects is TRUE, the associated POAs call
  etherealize for each active object associated with the POA once all currently executing requests have completed processing (if the POAs have the RETAIN and
  USE_SERVANT_MANAGER policies). Any queued requests are rejected and the
  POA gets rid of its registered servant manager object, if any. If the value is FALSE,
  no deactivations or etherealizations are attempted.

- State get_state();
  This operation returns the current state of the POA manager. State is an enumer-
  ated type (enum) with the enumerators HOLDING, ACTIVE, DISCARDING, and
  INACTIVE.

- string get_id();
  This operation returns the POAManager's identity. If it is invoked for POA manager
  of the root POA, the result "RootPOAManager" is returned.

`POAManager` instances may be created in two ways:

- implicitly, by invoking the operation `create_POA()` (as already discussed in Section 6.3.2, the `POAManager` parameter must be passed a `null` value) or
- explicitly, by using a `POAManagerFactory` object (this approach is not discussed here).

As previously mentioned, when the POA receives a request targeted at an inactive object, it employs a `ServantManager` object to activate the servants. The servant manager interface is itself empty:

```
local interface ServantManager{ };
```

It is inherited by two other interfaces, the `ServantActivator` and the `ServantLocator`.

6.3.4   Servant Activators

A POA configured with the `RETAIN` policy uses servant managers that are `ServantActivators` in order to activate servants permanently. The activated servants are placed in the Active Object Map. The servant activator interface has the following definition:

```
local interface ServantActivator : ServantManager
{
  Servant incarnate(in ObjectId oid, in POA adapter)
    raises(ForwardRequest);
  void etherealize(in ObjectId oid, in POA adapter,
    in Servant serv, in boolean cleanup_in_progress,
    in boolean remaining_activations);
};
```

The operation `incarnate()` is invoked by a POA (configured with the `RETAIN` and `USE_SERVANT_MANAGER` policies) whenever the POA receives a request for a servant that is not in the Active Object Map. Operation `etherealize()` provides the complementary functionality and is invoked by the POA whenever a servant is deactivated.

6.3.5   Servant Locators

`ServantLocators` are used by POA instances that employ the `NON_RETAIN` policy. Servants returned by this servant manager are only used for processing a single client request. The servant locator interface has the following definition:

```
local interface ServantLocator : ServantManager
{
  native Cookie;
  Servant preinvoke(in ObjectId oid, in POA adapter,
    in CORBA::Identifier operation, out Cookie the_cookie)
    raises(ForwardRequest);
  void postinvoke(in ObjectId oid, in POA adapter,
    in CORBA::Identifier operation, in Cookie the_cookie,
```

```
      in Servant the_servant);
};
```

The operation preinvoke() is invoked by a POA (configured with the NON_RETAIN and USE_SERVANT_MANAGER policies) whenever the POA receives a request for an object not currently active. The invocation returns a servant used to process the incoming request as well as a *cookie* (see the out parameter in the definition), which might be used in the corresponding postinvoke() invocation. The postinvoke() operation is invoked when the servant has completed the request.

6.3.6   Java Mapping of Interface POA

The POA interface is defined on the basis of regular IDL within the module Portable-Server. In accordance with the standard IDL to Java rules, it is mapped in the following way:

```
package org.omg.PortableServer;

public interface POA {
   ...
};
```

The first POA-related operation we introduced in Section 6.3.1 was create_POA(). It is invoked to generate new child POAs following policies other than the standard root POA. The resulting Java method is

```
public org.omg.PortableServer.POA create_POA(
   java.lang.String adapter_name,
   org.omg.PortableServer.POAManager a_POAManager,
   org.omg.CORBA.Policy[] policies) throws
      org.omg.PortableServer.POAPackage.AdapterAlreadyExists,
      org.omg.PortableServer.POAPackage.InvalidPolicy;
```

Examples for generating child POAs and configuring the desired policies are given in Chapter 16. In the context of operation create_POA(), we also discussed find_POA(), which finds existing POA instances. This operation is mapped to the Java method below:

```
public org.omg.PortableServer.POA find_POA(
   java.lang.String adapter_name,
   boolean activate_it) throws
      org.omg.PortableServer.POAPackage.AdapterNonExistent;
```

Generating new object references belongs to the primary tasks of a POA. To that end, the POA interface provides the operations create_reference() and create_reference_with_id(), introduced in Section 6.3.1. The corresponding Java methods are

```
public org.omg.CORBA.Object create_reference(
   java.lang.String intf) throws
      org.omg.PortableServer.POAPackage.WrongPolicy;
```

and

```
public org.omg.CORBA.Object create_reference_with_id(
    byte[] oid, java.lang.String intf) throws
        org.omg.PortableServer.POAPackage.WrongPolicy;
```

In both cases, the type of the object reference to be generated is determined by a Repo-sitoryId, which is passed as a String argument. The newly generated object references, however, are not yet associated with a servant; they are not activated. So far, only the "abstract" object and its reference exist, which can, for example, already be converted into its string representation or registered with the Naming Service.

For setting or getting references to ServantManager objects, we introduced the operations set_servant_manager() and get_servant_manager(). In Java they are represented by the methods

```
public void set_servant_manager(
    org.omg.PortableServer.ServantManager imgr) throws
        org.omg.PortableServer.POAPackage.WrongPolicy;
```

and

```
public org.omg.PortableServer.ServantManager
    get_servant_manager() throws
        org.omg.PortableServer.POAPackage.WrongPolicy;
```

Setting and getting references to Servant objects with the operations set_servant() and get_servant() follows the same pattern. In Java, the corresponding methods are

```
public void set_servant(
    org.omg.PortableServer.Servant p_servant) throws
        org.omg.PortableServer.POAPackage.WrongPolicy;
```

and

```
public org.omg.PortableServer.Servant get_servant() throws
    org.omg.PortableServer.POAPackage.NoServant,
    org.omg.PortableServer.POAPackage.WrongPolicy;
```

The fifth category of functionality provides means for activation, deactivation, and destruction of CORBA objects with the help of operations activate_object(), activate_object_with_id(), deactivate_object(), and destroy(). Their Java counterparts are

```
public byte[] activate_object(
    org.omg.PortableServer.Servant p_servant) throws
        org.omg.PortableServer.POAPackage.ServantAlreadyActive,
        org.omg.PortableServer.POAPackage.WrongPolicy;

public void activate_object_with_id(byte[] id,
    org.omg.PortableServer.Servant p_servant) throws
        org.omg.PortableServer.POAPackage.ServantAlreadyActive,
        org.omg.PortableServer.POAPackage.ObjectAlreadyActive,
        org.omg.PortableServer.POAPackage.WrongPolicy;
```

```
public void deactivate_object(byte[] oid) throws
    org.omg.PortableServer.POAPackage.ObjectNotActive,
    org.omg.PortableServer.POAPackage.WrongPolicy;

void destroy(boolean etherealize_objects,
    boolean wait_for_completion);
```

We further discussed the POA's conversion routines provided by the operations `servant_to_id()`, `servant_to_reference()`, `id_to_servant()`, `id_to_reference()`, `reference_to_servant()`, and `reference_to_id()`. They are mapped to the following Java methods:

```
public byte[] servant_to_id(
    org.omg.PortableServer.Servant p_servant) throws
        org.omg.PortableServer.POAPackage.ServantNotActive,
        org.omg.PortableServer.POAPackage.WrongPolicy;

public org.omg.CORBA.Object servant_to_reference(
    org.omg.PortableServer.Servant p_servant) throws
        org.omg.PortableServer.POAPackage.ServantNotActive,
        org.omg.PortableServer.POAPackage.WrongPolicy;

public org.omg.PortableServer.Servant id_to_servant(
    byte[] oid) throws
        org.omg.PortableServer.POAPackage.ObjectNotActive,
        org.omg.PortableServer.POAPackage.WrongPolicy;

public org.omg.CORBA.Object id_to_reference(
    byte[] oid) throws
        org.omg.PortableServer.POAPackage.ObjectNotActive,
        org.omg.PortableServer.POAPackage.WrongPolicy;

public org.omg.PortableServer.Servant
    reference_to_servant(org.omg.CORBA.Object reference)
        throws
        org.omg.PortableServer.POAPackage.ObjectNotActive,
        org.omg.PortableServer.POAPackage.WrongPolicy;

public byte[] reference_to_id(
    org.omg.CORBA.Object reference) throws
        org.omg.PortableServer.POAPackage.WrongAdapter,
        org.omg.PortableServer.POAPackage.WrongPolicy;
```

In the last category of POA functionality, we dealt with operations generating policy information. These operations, namely, `create_thread_policy()`, `create_lifespan_policy()`, `create_id_uniqueness_policy()`, `create_id_assignment_policy()`, `create_implicit_activation_policy()`, `create_servant_retention_policy()`, and `create_request_processing_policy()`, have the following Java mappings:

```
public org.omg.PortableServer.ThreadPolicy
    create_thread_policy(
        org.omg.PortableServer.ThreadPolicyValue value);
```

```
public org.omg.PortableServer.LifespanPolicy
  create_lifespan_policy(
    org.omg.PortableServer.LifespanPolicyValue value);

public org.omg.PortableServer.IdUniquenessPolicy
  create_id_uniqueness_policy(
    org.omg.PortableServer.IdUniquenessPolicyValue value);

public org.omg.PortableServer.IdAssignmentPolicy
  create_id_assignment_policy(
    org.omg.PortableServer.IdAssignmentPolicyValue value);

public org.omg.PortableServer.ImplicitActivationPolicy
  create_implicit_activation_policy(
    org.omg.PortableServer.ImplicitActivationPolicyValue
      value);

public org.omg.PortableServer.ServantRetentionPolicy
  create_servant_retention_policy(
    org.omg.PortableServer.ServantRetentionPolicyValue
      value);

public org.omg.PortableServer.RequestProcessingPolicy
  create_request_processing_policy(
    org.omg.PortableServer.RequestProcessingPolicyValue
      value);
```

Finally, according to the familiar rules, the readonly attributes defined in the POA interface are mapped to these get methods:

```
public byte[] id();

public java.lang.String the_name();

public org.omg.PortableServer.POA the_parent();

public org.omg.PortableServer.POA[] the_children();

public org.omg.PortableServer.POAManager the_POAManager();
```

6.4   Pseudo Interface CORBA::Object

The pseudo interface CORBA::Object serves as superinterface for all IDL interfaces defined with the intention of later implementing them through servants. Thus, all of its operations are available to all CORBA objects that application programmers develop.

6.4.1   IDL Operations of CORBA::Object

The interface CORBA::Object provides, amongst others, the following fundamental operations (note that discussion of operations pertaining to the DII are covered in Section 6.6.5).

- `Object duplicate();`
  This operation creates a copy of an object. The invocation returns an object reference to the newly generated duplicate.

- `void release();`
  When an object reference is no longer needed, its storage may be reclaimed by use of the operation `release()`. Operations `duplicate()` as well as `release()` play an important role for programming languages where programmers themselves are responsible for storage management and garbage collection like, for example, C or C++.

- `boolean is_nil();`
  With this operation, we can test whether an object's reference has the null value (more precisely: OBJECT_NIL) and, therefore, denotes no object. In that case, the invocation returns the result TRUE. Should the result be FALSE, one should nevertheless be cautious about presuming that the reference is valid since in the meantime (the return of the operation and the testing of its value) the object may have been destroyed.

- `boolean non_existent();`
  This operation may be used to test whether an object has been destroyed. It returns TRUE if the ORB knows that the object does not exist; otherwise, it returns FALSE. The latter result should, again, be interpreted with caution.

- `boolean is_a(in RepositoryID logical_type_id);`
  Operation `is_a()` tests whether an object is of a certain type. The string argument `logical_type_id` denotes the type to which it is to be compared; it is one of the types stored in the Interface Repository. If the invocation returns the result TRUE, the object is an instance of that type or of a subtype of that type. Should the result be FALSE, the types are not compatible. If the ORB cannot perform the test, e.g., it cannot contact a remote ORB or Interface Repository due to network problems, an exception in the calling application is raised.

- `boolean is_equivalent(in Object other_object);`
  This operation tests if two object references are equivalent. Two references are equivalent if they are identical. Two different object references referring to the same object are also equivalent. A return value of FALSE indicates that the references are not identical and that the ORB cannot determine whether they refer to the same object or not.

The CORBA standard specifies a number of additional interfaces and structures relevant for usage of the DII (in particular CORBA::NamedValue or CORBA::NVList), the DynAny interface, or the Interface Repository. These are discussed in subsequent chapters.

6.4.2 Java Mapping of Pseudo Interface CORBA::Object

CORBA::Object is the superinterface for all CORBA objects defined with the help of IDL. It provides the operations available to any CORBA object. They are implemented by the ORB local to the client of the service-providing object, often a remote object. In Java, the pseudo interface CORBA::Object is mapped in the following way:

```
package org.omg.CORBA;

public interface Object {
    ...
};
```

The two first operations duplicate() and release() from CORBA::Object, which were mentioned in Section 6.4.1, copy or release storage of CORBA objects. Although there is no necessity to invoke those methods in Java applications since the language provides automatic storage management for object references, they are provided for the sake of completeness. Note the underscores that had to be appended to the original IDL identifiers

```
org.omg.CORBA.Object _duplicate();
```

and

```
void _release();
```

With the operation is_nil(), one can test if an object reference is actually referencing an object or not. In the latter case, the reference has the value OBJECT_NIL and the operation returns the boolean value TRUE. Java uses the null value to indicate that a reference does not reference an object. For that reason, no Java mapping for the operation is_nil() is provided. The simple expression obj_ref == null yields the desired result without any method invocation. A corresponding Java code snippet could therefore read

```
if (obj_ref != null)
    obj_ref.op_x();
else
    ...
```

The operation non_existent(), which allows testing if a CORBA object has been destroyed, has the Java counterpart

```
boolean _non_existent();
```

The invocation might require the ORB to contact a remote server. Therefore, the application might throw an exception. The same holds for the operation is_a(), which tests if the object's type is compatible with the interface type specified in the argument. In Java, that operation is mapped to

```
boolean _is_a(String intf);
```

To compare two object references for equivalence, operation is_equivalent() may be invoked. In Java, the corresponding method is

```
boolean _is_equivalent(org.omg.CORBA.Object other_object);
```

Here, a false return value only indicates that the ORB does not know whether the referenced objects are identical or not.

6.5 Pseudo Interface CORBA::TypeCode

The pseudo interface CORBA::TypeCode makes it possible to represent type information on arbitrary IDL types. TypeCode instances are mainly needed in order to

- represent the data type and interface type specifications registered in an Interface Repository,
- determine the types of the actual arguments and the return type when compiling a dynamic operation invocation, or
- provide the value stored in an any with a type so that type safety is ensured during extraction of this value.

TypeCode instances are generated by invoking one of several similarly organized operations in the CORBA::ORB interface. The central type information stored in a TypeCode instance can be determined through an invocation of operation kind(), which returns a CORBA::TCKind instance as a result. TCKind is an enumerated type that defines enumerators for all kinds of TypeCodes. The set of admissible operation invocations for the object represented by the TypeCode is dependent on that code. The IDL definition for CORBA::TCKind is given below:

```
enum TCKind
{
    tk_null, tk_void, tk_short, tk_long,
    tk_ushort, tk_ulong, tk_float, tk_double, tk_boolean,
    tk_char, tk_octet, tk_any, tk_TypeCode, tk_Principal,
    tk_objref, tk_struct, tk_union, tk_enum, tk_string,
    tk_sequence, tk_array, tk_alias, tk_except, tk_longlong,
    tk_ulonglong, tk_longdouble, tk_wchar, tk_wstring,
    tk_fixed, tk_value, tk_value_box, tk_native,
    tk_abstract_interface, tk_local_interface, tk_component,
    tk_home, tk_event
};
```

In Java, the pseudo interface CORBA::TypeCode is represented by the public abstract class TypeCode in package org.omg.CORBA. The enumerated type CORBA::TCKind is mapped according to the rules discussed in Section 5.10 with the exception that no helper or holder classes are generated since that type is never used as argument of a remote operation invocation. Here, it should be sufficient to present only part of the Java implementation:

```
package org.omg.CORBA;

public class TCKind {
    public static final int _tk_null = 0;
    public static final TCKind tk_null =
        new TCKind(_tk_null);
    public static final int _tk_void = 1;
    TCKind tk_void = new TCKind(_tk_void);
    public static final int _tk_short = 2;
    ...
}
```

We chose not to describe in detail the specifics connected with TypeCodes and refer interested readers to the examples addressed in later chapters as well as to the CORBA specification and the IDL to Java Mapping documentation, where the complete definitions of the involved interfaces may be found.

6.6   Dynamic Invocation Interface

In Section 3.4.5, we explained the basics of the Dynamic Invocation Interfaces, which may be employed at run-time to execute remote operation invocations without resorting to the stub classes generated by an IDL compiler. The labeling DII is somewhat misleading since the DII is not a single, self-contained interface; rather, it is just a generic term for an aggregation of functional building stones, consisting of a number of specialized pseudo interfaces as well as several operations that are included in the already known pseudo interfaces CORBA::ORB and CORBA::Object. Before we go into these operations, we first describe the dedicated pseudo interfaces NamedValue and NVList, which, for their part, are used as types in these operations.

While working on this book, we came across a number of inconsistencies and errors in the CORBA specification 3.0.3 [OMG04c] we used pertaining to the DII's IDL to Java mapping [OMG02]. Obviously, during editing the revised version of the CORBA specification, the sections concerning the above pseudo objects were completely neglected with respect to updating and error correction. As an example, we could select the version of the pseudo interface NVList given in the specification. In the version presented there, this interface is rather useless since no operations are defined that are able to extract elements from the list once they were inserted. In the mapping document, however, a completely different but practical definition of NVLists is intended. We encountered similar problems in other parts of the specification and, therefore, recommend regarding the Java mapping document as a relevant reference in the context of specifying pseudo objects. Especially in view of practicability and runnability of example code, it can serve as a concrete basis for implementation of Java ORBs. Consequently, the PIDL particulars in the subsections below follow the definitions in the Java mapping document and not the CORBA specification. It can be expected that future versions of the CORBA standard resolve these inadequacies and, thus, set the record straight for application developers, ORB implementers, and programmers generally interested in middleware or CORBA technology.

6.6.1   Pseudo Interface CORBA::NamedValue

NamedValues are employed to describe the arguments and results of a dynamic operation invocation. Whereas in the actual CORBA specification and in previous specifications NamedValues are still defined as a struct data type, in the Java mapping document, they are specified through a PIDL pseudo interface CORBA::NamedValue. Its definition is

```
typedef unsigned long Flags;
typedef string Identifier;
const Flags ARG_IN = 1;
const Flags ARG_OUT = 2;
const Flags ARG_INOUT = 3;
```

```
const Flags CTX_RESTRICT_SCOPE = 15;

pseudo interface NamedValue
{
  readonly attribute Identifier name;
  readonly attribute any value;
  readonly attribute Flags flags;
};
```

The name attribute defines the name of a parameter needed for a dynamic operation invocation. The attribute value is used to store the corresponding argument value for that parameter. It also contains information on the concrete parameter type that is encapsulated here in the type any. The attribute flags of type Flags governs the direction in which the value is passed (note that this naming schema would be illegal in regular IDL). In accordance with the IDL keywords in, out, and inout, which may be used for static invocations, the following values are admissible:

- CORBA::ARG_IN
  This constant specifies that the argument be passed from client to server.
- CORBA::ARG_OUT
  This constant specifies that the argument be passed from server to client.
- CORBA::ARG_INOUT
  This constant specifies that the argument be passed in both directions.

Since on the IDL level neither the CORBA specification nor the Java mapping defines an operation to generate NamedValue instances, this had to be made up for on the programming language level. We introduce the corresponding Java method for that task in Section 6.6.6.

6.6.2   Pseudo Interface CORBA::NVList

The pseudo interface CORBA::NVList facilitates passing a number of arguments, which can be managed in a list of NamedValues. The Java mapping provides the following PIDL specification:

```
pseudo interface NVList
{
  readonly attribute unsigned long count;
  NamedValue add(in Flags flags);
  NamedValue add_item(in Identifier item_name,
    in Flags flags);
  NamedValue add_value(in Identifier item_name,
    in any val, in Flags flags);
  NamedValue item(in unsigned long index)
    raises(CORBA::Bounds);
  void remove(in unsigned long index)
    raises(CORBA::Bounds);
};
```

Three add...() operations are defined that insert new elements into an NVList instance. Note that, interestingly, the functionality of these operations goes beyond mere "add" semantics since they serve as constructors for NamedValue objects as well. It is important to be aware that no add...() operation is defined that can insert existing NamedValue objects and to this end provides an in parameter of type NamedValue.

All three variants first generate a new NamedValue object based on differing initialization arguments. This object is then automatically inserted into the NVList object that was the target of the invocation. The new NamedValue object is returned as a result of the invocation, as well. Normally, the last two variants are employed. In order to invoke operation add_value(), all relevant initialization information to generate the NamedValue must be given: parameter name, parameter value, and directional attribute. The operation add_item(), however, does without the possibility to provide a value, which predestines it to usage with parameters of type CORBA::ARG_OUT, which do not need an initializer value.

The pseudo interface NVList further specifies the two operations item() and remove() as well as an attribute count. Operation item() may be invoked to return a reference to the NamedValue object positioned at the given index in the list. With an invocation of operation remove(), the object at the specified position is removed from the list; one can see that NVLists are modifiable. At any time, the readonly attribute count stores the current number of entries in the list.

Instances of a CORBA::NVList can only be generated by the ORB operations create_ list() and create_operation_list() (see Section 6.6.4).

6.6.3   Pseudo Interface CORBA::Request

Request objects that can be generated by the ORB are needed in connection with dynamic operation invocations on objects where the IDL type is not known at compile-time of the application (see the interface Object and the operation create_request() in Section 6.6.5). A Request object contains all the information necessary for a dynamic invocation, namely, an object reference, an operation name, type information, and values for arguments. Thus, the client can send a request to an object analogous to the static approach that uses stub code. The pseudo interface Request provides the necessary operations to initialize and execute such an invocation:

```
pseudo interface Request
{
  readonly attribute Object target;
  readonly attribute Identifier operation;
  readonly attribute NVList arguments;
  readonly attribute NamedValue result;
  readonly attribute Environment env;
  readonly attribute ExceptionList exceptions;
  readonly attribute ContextList contexts;
  attribute Context ctx;
  any add_in_arg();
  any add_named_in_arg(in string name);
  any add_inout_arg();
```

```
    any add_named_inout_arg(in string name);
    any add_out_arg();
    any add_named_out_arg(in string name);
    void set_return_type(in TypeCode tc);
    any return_value();
    void invoke();
    void send_oneway();
    void send_deferred();
    void get_response();
    boolean poll_response();
};
```

The Request object is generated by invoking the Object operation create_request(). During its generation, values are provided for the attributes in the interface definition. The attribute target contains the reference to the object that has to execute the invocation. The attributes operation, arguments, and result contain the operation's name, its arguments, the return type of the expected result, and, after successful completion of the invocation, the result value. The attribute env stores the exceptions raised during the operation's execution. The TypeCodes of the user-defined exceptions that may be raised by the operation are given in the attribute exceptions. The attributes contexts and ctx are rarely used and make available additional information on the Request's execution context and on the names provided in the context clause of the operation definition, respectively.

The add...() operations are employed in order to add the different arguments to an existing Request object. For each argument, a new NamedValue instance has to be inserted into the NVList of the Request objects. After creating a new NamedValue instance, each add...() operation sets the appropriate flag in the NamedValue (see Section 6.6.1), and some also set the name.

Three different invocation models are distinguished for dynamic invocations. By means of the corresponding operations, synchronous, asynchronous, and *one-way* communication can be realized. The first two communication types can return a result value and, therefore, require that the expected return type be specified by means of invoking the operation set_return_type(). Subsequently, the methods to execute the operation and to retrieve the result may be called.

The first of these is operation invoke(), which puts into practice CORBA's standard communication model enabling blocking, synchronous invocations that do not return until the corresponding operation is completed. The caller now has to inspect the Request object's attribute env of type Environment and check whether the invocation has raised an exception. (Note that neither the CORBA specification nor the mapping document contains an IDL or PIDL specification of the type Environment. The Java mapping only defines a corresponding class; see Section 6.6.6.) If the method returned successfully, the result was placed in the attribute result of the Request object and the inout and out parameter in the attribute arguments of the Request object have also been updated correspondingly. Besides reading the value of the result attribute, one further possibility to access the result of the invocation is to employ the operation return_value(), which, however, does not provide a NamedValue instance but returns an any instance containing the proper value instead. Both possibilities are also available with the second invocation model, which is now examined closer.

The operation send_deferred() may be used to invoke an operation asynchronously. Unlike invoke(), send_deferred() returns control to the caller immediately without waiting for the operation to be finished by the target object. To enable the caller to access the results of the invocation at a later point in time, two additional operations are defined: get_response() and poll_response(). To determine whether the operation is done and the result, if any, is available, the caller must use poll_response(). In that case, the value TRUE is returned, otherwise FALSE. This approach is especially relevant to clients that should not block while waiting for a return result to be established. On the other hand, the operation get_response() can be invoked immediately; it blocks until the return result and all values of the inout and out parameters are available. get_response() then makes them ready in the corresponding attributes of the Request object where they can subsequently be accessed by the caller. If the poll_response() approach is used and the call has returned the result TRUE, then, get_response() must also be invoked in order to provide the results in the Request object.

The third alternative provides the opportunity to send requests one-way. In conformity with static IDL operation definitions specified oneway, return values, inout and out parameters, or exceptions must not be used here so that flow of control is indeed one-way (see Section 4.5.2). As a consequence, the Request object need not be accessed after such an invocation. The operation to be used for this purpose is operation send_oneway().

Additional possibilities exist for the last two invocation models. For example, more than one pre-initialized Request object may be used for dynamic invocations at the same time. The available operations are defined in the ORB interface and we therefore address them in Section 6.6.4.

6.6.4   ORB Operations for the Dynamic Invocation Interface

The ORB interface also provides a number of helper functions that are needed to generate dynamic operation invocations. In Section 6.2, we did not discuss them; however, they should be addressed here. These operations are required to generate an NVList's arguments for a Request object. The elements of that list are of type CORBA::NamedValue. In IDL syntax, the operations are defined as follows:

- Status create_list(in long count, out NVList new_list);
  This operation allocates an empty list; the specified count argument is a "hint" to help with storage allocation for the expected number of list elements. With the above described NVList operations add_item() and add_value(), list items can be inserted afterwards into the list.
- Status create_operation_list(in OperationDef op_def,
    out NVList new_list);
  This operation returns an NVList initialized with the argument descriptions (argument op_def of type OperationDef) for a given operation. The arguments of type NamedValue are returned in the same order as they were defined in the operation definition.

In addition to these two operations that generate NVList objects, the ORB interface defines four operations that make it possible to issue multiple requests.

- void send_multiple_requests_oneway(in RequestSeq req);
  This operation initiates more than one request in parallel. A sequence of pre-initialized Request objects must be provided to the operation as an argument of type RequestSeq. As indicated by the operation name, the oneway invocation model is employed. Since dynamic invocations following that model do not return any information, no subsequent operation invocations for retrieval of results are needed.

- void send_multiple_requests_deferred(in RequestSeq req);
  As above, more than one request is sent in parallel. And, again, a sequence of pre-initialized Request objects must be provided to the operation as argument of type RequestSeq. Here, the invocation follows the asynchronous model and, again, the operation returns to the caller immediately without waiting for the requests to finish. However, now reverse information flow is involved for the Request objects and the two following operations are of importance.

- boolean poll_next_response();
  This operation determines whether or not any request has been completed. A TRUE return indicates that at least one has; in that case, operation get_next_respon-se() may be invoked to retrieve the results.

- void get_next_response(out Request req);
  This operation returns the next request that is completed. The results (return value, inout and out arguments, and exceptions) are provided in the Request parameter. The operation blocks until the results of the next completed request are available.

In order to complete the description of the DII, we now only lack the operations supporting dynamic invocations that are provided by the Object interface. These operations are the topic of the next section.

6.6.5 Object Operations for the Dynamic Invocation Interface

We saw that objects of type Request are used to execute dynamic invocations in the COR-BA environment. To generate such a Request object, the operation create_re-quest(), defined in the interface Object, is invoked:

```
void create_request(in Context ctx,
    in Identifier operation, in NVList arg_list,
    inout NamedValue result, out Request request,
    in Flags req_flag);
```

This operation creates an ORB request and prepares a dynamic invocation. The arguments that have to be provided correspond to the attributes discussed in the context of the pseudo interface Request and are not repeated here. The actual invocation occurs by calling in-voke() or by using the send and get/poll_response calls.

One further operation from the Object interface relevant in connection with the Interface Repository should not remain unmentioned,

```
InterfaceDef get_interface();
```

In an Interface Repository, in which type information specified in IDL is available, the description of the interface of the CORBA object on which the operation was invoked can be determined dynamically. This kind of type information is represented by objects of IDL type CORBA::InterfaceDef. The operation get_interface() returns an object in the Interface Repository that describes the IDL type of the target object of the invocation.

6.6.6   Java Mapping of DII-related Pseudo Interfaces and Operations

We keep the following description of the Java mapping of the above-discussed DII-related pseudo interfaces and operations rather brief since at this point one should be familiar with all central information.

We introduced the pseudo interface CORBA::NamedValue in Section 6.6.1; in Java, it is represented by the public and abstract class NamedValue declared in the package org.omg.CORBA. Recall that IDL constants, which are defined at module scope, are in Java mapped to interfaces of the same name (see Section 5.7).

```
package org.omg.CORBA;

public interface ARG_IN {
  public static final int value = 1;
}

public interface ARG_OUT {
  public static final int value = 2;
}

public interface ARG_INOUT {
  public static final int value = 3;
}

public interface CTX_RESTRICT_SCOPE {
  public static final int value = 15;
}

public abstract class NamedValue {
  public abstract String name();
  public abstract Any value();
  public abstract int flags();
}
```

Instances of a NamedValue can be created using the following ORB method:

```
public abstract NamedValue create_named_value(
  String name, Any value, int flags);
```

A call to this method constructs a new NamedValue object using the given name, value, and argument mode flags.

As discussed in Section 6.6.2, lists of NamedValue instances are realized through instances of type NVList. In Java, the IDL type NVList is mapped to the public and abstract declared class NVList in package org.omg.CORBA.

```
package org.omg.CORBA;

public abstract class NVList {
  public abstract int count();
  public abstract NamedValue add(int flags);
  public abstract NamedValue add_item(String item_name,
    int flags);
  public abstract NamedValue add_value(String item_name,
    Any val, int flags);
  public abstract NamedValue item(int index)
    throws org.omg.CORBA.Bounds;
  public abstract void remove(int index)
    throws org.omg.CORBA.Bounds;
}
```

The central pseudo interface that enables dynamic invocations is the interface CORBA::Request, which we introduced in Section 6.6.3. Its Java mapping is designed as follows:

```
package org.omg.CORBA;

public abstract class Request {
  public abstract org.omg.CORBA.Object target();
  public abstract String operation();
  public abstract NVList arguments();
  public abstract NamedValue result();
  public abstract Environment env();
  public abstract ExceptionList exceptions();
  public abstract ContextList contexts();
  public abstract Context ctx();
  public abstract void ctx(Context c);
  public abstract Any add_in_arg();
  public abstract Any add_named_in_arg(String name);
  public abstract Any add_inout_arg();
  public abstract Any add_named_inout_arg(String name);
  public abstract Any add_out_arg();
  public abstract Any add_named_out_arg(String name);
  public abstract void set_return_type(TypeCode tc);
  public abstract Any return_value();
  public abstract void invoke();
  public abstract void send_oneway();
  public abstract void send_deferred();
  public abstract void get_response()
    throws org.omg.CORBA.WrongTransaction;
  public abstract boolean poll_response();
}
```

With one exception, this Java mapping does not show any noteworthy particularities. Contrary to the guideline in the PIDL definition, where the operation get_response() cannot raise any exceptions, in the Java mapping, it is possible that an exception of type org.omg.CORBA.WrongTransaction is thrown. This exception belongs to the class of CORBA User Exceptions. Such an exceptional situation can occur if OMG's *Transaction Service* [OMG03a] comes into operation and the transaction context for delivery of the original `Request` differs from that pertaining to the subsequent invocation of operation `get_response()`.

There is only one thing that needs to be discussed here: the Java mapping of the type `Environment` already envisaged above. This type, which is not specified in IDL or PIDL, serves to make information on raised exceptions available. The method `env()` declared in class `Request` has the corresponding Java class `Environment` as a return type. The Java mapping prescribes the following implementation of this data type:

```
package org.omg.CORBA;

public abstract class Environment {
  public abstract void exception(
    java.lang.Exception except);
  public abstract java.lang.Exception exception();
  public abstract void clear();
}
```

The effects of invoking these methods should be largely self-explanatory. With a call of the method `exception()`, which expects an `Exception` object as an argument, an invoked operation can supply a raised exception in the `Environment` object; and, with the parameter-free `exception()` method, the caller can afterwards access that information. By means of method `clear()`, the `Environment` object may be reset for future use.

After having described the pseudo interfaces dedicated for the DII, we discussed the operations from the `ORB` and the `Object` interfaces that are also relevant in the context of dynamic operation invocations. We keep to the order chosen above and begin with the presentation of the Java mapping of the `ORB` operations corresponding to Section 6.6.4. There, we first of all illustrated the two operations `create_list()` and `create_operation_list()`, which generate `NVList` objects. In Java, these operations become the methods

```
public abstract NVList create_list(int count);
```

and

```
public NVList create_operation_list(
  org.omg.CORBA.Object oper);
```

Some minor irregularities concerning OMG's general mapping rules of IDL operations can be noticed here. As opposed to the IDL definition, where both operations have a return type `Status`, this result is completely ignored in the Java versions. Instead, both Java methods return the newly created `NVList` object and, thus, replace the `out` parameter of the same name provided in the operation's IDL definition.

The two `create()` methods are supplemented by a method `create_environment()`, which can construct objects of the additional type `Environment`, discussed above. It is declared with this signature:

```
public abstract Environment create_environment();
```

We saw that operations send_multiple_requests_oneway(), send_multiple_
requests_deferred(), poll_next_response(), and get_next_respon-
se() make it possible to issue multiple requests by means of a single operation invocation.
Subsequently, the return results, if any, can be retrieved request by request. The Java equiva-
lents of these operations go like this:

```
public abstract void send_multiple_requests_oneway(
  Request[] req);

public abstract void send_multiple_requests_deferred(
  Request[] req);

public abstract boolean poll_next_response();

public abstract Request get_next_response()
  throws org.omg.CORBA.WrongTransaction;
```

With respect to the exception class org.omg.CORBA.WrongTransaction, our explanations pertaining to the method get_response() of class Request are valid analogously.

The last group of operations that is required for employment of the Dynamic Invocation Interface is provided through the Object interface. By invoking operation create_re-
quest(), a client may generate Requests. On the Java level, a Request object is constructed through calling one of the next three methods on an object reference of type
org.omg.CORBA.Object:

```
Request _create_request(Context ctx, String operation,
  NVList arg_list, NamedValue result);

Request _create_request(Context ctx, String operation,
  NVList arg_list, NamedValue result,
  ExceptionList exclist, ContextList ctxlist);

Request _request(String operation);
```

One can see that the parameter Flags of the IDL definition of operation create_re-
quest() is not mapped to Java. It is useful for purposes of storage management in some
programming languages. In Java however, with its built-in garbage collection mechanism, it
is not needed. While the first two methods only differ in that the second version can also
process additional type information, the third method was supplemented in order to produce
partially pre-initialized Request objects. The first two methods have the four arguments in
common. Arguments ctx, operation, arg_list, and result are passed the execution context of the request, the name of the operation to be invoked, and the argument list for
the invocation as well as the expected result type. In addition, for the second method, the
TypeCodes of user-defined exceptions that may be thrown by the operation and the names
in the context clause of the operation may be specified in the arguments exclist und
ctxlist.

At the end of Section 6.6.5, we mentioned operation `get_interface()`, which is also defined in the pseudo interface `CORBA::Object`. When invoked, it dynamically gets a `CORBA::InterfaceDef` object from the Interface Repository and describes a CORBA object by providing details on the data types, operations, and attributes supported by that object's type. In Java, this operation is mapped to the method

```
org.omg.CORBA.Object _get_interface_def();
```

Some characteristics of this mapping to Java have to be mentioned here as well. On the one hand, they concern the method's name and, on the other, its return type. Since, due to specific Java-related reasons, the return type is the general `org.omg.CORBA.Object` type, the result must be cast to the type `org.omg.CORBA.InterfaceDef` with the well-known method `narrow()` from the corresponding helper class.

6.7   Dynamic Skeleton Interface

Through the DII, we became acquainted with a mechanism that allows clients to invoke operations on CORBA objects at run-time without knowing the interface type of that object at compile-time. The Dynamic Skeleton Interface provides an analogue for the server side. The DSI enables an ORB to dynamically invoke an object implementation such that, rather than being accessed through a skeleton that is specific to the particular operation and known at compile-time, the object is reached through an interface. Just as the implementation of an object cannot distinguish whether its client is using type-specific stubs or the DII, it makes no difference for the object and it is not even perceptible whether an invocation was triggered through a compiler-generated skeleton class or through the DSI. The functionality of the DSI essentially relies on the basic idea of providing the same call up routine for arbitrary requests. In the Java mapping, this is the generic method `invoke()`, declared in the abstract class `DynamicImplementation`. All relevant information concerning the request (operation to be invoked and arguments) is passed to this method. For that purpose, a pseudo object of type `ServerRequest` is used; it brings to mind the `Request` type that is known from the DII context.

6.7.1   Pseudo Interface `CORBA::ServerRequest`

In the CORBA specification, the pseudo interface `ServerRequest` is defined as follows (note that instead of using the IDL type `any`, the standard wrongly employs the Java type `Any`):

```
module CORBA
{
  ...

  interface ServerRequest
  {
    readonly attribute Identifier operation;
    void arguments(inout NVList nv);
    Context ctx();
    void set_result(in any val);
```

```
        void set_exception(in any val);
    };
};
```

The `operation` attribute provides the identifier naming the operation being invoked. Operation parameter types are specified and `in` and `inout` argument values are retrieved with the operation `arguments()`. An `NVList` instance, initialized with the `TypeCodes` and `Flags` describing the parameter types for the operation in the order in which they appear in the IDL specification, is passed into `arguments()`. The ORB enters the argument values into the `NVList` instance for subsequent usage by the server. The same `NVList` instance is also used to return new values for the `inout` and `out` parameters once the server has finished processing.

When the operation's IDL definition contains a context expression, the operation `ctx()` returns the specified context information. The `set_result()` operation is used to specify a return value for the value of the call in the form of an `any` instance. And, the operation `set_exception()` is called any time the server has to return an exception to the client instead of providing a return result.

6.7.2   Java Mapping of the DSI

In the DSI's Java mapping, the public abstract class `DynamicImplementation` of package `org.omg.PortableServer` is described. This class has no corresponding IDL or PIDL specification. A server intending to use the DSI has to implement that class. It inherits from the `Servant` class (see Section 6.8), which is superclass for any object implementation.

```
package org.omg.PortableServer;

public abstract class DynamicImplementation
    extends Servant {
    abstract public void invoke(
        org.omg.CORBA.ServerRequest request);
}
```

The `invoke()` method receives requests issued to any CORBA objects incarnated by the DSI servant and performs the processing necessary to execute the request. The server can access the `request` argument of `invoke()` in order to determine the operation's name and its invocation arguments and to, finally, provide the results of the execution. The `ServerRequest` pseudo interface maps to the following Java class:

```
package org.omg.CORBA;

public abstract class ServerRequest {
    public String operation() {
        throw new org.omg.CORBA.NO_IMPLEMENT();
    }
    public abstract Context ctx();
    public void arguments(NVList nv) {
        throw new org.omg.CORBA.NO_IMPLEMENT();
    }
```

```
public void set_result(Any val) {
  throw new org.omg.CORBA.NO_IMPLEMENT();
}
public void set_exception(Any val) {
  throw new org.omg.CORBA.NO_IMPLEMENT();
}
}
```

As to be expected, the class is named `ServerRequest`. It is declared public and abstract and is declared in package `org.omg.CORBA`. However, due to the reasons already discussed in Section 6.2.5, not all methods are declared abstract; rather, some of them define default implementations that throw an `org.omg.CORBA.NO_IMPLEMENT` exception. These method implementations have to be suitably overridden.

6.8   Java Class `Servant`

The class `Servant`, which implements the IDL type `PortableServer::Servant`, is an abstract class declared in package `org.omg.PortableServer`. It is the superclass for all servant implementations and provides methods that may be called by application developers as well as methods that are invoked by the POA itself and may be overridden by users in order to adapt specific aspects of the servant's behavior according to their requirements.

With the exception of the `_all_interfaces()` and `_this_object()` methods, all methods defined in the `Servant` class may only be invoked after the servant has been associated with an ORB instance. Otherwise, an `org.omg.CORBA.BAD_INV_ORDER` exception is raised. At any point in time, a servant may be associated to, at most, one ORB instance. Via several means, a servant may be associated with the specified ORB:

- through a call to `_this_object()`, passing an ORB instance as parameter; the servant becomes associated with the specified ORB;
- by explicitly activating a servant with a POA by calling one of the POA methods `activate_object()` or `activate_object_with_id()` (see Section 6.3.2); this associates the servant with the ORB instance, which contains the POA on which the servant has been activated;
- by requesting a `Servant` instance from a `ServantManager`; the servant returned from a `ServantActivator`'s method `incarnate()` or a `ServantLocator`'s method `preinvoke()` is associated with the ORB instance that contains the POA on which the `ServantManager` is installed;
- by installing the servant as a default servant on a POA; the servant becomes associated with the ORB instance, which contains the POA for which the servant is acting as a default servant; and
- by explicitly setting the servant by calling `org.omg.CORBA_2_3.ORB.set_delegate()` on an ORB instance that is passed this servant.

The Java class Servant is declared as follows:

```java
package org.omg.PortableServer;

import org.omg.CORBA.ORB;
import org.omg.PortableServer.POA;

abstract public class Servant {
  // Convenience methods for application programmer
  final public org.omg.CORBA.Object _this_object() {
    return _get_delegate().this_object(this);
  }

  final public org.omg.CORBA.Object _this_object(ORB orb) {
    try {
      ((org.omg.CORBA_2_3.ORB)orb).set_delegate(this);
    }
    catch(ClassCastException e) {
      throw new org.omg.CORBA.BAD_PARAM(
        "POA Servant requires an instance of "
        + "org.omg.CORBA_2_3.ORB");
    }
    return _this_object();
  }

  final public ORB _orb() {
    return _get_delegate().orb(this);
  }

  final public POA _poa() {
    return _get_delegate().poa(this);
  }

  final public byte[] _object_id() {
    return _get_delegate().object_id(this);
  }

  // Methods which may be overridden by the
  // application programmer
  public POA _default_POA() {
    return _get_delegate().default_POA(this);
  }

  public boolean _is_a(String repository_id) {
    return _get_delegate().is_a(this, repository_id);
  }

  public boolean _non_existent() {
    return _get_delegate().non_existent(this);
  }

  public org.omg.CORBA.Object _get_interface_def() {
    return _get_delegate().get_interface_def(this);
  }
```

```
// methods for which the skeleton or application
// programmer must provide an an implementation

abstract public String[] _all_interfaces(
  POA poa, byte[] objectId);

// private implementation methods

private transient org.omg.PortableServer.portable.Delegate
  _delegate = null;

final public org.omg.PortableServer.portable.Delegate
  _get_delegate() {
    if (_delegate == null) {
      throw new org.omg.CORBA.BAD_INV_ORDER(
        "The Servant has not been associated with an "
        + "ORBinstance");
    }
    return _delegate;
  }

final public void _set_delegate(
  org.omg.PortableServer.portable.Delegate delegate) {
    _delegate = delegate;
  }
}
```

We do not discuss the entire functionality of the servant class here. However, we give the description of a number of selected, often used methods. For example, the methods _orb(), _poa(), and _object_id() return the instance of the ORB currently associated with the servant, the servant's POA, and the servant's object ID, respectively. The latter is returned in an array of type byte[].

The method _default_POA() may be invoked at any time to determine the servant's POA. By default, the root POA from the ORB instance associated with the servant is returned. If a child POA is in use, developers should override this method since, otherwise, objects might erroneously be activated by the root POA that is returned by default.

Finally, the method _all_interfaces() should be overridden. It is used by the ORB to obtain complete type information, i.e., a list of all interfaces implemented, from the servant.

6.9   Exercises

1. Which combination of the following implementation possibilities is admissible when writing a CORBA application?

    - client using stubs   - client using skeletons   - client using DII
    - client using DSI   - server using stubs   - server using skeletons
    - server using DII   - server using DSI

2. When using the DII, a client is implemented without knowing the interface definition of the server object. Identify real-world applications where that scenario would be interesting.

3. When using the DSI, a server is implemented without knowing the interface definition of the server object. Identify real-world applications where that scenario would be interesting.

7   A First Example

Our first practical example is presented with the aid of three ORBs available free of charge: first of all with the ORB included with the Java Software Development Kit, then with the ORBs JacORB and OpenORB, which were developed within the framework of open source activities. Installation instructions for JacORB and OpenORB may be found in Appendix E. All the examples presented in this book assume that a command-line environment is available. Under Windows (95, 98, ME, NT, 2000, XP), the command window COMMAND.COM or CMD.COM is required (see Figure 10); in the case of Unix-based systems, a shell, for example, ksh, bash, csh, or tcsh, has to be employed.

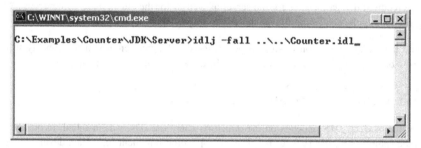

Figure 10: Invocation of JDK's IDL Compiler under Windows XP

The development of a CORBA-based application always starts with the specification of the IDL interface definition; we already discussed IDL fundamentals in Chapter 4. In the first example we just specify a simple counter. The counter is provided with an attribute value of IDL type long. The value should not be manipulated directly and, therefore, is specified readonly. In addition, the counter has the two operations inc() and dec(), which may be invoked to increment and decrement the current counter value, respectively. Based on these requirements, the IDL file Counter.idl has the following structure:

```
// Counter.idl

interface Counter
{
  readonly attribute long value;
  void inc();
  void dec();
};
```

This IDL specification can now be translated with the help of an IDL compiler. The IDL compiler used has product-specific characteristics and is bound to a specific platform (hardware, operating system) as well as to a specific programming language. In order to ease one's approach to this material, we briefly explain in the following how the IDL compilers shipped with the JDK, JacORB, and OpenORB are invoked.

7.1   JDK's IDL Compiler

If we want to translate the `Counter` example with the IDL compiler contained in Sun Microsystems' Java Software Development Kit, the invocation is

```
idlj -fall Counter.idl
```

The parameter `-fall` achieves that stubs (the client-side proxies) as well as skeletons (the server-side proxies) are generated. Should we only need the client-side files, this can be accomplished by specifying the `-fclient` parameter. Setting the `-fserver` parameter, by analogue, only generates the server-side files. If one intends to implement the delegation approach (see Section 5.14.1), the necessary parameter specifications are `-fallTIE`, to generate the required delegation files for the server as well as for the client, and `-fserverTIE`, to generate only the delegation file for the server, respectively.

Should the `idlj` invocation produce an error, the development environment probably still needs to be adapted. Under Windows, this can be done by setting the path variable:

```
set JDK_DIR=JDK_DIR
set PATH=%JDK_DIR%\bin;%PATH%
```

The value of `JDK_DIR` depends on the directory where the JDK was installed; in our system, the value is `c:\jdk1.5.0_01`. The corresponding statement for a Unix development platform and the shells `ksh` or `bash` is

```
export PATH=JDK_DIR/bin:$PATH
```

If, however, a `csh` or `tcsh` is used, the statement is

```
setenv PATH JDK_DIR/bin:$PATH
```

Unless one intends to enter that statement repeatedly before each compiler invocation or to adjust the path variable correspondingly as a default setting, it is recommended that the above lines be stored in a batch file, such as, e.g., `environment.bat` (for Windows) or simply `environment` (for Unix, with read and execute permissions being set appropriately). This batch file can then be executed as required, for example, once, before beginning with application development. For Unix operating systems, the necessary file permissions (read/write/execute) for the batch file can be modified with the `chmod` command.

When the parameter setting `-fall` is chosen, the JDK's IDL to Java compiler generates the following files:

```
CounterPOA.java
_CounterStub.java
CounterHolder.java
CounterHelper.java
Counter.java
CounterOperations.java
```

All these files are needed to implement the server application. The client application needs all files except `CounterPOA.java`.

7.2   JacORB's IDL Compiler

The IDL compiler of JacORB is invoked, for example, with the command

```
idl Counter.idl
```

The same holds as above; should the `idl` command not be found, the environment variables have to be adjusted. JacORB's IDL compiler is located in the `bin` subdirectory of the JacORB installation directory. Assuming that JacORB is installed in the directory *Jac-ORB_DIR*, then the Windows path must be set like this:

```
set JDK_DIR=JDK_DIR
set JacORB_DIR=JacORB_DIR
set PATH=%JacORB_DIR%\bin;%JDK_DIR%\bin;%PATH%
```

In our system, the value for the placeholder *JacORB_DIR* is `c:\JacORB_2_2_1`. Again, we recommend installing a batch file that contains the above statements. For a Unix-based operating system, the settings must be provided analogous to the instructions in the preceding section, Section 7.1. In the following, we limit our example specifications to Windows.

In addition to the six files generated from the JDK's IDL compiler, JacORB automatically produces the file `CounterPOATie.java`, which is needed to implement the delegation approach.

We recommend creating two additional batch files: one for translating example applications with the Java compiler and one for executing the examples with the Java interpreter. In the following, we name those files `jmake.bat` and `jrun.bat`. They were written in a way that allows us to use them unmodified for subsequent examples. The file `jmake.bat` contains one single line,

```
javac -classpath "%JacORB_DIR%\lib\jacorb.jar;." %*
```

The main differences in file `jrun.bat` are that, first of all, the Java interpreter instead of the Java compiler is invoked. Secondly, we provide the interpreter with the JacORB-specific property information mentioned in Section 6.2.5.

```
java -Dorg.omg.CORBA.ORBClass=org.jacorb.orb.ORB
-Dorg.omg.CORBA.ORBSingletonClass=
org.jacorb.orb.ORBSingleton
-cp "%JacORB_DIR%\lib\jacorb.jar;
%JacORB_DIR%\lib\avalon-framework-4.1.5.jar;
%JacORB_DIR%\lib\logkit-1.2.jar;." %*
```

Note that the above `java` invocation must be entered in its entirety on one single line without any line feeds. It is just one single rather long statement. When a different JacORB version is used, the version numbers of the `jar` files also differ; they have to be looked up in the *JacORB_DIR*\lib directory. When writing the batch files, one should not forget to provide values for the placeholders *JacORB_DIR* and *JDK_DIR* in the environment settings that correspond to one's installation.

7.3   OpenORB's IDL Compiler

Setting up the environment for OpenORB requires more work than in the first two cases. The reason is that OpenORB's IDL compiler is only provided in the form of Java classes and that no dedicated batch processing file, as, for example, with JacORB, is available. Therefore, as a first step, one should build one's own batch file idl.bat; otherwise, the compiler invocation is cumbersome and prone to errors. Assume, again, that *OpenORB_DIR* denotes the installation directory (in our system c:\OpenORB-1.3.1). Then, this batch file looks like this:

```
java -cp "%OpenORB_DIR%\lib\avalon-framework.jar;
%OpenORB_DIR%\lib\excalibur-configuration.jar;
%OpenORB_DIR%\lib\junit.jar;
%OpenORB_DIR%\lib\logkit.jar;
%OpenORB_DIR%\lib\openorb-1.3.1.jar;
%OpenORB_DIR%\lib\openorb_tools-1.3.1.jar;
%OpenORB_DIR%\lib\xerces.jar;."
org.openorb.compiler.IdlCompiler %*
```

When building that file, note that the above java invocation must be entered in one single line as a whole without any line feeds. Note also that, when a different OpenORB version is used, the version numbers of the jar files also differ; they have to be looked up in the *OpenORB_DIR*\lib directory. We suggest storing this batch file in directory *OpenORB_DIR*\bin; otherwise, it is needed in the current directory when one intends to invoke the IDL compiler.

Before the IDL compiler can be invoked, the environment has to, again, be adjusted by means of

```
set JDK_DIR=JDK_DIR
set OpenORB_DIR=OpenORB_DIR
set PATH=%OpenORB_DIR%\bin;%JDK_DIR%\bin;%PATH%
```

Now, the interface definition of the Counter example can be compiled with the invocation

```
idl -d . Counter.idl
```

Specifying the parameter "-d ." has the result that the compiler-generated files are written to the current directory ".". Similar to JacORB, OpenORB automatically produces the file CounterPOATie.java for implementations following the tie approach.

Like JacORB, the OpenORB needs a batch file jmake.bat, which translates an application and contains one single line:

```
javac -classpath "%OpenORB_DIR%\lib\openorb-1.3.1.jar;
%OpenORB_DIR%\lib\openorb_tools-1.3.1.jar;." %*
```

It also needs a batch file jrun.bat, which runs the application:

```
java -Dorg.omg.CORBA.ORBClass=org.openorb.CORBA.ORB
   -Dorg.omg.CORBA.ORBSingletonClass=
   org.openorb.CORBA.ORBSingleton
```

```
-cp "%OpenORB_DIR%\lib\avalon-framework.jar;
%OpenORB_DIR%\lib\logkit.jar;
%OpenORB_DIR%\lib\openorb-1.3.1.jar;
%OpenORB_DIR%\lib\openorb_tools-1.3.1.jar;
%OpenORB_DIR%\lib\xerces.jar;." %*
```

When one wants to use the batch files, one should not forget to provide current values of one's installation for the placeholders OpenORB_DIR and JDK_DIR.

7.4   Recommended File Organization

In order to implement and test the Counter and the subsequent examples in a realistic environment, we recommend using at least two TCP/IP-connected hosts: a server host and one or more client hosts. Also, to obtain a running application fast, we suggest using the file structure described below in Figure 11 for deployment of the various IDL, batch, Java, and class files on the server host. We store the Counter's IDL file in the directory \Examples\Counter and place the environment, jmake, and jrun batch files in the matching ORB directories, according to the discussion in Sections 7.1 – 7.3.

```
Examples
   Counter
      Counter.idl
      JDK
         environment.bat
         Server
            CounterImpl.java
            Server.java
            & files generated by the IDL compiler
      JacORB
         environment.bat
         Server
            jmake.bat
            jrun.bat
            CounterImpl.java
            Server.java
            & files generated by the IDL compiler
      OpenORB
         environment.bat
         Server
            jmake.bat
            jrun.bat
            CounterImpl.java
            Server.java
            & files generated by the IDL compiler
```

Figure 11: Suggested File Structure for the Server Host

For the client side, a similar structure is suggested (see Figure 14). If only a single host is available, one should at least compile and run the server and the clients in their own command windows, each with its specific environment variable setting.

7.5   Implementing `Counter` Using the Inheritance Approach

We compile the `Counter`'s IDL file by setting the needed environment variables and invoking the IDL compiler as follows:

- JDK
  In `\Examples\Counter\JDK`, execute the batch file `environment.bat`. Change the directory to `\Examples\Counter\JDK\Server` and invoke the IDL compiler through `idlj -fall ..\..\Counter.idl`.
- JacORB
  In `\Examples\Counter\JacORB`, execute the batch file `environment.bat`. Change the directory to `\Examples\Counter\JacORB\Server` and invoke the IDL compiler through `idl ..\..\Counter.idl`.
- OpenORB
  In `\Examples\Counter\OpenORB`, execute the batch file `environment.bat`. Change the directory to `\Examples\Counter\OpenORB\Server` and invoke the IDL compiler through `idl -d . ..\..\Counter.idl`.

After these steps, the Java files generated by the IDL compiler are stored in the `Server` subdirectory. Now, the actual `Counter` has to be implemented. If we follow the common inheritance approach, the compiler-generated class `CounterPOA` acts as a superclass of the implementation provided by programmers. We name our implementation class `Counter-Impl` and thus follow the CORBA style to use the class names `<Interface>Impl` or `<Interface>_Impl`.

`CounterPOA` is an abstract class that implements the operations interface `CounterOperations` but does not provide any method declarations for the inherited methods. The class `CounterImpl`, therefore, must implement all methods declared in the operations interface (see Section 5.14). It is recommended to first inspect the declaration of the operations interface that the IDL compiler generates. In the example, `CounterOperations.java` is stored in the `Server` directory; it has the following form:

```
// CounterOperations.java

public interface CounterOperations {
    int value();
    void inc();
    void dec();
}
```

Therefore, one possible implementation of the `CounterImpl` class would declare an instance variable `count` for the `Counter`'s value as well as the get method and the two increment and decrement methods. The IDL type `long` of the readonly attribute `value` is mapped to the Java type `int`, as defined in Table 8:

```
// CounterImpl.java

public class CounterImpl extends CounterPOA {
```

```
private int count;
public CounterImpl() {
  count = 0;
}
public void inc() {
  count++;
}
public void dec() {
  count--;
}
public int value() {
  return count;
}
}
```

Since `value` is defined as readonly, no set method is necessary; that method would be declared as `void value(int v);` in the operations interface. We store the Counter-Impl file in the server directory (see Figure 11).

The UML class diagram in Figure 12 shows the dependencies between the Java classes and interfaces generated by the IDL compiler on the one hand and the implementation class CounterImpl on the other.

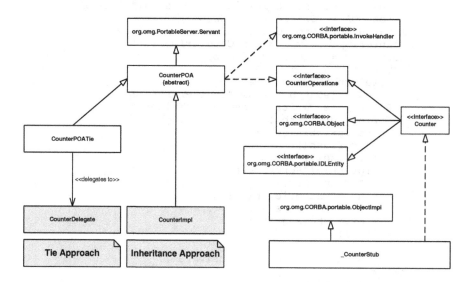

Figure 12: Dependencies between the Generated Classes and the Implementation Class

7.6   Implementing the Server Application for the Inheritance Approach

After having provided a Java implementation for the IDL specification of the Counter, the server side for the distributed CORBA application has to be implemented. When using the JDK's ORB, the server might be implemented as follows:

```java
// Server.java

import java.io.*;
import java.util.Properties;
import org.omg.CORBA.*;
import org.omg.PortableServer.*;
import static java.lang.System.*;

public class Server {
  public static void main(String[] args) {
    try {
      Properties props = getProperties();
      ORB orb = ORB.init(args, props);
      org.omg.CORBA.Object obj = null;
      POA rootPOA = null;
      try {
        obj = orb.resolve_initial_references("RootPOA");
        rootPOA = POAHelper.narrow(obj);
      } catch (org.omg.CORBA.ORBPackage.InvalidName e) { }
      CounterImpl c_impl = new CounterImpl();
      Counter c = c_impl._this(orb);
      try {
        FileOutputStream file =
          new FileOutputStream("Counter.ref");
        PrintWriter writer = new PrintWriter(file);
        String ref = orb.object_to_string(c);
        writer.println(ref);
        writer.flush();
        file.close();
        out.println("Server started."
          + " Stop: Ctrl-C");
      } catch (IOException ex) {
        out.println("File error: "
          + ex.getMessage());
        exit(2);
      }
      rootPOA.the_POAManager().activate();
      orb.run();
    } catch(Exception ex) {
      out.println("Exception: " + ex.getMessage());
      exit(1);
    }
  }
}
```

In method main(), we at first initialize the ORB (ORB.init()) and determine the reference to the root POA (orb.resolve_initial_references()). Then, by means of method `narrow()` of class `POAHelper`, we cast the type of the reference from type `org.omg.CORBA.Object` to type `org.omg.PortableServer.POA`. Subsequently, we create a `CounterImpl` instance (our servant), associate it with the ORB that contains the root POA, and implicitly activate it (`_this()`). As an alternative to writing

```
Counter c = c_impl._this(orb);
```

the two statements

```
byte[] servantId = rootPOA.activate_object(c_impl);
org.omg.CORBA.Object c =
  rootPOA.id_to_reference(servantId);
```

could be used. The first line explicitly activates the servant and provides an object ID. The methods `activate_object()` and `activate_object_with_id()` can be invoked here (see Section 6.3.2). Once the servant is activated, the server application can associate it with its corresponding reference, either by employing the method `servant_to_refer-ence()` or, as above, via `id_to_reference()`. (There is even a third alternative for servant activation, see Exercise 2 at the end of the chapter.) We transform the IOR of the constructed `CounterImpl` instance into its string representation (`orb.object_to_string()`) and store the string in a file `Counter.ref`. Then, the reference to the POA's `POAManager` is determined and the manager is activated. Finally, invoking `orb.run()` has the effect that the server application is ready for accepting client requests. We store the file `Server.java` in the server host's `Server` directory (see Figure 11). It is a typical implementation for a simple CORBA server and many of our examples below are similar.

In the case of JacORB, the server declaration above can be used unmodified when we provide the initialization information for the ORB (Section 6.2.5) with the "-D" options in file `jrun.bat` as shown in Section 7.2. Otherwise, the server needs the following lines at the beginning of the first `try` block:

```
Properties props = getProperties();
props.put("org.omg.CORBA.ORBClass",
  "org.jacorb.orb.ORB");
props.put("org.omg.CORBA.ORBSingletonClass",
  "org.jacorb.orb.ORBSingleton");
setProperties(props);
ORB orb = ORB.init(args, props);
```

Corresponding additions are necessary when OpenORB is selected and the "-D" options are omitted from `jrun.bat` in Section 7.3. In that case, the following lines are inserted at the same location:

```
Properties props = getProperties();
props.put("org.omg.CORBA.ORBClass",
  "org.openorb.CORBA.ORB");
props.put("org.omg.CORBA.ORBSingletonClass",
  "org.openorb.CORBA.ORBSingleton");
setProperties(props);
ORB orb = ORB.init(args, props);
```

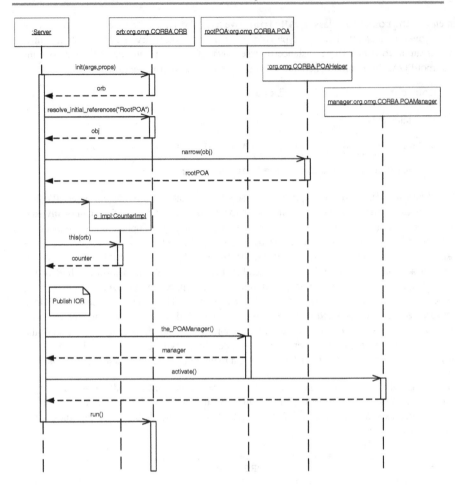

Figure 13: UML Sequence Diagram for the Server Application

In Section 6.2.5, we explained the necessity of these additional specifications. Sun's JDK already contains declarations of the CORBA classes `org.omg.CORBA.ORBClass` and `org.omg.CORBA.ORBSingletonClass`, which need to be "hidden" so that the correct ORB-specific classes are employed. The names of the respective product-specific classes must be fully qualified, for example, `org.jacorb.orb.ORB` for JacORB or `org.openorb.CORBA.ORB` in the case of OpenORB.

7.7   Compiling the Server Application

We compile the server application by invoking the Java compiler as follows:

- JDK
  In `\Examples\Counter\JDK\Server`, invoke the Java compiler through

javac Server.java. (The batch file environment.bat must have been previously executed in \Examples\Counter\JDK.)

- JacORB
  In \Examples\Counter\JacORB\Server, invoke the Java compiler through jmake Server.java. (The batch file environment.bat must have been previously executed in \Examples\Counter\JacORB.)

- OpenORB
  In \Examples\Counter\OpenORB\Server, invoke the Java compiler through jmake Server.java. (The batch file environment.bat must have been previously executed in \Examples\Counter\OpenORB.)

After successful compilation, the server is now ready to be started. Figure 13 demonstrates the dynamics of the server application by means of a UML sequence diagram.

7.8 Implementing the Client Application

Now, we are finally able to implement a client application. We recommend organizing the files on the client host similar to the structure on the server host shown in Figure 11.

```
Examples
    Counter
        Counter.idl
        JDK
            environment.bat
            Client
                Client.java
                & files generated by the IDL compiler
        JacORB
            environment.bat
            Client
                jmake.bat
                jrun.bat
                Client.java
                & files generated by the IDL compiler
        OpenORB
            environment.bat
            Client
                jmake.bat
                jrun.bat
                Client.java
                & files generated by the IDL compiler
```

Figure 14: Suggested File Structure for the Client Host

Note that a servant (the CounterImpl class) is not needed on the client side. A very simple command-line version of a client that is implemented for the JDK ORB could look as follows:

```java
// Client.java

import java.io.*;
import java.util.*;
import org.omg.CORBA.*;
import static java.lang.System.*;

public class Client {
  public static void main(String[] args) {
    try {
      Properties props = getProperties();
      ORB orb = ORB.init(args, props);
      String ref = null;
      org.omg.CORBA.Object obj = null;
      try {
        Scanner reader =
          new Scanner(new File("Counter.ref"));
        ref = reader.nextLine();
      } catch (IOException ex) {
        out.println("File error: " + ex.getMessage());
        exit(2);
      }
      obj = orb.string_to_object(ref);
      if (obj == null) {
        out.println("Invalid IOR");
        exit(4);
      }
      Counter c = null;
      try {
        c = CounterHelper.narrow(obj);
      } catch (BAD_PARAM ex) {
        out.println("Narrowing failed");
        exit(3);
      }
      int inp = -1;
      do {
        out.print("Counter value: " + c.value()
          + "\nAction (+/-/e)? ");
        out.flush();
        do {
          try {
            inp = in.read();
          } catch (IOException ioe) { }
        } while (inp != '+' && inp != '-' && inp != 'e');
        if (inp == '+')
          c.inc();
        else if (inp == '-')
          c.dec();
      } while (inp != 'e');
    } catch (Exception ex) {
      out.println("Exception: " + ex.getMessage());
      exit(1);
    }
  }
}
```

Like the server application, the client has to initialize the ORB first (ORB.init()). The POA is not needed here since we write a pure client application, which does not instantiate CORBA objects but instead relies on the functionality offered by the server object. Next, the IOR of the server object is read from the file Counter.ref and converted from its stringified form (orb.string_to_object()). Finally, the type of the reference is cast from type org.omg.CORBA.Object to type Counter with the help of the CounterHelper method narrow(). The ORB-related preparations are now complete and the user can invoke the remote counter's methods with the inputs '+' or '-'.

If JacORB or OpenORB are to be used instead of the JDK ORB, the client ORB has to be informed of the ORBClass and ORBSingletonClass to use analogous to the procedure for the server discussed in Section 7.6. We store the file Client.java in the client hosts Client directory (see Figure 14).

7.9 Compiling the Client Application

On the client host, we compile the IDL specification of the Counter and the client application as follows:

- JDK
  In \Examples\Counter\JDK, execute the batch file environment.bat. Change the directory to \Examples\Counter\JDK\Client and invoke the IDL compiler through idlj -fall ..\..\Counter.idl. Invoke the Java compiler through javac Client.java.

- JacORB
  In \Examples\Counter\JacORB, execute the batch file environment.bat. Change the directory to \Examples\Counter\JacORB\Client and invoke the IDL compiler through idl ..\..\Counter.idl. Invoke the Java compiler through jmake Client.java.

- OpenORB
  In \Examples\Counter\OpenORB, execute the batch file environment.bat. Change the directory to \Examples\Counter\OpenORB\Client and invoke the IDL compiler through idl -d . ..\..\Counter.idl. Invoke the Java compiler through jmake Client.java.

After successful compilation, the client is also ready to be started.

7.10 Running the Application

We first turn to the server host, set the environment variables as needed, and start the server by entering

```
java Server in \Examples\Counter\JDK\Server,
jrun Server in \Examples\Counter\JacORB\Server, or
jrun Server in \Examples\Counter\OpenORB\Server, respectively.
```

The server is started and the IOR of the server object is written to the file `Counter.ref` in the current `Server` subdirectory. As discussed in Section 3.4.2, the IOR contains all the information that a remote client needs in order to localize the server object and to invoke operations on it: IP address and port number of the server host, repository ID of the server object, object ID, etc. JacORB provides a tool, `dior`, which displays the IOR and enables us to inspect its content by the command `dior -f Counter.ref`.

The file `Counter.ref` must now be copied to the client host, more precisely to the directory where the client application is started, i.e., `\Examples\Counter\JDK\Client`, `\Examples\Counter\JacORB\Client`, or `\Examples\Counter\OpenORB\Client`, respectively. One can transfer the file via FTP, provide it on an FTP or HTTP server for download, send it by e-mail, or use any other means. This procedure is rather cumbersome and time-consuming. However, since CORBA version 2.0, usage of the Naming Service offers a far better alternative, which we present in Chapter 17. As soon as the client has access to the IOR, it can be started. This is done by invoking

```
java Client in \Examples\Counter\JDK\Client,
jrun Client in \Examples\Counter\JacORB\Client, or
jrun Client in \Examples\Counter\OpenORB\Client, respectively.
```

The complete application can now be tested, provided that the server is up and running.

7.11   Implementing `Counter` Using the Delegation Approach

The delegation approach is used when the implementation class needs to inherit from a superclass different than the servant class. Due to Java's single inheritance property, the inheritance approach demonstrated in Section 7.5 is then out of the question. In our example, we now provide a GUI for the server-side `Counter`, to be realized in class `CounterDelegate`. To be able to add this user interface to any top-level window, such as `JApplet`, `JDialog`, or `JFrame`, we use the `JPanel` as a superclass. We recommend having a look at the file `CounterPOATie.java` that the IDL compiler generates before starting the implementation. (In the case of the JDK ORB, remember to invoke `idlj` with the parameter `-fallTIE` or `-fserverTIE`.)

```
// CounterPOATie.java

public class CounterPOATie extends CounterPOA {
  private CounterOperations _impl;
  public CounterPOATie(CounterOperations delegate) {
      this._impl = delegate;
  }
  public int value() {
    return _impl.value();
  }
  public void inc() {
    _impl.inc();
  }
  public void dec() {
```

```
    _impl.dec();
  }
  ...
}
```

Three properties of that class are noticeable: it declares an instance variable _impl of type CounterOperations; it has a one-argument constructor that sets this variable; and all three interface methods, value(), inc(), and dec(), simply delegate execution to the CounterOperations object. These properties are typical for any IDL compiler-generated tie class. As a consequence, developers must write an implementation class that implements the operations interface. In the server application, an instance of the implementation class is instantiated and passed to the constructor of the tie class. In our example, an implementation could look as follows:

```
// CounterDelegate.java

import javax.swing.*;

public class CounterDelegate extends JPanel
    implements CounterOperations {
  private int count;
  private JTextField value;
  public CounterDelegate() {
    count = 0;
    add(new JLabel("Counter value: ", JLabel.RIGHT));
    add(value =
      new JTextField((String.valueOf(count)), 10));
    value.setEditable(false);
  }
  public void inc() {
    value.setText(String.valueOf(++count));
  }
  public void dec() {
    value.setText(String.valueOf(--count));
  }
  public int value() {
    return count;
  }
}
```

In the constructor, the counter (count) is initialized and the GUI is created. The methods inc(), dec(), and value() implement the operations interface and display the new counter value.

7.12   Implementing the Server Application for the Delegation Approach

The delegation-based server application only differs in two significant ways from the inheritance-based server application described in Section 7.6. A CounterPOATie instance is used where, before, a CounterImpl was needed. And, a CounterDelegate instance is created and passed to the CounterPOATie constructor. The CounterPOATie can then delegate all remote invocations to the delegate. Furthermore, a JFrame is created, packed, and set visible; the panel (the CounterPOATie) is added to that frame.

The server application then looks as follows:

```java
// DelegationServer.java

import java.io.*;
import java.util.Properties;
import org.omg.CORBA.*;
import org.omg.PortableServer.*;
import javax.swing.*;
import static java.lang.System.*;

public class DelegationServer {
  public static void main(String[] args) {
    try {
      CounterDelegate cd;
      JFrame f = new JFrame("Counter Server");
      f.getContentPane().add(cd = new CounterDelegate());
      f.pack();
      f.setDefaultCloseOperation(JFrame.EXIT_ON_CLOSE);
      f.setVisible(true);
      Properties props = getProperties();
      ORB orb = ORB.init(args, props);
      org.omg.CORBA.Object obj = null;
      POA rootPOA = null;
      try {
        obj = orb.resolve_initial_references("RootPOA");
        rootPOA = POAHelper.narrow(obj);
      } catch (org.omg.CORBA.ORBPackage.InvalidName e) { }
      CounterPOATie c_impl = new CounterPOATie(cd);
      Counter c = c_impl._this(orb);
      try {
        FileOutputStream file =
          new FileOutputStream("Counter.ref");
        PrintWriter writer = new PrintWriter(file);
        String ref = orb.object_to_string(c);
        writer.println(ref);
        writer.flush();
        file.close();
        out.println("Server started."
          + " Stop: Close-Button");
      } catch(IOException ex) {
        err.println("File error: " + ex.getMessage());
        exit(2);
      }
      rootPOA.the_POAManager().activate();
      orb.run();
    } catch(Exception ex) {
      out.println("Exception: " + ex.getMessage());
      exit(1);
    }
  }
}
```

The above implementation is written for the JDK's ORB. If another ORB is to be used, the information on the two ORB-specific classes has to be provided in the same way as in the inheritance example ("-D" options in `jrun` or `props.put()` in the Java sources). After storing the `DelegationServer` and the `CounterDelegate` in the `Server` subdirectory on the server host, we can compile and run the server application exactly as described above in Section 7.7. The `DelegationServer` can be combined with any number of our client applications.

Figure 15: GUI for the Server Application

7.13   A GUI for the Client Application

We now show how the client can be equipped with a graphical user interface. The following implementation consists mainly of three methods: `initializeORB()`, `getRef()`, and `createGUI()`. The first two methods combine all CORBA-specific statements like the `main()` method of the command-line client presented in Section 7.8. `createGUI()`, on the other hand, contains the GUI specifics: a label for the current `Counter` value, an "Increment" and a "Decrement" button, and the corresponding `ActionListeners` that trigger the respective remote `inc()` and `dec()` invocations. The constructor, therefore, first initializes the middleware, then reads and casts the server object's reference, and then creates the GUI. The `main()` method simply creates a `JFrame`, adds a new `GUIClient`, packs the frame, and sets it visible.

```java
// GUIClient.java

import java.awt.GridLayout;
import java.awt.event.*;
import java.io.*;
import java.util.*;
import javax.swing.*;
import org.omg.CORBA.*;
import static java.lang.System.*;

public class GUIClient extends JPanel {
  private ORB orb;
  private Counter c;
  private void initializeORB(String[] args) {
    Properties props = getProperties();
    orb = ORB.init(args, props);
  }
  private org.omg.CORBA.Object getRef(String refFile) {
    String ref = null;
    try {
      Scanner reader = new Scanner(new File(refFile));
      ref = reader.nextLine();
    } catch (IOException ex) {
      out.println("File error: "
```

```
         + ex.getMessage());
      exit(2);
   }
   org.omg.CORBA.Object obj = orb.string_to_object(ref);
   if (obj == null) {
      out.println("Invalid IOR");
      exit(4);
   }
   return obj;
}
private void createGUI() {
   setLayout(new GridLayout(2, 1));
   JPanel p = new JPanel();
   final JLabel value;
   p.add(new JLabel("Counter value: ", JLabel.RIGHT));
   p.add(value = new JLabel(String.valueOf(c.value())));
   add(p);
   p = new JPanel();
   JButton inc, dec;
   p.add(inc = new JButton("Increment"));
   p.add(dec = new JButton("Decrement"));
   add(p);
   inc.addActionListener(new ActionListener() {
      public void actionPerformed(ActionEvent e) {
         c.inc();
         value.setText(String.valueOf(c.value()));
      }
   });
   dec.addActionListener(new ActionListener() {
      public void actionPerformed(ActionEvent e) {
         c.dec();
         value.setText(String.valueOf(c.value()));
      }
   });
}
public GUIClient(String[] args, String refFile) {
   initializeORB(args);
   org.omg.CORBA.Object obj = getRef(refFile);
   try {
      c = CounterHelper.narrow(obj);
   } catch (BAD_PARAM ex) {
      out.println("Narrowing failed");
      exit(3);
   }
   createGUI();
}
public static void main(String[] args) {
   try {
      String refFile = "Counter.ref";
      JFrame f = new JFrame("Counter Client");
      f.getContentPane().add(
         new GUIClient(args, refFile));
      f.pack();
      f.setDefaultCloseOperation(JFrame.DISPOSE_ON_CLOSE);
      f.setVisible(true);
```

```
        } catch (Exception ex) {
          out.println("Exception: " + ex.getMessage());
          exit(1);
        }
    }
}
```

One or more instances of the GUIClient can be started together with one or more instances of the command-line Client. They may be provided with the IOR of the Server
or the DelegationServer discussed above. Figure 16 below demonstrates the look of
the user interface on a client host running Windows. Again, the above code is based on the
JDK ORB; if another ORB is to be used, information on the ORBClass and the ORB-
SingletonClass must be passed in one of the ways discussed in Section 7.6.

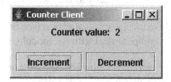

Figure 16: GUI for the Client Application

7.14   Using Different ORBs

Sometimes it may be useful to install several different ORBs on the hosts in one's system,
for example, when a CORBA application has to be checked for its portability or when
CORBA's interoperability is to be tested. This does not pose any problems if the simple ad-
vice given in this chapter is followed. For each ORB, its own subdirectories (see Figure 11
and Figure 14), with its own environment, jmake, and jrun files (see Sections 7.1, 7.2,
and 7.3), should be provided so that each component of the distributed application can access
only the classes that it really needs. Otherwise, a "mix" of different CORBA classes might
result and yield unexpected system behavior.

7.15   Modules

In Section 4.8, we mentioned the OMG's style guide recommendations to renounce the use
of file-level definitions and the request to always embed interface declarations and other
definitions in modules. Throughout this chapter, we have so far ignored these recommendations for reasons of simplicity. However, now, with the first simple examples running, we
can remedy these shortcomings.

We still deal with the Counter example but, now, we begin with the following IDL specification, where the Counter's interface is defined in module scope:

```
// Counter.idl

module Count
  {
```

```
interface Counter
{
  readonly attribute long value;
  void inc();
  void dec();
};
};
```

In order to distinguish between our implementations, we create a new subdirectory Mod-
Counter below the Examples directory, store the new IDL specification there, and create
ORB and client/server subdirectories below ModCounter completely analog to the directory structures shown in Figure 11 and Figure 14. The batch files for setting environment
variables and for invoking the IDL compiler, the Java compiler, and the Java interpreter can
be reused from Sections 7.1, 7.2, and 7.3 exactly as they were specified there.

In accordance with the IDL to Java mapping specification (see Section 5.6), the JDK ORB's,
JacORB's, and OpenORB's IDL compiler deal with the module definition in the same way.

- A subdirectory Count is generated below the Server or Client directory, respectively, and the Java classes and interfaces Counter, CounterHelper, etc., are
  stored there.
- The class and interface declarations begin with a package declaration, for example,

```
// CounterOperations.java

package Count;

public interface CounterOperations {
  int value();
  void inc();
  void dec();
}
```

Now, to implement the Counter using the inheritance approach, we store the implementation class in the Count directory and begin it with the package declaration

```
// CounterImpl.java

package Count;

public class CounterImpl extends CounterPOA {
  private int count;
  public CounterImpl() {
    count = 0;
  }
  ... rest as above
}
```

It is essential to declare the class, its constructor, and all methods public so that they can
be accessed from outside the Count package. We suggest storing the server application in
the Server directory. The only difference to the implementation given in Section 7.6 is that
it has to begin with an import declaration:

```
// Server.java

import Count.*;
import ...

public class Server { ... as above }
```

Analogously, we store the client application in the `Client` directory, begin it with an import declaration, and reuse the implementation given in Section 7.8:

```
// Client.java

import Count.*;
import ...

public class Client { ... as above }
```

The steps for compiling and running server and client and copying the server IOR are no different than as described above.

7.16   Exercises

1. Implement a server with an operation dump() that simply writes any input in the client's command window to the server's command window.

2. Check that a third alternative for servant activation exists: in `Servant.java`, replace the statement

   ```
   Counter c = c_impl._this(orb);
   ```

   with

   ```
   org.omg.CORBA.Object c =
       rootPOA.servant_to_reference(c_impl);
   ```

3. Implement a server with the following features:

   a) A subdirectory `glossary` exists relative to the `Server` directory. The `glossary` contains a number of simple textiles such as `adapter`, `interface`, `orb`, `reference`, etc. And, each of these files contains a text explaining the term used as file name.

   b) The server provides two operations. Operation `list()` returns the `glossary` file names as a sequence of `strings`. Operation `display()` returns the content of a file; the file name is passed as an `in` parameter. If anything is wrong with the glossary's file structure, an exception is raised.

4. Implement a server for the following IDL specification:

   ```
   // Stocks.idl
   ```

```
module Stocks
{
  typedef string Share;
  typedef sequence<Share> ShareSeq;
  exception NotFound { Share s; };
  interface StockServer
  {
    double price(in Share s) raises(NotFound);
    ShareSeq shares();
  };
};
```

In the implementation of the StockServer interface, one might provide Shares and their prices in this way:

```
private SortedMap<String, Double> prices;
  public StockServerImpl() {
    prices = new TreeMap<String, Double> ();
    prices.put("Am. Java", 26.65);
    prices.put("SciComp", 14.68);
    ...
  }
  ...
}
```

8   Generating Remote Objects

When developing applications accessing distributed objects, it is often important to equip the client with the possibility of constructing and destroying server-side objects on demand. In distributed, object-oriented systems, where resource user and resource manager reside on different, locally remote hosts, a new remote object cannot be created as usual by simply invoking new(). Often, the "Factory" pattern is implemented to provide the client with the means of generating and invoking server-side objects at run-time.

In this section, we describe how such factory objects can be implemented within the CORBA framework. The following example falls back to our Counter example as it was in Section 7.15. We begin with the implementation of the server and assume that a directory structure is prepared analogous to Figure 11, i.e., Counter.idl and CounterFactory.idl are stored in \Examples\CounterFactory.

The IDL interface of a CounterFactory may be defined as follows:

```
// CounterFactory.idl

#include "\Examples\CounterFactory\Counter.idl"

module CFactory
{
  interface CounterFactory
  {
    enum Kind { SHARED, UNSHARED };
    Count::Counter create(in Kind k);
    void destroy(in Count::Counter c);
  };
};
```

The #include directive causes the compiler to read the IDL file Counter.idl before starting with the translation of CounterFactory.idl. This step is necessary since the CounterFactory interface uses the Counter type. As the Counter interface is defined in module Count, its name must be qualified with the module name (see Section 4.8). In the CounterFactory, an enumerated type Kind is defined with the enumerators SHARED and UNSHARED. Further, two operations create() and destroy() are defined, which create a new Counter instance and destroy it, respectively. With the create() operation's Kind parameter, we specify whether the newly created Counter is exclusively made available for the invoking client application (UNSHARED), or whether it is meant to be used by other clients as well (SHARED). All the Counters in the preceding chapter, Chapter 7, were of type SHARED.

8.1   Implementing the `CounterFactory` Servant

After setting the environment variables as needed (see Chapter 7), we compile the CounterFactory as follows:

- JDK
  In \Examples\CounterFactory\JDK\Server, invoke the IDL compiler through idlj –fall –emitAll ..\..\CounterFactory.idl.
- JacORB
  In \Examples\CounterFactory\JacORB\Server, invoke the IDL compiler through idl -all ..\..\CounterFactory.idl.
- OpenORB
  In \Examples\CounterFactory\OpenORB\Server, invoke the IDL compiler through idl –d . -all ..\..\CounterFactory.idl.

The additional parameters –emitAll and –all, respectively, make sure that the Java files for the Counter are also generated. After these steps, the files generated by the IDL compiler are stored in the Server subdirectories Count, CFactory, and CFactory\CounterFactoryPackage. If they do not yet exist, these subdirectories are created.We reuse CounterImpl.java, implementing the Counter interface from Section 7.15, and, again, store that file in the Count subdirectory below the Server directory.

For the implementation of the CounterFactory interface, we also follow the inheritance approach:

```
// CounterFactoryImpl.java

package CFactory;

import CFactory.CounterFactoryPackage.*;
import Count.*;
import org.omg.CORBA.*;
import org.omg.PortableServer.*;

public class CounterFactoryImpl
    extends CounterFactoryPOA {
  private ORB orb;
  private POA poa;
  private Counter singleton;
  public CounterFactoryImpl(ORB orb, POA poa) {
    this.orb = orb;
    this.poa = poa;
    CounterImpl c_impl = new CounterImpl();
    singleton = c_impl._this(orb);
  }
  public Counter create(Kind k) {
    if (k == Kind.SHARED)
      return singleton;
    else {
      CounterImpl c_impl = new CounterImpl();
      Counter unshared = null;
```

```
      try {
        byte[] oid = poa.activate_object(c_impl);
        unshared = CounterHelper.
          narrow(poa.id_to_reference(oid));
      } catch (Exception ex) { }
      return unshared;
    }
  }
  public void destroy(Counter c) {
    if (!orb.object_to_string(singleton).
        equals(orb.object_to_string(c))) {
      try {
        byte[] oid = poa.reference_to_id(c);
        poa.deactivate_object(oid);
      } catch (Exception ex) {
        System.out.println("Object not found.");
      }
      c._release();
    }
  }
}
```

As usual for the inheritance approach, the implementation class extends the corresponding POA class, here the CounterFactoryPOA. The instance variable orb is used to activate the SHARED instance of the Counter in the constructor as well as for comparison of references in the method destroy(). This shared Counter variant is treated as a *Singleton*, therefore, only a single instance (singleton) exists, which is created, activated, and associated with the POA in the constructor. The variable poa is used to activate or deactivate Counter instances and to obtain their IOR. The UNSHARED variants of the Counter are only created through explicit create() invocations; their activation does not follow the familiar approach:

```
CounterImpl c_impl = new CounterImpl();
Counter unshared = c_impl._this(orb);
```

Instead, here, we had to write

```
CounterImpl c_impl = new CounterImpl();
Counter unshared = null;
try {
  byte[] oid = poa.activate_object(c_impl);
  unshared = CounterHelper.
    narrow(poa.id_to_reference(oid));
} catch (Exception ex) { }
```

because, as opposed to JacORB and OpenORB, the JDK ORB causes problems with the first approach; the application compiles properly but causes communication problems at run-time. For portability reasons, we recommend implementing the second approach since it works well with all ORBs that we examined.

The method destroy() demonstrates how destruction of an unshared servant must be handled. At first, the servant must be deactivated; then, it can be released and removed from the set.

We store this file in the subdirectory CFactory below the Server directory; note the package declaration at its beginning.

8.2   Implementing the CounterFactory Server

The implementation of the server application that creates a CounterFactory instance is rather straightforward. We can reuse our implementation from Section 7.6 to a large extent. Here, we quote the source code in its entirety. However, we group those parts that are relevant for future examples into two methods, initializeORB() and putRef(), whose bodies are not repeated time and again.

For the above example, the implementation could look like this (note the package declarations at the beginning):

```java
// CFServer.java

import Count.*;
import CFactory.*;
import java.io.*;
import java.util.Properties;
import org.omg.CORBA.*;
import org.omg.PortableServer.*;
import static java.lang.System.*;

public class CFServer {
  private ORB orb;
  private POA rootPOA;
  private void initializeORB(String[] args) {
    Properties props = getProperties();
    orb = ORB.init(args, props);
    try {
      rootPOA = POAHelper.narrow(orb.
        resolve_initial_references("RootPOA"));
    } catch (org.omg.CORBA.ORBPackage.InvalidName ex) { }
  }
  private void putRef(org.omg.CORBA.Object obj,
      String refFile) {
    try {
      FileOutputStream file =
        new FileOutputStream(refFile);
      PrintWriter writer = new PrintWriter(file);
      String ref = orb.object_to_string(obj);
      writer.println(ref);
      writer.flush();
      file.close();
      out.println("Server started. Stop: Ctrl-C");
    } catch (IOException ex) {
      out.println("File error: "
        + ex.getMessage());
      exit(2);
    }
  }
```

```
public CFServer(String[] args, String refFile) {
  try {
    initializeORB(args);
    CounterFactoryImpl cf_impl =
      new CounterFactoryImpl(orb, rootPOA);
    CounterFactory cf = cf_impl._this(orb);
    putRef(cf, refFile);
    rootPOA.the_POAManager().activate();
    orb.run();
  } catch (Exception ex) {
    out.println("Exception: " + ex.getMessage());
    exit(1);
  }
}
public static void main(String[] args) {
  String refFile = "CounterFactory.ref";
  new CFServer(args, refFile);
}
}
```

We store this file in the Server directory and compile it as usual by invoking javac CF-Server.java (JDK) or jmake CFServer.java (JacORB and OpenORB) in that current directory.

8.3   Implementing the CounterFactory Client

We now continue on the client host and carry out the necessary preparatory steps. We create a directory structure analogous to Figure 14. We store the IDL files Counter.idl and CounterFactory.idl in \Examples\CounterFactory. And, we translate the CounterFactory by invoking the IDL compiler in the respective Client subdirectory in the same way as described above in Section 8.1.

The actual client implementation also differs only slightly from the client applications discussed in Chapter 7. For reasons of completeness, we, once again, quote it in its entirety. However, as above, we group the parts initializing the ORB and getting the server object's reference that are reusable in future examples in separate methods initializeORB() and getRef(). Again, note the package declarations at the beginning of the file.

```
// CFClient.java

import Count.*;
import CFactory.*;
import CFactory.CounterFactoryPackage.*;
import java.io.*;
import java.util.*;
import org.omg.CORBA.*;
import static java.lang.System.*;

public class CFClient {
  private ORB orb;
  private void initializeORB(String[] args) {
    Properties props = getProperties();
```

```
    orb = ORB.init(args, props);
  }
  private org.omg.CORBA.Object getRef(String refFile) {
    String ref = null;
    try {
      Scanner reader = new Scanner(new File(refFile));
      ref = reader.nextLine();
    } catch (IOException ex) {
      out.println("File error: "
        + ex.getMessage());
      exit(2);
    }
    org.omg.CORBA.Object obj = orb.string_to_object(ref);
    if (obj == null) {
      out.println("Invalid IOR");
      exit(4);
    }
    return obj;
  }
  public CFClient(String[] args, String refFile) {
    try {
      initializeORB(args);
      org.omg.CORBA.Object obj = getRef(refFile);
      CounterFactory cf =
        CounterFactoryHelper.narrow(obj);
      Counter c;
      if (args[0].equalsIgnoreCase("Shared"))
        c = cf.create(Kind.SHARED);
      else
        c = cf.create(Kind.UNSHARED);
      int inp = -1;
      do {
        out.print("Counter value: " + c.value()
          + "\nAction (+/-/e)? ");
        out.flush();
        do {
          try {
            inp = in.read();
          } catch (IOException ioe) { }
        } while (inp != '+' && inp != '-' && inp != 'e');
        if (inp == '+')
          c.inc();
        else if (inp == '-')
          c.dec();
      } while (inp != 'e');
      cf.destroy(c);
    } catch (BAD_PARAM ex) {
      out.println("Narrowing failed");
      exit(3);
    } catch (Exception ex) {
      out.println("Exception: " + ex.getMessage());
      exit(1);
    }
  }
}
```

```
public static void main(String[] args) {
    if (args.length < 1) {
        out.println("Start with"
            + "\n\tjava/jrun CFClient Shared\nor"
            + "\n\tjava/jrun CFClient Unshared");
        return;
    }
    String refFile = "CounterFactory.ref";
    new CFClient(args, refFile);
}
}
```

The client has to be provided with a command-line argument when the Java interpreter is invoked. When started in the form

```
java CFClient SharedCounter
```

the existing SHARED Counter is used; otherwise, an UNSHARED Counter is created. For a JacORB or an OpenORB implementation, java is to be replaced by jrun.

This file goes to the Client directory and is compiled as usual by invoking javac CF-Client.java (JDK) or jmake CFClient.java (JacORB and OpenORB) in that current directory.

8.4 Running the Application

The steps necessary for testing the complete application are completely analogous to the procedure for the first example (see Section 7.10).

- On the server host, start the server by invoking java CFServer (JDK) or jrun CFServer (JacORB and OpenORB) in the Server directory.
- Copy the file containing the CFServer's IOR to the client host. The file name is CounterFactory.ref; it has to be stored in the Client directory.
- On the client hosts, start the CFClients. Invoke java CFClient Shared or java CFClient Unshared (JDK). Invoke jrun CFClient Shared or jrun CFClient Unshared (JacORB and OpenORB). These commands must be entered in the Client directory.

It is worthwhile to experiment with several shared and unshared clients that operate concurrently to see how the same or a new Counter is modified by the remote invocations.

8.5 Exercises

1. Implement a GUI version for the CFClient.

2. Implement a "bounded" variant of the CounterFactory that ensures that a given maximum number of unshared Counter objects are not exceeded on the server host. If

the maximum is reached and a client tries to create another unshared `Counter`, let the
`CounterFactory` throw a `TooManyObjects` exception. Test the implementation
with a very small maximum, e.g., 2.

9 Alternatives for Designing IDL Interfaces

In IDL, an interface with a specific function can be specified in various different ways that resemble each other. To discuss the possibilities, we examine an application providing the current time of a system clock. The simplest procedure for determining and managing the chronological sequence of events in distributed systems is based on a central system clock. In this chapter, we concentrate on the discussion of the alternative possibilities offered by IDL for that task and neglect the existing sophisticated algorithms that may be used for synchronization of the clocks in a distributed system.

9.1   Attributes vs. Operations

The first solution for specifying a central, server-side clock with IDL could look as follows:

```
// TimeServer.idl
// Version 1

module Timer
{
  interface TimeServer
  {
    readonly attribute unsigned long hours;
    readonly attribute unsigned long minutes;
    readonly attribute unsigned long seconds;
  };
};
```

Here, we use three `readonly` attributes. Following the pattern outlined in Figure 11, we store the IDL file in a directory `\Examples\TimeServer\1` on the server host. After invoking the IDL compiler, we inspect the operations interface `TimeServerOperations`, which is generated in the package subdirectory `Timer` below the `Server` directory. A suitable implementation of the interface would be

```
// TimeServerImpl.java

package Timer;

import static java.util.Calendar.*;

public class TimeServerImpl extends TimeServerPOA {
  public int hours() {
    return getInstance().get(HOUR_OF_DAY);
  }
  public int minutes() {
```

```
      return getInstance().get(MINUTE);
    }
  public int seconds() {
    return getInstance().get(SECOND);
    }
}
```

The import declaration for package java.util is included for accessing the class Calendar, which we need to obtain the hour, minute, and second components of a calendar instance. As before, we store this file in subdirectory Timer.

The corresponding server application can be copied almost entirely from Section 8.2; we only make minor changes to class names in the constructor and the main() method and store
the file in the Server directory, as usual:

```
// TServer.java

import Timer.*;
import java.io.*;
import java.util.Properties;
import org.omg.CORBA.*;
import org.omg.PortableServer.*;
import static java.lang.System.*;

public class TServer {
  private ORB orb;
  private POA rootPOA;
  private void initializeORB(String[] args) {
    ... as above in Section 8.2
  }
  private void putRef(org.omg.CORBA.Object obj,
    String refFile) {
    ... as above in Section 8.2
  }
  public TServer(String[] args, String refFile) {
    try {
      initializeORB(args);
      TimeServerImpl t_impl = new TimeServerImpl();
      TimeServer t = t_impl._this(orb);
      putRef(t, refFile);
      rootPOA.the_POAManager().activate();
      orb.run();
    } catch (Exception ex) {
      out.println("Exception: " + ex.getMessage());
      exit(1);
    }
  }
  public static void main(String[] args) {
    String refFile = "TimeServer.ref";
    new TServer(args, refFile);
  }
}
```

The client application is just as simple. We can copy most of its code from the client in Section 8.3 and thus complete the first example.

```
// TClient.java

import Timer.*;
import java.io.*;
import java.util.*;
import org.omg.CORBA.*;
import static java.lang.System.*;

public class TClient {
  private ORB orb;
  private void initializeORB(String[] args) {
    ... as above in Section 8.3
  }
  private org.omg.CORBA.Object getRef(String refFile) {
    ... as above in Section 8.3
  }
  public TClient(String[] args, String refFile) {
    try {
      initializeORB(args);
      org.omg.CORBA.Object obj = getRef(refFile);
      TimeServer t = TimeServerHelper.narrow(obj);
      int h = t.hours(), m = t.minutes(), s = t.seconds();
      out.println("Time on Server: " + h
        + ((m < 10)? ":0": ":") + m
        + ((s < 10)? ":0": ":") + s);
    } catch (BAD_PARAM ex) {
      out.println("Narrowing failed");
      exit(3);
    } catch (Exception ex) {
      out.println("Exception: " + ex.getMessage());
      exit(1);
    }
  }
  public static void main(String[] args) {
    String refFile = "TimeServer.ref";
    new TClient(args, refFile);
  }
}
```

An alternative to the first interface specification would be the second version below, which, according to our file system structure, goes to the \Examples\TimeServer\2 directory on the server host:

```
// TimeServer.idl
// Version 2

module Timer
{
  interface TimeServer
  {
    unsigned long hours();
    unsigned long minutes();
```

```
   unsigned long seconds();
  };
};
```

Even though the interface definitions differ, their Java mapping is exactly the same. Therefore, we can reuse the above-described implementations of servant, server application, as well as client application entirely. These sources, TimeServerImpl.java, TServer.java, and TClient.java, should be stored in directories named in correspondence with the first version; in the remainder of this chapter, we do not go into more detail regarding the directory structure.

The two first alternatives are rather inefficient since they both invoke three remote methods, hours(), minutes(), and seconds(), in order to determine the server's time. These invocations should be combined into one single invocation. There are at least three different approaches that return the hours, minutes, and seconds with one single method call.

9.2   Returning Results From an Operation

Our third TimeServer version achieves this by defining an operation get_time() with three out parameters:

```
// TimeServer.idl
// Version 3

module Timer
{
  interface TimeServer
  {
    void get_time(
      out unsigned long hours,
      out unsigned long minutes,
      out unsigned long seconds);
  };
};
```

A look at Section 5.17 for the mapping of out parameters and inspection of the operations interface shows us that, now, a method with three IntHolder parameters has to be implemented. Holder classes for basic types, such as int, are already available in package org.omg.CORBA (see Section 5.4). They are all defined following the same pattern, providing a public instance variable value of the type they hold, a public default constructor, and a public one-argument constructor that initializes the value.

The Java implementation of the operations interface can, therefore, look as follows:

```
// TimeServerImpl.java

package Timer;

import static java.util.Calendar.*;
import org.omg.CORBA.*;
```

```
public class TimeServerImpl extends TimeServerPOA {
   public void get_time(IntHolder hours,
        IntHolder minutes, IntHolder seconds) {
     hours.value = getInstance().get(HOUR_OF_DAY);
     minutes.value = getInstance().get(MINUTE);
     seconds.value = getInstance().get(SECOND);
   }
}
```

We construct a Calendar object, extract the desired current time values from it, and set the holder values of the IntHolder parameters correspondingly.

There are no revisions necessary to the server application; its code can be once again reused entirely. The main difference to alternatives one and two is that, now, some changes are to be made to the code of the client application. Clients invoke the method get_time() and, before the remote invocation can be executed, a client has to provide an instance for each out parameter (see Section 5.17). The corresponding Java code for the TClient's constructor is therefore

```
IntHolder hours = new IntHolder(),
   minutes = new IntHolder(), seconds = new IntHolder();
t.get_time(hours, minutes, seconds);
out.println("Time on Server: " + hours.value
   + ((minutes.value < 10)? ":0": ":") + minutes.value
   + ((seconds.value < 10)? ":0": ":") + seconds.value);
```

Since hours, minutes, and seconds are out parameters, they obtain suitable values through the server and default initialization on the client side, through the default constructor, is sufficient.

Alternative four provides a similar solution with a single remote invocation, this time falling back on a constructed type Time, a structure with the elements hours, minutes, and seconds. Operation get_time() returns a Time instance. The IDL definition looks as follows:

```
// TimeServer.idl
// Version 4

module Timer
{
   interface TimeServer
   {
     struct Time {
       unsigned long hours;
       unsigned long minutes;
       unsigned long seconds;
     };
     Time get_time();
   };
};
```

The servant implementation for the above interface could be realized like this:

```
// TimeServerImpl.java

package Timer;

import Timer.TimeServerPackage.*;
import static java.util.Calendar.*;

public class TimeServerImpl extends TimeServerPOA {
  public Time get_time() {
    return new Time(getInstance().get(HOUR_OF_DAY),
      getInstance().get(MINUTE),
      getInstance().get(SECOND));
  }
}
```

The first obvious difference is that, now, a new package, TimeServerPackage, has to be imported. This is the package the IDL compiler generates below the module package Timer to store the Java class Time to which the structure is mapped. The class declares three public int instance variables, hours, minutes, and seconds, a default constructor, and a constructor with three int parameters (see Section 5.9 and also inspect Timer\TimeServerPackage\Time.java). We use the IDL compiler-generated constructor to initialize a new Time instance with the current time values and immediately return that object as a result of the invocation of method get_time(). The server application itself can, again, remain unchanged.

The class Time is also needed on the client side. Therefore, a corresponding import declaration must be included at the beginning of TClient.java:

```
import Timer.TimeServerPackage.*;
```

And in the client's constructor, we invoke get_time() as follows:

```
Time hms = t.get_time();
out.println("Time on Server: " + hms.hours
  + ((hms.minutes < 10)? ":0": ":") + hms.minutes
  + ((hms.seconds < 10)? ":0": ":") + hms.seconds);
```

The rest of the client application can be copied; as above, the variable t holds a reference to the TimeServer.

As a last alternative, we change the interface such that, instead of returning the Time structure as usual as the invocation's result, we provide it in the form of an out parameter. In that case, we define the interface specification below:

```
// TimeServer.idl
// Version 5

module Timer
{
  interface TimeServer
  {
```

```
      struct Time {
        unsigned long hours;
        unsigned long minutes;
        unsigned long seconds;
      };
      void get_time(out Time hms);
    };
};
```

In Section 5.17, we discussed that out parameters of user-defined types are mapped to their corresponding holder classes. Therefore, in the TimeServerOperations interface, we find the following method:

```
void get_time(Timer.TimeServerPackage.TimeHolder hms);
```

As in our example's version four, the TimeHolder is generated in the TimeServer-Package; however, now we have to use it to return the current time back to the client. The structure of holder classes was explained in Section 5.4, one might also want to read Timer\TimeServerPackage\TimeHolder.java to recall how the class declares a public instance variable value of type Time. When writing the servant, one should recall (Section 5.17) that an object for an out parameter must be created and is owned by the receiver of the call. An implementation of the interface can, therefore, have the form

```
// TimeServerImpl.java

package Timer;

import Timer.TimeServerPackage.*;
import static java.util.Calendar.*;

public class TimeServerImpl extends TimeServerPOA {
  public void get_time(TimeHolder hms) {
    Time tim = new Time(getInstance().get(HOUR_OF_DAY),
      getInstance().get(MINUTE),
      getInstance().get(SECOND));
    hms.value = tim;
  }
}
```

We create a Time object exactly as in alternative four. But, now, we do not pass it to the client with a return statement; instead, we insert it into the TimeHolder by setting its value.

The code of the server application can be reused entirely. However, due to the change in the specification of method get_time(), the client application has to be adapted. First, an import statement for the Timer.TimeServerPackage is needed. And second, as for alternative three, the client has to provide an instance for the out parameter. Since the server creates the actual value of type Time, we can simply call the TimeHolder's default constructor

```
TimeHolder hms = new TimeHolder();
t.get_time(hms);
Time tim = hms.value;
```

```
out.println("Time on Server: " + tim.hours
  + ((tim.minutes < 10)? ":0": ":") + tim.minutes
  + ((tim.seconds < 10)? ":0": ":") + tim.seconds);
```

After completion of the call, we access the hours, the minutes, and the seconds via the value of the out parameter.

As we saw in this chapter, designing IDL interfaces often involves decisions for or against different design alternatives. The developer should be aware of the consequences that a particular approach might imply, e.g., with respect to network communication overhead, maintainability, and other relevant aspects. After carefully trading off these consequences, the developer is then able to choose the best solution with respect to the requirements at hand.

9.3   Exercises

1. Implement a server with an operation x1x2 () that passes two doubles p and q and calculates and returns the two results

$$x_1 = -\frac{p}{2} + \sqrt{\frac{p^2}{4} - q} \, , \quad x_2 = -\frac{p}{2} - \sqrt{\frac{p^2}{4} - q}$$

i.e., the two roots of the equation $x^2 + px + q = 0$.

For the DoubleHolder class, see Section 5.4; for the creation and "ownership" of in, out, and inout parameters, see Section 5.17; for Pair and PairHolder, read the files generated from the IDL compiler.

a) Use the following interface definition:

```
interface Roots
{
  exception Complex { };
  void x1x2(in double p, in double q,
     out double x1, out double x2) raises(Complex);
};
```

b) Use the following interface definition:

```
interface Roots
{
  exception Complex { };
  struct Pair
  {
    double a;
    double b;
  };
  void x1x2(in Pair pq, out Pair roots)
    raises(Complex);
};
```

c) Use the following interface definition:

```
interface Roots
{
  exception Complex { };
  struct Pair
  {
    double a;
    double b;
  };
  void x1x2(inout Pair pqroots) raises(Complex);
};
```

2. The method `System.currentTimeMillis()` returns the current time at the host as a `long`. For each of the five alternatives discussed above, get the time on the server host 1,000 times (5,000 times or 10,000 times, etc.) and use `currentTimeMillis()` to compare the respective run-times.

3. Implement a sixth `TimeServer` version where `get_time()` returns a sequence with three `unsigned longs`.

4. Implement a seventh `TimeServer` version where `get_time()` returns an array with three `unsigned longs`.

5. Given the following IDL interfaces, each containing an operation `compute()` with an `in` parameter of different types, compile the interfaces and have a look at the signatures of the resulting Java methods. Which conclusion(s) with respect to the design of the IDL interfaces can be drawn from the findings?

```
interface ArrXmpl
{
  typedef long larr[10];
  long compute(in larr l);
};
interface BSeqXmpl
{
  typedef sequence<long,50> lseq;
  long compute(in lseq l);
};
interface UnBSeqXmpl
{
  typedef sequence<long> luseq;
  long compute(in luseq l);
};
```

10 Inheritance and Polymorphism

The most powerful object-oriented concepts known to those programming in object-oriented languages are inheritance and the related possibility of invoking operations or methods polymorphically. For example, in Java, classes and interfaces can be organized in an inheritance hierarchy and inherit members from their supertypes. While in Java a class can have at most one direct superclass, interfaces may have an arbitrary number of superinterfaces. Therefore, in Java, multiple inheritance is only permitted on the interface level. In addition to the possibility of overloading methods, i.e., declaring methods with the same name and same return type but different signatures, in Java, it is allowed to override methods inherited from superclasses or superinterfaces. Recall that a method overrides a method inherited from a superclass when it is declared with a new method body but the same signature and return type. References to objects of such a class can now be managed through references of the superclass type by implicitly casting up the type hierarchy. Calling an overridden method with a reference of the superclass type now results in executing the method body belonging to the class with which the object was originally constructed. Method invocations with the same name, therefore, can result in different kinds of behavior, depending on the type of the referenced object; they are *polymorphic*.

If we examine the realization of the concepts of inheritance and polymorphism in CORBA, we have to bear in mind that, there, we find an even stricter separation of interface and implementation. On the IDL level, we never deal with implementation aspects. These are realized through the mapping to a programming language that is not necessarily object-oriented and whose concepts are not influenced by the CORBA standard itself. In order to guarantee the object-oriented approach, CORBA embeds the concepts of inheritance and polymorphism already in IDL. Similar to the rules for Java interfaces, multiple inheritance is allowed for IDL interfaces; therefore, an IDL interface can have several direct superinterfaces. However, in contrast to Java, it is not allowed in IDL to overload operations nor to override them in a subinterface. This fact could support the assumption that, in CORBA, polymorphism cannot be realized, an assumption that is not true as we see later. All IDL operations support late binding, irrespective of the concrete programming language chosen for their implementation. Depending on the type of the referenced object, the CORBA runtime selects the corresponding implementation for the invoked operation. And, since the same IDL operation can be provided with a new implementation on each level of the inheritance hierarchy, nothing gets in the way of polymorphic behavior in CORBA.

Let us begin with a simple example that we realize in two variants in order to illustrate inheritance on the interface and implementation levels. At the end of the chapter, we also practically test an example with polymorphic method calls.

10.1   IDL Definition of `DateTimeServer`

For the first example, which is first implemented with the inheritance approach and later
with the delegation approach, we come back to the `TimeServer` example from Chapter 9.
Assume that, in addition to the simple `TimeServer`, which provides the current time in a
structure `Time` with members holding hours, minutes, and seconds, we now want to implement a more specialized `DateTimeServer`, which can additionally return the current date
in a structure `DateTime` holding day, month, and year in addition to the current time. Inspect the following IDL definition of the module `Timer`.

```
// DateTimeServer.idl

module Timer
{
    interface TimeServer
    {
        struct Time {
            unsigned long hours;
            unsigned long minutes;
            unsigned long seconds;
        };
        Time get_time();
    };
    interface DateTimeServer : TimeServer
    {
        struct DateTime {
            unsigned long day;
            unsigned long month;
            unsigned long year;
            Time hms;
        };
        DateTime get_date_time();
    };
};
```

The module `Timer` contains the interface `TimeServer`, known from Section 9.2, in version 4. The interface `DateTimeServer` is new; it extends the `TimeServer` interface
and, thus, inherits the structure `Time` and the method `get_time()` from its superinterface
`TimeServer`. These elements need not be redefined. The structure `DateTime` and the operation `get_date_time()`, which returns a current `DateTime` instance, are new. In addition to the three `unsigned long` values for day, month, and year, `DateTime` contains
a member of the inherited type `Time` to be able to store the current time. Here, interface inheritance is used to avoid redundancies in the IDL specification. Inheritance also enables us
to treat objects of the subinterface type (here, `DateTimeServer`) like objects of the superinterface type (here, `TimeServer`); we demonstrate this below.

On the server host and the client hosts, one should now create directories `\Examples\In-
heritance` and three subdirectories, 1, 2, and 3, where the following three examples can
be stored. As before, create the subdirectories `YourORB\Client` on the client hosts and
`YourORB\Server` on the server host. Store the file `DateTimeServer.idl` on each
host in `\Examples\Inheritance\1` and in `\Examples\Inheritance\2`. (We use

the same IDL specification for the first two examples.) After setting the environment variables, one can now invoke the IDL compiler in the respective `Server` or `Client` subdirectory.

The IDL compiler creates a subdirectory and a Java package `Timer` for the module `Timer`, where the usual files for the two interfaces `TimeServer` and `DateTimeServer` are stored. For the two structures `Time` and `DateTime`, two Java packages, `TimeServer-Package` and `DateTimeServerPackage`, and the corresponding subdirectories of the `Timer` directory are generated. The Java classes `Time` and `DateTime`, as well as the appropriate helper and holder classes, are created and stored there.

10.2   Implementing the Inheritance Approach

We now examine how interface inheritance on the IDL level influences the implementation of the interfaces. To do that, we follow the inheritance approach first and then implement the delegation approach consecutively.

10.2.1   Implementing `TimeServer`

We start with the `TimeServer`'s implementation and reuse the code from version 4, discussed in Section 9.2, entirely:

```
// TimeServerImpl.java

package Timer;

import Timer.TimeServerPackage.*;
import static java.util.Calendar.*;

public class TimeServerImpl extends TimeServerPOA {
   public Time get_time() {
      return new Time(getInstance().get(HOUR_OF_DAY),
         getInstance().get(MINUTE),
         getInstance().get(SECOND));
   }
}
```

As before, store the file `TimeServerImpl.java` in the directory `\Examples\Inheritance\1\`*YourORB*`\Server\Timer`.

10.2.2   Implementing `DateTimeServer`

Analogously, implementing the inheritance approach, we declare the `DateTimeServer`'s implementation class as a subclass of the `DateTimeServerPOA` class as follows:

```
// DateTimeServerImpl.java

package Timer;
```

```
import Timer.DateTimeServerPackage.*;
import Timer.TimeServerPackage.*;
import static java.util.Calendar.*;

public class DateTimeServerImpl
    extends DateTimeServerPOA {
  public Time get_time() {
    return new Time(getInstance().get(HOUR_OF_DAY),
      getInstance().get(MINUTE),
      getInstance().get(SECOND));
  }
  public DateTime get_date_time() {
    return new DateTime(getInstance().get(DAY_OF_MONTH),
      getInstance().get(MONTH) + 1,
      getInstance().get(YEAR),
      get_time());
  }
}
```

Method get_time() is implemented with exactly the same body as in the TimeServer-Impl class. This shows that IDL inheritance resulted in duplicating the code of the Java implementation of the inherited method. On the code level, we did not gain any benefit from the inheritance principle. (See Exercise 1 for a way that goal can, nevertheless, be reached.) In that way, CORBA inheritance can be implemented with non-object-oriented programming languages that do not know the inheritance concept. It can also be seen that the method get_time() could have been re-declared with an arbitrary new method body in class DateTimeServerImpl. The implementation of the new method get_date_time() is straightforward; once again, we fall back on the functionality of the Calendar class.

The file DateTimeServerImpl.java also goes to the directory \Examples\Inheritance\1\YourORB\Server\Timer.

10.2.3   Implementing the Server Application

The server-side application of the inheritance example could be implemented as follows:

```
// TServer.java

import Timer.*;
import java.io.*;
import java.util.Properties;
import org.omg.CORBA.*;
import org.omg.PortableServer.*;
import static java.lang.System.*;

public class TServer {
  private ORB orb;
  private POA rootPOA;
  private void initializeORB(String[] args) {
    ... as above in Section 8.2
  }
  private void putRef(org.omg.CORBA.Object obj,
```

```
     ... as above in Section 8.2
   }
   public TServer(String[] args, String refFile) {
     if (args.length < 1) {
       out.println("Start with\n\tjava/jrun TServer Time"
         + "\nor\n\tjava/jrun TServer DateTime");
       return;
     }
     try {
       initializeORB(args);
       if (args[0].equalsIgnoreCase("Time"))
         putRef(new TimeServerImpl()._this(orb), refFile);
       else
         putRef(new DateTimeServerImpl()._this(orb),
           refFile);
       rootPOA.the_POAManager().activate();
       orb.run();
     } catch (Exception ex) {
       out.println("Exception: " + ex.getMessage());
       exit(1);
     }
   }
   public static void main(String[] args) {
     String refFile = "TimeServer.ref";
     new TServer(args, refFile);
   }
 }
```

Apart from minor modifications in the TServer() constructor, this implementation is identical to the one used above in Section 9.1. In the constructor, the method putRef() is called to write the reference to a newly created and activated TimeServerImpl or DateTimeServerImpl object to the file TimeServer.ref; the object's type is determined by the command-line argument. The rest of the constructor, with the ORB's initialization, the POAManager's activation, and the passing of the control flow to the ORB, should now be customary.

After storing the file TServer.java on the server host in \Examples\Inheritance\1\YourORB\Server, one can now translate and start the server. Finally, one should not forget to transfer the file TimeServer.ref containing the server IOR to the client hosts.

10.2.4   Implementing the Client Application

At last, we implement the client application with the Java code given below:

```
// TClient.java

import Timer.*;
import Timer.TimeServerPackage.*;
import Timer.DateTimeServerPackage.*;
import java.io.*;
import java.util.*;
```

```java
import org.omg.CORBA.*;
import static java.lang.System.*;

public class TClient {
  private ORB orb;
  private void initializeORB(String[] args) {
    ... as above in Section 8.3
  }
  private org.omg.CORBA.Object getRef(String refFile) {
    ... as above in Section 8.3
  }
  public TClient(String[] args, String refFile) {
    try {
      initializeORB(args);
      org.omg.CORBA.Object obj = getRef(refFile);
      TimeServer t = null;
      DateTimeServer dt = null;
      try {
        t = TimeServerHelper.narrow(obj);
      } catch (BAD_PARAM ex) {
        out.println("Narrowing failed");
        exit(3);
      }
      Time hms = t.get_time();
      out.println("Time on Server: " + hms.hours
        + ((hms.minutes < 10)? ":0": ":") + hms.minutes
        + ((hms.seconds < 10)? ":0": ":") + hms.seconds);
      try {
        dt = DateTimeServerHelper.narrow(t);
      } catch (BAD_PARAM ex) { }
      if (dt != null) {
        DateTime dmy = dt.get_date_time();
        out.println("Date on Server: "
          + ((dmy.day < 10)? "0": "")+ dmy.day
          + ((dmy.month < 10)? ".0": ".") + dmy.month
          + "." + dmy.year);
      }
    } catch (Exception ex) {
      out.println("Exception: " + ex.getMessage());
      exit(1);
    }
  }
  public static void main(String[] args) {
    String refFile = "TimeServer.ref";
    new TClient(args, refFile);
  }
}
```

While methods main() as well as initializeORB() and getRef() are coded in the
familiar way, the constructor TClient() deserves a further look. As usual, the ORB is initialized and the server object's reference string is read. Since there are two options to start
the server, the client has no information on the actual type of the server object; TimeServer or DateTimeServer, at that time.

At this point, it might be useful to recapitulate how the narrowing of CORBA object references is carried through (see also Section 5.5 on helper classes.) From the previous examples, it is known that `getRef()` returns the IOR read from a file as a reference to the generic supertype `org.omg.CORBA.Object`. This type cast up the inheritance hierarchy is always unproblematic since the concrete subtype has at least all the properties of the supertype. To come back to our example, a `DateTimeServer` object is also a `TimeServer` object. Casts in the other direction, the narrowing of references, are only appropriate when the referenced object's type is indeed the subtype since potential additional properties (attributes or methods) are expected that the supertype does not provide. A `TimeServer` object is not by any means a `DateTimeServer` object, which can also determine the date. Therefore, to be able to use the read object reference for invocations on the remote server object, this reference has to be narrowed to the correct type, as in the previous examples. To provide a language-spanning mechanism for that task, the CORBA standard defines the IDL operation `narrow()` for a type's helper class; in Java, this operation is mapped to a method with the same name. In order to guarantee type safety, the ORB's difficulty is that it has to decide whether the narrowing is appropriate or not; for that decision, it needs information on the type hierarchy. The ORB obtains this information automatically, either locally from the current stub code or, if this is not available, dynamically by a remote call. The latter should definitely be avoided since it slows down the client and, in the worst case, could even produce a deadlock. Should narrowing of a type be inadmissible, the method `narrow()` throws a system exception of type `org.omg.CORBA.BAD_PARAM`.

Against this background, we can now take a closer look at the next statements in the `TClient` constructor. Due to the design of the server application, the reference returned by `getRef()` is either of type `TimeServer` or of type `DateTimeServer`. Since the latter is a subtype of the `TimeServer`, we can always try a cast to the `TimeServer` type by means of `TimeServerHelper.narrow()`. Should this attempt fail, the reference does not have one of the two `TimeServer` types, a `BAD_PARAM` exception is thrown and the program is terminated in the exception handler. Otherwise, irrespective of its actual type, we treat the object as a `TimeServer`, call `get_time()`, and print the time values. Subsequently, we try a second cast to the type `DateTimeServer`. If this succeeds, the object is truly of that type and we can invoke the `DateTimeServer`'s method `get_date_time()` and print the date. Otherwise, if the object was "only" of type `TimeServer` and the narrowing fails, we can simply ignore the exception thrown.

The file `TClient.java` can now be stored in the directory `\Examples\Inheritance\1\`*YourORB*`\Client` on one's client hosts and the complete application can be translated and tested as accustomed. The client is also used in unrevised form for the next, second, variation of the inheritance example and `TClient.java` should also be stored in one's client hosts' directory `\Examples\Inheritance\2\`*YourORB*`\Client`.

10.3 Implementing the Example with the Delegation Approach

For a second variation of the example, we now rely on the delegation approach. Here, it is noticeable that, also on the programming language level, we can make good use of the inheritance principle since Java, as an object-oriented language, provides the opportunity to do so. The above-described first variation was characterized by inheritance on the IDL level, coupled with code duplication on the implementation level. Duplicated code is hard to maintain and not elegant from an object-oriented point of view; but, it at least offers some performance gain with respect to the method invocations since the additional level of indirection that the delegation approach brings about is not needed.

We use the same IDL specification `DateTimeServer.idl` as a starting point. It should already be stored in the correct directories for the second example and may now be translated. Since the delegation approach is now followed, the IDL compiler has to be invoked such that, on the server host, tie classes are generated as well.

Next to the `DateTimeServer.idl`'s IDL specification, the client application, file `TClient.java`, can also be reused without any changes.

10.3.1 Implementing `TimeServer`

It is the characteristic of the delegation approach to implement the CORBA objects specified in IDL by means of the delegate classes. This way to proceed should already be known so further details on the `TimeServerDelegate`'s Java code can be spared:

```
// TimeServerDelegate.java

package Timer;

import Timer.TimeServerPackage.*;
import static java.util.Calendar.*;

public class TimeServerDelegate
    implements TimeServerOperations {
  public Time get_time() {
    return new Time(getInstance().get(HOUR_OF_DAY),
      getInstance().get(MINUTE),
      getInstance().get(SECOND));
  }
}
```

Store this file in the directory `\Examples\Inheritance\2\YourORB\Server\Timer`.

10.3.2 Implementing `DateTimeServer`

The implementation of the `TimeServerDelegate`'s subtype `DateTimeServerDelegate` is given below:

```
// DateTimeServerDelegate.java

package Timer;

import Timer.DateTimeServerPackage.*;
import Timer.TimeServerPackage.*;
```

```
import static java.util.Calendar.*;

public class DateTimeServerDelegate
      extends TimeServerDelegate
      implements DateTimeServerOperations {
   public DateTime get_date_time() {
      return new DateTime(getInstance().get(DAY_OF_MONTH),
        getInstance().get(MONTH) + 1,
        getInstance().get(YEAR),
        get_time());
   }
}
```

The essential advantage of the delegation approach, as opposed to the inheritance approach, is that, now, the implementation class is not forced to subclass the corresponding POA class and, therefore, does not use up Java's single possibility of declaring a subclass. Instead, here, only the operations interface is implemented so that the delegate class can, in principle, inherit from any other Java class. We exploit this possibility by declaring DateTimeServerDelegate as a subclass of TimeServerDelegate and, thus, make use of all advantages of implementation inheritance so that code duplication, especially, is avoided.

The file DateTimeServerDelegate.java should be stored in the same directory as TimeServerDelegate.java.

10.3.3   Modifying the Server Application

The implementation of the server application can also be kept almost entirely from the first example. The only modification that the file TServer.java needs concerns the construction of the server objects once the ORB is initialized. The if statement

```
if (args[0].equalsIgnoreCase("Time"))
   putRef(new TimeServerImpl()._this(orb), refFile);
else
   putRef(new DateTimeServerImpl()._this(orb), refFile);
```

in the constructor now has to be replaced by the construction

```
if (args[0].equalsIgnoreCase("Time"))
   putRef(new TimeServerPOATie(
     new TimeServerDelegate())._this(orb), refFile);
else
   putRef(new DateTimeServerPOATie(
     new DateTimeServerDelegate())._this(orb), refFile);
```

One can store this file, as usual, in the Server directory, compile it, and start it with the desired command-line argument. After copying the object reference to a client host, one can start the client and test the complete application.

10.4   An Example for Polymorphism

We now come back to the subject of polymorphic method calls. In order to concentrate on
the essentials, we discuss a very simple, abstract example that is nevertheless well-suited to
practically demonstrate the possibilities CORBA and Java offer.

Consider the following IDL specification of a module XYZ with interfaces X, Y, and Z:

```
// XYZ.idl

module XYZ
{
   interface X
   {
     void m();
     void l();
   };
   interface Y : X
   {
   };
   interface Z : Y
   {
   };
};
```

These interfaces are arranged in a three-level inheritance hierarchy, where Z inherits from Y
and Y inherits from X. In X, two operations, m() and l(), with empty parameter lists and
void return types, are defined. As repeatedly mentioned, IDL allows neither overloading nor
overriding of operations. And, since the IDL level is still completely implementation-
independent, it cannot be indicated whether one of the subtypes of X should provide another
implementation of one of X's operations or not. Let us assume that operation m() shall have
its own specific implementation on each hierarchy level while, on the other hand, the implementation of l() shall be identical for all three types.

Figure 17 clearly demonstrates the IDL interfaces of module XYZ once again in UML notation. Store and compile the IDL file on server and client hosts as usual and take care to generate the tie classes necessary for the delegation approach.

On the server host, we now implement XDelegate, YDelegate, and ZDelegate according to the delegation approach; we begin with the file XDelegate.java:

```
// XDelegate.java

package XYZ;

public class XDelegate implements XOperations {
   public void m() { System.out.println("X::m()"); }
   public void l() { System.out.println("X::l()"); }
}
```

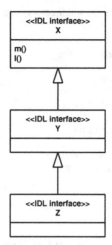

Figure 17: IDL Level Inheritance Hierarchy

The only purpose of the two methods m() and l() is to write their names to the console so that we can later understand which concrete implementation is executed when they are called by a client.

The implementation class for the YDelegate follows; it is declared as a subclass of class XDelegate:

```
// YDelegate.java

package XYZ;

public class YDelegate extends XDelegate
    implements YOperations {
  public void m() { System.out.println("Y::m()"); }
}
```

Overriding a method's implementation on the Java level does not pose any problems. Therefore, we declare a new method body for YDelegate's method m() while not providing a new implementation for l(), thus, leaving it unrevised.

The implementation of the ZDelegate class follows the same scheme, "overriding" m() while simply inheriting l().

```
// ZDelegate.java

package XYZ;

public class ZDelegate extends Ydelegate
    implements ZOperations {
  public void m() { System.out.println("Z::m()"); }
}
```

Store these files on the server host in the subdirectory XYZ of one's Server directory for the third example.

Now, we turn to the server application.

```
// DelegationServer.java

import XYZ.*;
import java.io.*;
import java.util.Properties;
import org.omg.CORBA.*;
import org.omg.PortableServer.*;
import static java.lang.System.*;

public class DelegationServer {
  public static void main(String args[]) {
    ORB orb = null;
    try {
      Properties props = getProperties();
      orb = ORB.init(args, props);
      org.omg.CORBA.Object obj;
      POA rootPOA;
      FileOutputStream file =
        new FileOutputStream("XYZ.ref");
      PrintWriter writer = new PrintWriter(file);
      obj = orb.resolve_initial_references("RootPOA");
      rootPOA = POAHelper.narrow(obj);
      String ref;
      ref = orb.object_to_string(
        new XPOATie(new XDelegate())._this(orb));
      writer.println(ref);
      ref = orb.object_to_string(
        new YPOATie(new YDelegate())._this(orb));
      writer.println(ref);
      ref = orb.object_to_string(
        new ZPOATie(new ZDelegate())._this(orb));
      writer.println(ref);
      writer.flush();
      file.close();
      rootPOA.the_POAManager().activate();
    } catch(Exception ex) {
      out.println("Exception:" + ex);
      exit(5);
    }
    out.println("Server started. Stop: Ctrl-C");
    orb.run();
  }
}
```

The main difference compared to our previous examples is that, now, three server objects of types X, Y, and Z are created and stored via their stringified references in the file XYZ.ref. In order to keep the code very short, we do not factor out the code previously grouped in the methods initializeORB() and getRef(). The remaining statements in the main() method should all be familiar.

One can store and compile the server application according to the usual conventions.

As the last element of the distributed test application, we implement the client application; with its help, we intend to demonstrate how polymorphic method calls can be performed.

```java
// Client.java

import XYZ.*;
import java.io.*;
import java.util.*;
import org.omg.CORBA.*;
import static java.lang.System.*;

public class Client {
    public static void main(String[] args) {
        try {
            Properties props = getProperties();
            ORB orb = ORB.init(args, props);
            org.omg.CORBA.Object obj;
            Scanner reader = new Scanner(new File("XYZ.ref"));
            String ref;
            X[] x = new X[3];
            for (int i = 0; i < x.length; i++) {
                ref = reader.nextLine();
                obj = orb.string_to_object(ref);
                x[i] = XHelper.narrow(obj);
            }
            reader.close();
            for (int i = 0; i < x.length; i++) {
                x[i].m();
                x[i].l();
            }
        } catch(Exception ex) {
            out.println("System error!");
            exit(1);
        }
    }
}
```

Again, the application is kept very simple and short. We read the three object references from the file XYZ.ref and narrow them to the type X, as discussed in Section 10.2.4. The results are stored in an array of type X[] with length three. And, finally, we call m() and, subsequently, l() for each element of this array. On the console of the server host, the following output is printed:

```
X::m()
X::l()
Y::m()
X::l()
Z::m()
X::l()
```

It can be seen that, depending on the actual type of the referenced server-side object, the correct implementation of methods m() and l() is executed, respectively. While the calls of m() are polymorphic because, on the code level, m() was newly implemented each time (and in Java actually overridden), the calls of l() always yield the same result since l() was only implemented in the XDelegate class and was simply inherited in its original form in the subclasses.

The inheritance and implementation relationships between the classes and the interfaces of this simple example are relatively complex. Part of them is demonstrated for the Java level in the UML diagram shown in Figure 18. Note that, when portraying the Java classes YDelegate and ZDelegate on the left side of the figure, overriding of method m() was indicated by repeatedly displaying m(), which was not possible on IDL level; see Figure 17.

10.5 Exercises

1. One disadvantage of the first example in this chapter is its duplication of Java code. How could this code duplication be prevented and nevertheless be profited from inheritance between Java classes without falling back on the delegation approach? Implement and test your solution and discuss advantages and disadvantages of both approaches from a performance-oriented view.

    Hint: Write a very lightweight implementation that mimics the delegation approach without the overhead of the IDL compiler-generated classes.

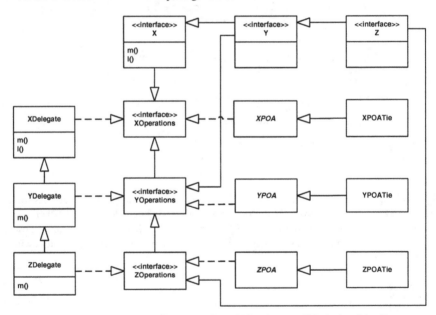

Figure 18: Partial Overview of "extends" and "implements" Relationships Between Java Classes and Interfaces Involved in the Example

2. Starting from the original `Counter` in the version discussed in Chapter 7, implement an
    `InvCounter` with the following IDL interface:

    ```
    interface InvCounter  : Counter
    {
      void invert();
    };
    ```

    It is the purpose of operation `invert()` to change the sign of the current `Counter`
    value. Write a test application that implements the delegation approach.

11 Implementing Distributed Callbacks

In the preceding chapters, we discussed examples that all implemented a rather strict allocation of the server and the client application roles. Communication was one-sided since only the clients invoked operations on the server objects. There are occasions, however, when requests on the design of the desired distributed system make it necessary that clients and servers change their roles, temporarily.

A typical situation in which a client application takes over server functionality for a dedicated period of time is one where the client is waiting for specific events that might occur at a server-side object and that require suitable reactions. On the other hand, a server might need to contact its clients to invoke certain update operations on them. In principle, a client can send a request to the server in regular intervals in order to determine whether an event that is of interest has occurred or not. This "Polling" or "Busy Waiting" technique, however, only unnecessarily consumes computing time on the client host and, for a larger number of clients, also increases load on the server host as well as network traffic. A solution to that problem is implementing the *Callback* technique ([MM97], pp.83), where the server itself informs the client about the occurrence of events.

To realize distributed callbacks and to enable the intended role change, the two following hints should be taken into consideration:

- The client application must provide a CORBA object, i.e., an IDL interface has to be specified and the corresponding servant has to be implemented for the client, so that the client as well can be invoked via the CORBA infrastructure and is enabled to receive and process the server's callback.
- The server object from which the client expects to be called back must offer an operation for registering the object reference of the client object so that the receiver of the callback can be communicated to the server. This operation must be defined in the server's IDL interface and has to be implemented suitably in the servant.

In the following, we describe a simple example that demonstrates the employment of a callback. It is based on our initial Counter example, which is unsatisfactory because the value displayed in the client application would temporarily be outdated when several clients are active. The command window could, for example, look like

```
Counter value: 3
Action (+/-/e)? +
Counter value: 6
Action (+/-/e)?
```

because during the time the client application waited for the user's input, executed the inc() operation, and accessed the new value, the actions of other clients finally yielded a value of six. We now implement a client immediately informed by a callback whenever an operation changes the `Counter` object's value. The callback then displays the current value on the client's command line.

11.1   Defining IDL Interfaces

As usual, we begin with the IDL definitions. We reuse the existing `Counter` interface from Chapter 7 and first add two operations `add()` and `remove()`, which a client can invoke to be registered with the server for receiving callbacks. Both operations have to be invoked with an argument referencing a `CounterClient`, which stands for the client to be called back. This implies that we also have to define an interface for the client application, the `CounterClient` interface, to guarantee it also implements a CORBA object. The operation invoked during a callback of the server object is the operation `update()`; the current `Counter` value is passed to it when invoked.

We combine both IDL interfaces in the module `CBCount` as follows:

```
// CBCounter.idl

module CBCount
{
  interface CounterClient
  {
    void update(in long value);
  };
  interface Counter
  {
    readonly attribute long value;
    void inc();
    void dec();
    void add(in CounterClient cc);
    void remove(in CounterClient cc);
  };
};
```

If one adheres to the file structure suggested for server host (Figure 11) and client host (Figure 14), one saves that module definition in a file `CBCounter.idl` in the directory `\Examples\Callback`.

11.2   Implementing the `Counter` Servant

We begin with server-side development, execute the appropriate batch file to set the environment variables, and translate module CBCount as usual by invoking the IDL compiler in the `Server` subdirectory on the server host. To implement the `Counter` interface, we employ the inheritance approach and, possibly after inspecting the operations interface `CounterOperations.java`, provide the following implementation:

```java
// CounterImpl.java

package CBCount;

import java.util.*;

public class CounterImpl extends CounterPOA {
  private int count;
  private List<CounterClient> clients =
    new ArrayList<CounterClient>();
  public CounterImpl() {
    count = 0;
  }
  public void inc() {
    count++;
    _notify();
  }
  public void dec() {
    count--;
    _notify();
  }
  public int value() {
    return count;
  }
  public synchronized void add(CounterClient cc) {
    clients.add(cc);
  }
  public synchronized void remove(CounterClient cc) {
    clients.remove(cc);
  }
  private synchronized void _notify() {
    for (CounterClient cc: clients) {
      if (cc != null)
        try {
          cc.update(count);
        } catch (Exception ign) { }
    }
  }
}
```

There are some notable differences when comparing this implementation with our first, simple version of the class CounterImpl discussed in Section 7.5. A new private instance variable clients of type List<CounterClient> is added to manage the references to those client objects interested in callbacks and register with the server by means of the add() method. Analogously, remove() is the method for removing CounterClients from the callback list.

add(), remove(), and _notify() have to be specified synchronized so that the attempt of several client threads to access and change the clients list at the same time is serialized and the list remains in a consistent state. Recall that a synchronized Java method can only be executed by one thread at a certain time and all other synchronized instance methods of the same object (in our case the CounterImpl object, the servant) are blocked until execution is completed. For details on Java Threads and synchronization, we refer our readers to the relevant literature.

Finally, we have to deal with method _notify(). It is only used in the bodies of the CounterImpl methods inc() and dec() and therefore has no counterpart in the Counter interface (for the necessity of the leading underscore see Section 5.2). It is this method's task to invoke the callback on all CounterClient objects registered. To do that, for each object in the clients list, method update() is invoked.

Store the file CounterImpl.java in the package directory CBCount on the server host, i.e., in directory \Examples\Callback*YourORB*\Server\CBCount, where *Your-ORB* stands for JacORB, JDK, or OpenORB.

11.3   Implementing the CBCount Server

The implementation of the server application that instantiates a CounterImpl object contains nothing new. Object creation takes place as usual; the stringified object reference is written to a file that must be copied to the clients so they can find and access the remote server (see Section 8.2). The file Server.java is stored and compiled in the Server directory on the server host.

```
// Server.java

import CBCount.*;
import java.io.*;
import java.util.Properties;
import org.omg.CORBA.*;
import org.omg.PortableServer.*;
import static java.lang.System.*;

public class Server {
  private ORB orb;
  private POA rootPOA;
  private void initializeORB(String[] args) {
    ... as above in Section 8.2
  }
  private void putRef(org.omg.CORBA.Object obj,
      String refFile) {
    ... as above in Section 8.2
  }
  public Server(String[] args, String refFile) {
    try {
      initializeORB(args);
      CounterImpl c_impl = new CounterImpl();
      Counter c = c_impl._this(orb);
      putRef(c, refFile);
      rootPOA.the_POAManager().activate();
      orb.run();
    } catch(Exception ex) {
      out.println("Exception: "
        + ex.getMessage());
```

```
      exit(1);
    }
  }
  public static void main(String args[]) {
    String refFile = "CBCounter.ref";
    new Server(args, refFile);
  }
}
```

11.4 Implementing the `CounterClient` Servant

We now continue on the client side. As already mentioned, the client application also must instantiate a CORBA object on which the server can invoke the callbacks, in this example the update() operations. The needed servant is the CounterClient. Since this example only shall demonstrate the principles of a callback, we keep it rather simple and, again, implement an inheritance approach. After invoking the IDL compiler in the Client subdirectory on the client host, we see from the operations interface CounterClientOperations that a suitable method body for the callback method update() must be provided. As usual, we name the servant class CounterClientImpl, and we simply print the Counter value passed to the update() method:

```
// CounterClientImpl.java

package CBCount;

public class CounterClientImpl extends CounterClientPOA {
  public void update(int value) {
    System.out.println("Server information. "
      + "New Counter value: " + value);
  }
}
```

This file should be stored and compiled in the subdirectory Client\CBCount on the client host.

11.5 Implementing the Client Application

Finally, we implement the client application, which is now clearly more complex than in previous examples. It contains elements of our former pure client application discussed in Section 7.8 but also includes elements of a typical server application since a CORBA object must be created and prepared for incoming CORBA requests.

```
// Client.java

import CBCount.*;
import java.io.*;
import java.util.*;
import org.omg.CORBA.*;
```

```java
import org.omg.PortableServer.*;
import static java.lang.System.*;

public class Client {
  private ORB orb;
  private POA rootPOA;
  private void initializeORB(String[] args) {
    ... as above in Section 8.2
  }
  private org.omg.CORBA.Object getRef(String refFile) {
    ... as above in Section 8.3
  }
  private void businessLogic(final Counter c,
      final CounterClient cc) {
    new Thread(new Runnable() {
      public void run() {
        c.add(cc);
        int inp = -1;
        do {
          out.print("Counter value: " + c.value()
            + "\nAction (+/-/e)? ");
          out.flush();
          do {
            try {
              inp = in.read();
            } catch (IOException ioe) { }
          } while (inp != '+' && inp != '-'
            && inp != 'e');
          if (inp == '+')
            c.inc();
          else if (inp == '-')
            c.dec();
        } while (inp != 'e');
        c.remove(cc);
        exit(0);
      }
    }).start();
  }
  public Client(String[] args, String refFile) {
    try {
      initializeORB(args);
      org.omg.CORBA.Object obj = getRef(refFile);
      Counter c = CounterHelper.narrow(obj);
      CounterClientImpl cc_impl =
        new CounterClientImpl();
      CounterClient cc = cc_impl._this(orb);
      rootPOA.the_POAManager().activate();
      businessLogic(c, cc);
      orb.run();
    } catch (BAD_PARAM ex) {
      out.println("Narrowing failed");
      exit(3);
    } catch (Exception ex) {
      out.println("Exception: "
        + ex.getMessage());
```

```
      exit(1);
    }
  }
  public static void main(String[] args) {
    String refFile = "CBCounter.ref";
    new Client(args, refFile);
  }
}
```

Like in many of our above examples, in method main(), only the name of the file needed for reading the server object's ID is established and then a Client object is created.

In the Client's constructor, we, as usual, initialize the ORB. Differing from our previous client applications, now a reference to the root POA must be obtained since the application has to instantiate a CORBA object. Therefore, we copy the initialize() body from Section 8.2 and not from Section 8.3 as for the clients before. Next, as usual, we read the reference to the Counter with the help of method getRef(). This reference is cast to the correct type (Counter). The three following statements make it clear that the application occasionally assumes the server role: a CounterClient instance is constructed, associated with the ORB containing the root POA, and activated implicitly. Then, the POA manager is activated.

The two last statements in the constructor body also need to be discussed in some detail. We have to bear in mind that the client application must carry out two tasks not easily compatible with each other. On the one hand, in a method we called businessLogic(), the usual client functionality must be provided. Here, this is about repeatedly accepting user input and invoking the requested inc() or dec() method on the remote Counter object residing on the server host. On the other hand, the application must be enabled to adopt the server role and accept callbacks. This is intended by the call orb.run(), which, however, as we know from Section 6.2.4, blocks the application's main thread. We, therefore, start a new thread in the method businessLogic(), which is invoked earlier so that the client's first task, the "business logic", runs independently of its second task, the update functionality controlled by the Counter object. To do this efficiently, we create a Thread object, which controls an anonymous Runnable object and which is started immediately after its construction. The statements to be executed by the new thread go into the body of the Runnable's run() method; again, we refer the readers to the existing literature for the usage of this standard Java technique.

The first step in the implementation of run() is registering the CounterClient instance cc with the Counter object c with the help of the add() method. The last step is to remove the client when a user terminates the input loop by entering an 'e'. The remainder of the code corresponds to the input loop known from Section 7.8. With the new callback version of the Counter, the command window for the above example could look like this:

```
Counter value: 3
Action (+/-/e)? Server information. New Counter value: 4
Server information. New Counter value: 5
Server information. New Counter value: 4
Server information. New Counter value: 5
```

```
+
Server information. New Counter value: 6
Counter value: 6
Action (+/-/e)?
```

Now, all operations changing the server's `Counter` value are displayed in each client's command window.

11.6   Further Usages of the Callback Technique

The above-discussed example for an application using distributed callbacks is, strictly speaking, an implementation of a widely used, more specific design pattern known under the names "Observer" [GHJV95], "Subject-Observer", "Observer-Observable", or "Publish-Subscribe". The common goal of these patterns is to define a one-to-many dependency between objects so that, when one object changes state, all its dependents are notified and updated automatically.

The "Distributed Callback" design pattern can also be very useful in other contexts. For example, Mowbray and Malveau [MM97] describe its usage in order to maximize parallelism in distributed applications. The idea is to reduce the length of time a client spends waiting for an operation to be completed by converting a synchronous operation to an asynchronous operation. The server invokes a callback routine on the client when the operation is completed. This approach is especially favorable when object operations take a long time and the client application cannot afford to suspend processing waiting for results. To enable asynchronous communication, in that case, the respective operations in the server object's IDL interface have to be specified `oneway`. Attention should, again, be paid to the syntactical restrictions and to our practical experiences with `oneway` operations and their support through currently existing ORB products, as previously mentioned in Section 4.5.2.

11.7   Exercise

1. Re-implement the dump server example of Chapter 7, Exercise 1.

    a) The server now shall also write the input of a client together with the name of that client to the command window of any client currently registered with the server. When registering, clients have to pass their name to the server. This name can be provided upon startup of the client application, e.g., via `args[0]`. Reuse as much as possible of the code from the callback example discussed in Chapter 10.

    b) Now, provide a GUI for the clients (see Figure 19). This might be a `JTextArea`, a `JTable`, etc., together with a `JTextField` as demonstrated in the figure below. In order to enable the implementation of the client's operations interface to "dump" to the client-side GUI, this implementation class needs an instance variable referencing the component to be updated. To prevent deadlocking, one might want to wrap the dump invocation triggered by the server application into a piece of code like this:

```
SwingUtilities.invokeLater(new Runnable() {
  public void run() {
    ... dump invocation
  }
});
```

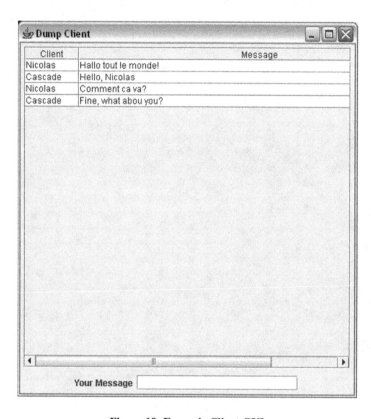

Figure 19: Example Client GUI

12 Utilizing Value Types

For most application scenarios in distributed, CORBA-based systems, the best solution is the call-by-reference semantics employed to pass normal CORBA objects of a type defined through an IDL interface during an operation invocation. However, there are a number of situations where it might be favorable to pass an instance by value and to provide a local implementation on the side of the receiver. When only working with references to remote implementations, this implies, e.g., that any invocation of a CORBA object is potentially routed via the network, thus causing significant overhead for marshaling, unmarshaling, etc. This fact negatively influences the overall performance of the system. In the case of local invocations, this overhead is not generated so that they can altogether be executed faster.

In Section 4.6, we already briefly discussed the concept of value types, introduced in CORBA version 2.3. In principle, objects of such a type are as powerful as normal IDL interface types. However, while regular CORBA objects, i,e., objects implementing an interface type, are only passed by reference during an operation invocation, value type objects are passed by value; their state is serialized, transmitted to the receiver, deserialized, and copied into a local value type instance. On the side of the receiver, we then have available a complete instance with a local implementation able to accept and execute local operation invocations. To recall the various details of the different kinds of value types, we refer readers to Section 4.6.

In this chapter, we demonstrate the practical usage of value types on the basis of a simplified example. Here, we fall back on the principle of distributed callbacks, which we explained in Chapter 11. Our example presents an implementation of the "Publish-Subscribe" design pattern [BMRS96], discussed previously in its "Observer" pattern variation in the `Counter` example in Chapter 11. Now, the distributed application consists of a `Publisher` object where any number of `Subscriber` objects can register in order to be provided with information repeatedly distributed by the `Publisher`. The `Publisher` object could reside on a server host in the network; whereas, the `Subscriber` objects are typically generated on client hosts.

In its simplest form, the `Publisher` administers a list of its registered `Subscriber`s and contacts and informs these objects whenever a new event needing to be published occurs. For a more realistic scenario, assume that individual `Subscriber` objects are only interested in specific types of events and should not necessarily be informed of all the events the `Publisher` object could publish. Then, whenever the `Publisher`, on the server side, traverses its list and informs all registered `Subscriber` objects on the client hosts, these have to decide locally whether they are going to process the corresponding event or not. Such a design would unnecessarily entail an increase in network load since many publication messages would be sent via the network to `Subscriber` objects that are not at all interested in these publications.

One approach to improve this situation would be to introduce individually adapted `Filter` objects that are created and initialized by the `Subscriber` objects and are responsible for their respective Subscriber on a one-to-one basis. If those Filter objects reside on the server host and are accessible to the Publisher, then, with their help, unneeded messages could be filtered out directly at their point of origin and would not have to be communicated via the network.

During the design of such Filter objects, the problem of regular CORBA objects, which can only be passed by reference becomes apparent. If the Filter objects are implemented as CORBA objects of an interface type individually generated by the different Subscriber objects residing on their client hosts, then the Filters can only be sent to the Publisher object in the form of references; recall that the Publisher is residing on the server host. This design, therefore, has the severe disadvantage that the Filters remain on the client hosts and any operation invocation of Publisher initiating the "filtering" process would, again, be routed via the network so that the intended performance gain would not be realized.

Thus, the best solution in this application scenario would be to use value types to define the Filter instances. It is then guaranteed that a local implementation exists and filtering can effectively take place locally on the server host although the original Filter objects are created on their respective client hosts. Each Subscriber object can generate a suitable Filter value type instance, initialize it with the needed filtering logic, and send it to the Publisher object during registration. Since value types are passed by value, filtering of the publication events can now be performed on the side of the Publisher, the event generator. If a Subscriber wants to change its filtering rules, it simply has to create a new value type instance and send it to the Publisher. No changes in the code of the Publisher's implementation are necessary in that case.

12.1　Defining IDL Module PublishSubscribe

We begin, as usual, with the IDL definitions for the new example:

```
// Filtering.idl

module PublishSubscribe
{
  interface Subscriber
  {
    void notify(in unsigned long value);
  };

  valuetype Filter
  {
    private Subscriber sub;
    private unsigned long min;
    private unsigned long max;
    factory init(in Subscriber s,
      in unsigned long min,
      in unsigned long max);
    void notify(in unsigned long value);
  };
```

```
interface Publisher
{
    void add(in Filter f);
  };
};
```

The type definitions for this example are grouped into the module PublishSubscribe. Interface Subscriber, which specifies the event receiver's type, defines a single operation notify(). This operation is invoked by the Publisher object to communicate a publication event, which, in our example, simply consists of a new unsigned long value. The Publisher interface defines the type of the event generator. It specifies an operation add() that is invoked to register a new Filter instance, which is able to perform the filtering for its corresponding Subscriber object in the case of a publication event. If the filtering criterion is not met, the event is not filtered out and the Subscriber is notified by an invocation of operation notify().

Filter is a regular value type. It defines three private state members, sub, min, and max as well as an operation notify() and an initializer init(). In sub, a reference to the Filter's Subscriber object is stored. The values min and max are the upper and the lower bounds of an interval that defines the filtering rule: the Subscriber using that Filter is only interested in values falling within the interval, including its bounds. We use this rule in order to keep the example simple and concentrate on the value type specifics. The Filter's operation notify() is invoked by the Publisher and is provided with the publication event, which, in our case, consist of an unsigned long value. Should that event pass the filtering process, i.e., the value lies in the interval [min, max], the operation notify() is invoked on the Subscriber object sub. The factory operation init() assumes the role of a constructor for instances of the Filter value type, as it was described in Section 4.6.

One should now generate the directory structures analogous to those described in Figure 11 (for the server host) and Figure 14 (for the client hosts) and store the file Filtering.idl on each host in directory \Examples\Values.

12.2 Implementing Value Type Filter

We now begin with the implementation of the distributed application and, as usual, start on the server host. After setting the environment variables, we proceed analogous to the previous examples, change the current directory to \Examples\Values\YourORB\Server, and invoke the IDL compiler to translate the definitions in Filtering.idl.

According to the mapping rules for modules, the IDL compiler creates a new Java package, PublishSubscribe, and writes the compiled interfaces and classes to a subdirectory of the Server directory. By now, one should be familiar with the content of the generated interfaces, Publisher and Subscriber.

The result for the value type Filter is new and deserves a closer look. In Section 5.15.1, one saw that a regular value type like Filter is mapped to an abstract Java class with the same name that implements the org.omg.CORBA.portable.StreamableValue interface. The class declaration is given below; note how the state members sub, min, and max are mapped to instance variables and where they appear in the method declarations.

```
// Filter.java

package PublishSubscribe;

public abstract class Filter implements
    org.omg.CORBA.portable.StreamableValue {
  protected PublishSubscribe.Subscriber sub = null;
  protected int min = (int)0;
  protected int max = (int)0;
  private static String[] _truncatable_ids = {
    PublishSubscribe.FilterHelper.id()
  };
  public String[] _truncatable_ids() {
    return _truncatable_ids;
  }
  public abstract void _notify(int value);
  public void _read(org.omg.CORBA.portable.
      InputStream istream) {
    this.sub = PublishSubscribe.
      SubscriberHelper.read(istream);
    this.min = istream.read_ulong();
    this.max = istream.read_ulong();
  }
  public void _write(org.omg.CORBA.portable.OutputStream
      ostream) {
    PublishSubscribe.SubscriberHelper.write(ostream,
      this.sub);
    ostream.write_ulong(this.min);
    ostream.write_ulong(this.max);
  }
  public org.omg.CORBA.TypeCode _type() {
    return PublishSubscribe.FilterHelper.type();
  }
}
```

The interface StreamableValue is itself a subinterface of org.omg.CORBA.portable.ValueBase that declares the method _truncatable_ids(). The Filter class provides an implementation of that method. The intention is to return a String array with the repository IDs of all supertypes that can be narrowed to the respective value type. Remember that a repository ID is the unique identifier string associated with a named IDL type and thus represents a unique type identifier. If one inspects the FilterHelper, one finds that, in our example, the array contains only one element: "IDL:PublishSubscribe/Filter:1.0". Since the internally needed methods _read(), _write(), and _type() are also generated, the only method that remains to be implemented is _notify(), the outcome of translating the IDL operation notify().

In the Filter's IDL definition, an initializer operation init() is specified. As a consequence, a Java interface FilterValueFactory is created. This value factory interface declares one single method, init(), that constructs and returns a Filter instance. The FilterValueFactory is a subinterface of org.omg.CORBA.portable.Value-

Factory, which declares one method, read_value(), that is invoked by the ORB run-time when unmarshaling a Filter value.

In addition, the IDL compiler generates the usual helper and holder classes, FilterHelper and FilterHolder. One difference to the schema used up until now is that, for each factory operation, a static method with the same name, a corresponding parameter list, and an additional first parameter of type org.omg.CORBA.ORB is declared. When this method is invoked, the ORB first looks up a value type factory and then delegates instance construction to it.

In summary, the following tasks to be carried out still remain:

- write a non-abstract subclass of class Filter; as usual, we name that class FilterImpl and
- implement the FilterValueFactory interface in the form of a class FilterValueFactoryImpl or test whether the IDL compiler-generated standard implementation FilterDefaultFactory is sufficient for the intended application.

12.2.1 Implementing the FilterImpl Class

The implementation of class FilterImpl is rather straightforward:

```
// FilterImpl.java

package PublishSubscribe;

public class FilterImpl extends Filter {
  public FilterImpl() { }
  public FilterImpl(Subscriber sub, int min, int max) {
    this.sub = sub;
    this.min = min;
    this.max = max;
  }
  public void _notify(int value) {
    if (min <= value && value <= max)
      sub._notify(value);
  }
}
```

The interesting part is the body of method _notify(). Here, the concrete filtering mechanism is implemented. We have to test whether the publication event should be passed to the Subscriber or not. In our example, this task is reduced to comparing the value to the bounds min and max. If the event value lies within the bounds, the event is communicated to the Subscriber by invoking _notify() on sub. Otherwise, no publishing activity is necessary, no remote method is invoked, and the event is filtered out. The FilterImpl's default constructor must be declared so that the standard implementation FilterDefaultFactory of the Filter value factory can also be used (see the next section).

At the moment, we develop the server part of the application. It should be noted that also the Subscriber objects on the client hosts need the FilterImpl class since they have to be able to create `Filter` instances according to their filtering strategy. Therefore, we can now copy the file `FilterImpl.java` to the `PublishSubscribe` subdirectory of the `Client` directory on the client hosts. Since value type instances are passed by value, the server application on the server host must also provide a local implementation of that type. Otherwise, the serialized state values transmitted via the network could not be reconstructed into concrete instances of the value type. The value type factories, discussed in the next section, are employed specifically for that purpose. We also store the `FilterImpl.java` file in the `Server/PublishSubscribe` subdirectory on the server host.

12.2.2   Using Class `FilterDefaultFactory`

As mentioned above, a special mechanism is employed to reconstruct a value type instance passed to the receiver object in a CORBA system. The concept is based on a value factory. The ORB on the receiver side must create a new, local instance of the value type and initialize it with the transmitted state values. To that aim, it locates a suitable factory object and invokes operation `read_value()` on it. Therefore, all Java-based value factories have to implement the interface `org.omg.CORBA.portable.ValueFactory`, which results from the mapping of IDL interface `CORBA::ValueFactory`, introduced in CORBA 2.3.

```
package org.omg.CORBA.portable;

public interface ValueFactory {
  java.io.Serializable read_value(
    org.omg.CORBA_2_3.portable.InputStream is);
};
```

The implementation of the `ValueFactory` is achieved indirectly by implementing the subinterface `FilterValueFactory`, generated by the IDL compiler; we briefly discussed both interfaces above at the beginning of Section 12.2.

There are two ways for an ORB to obtain a value type's value factory. Either a standard implementation is available or a specific factory implementation was explicitly registered for the value type's repository ID. The standard implementation an IDL compiler generates for the `Filter` value type is the class `FilterDefaultFactory`, which has the following declaration:

```
// FilterDefaultFactory.java

package PublishSubscribe;

public class FilterDefaultFactory implements
    FilterValueFactory {
  public Filter init(PublishSubscribe.Subscriber s,
      int min, int max) {
    return new FilterImpl(s, min, max);
  }
  public java.io.Serializable read_value(
      org.omg.CORBA_2_3.portable.InputStream is) {
    return is.read_value(new FilterImpl());
  }
}
```

It can be seen how the init() method is implemented and how it creates and initializes a new FilterImpl instance and returns it with a reference of type Filter. It can also be seen that it is expected that we follow the naming conventions and use the name Filter-Impl for the Filter's implementation class. Finally, it can be seen why a default constructor had to be declared for the FilterImpl class; it is invoked in method read_value(). For our purposes, this standard implementation is perfectly sufficient. It is easy to use and has the advantage that no explicit registration is necessary. A precondition for its employment is, however, that the repository not be modified by means of #pragma prefix directives or typeprefix statements since the ORB determines the name of the default factory simply through trimming the repository ID string and appending De-faultFactory. In case of repository modifications or when a specific factory implementation is required, the corresponding class has to be registered with the ORB.

Since CORBA version 2.3, the Java mapping of the ORB interface provides the methods register_value_factory(), unregister_value_factory(), and lookup_value_factory() for the purpose of registering, unregistering, or finding a factory implementation. Note the package declaration in the following code snippet. Note also, that the mapping declares the class abstract and provides only dummy implementations that ORB vendors shall have to complete.

```
package org.omg.CORBA_2_3;

public abstract class ORB extends org.omg.CORBA.ORB {
   public org.omg.CORBA.portable.ValueFactory
     register_value_factory(String id,
       org.omg.CORBA.portable.ValueFactory factory) {
     throw new org.omg.CORBA.NO_IMPLEMENT();
   }
   public void unregister_value_factory(String id) {
     throw new org.omg.CORBA.NO_IMPLEMENT();
   }
   public org.omg.CORBA.portable.ValueFactory
       lookup_value_factory(String id) {
     throw new org.omg.CORBA.NO_IMPLEMENT();
   }
   ...
}
```

We discuss the usage of method register_value_factory() below when implementing the server application.

Should the default implementation FilterDefaultFactory not be suitable for the requirements of an application, it is possible to develop one's own factory implementation, for example, in the form of a class FilterValueFactoryImpl. In order to enable the ORB to use this specific factory, it must be explicitly registered with an invocation of the method register_value_factory().

The easiest way to do develop one's own factory is to declare the class FilterValue-FactoryImpl as a subclass of the FilterDefaultFactory, e.g.:

```
// FilterValueFactoryImpl.java

package PublishSubscribe;

public class FilterValueFactoryImpl extends
    FilterDefaultFactory {
  public Filter init(Subscriber sub, int min, int max) {
    ...perform required calculations
        and return suitable new FilterImpl object
  }
}
```

If intending to use one's own implementation, the file FilterValueFactory-
Impl.java should be stored in the PublishSubscribe subdirectory of the Server
directory on the server host. In our simple example, there is no need to extend the default
implementation written by the IDL compiler to that directory.

12.3   Implementing Class PublisherImpl

Apart from the above-mentioned Java class FilterImpl and, possibly, the specific FilterValueFactoryImpl, the following classes have to be implemented to install our distributed application:

- PublisherImpl.java,
- PublisherApp.java,
- SubscriberImpl.java, and
- SubscriberApp.java.

At the moment, we remain on the server host and, therefore, begin with the first two classes.
The purpose of the PublisherImpl class is to implement the IDL interface Publisher.
As always, the operations that need to be defined and, especially, their signatures can be loo-
ked up in the operations interface PublisherOperations.

```
// PublisherImpl.java

package PublishSubscribe;

import java.util.*;

public class PublisherImpl extends PublisherPOA {
  private List<Filter> filters = new ArrayList<Filter>();
  public synchronized void add(Filter f) {
    filters.add(f);
  }
  public List<Filter> getFilters() {
    return filters;
  }
}
```

In this example, we use the inheritance approach. The only method that must be implemented is the method add(), which has a corresponding counterpart on the IDL level. Its purpose is to register Filters with the Publisher. We declare an instance variable filters of type List<Filter>, initialize it with an ArrayList object, and simply insert the Filter instance into the list whenever add() is called. Access to the list must be synchronized so that concurrent insertions do not result in unexpected behavior. Since a servant class is not restricted to implementing only the IDL-specified operations, it is convenient to declare an additional method, getFilters(), which can be invoked locally and returns the list of currently registered Filters.

The servant, PublisherImpl.java, should also be stored in the Server\Publish-Subscribe subdirectory on the server host.

12.4   Implementing the Server Application

The last step to be carried out on the server side concerns the server application, implemented through a class PublisherApp:

```
// PublisherApp.java

import PublishSubscribe.*;
import java.io.*;
import java.util.*;
import org.omg.CORBA.*;
import org.omg.PortableServer.*;
import static java.lang.System.*;

public class PublisherApp {
  private ORB orb;
  private POA rootPOA;
  private void initializeORB(String[] args) {
    ... as above in Section 8.2
  }
  private void putRef(org.omg.CORBA.Object obj,
      String refFile) {
    ... as above in Section 8.2
  }
  private void businessLogic(final PublisherImpl p_impl) {
    new Thread(new Runnable() {
      public void run() {
        for (;;) {
          int message = (int)(1000*Math.random());
          out.println("Sending message: " + message);
          for (Filter f: p_impl.getFilters()) {
            if (f != null)
              try {
                f._notify(message);
              } catch (Exception ex) { }
          }
          try {
            Thread.sleep(1000);
          } catch (InterruptedException ign) { }
```

```
        }
      }
    }).start();
  }
  public PublisherApp(String[] args, String refFile) {
    try {
      initializeORB(args);
      PublisherImpl p_impl = new PublisherImpl();
      Publisher p = p_impl._this(orb);
      putRef(p, refFile);
      rootPOA.the_POAManager().activate();
      businessLogic(p_impl);
      orb.run();
    } catch (Exception ex) {
      out.println("Exception: " + ex.getMessage());
      exit(1);
    }
  }
  public static void main(String[] args) {
    String refFile = "Publisher.ref";
    new PublisherApp(args, refFile);
  }
}
```

The file PublisherApp.java is stored in the Server directory on the server host. The methods initializeORB() and putRef() can be reused entirely from our previous examples. Also, the constructor and the main() method should, by now, look familiar: the ORB is initialized, a servant object is created and activated, and its IOR is written in string form to a file. Then, method businessLogic() is called and, through orb.run(), the control flow is passed to the ORB so that it can wait for clients requesting registration of new Filter instances.

The realization of the server's businessLogic() bears some resemblance to the server application in the callback example of Chapter 11. In order to enable the Publisher to publish new values from time to time, we start a new thread. The run() method is implemented such that, repeatedly (every second; see the Thread.sleep(1000) statement), a new publication event is generated. In our simple example, this is just a random int value between 0 (inclusive) and 1,000 (exclusive). Afterwards, this value is passed to all Filters in the list filters through a call of method _notify(). The way a Filter handles such a call was already discussed above in Section 12.2.

In this form, our implementation relies on the FilterDefaultFactory. This approach has the advantage that it is not necessary to write one's own value factory and no explicit registration with the ORB is needed. Should one want to use a specific value factory that one provides in a class FilterValueFactoryImpl, then the two following statements have to be included directly before the putRef(p, refFile) statement in the Publisher-App constructor:

```
FilterValueFactoryImpl factory =
  new FilterValueFactoryImpl();
((org.omg.CORBA_2_3.ORB)orb).register_value_factory(
  FilterHelper.id(), factory);
```

Here, a new value factory object is created and then the method `register_value_fac-tory()` is called for its registration. This method is only available since CORBA version 2.3, hence, the cast of the variable `orb`. The first argument of the registration method is the repository ID of the value type; the second is the factory instance to be registered.

The server application and the necessary components are now completed. In order to translate them, invoke the Java compiler from the directory `\Examples\Values\Your-ORB\Server` on the server host. After successful compilation, the server is ready to be started.

When using the default value factory, here the `FilterDefaultFactory`, note that the corresponding class is not automatically compiled since it is not explicitly used in the server application. Therefore, one has to compile it separately, e.g., by invoking `javac Pub-lishSubscribe\FilterDefaultFactory.java` in the `Server` directory. Otherwise, it is possible to run the server but as soon as a client tries to register a filter it crashes.

12.5 Implementing Class `SubscriberImpl`

Having discussed the implementation of the server-side details of the `Publisher` component, we concentrate on the characteristic features of the client-side `Subscriber` part of the distributed CORBA application in the following. As a first step, as always, one should compile the IDL definitions in file `Filtering.idl`. Next, we begin defining the client application by providing an implementation of the `Subscriber` interface. The corresponding class, `SubscriberImpl`, might be declared as follows:

```
// SubscriberImpl.java

package PublishSubscribe;

public class SubscriberImpl extends SubscriberPOA {
   public void _notify(int value) {
      System.out.println("Received message: " + value);
   }
}
```

Again, we implement the inheritance approach and extend the `SubscriberPOA` class. Inspection of the `SubscriberOperations` interface shows that only the Java counterpart `_notify()` of the IDL operation `notify()` has to be declared. In this simple example, we only print the published value to the console window.

12.6 Implementing the Client Application

To complete the Publish/Subscribe application, at this point, only the `SubscriberApp` class has to be declared; it takes on the role of the client application. In analogy to the callback example, the notion client is not absolutely correct since `SubscriberApp` is not a "pure" client application. A CORBA object of type `Subscriber` is created on the client host. This object is informed of the publication events that pass the filter and, thus, also provides server functionality.

Reusing as much as possible from the code of previous clients, the SubscriberApp class could be declared in this way:

```java
// SubscriberApp.java

import PublishSubscribe.*;
import java.io.*;
import java.util.*;
import org.omg.CORBA.*;
import org.omg.PortableServer.*;
import static java.lang.Math.*;
import static java.lang.System.*;

public class SubscriberApp {
  private ORB orb;
  private POA rootPOA;
  private void initializeORB(String[] args) {
    ... as above in Section 8.2
  }
  private org.omg.CORBA.Object getRef(String refFile) {
    ... as above in Section 8.3
  }
  public SubscriberApp(String[] args, String refFile) {
    try {
      int lo = Integer.valueOf(args[0]),
        hi = Integer.valueOf(args[1]);
      int min = min(max(lo, 0), min(hi, 1000)),
        max = max(max(lo, 0), min(hi, 1000));
      initializeORB(args);
      SubscriberImpl s_impl = new SubscriberImpl();
      Subscriber s = s_impl._this(orb);
      FilterImpl f_impl = new FilterImpl(s, min, max);
      org.omg.CORBA.Object obj = getRef(refFile);
      Publisher p = PublisherHelper.narrow(obj);
      p.add(f_impl);
      out.println("Activating Subscriber filtering with "
        + min + " and " + max);
      rootPOA.the_POAManager().activate();
      orb.run();
    } catch (BAD_PARAM ex) {
      out.println("Narrowing failed");
      exit(3);
    } catch (Exception ex) {
      out.println("Exception: " + ex);
      exit(1);
    }
  }
  public static void main(String[] args) {
    if (args.length < 2) {
      out.println("Start with"
        + "\n\tjava/jrun SubscriberApp <min> <max>,"
        + " 0 <= min < max <= 1000");
```

```
   return;
 }
 String refFile = "Publisher.ref";
 new SubscriberApp(args, refFile);
}
}
```

This file should be stored in the directory \Examples\Values*YourORB*\Client on the client hosts.

Most of the above statements need no further discussion since we used them in a similar form in previous examples. Besides the classes and interfaces generated by the IDL compiler, the application needs the implementations of the FilterImpl and the SubscriberImpl. These have to be present in each client's PublishSubscribe subdirectory. However, the implementations of the Publisher interface (PublisherImpl) and the Filter value factory (FilterDefaultFactory or FilterValueFactoryImpl) are not needed. While the former is immediately clear, the latter is due to the fact that, on the client host, the initial Filter objects are created with the help of the FilterImpl class. Only the server application needs to be able to recreate serialized Filter instances sent to it; and, therefore, it requires a factory implementation.

The SubscriberApp is started with two integer command-line arguments, min and max, which define the filtering criteria for the new client object. The rest of the class declaration deserves no further explanations.

Compilation of the client application on the client hosts occurs analogous to the server application. After setting the required environment variables, the Java compiler for the respective ORB is invoked in the Client directory.

Finally, the application can be started in the usual sequence of steps:

- start the server application;
- copy the file "Publisher.ref", which contains the reference to the Publisher object, to the client hosts and store it in the directory where the client application is invoked; and
- start the client application, providing the min and des max values.

When running the application, one notes that no method for appropriate termination of the clients is provided and that simply stopping them with Control-C causes the Publisher's list of registered filters to become obsolete (see Exercise 4 below).

12.7   Exercises

1. How might a delegation-based variation of the Publisher look? What are the advantages or disadvantages?
2. Design a value type-based variant of the TimeServer example introduced in Chapter 9. Which advantages and disadvantages with respect to the earlier version can be recognized?

3. What would be the consequences of removing the following `try` statement from the class `PublisherApp` and calling `_notify()` directly?

```
try {
  f._notify(message);
}
catch(Exception e) { }
```

4. Provide the `SubscriberApp` with a third command-line argument that specifies the duration (in seconds) a subscriber is registered with the publisher. After this time, remove the subscriber's filter from the publisher's list. Note that one cannot simply implement a remote `remove(Filter f)` call for the filter inserted into the list because the argument to `remove()` is only passed by value and is not found in the list. Therefore implement the following IDL definition for the `Publisher`:

```
interface Publisher
{
  long add(in Filter f);
  void remove(in long index);
};
```

In the `PublisherImpl`'s `add()` method, return the index where the filter was inserted into the list, pass this index when `remove()` is called, and replace the corresponding entry in the `filters` list by `null`. Test your implementation with more than one client.

5. The IDL definitions of the `Subscriber` and the `Filter` contain an operation `notify()`. An IDL designer suggests to define the `Filter` value type such that it supports the `Subscriber` interface and also to change the signature of the `Publisher`'s `add()` operation to `add(in Subscriber s)`. Discuss advantages and disadvantages of that design.

13 Utilizing Interfaces of the DynamicAny Module

From Section 5.16, we are already familiar with the generic container type `any` and its mapping to Java with the class `org.omg.CORBA.Any`. If we use an `any` as parameter or return type in IDL operations, we gain maximum flexibility when passing arguments or receiving result values since the actual types of the arguments or the result can be dynamically determined at run-time. An `any` instance contains not only a value but also type information for that value in the form of a `TypeCode` (see Section 6.5); therefore, it is completely self-describing and type safe. Utilizing `any`s, however, generates additional marshaling overhead so they should only be employed when a significant advantage is achieved. Examples could be operations with parameters needing to process a large number of different types or of complex, recursively defined data structures. In order to develop generic programs, such as CORBA *bridges* or *messaging services*, where, at compile-time, it is unknown which data types need to be passed to or from certain operations at run-time, the flexibility offered by the `any` type might prove to be very helpful.

The mapping of the IDL type `any` to the Java class `org.omg.CORBA.Any` has one serious disadvantage. In order to insert the value of a non-basic type into an `Any` object or to extract it from such an object, it is mandatory to fall back on the compiler-generated stub code for that user-defined type. There are situations where very generic programs shall be developed so that it is not possible to provide the compiled stubs for all the potentially useful data types. In these situations, the interfaces of the `DynamicAny` module provide a flexible means for dynamic type manipulation. Before we discuss this module in detail, we first recapitulate the basic elements of dealing with `Any`s and `TypeCode`s.

13.1 Usage of Anys and TypeCodes

Recall that in Section 5.16 we briefly described the two ways for accessing an `Any` object in Java: insertion or extraction of a value. Depending on whether the value is of a pre-defined type or a user-defined type, we directly invoke the methods of class `Any` (see Table 10) or the methods of the corresponding helper class (see Section 5.5).

In the following, we demonstrate both type categories with the aid of a first example. There, a simple, distributed application is developed where the client application inserts the `string` value `"12:00:00"` and, consecutively, the same time 12:00:00, represented by the `Time` structure we have repeatedly used above, into an `Any` object. This object is then passed as an argument to a server object's method `display_any()`.

Examine the following IDL file `AnyServer.idl`, which should be stored on one's client and server hosts in directory `\Examples\Any` and compiled, as usual, from the respective `Client` and `Server` subdirectories.

```
// AnyServer.idl

module AnyTest
{
  struct Time
  {
    unsigned long hours;
    unsigned long minutes;
    unsigned long seconds;
  };
  interface AnyServer
  {
    void display_any(in any a);
  };
};
```

In module AnyTest, at first, the well-known structure Time is defined. Then, the interface AnyServer is specified; it defines the operation display_any(), which contains an in parameter of type any.

We now turn to the client application. Here, the string object and, afterwards, the Time object are inserted into an Any object. This object is then passed to the server's method display_any(), which is invoked twice. The structure of the client application AClient.java resembles the previous implementations. It should be stored and compiled as usual in directory \Examples\Any\YourORB\Client.

```
// AClient.java

import AnyTest.*;
import java.io.*;
import java.util.*;
import org.omg.CORBA.*;
import static java.lang.System.*;

public class AClient {
  private ORB orb;
  private void initializeORB(String[] args) {
    ... as above in Section 8.3
  }
  private org.omg.CORBA.Object getRef(String refFile) {
    ... as above in Section 8.3
  }
  public AClient(String[] args, String refFile) {
    try {
      initializeORB(args);
      org.omg.CORBA.Object obj = getRef(refFile);
      AnyServer as = AnyServerHelper.narrow(obj);
      Any any = orb.create_any();
      any.insert_string("12:00:00");
      as.display_any(any);
      Time t = new Time(12, 0, 0);
      TimeHelper.insert(any, t);
      as.display_any(any);
    } catch (BAD_PARAM ex) {
```

```
    out.println("Narrowing failed");
    exit(3);
  } catch (Exception ex) {
    out.println("Exception: " + ex.getMessage());
    exit(1);
  }
}
public static void main(String[] args) {
  String refFile = "AnyServer.ref";
  new AClient(args, refFile);
}
}
```

The standard approach of initializing the ORB and accessing the reference to the server object need not be explained anew. Interesting is the insertion of the two values of the IDL types string and Time into the newly constructed Any object. At first, we invoke the ORB's method create_any(), to obtain the Any object. Then, we call the Any method insert_string() and the TimeHelper method insert() to insert the string value and the Time value, respectively.

The task of the AnyServer servant and its method display_any() is to extract and display the value contained in the received Any object. Store the file AnyServer-Impl.java in the directory \Examples\Any\YourORB\Server\AnyTest on the server host:

```
// AnyServerImpl.java

package AnyTest;
import org.omg.CORBA.*;
import static java.lang.System.*;

public class AnyServerImpl extends AnyServerPOA {
  public void display_any(Any any) {
    if ((any.type()).kind() == TCKind.tk_string) {
      String s = any.extract_string();
      out.println("Server decomposed string value "
      + s + " from Any object!");
    }
    else if ((any.type()).equivalent(TimeHelper.type())) {
      Time t = TimeHelper.extract(any);
      out.println("Server decomposed Time value "
        + t.hours
        + ((t.minutes < 10)? ":0": ":") + t.minutes
        + ((t.seconds < 10)? ":0": ":") + t.seconds
        + " from Any object!");
    }
    else {
      out.println("Type in Any object unknown");
    }
  }
}
```

Note that to extract the value contained in the `Any` object any, we call the `Any` method `extract_string()` (for the `string`-value) and the `TimeHelper` method `extract()` (for the `Time` value).

The test that determines which type is actually contained in the `Any` object is carried out in two steps. First, we invoke the `Any` method `type()` and obtain the type code of the value stored in the object any. The result is of type `org.omg.CORBA.TypeCode` (see Section 6.5). This type code is then compared to the two types we expect. In the first case, we compare to the pre-defined CORBA type `string` and, to that end, invoke the `TypeCode` object's method `kind()`. The result is an enumerator of type `org.omg.CORBA.TCKind`, which can immediately be compared to the value in question, here `org.omg.CORBA.TCKind.tk_string`. The complete list of `TCKind` enumerators is displayed in Section 6.5.

In the second case of a user-defined type, we invoke the `TypeCode` object's method `equivalent()` and pass the type code to compare to as an argument. Since the type code of a user-defined type can be obtained by invoking the method `type()` of the corresponding helper class, the test expression in this case has the form

```
(any.type()).equivalent(TimeHelper.type())
```

To complete the server side of the application, we now only need to implement the usual pattern demonstrated in Section 8.2: create an `AnyServer` object, write the reference to a file, which is sent to the clients, etc. The server application could be named `AServer.java` and stored and compiled in directory `\Examples\Any\`*YourORB*`\Server` on one's server host. Once the complete application is running, the following output should be obtained on one's server console whenever a client is started:

```
Server decomposed string value 12:00:00 from Any object!
Server decomposed Time value 12:00:00 from Any object!
```

13.2   DynamicAny API

The example in the preceding section demonstrated that the standard usage of the Java equivalent of the IDL type any for user-defined data types is based on methods in the helper classes of these types. If, at compile-time, no knowledge concerning the respective IDL definitions is accessible, a way must be found to, nevertheless, compose any instances containing such values at run-time and to retrieve values from them. This situation might occur when generic applications such as debuggers, flexible user interfaces, messaging services, etc., are to be developed. Also in the context of employing functionality provided by the Dynamic Invocation Interface or the Dynamic Skeleton Interface, such problems might need to be solved.

The solution is offered by the `DynamicAny` API, which, in CORBA 2.3, is embedded in its own module `DynamicAny`. `DynamicAny`s were first introduced in version 2.2; at that time, however, they were part of the `CORBA` module. There are also some conceptual differences that make it necessary to adapt applications based on CORBA 2.2 should they rely on the `DynamicAny` functionality.

The DynamicAny module specifies eleven local IDL interfaces. Interface DynAny is the DynamicAny API's central interface. DynAny enables a CORBA application to compose a value at run-time whose type is unknown at compile-time and to pass it to a remote program in an any instance. Reciprocally, an application that receives an any object is able to, both, interpret the contained type by means of the TypeCode interface and to extract the contained value by means of the DynAny interface as well; interpretation and extraction are possible without having static knowledge of the corresponding IDL types. In order to create an any value dynamically, first a DynAny object must be constructed and initialized with the value it shall encapsulate; then, the desired any object can be generated from the DynAny. Similarly, to decompose an any value dynamically, first, a DynAny object is initialized with this any and, after that, the DynAny's operations are invoked in order to extract the original value. Even though this approach might seem complicated, it must be followed whenever dynamic value insertion or extraction is desired.

The list below is a compilation of important functionality provided by the DynamicAny API. Seven categories of operations are available:

- factory operations for DynAny objects,
- life cycle operations copying or destroying DynAny objects,
- TypeCode operations for inserting or extracting TypeCodes into or from DynAny objects,
- insert operations for inserting values of basic types into a DynAny object or for composing more complex DynAny objects from other DynAny objects,
- extract operations for getting basic values from DynAny objects or for decomposing them,
- iterator operations for navigating from one component within a complex DynAny object to the next component, and
- conversion operations for generating an any from a DynAny object or for initializing a DynAny object from an any value.

Figure 20 gives an overview of these operations and their interfaces. Besides the central interface DynAny, the module DynamicAny defines ten additional interfaces. Among these are the interface DynAnyFactory, which is used for creating DynAny objects, and interfaces such as DynStruct or DynSequence, which are subinterfaces of DynAny representing structures or sequences. In the next section, all eleven interfaces are presented briefly.

Note that all of module DynamicAny's interfaces are specified local; they are "locality constrained" and their instances cannot be transferred via remote invocations nor can references to such instances be stringified via object_to_string().

13.2.1   DynAnyFactory Interface

Let us begin discussion of the DynamicAny API with the interface DynAnyFactory; it provides the factory operations for creating DynAny objects.

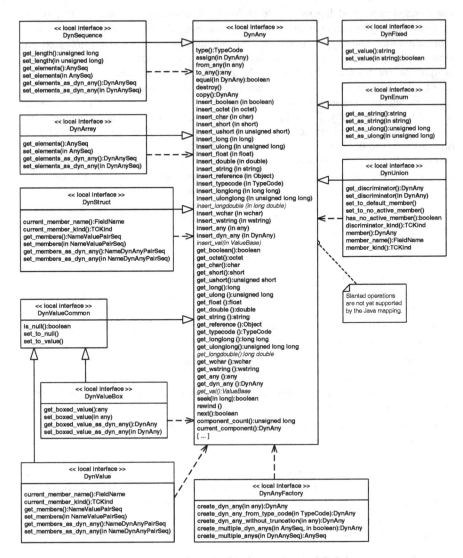

Figure 20: Interfaces in the DynamicAny Module

Practical usage of the DynAny factory requires an application has, previously, obtained a corresponding initial reference to that factory. To that purpose, the well-known ORB operation resolve_initial_references() may be invoked with the argument "DynAnyFactory".

Here is the IDL specification of the `DynAnyFactory` interface:

```
module DynamicAny
{
   ...
   local interface DynAnyFactory
   {
      exception InconsistentTypeCode { };
      DynAny create_dyn_any(in any value)
        raises(InconsistentTypeCode);
      DynAny create_dyn_any_from_type_code(
        in CORBA::TypeCode type)
          raises(InconsistentTypeCode);
   };
};
```

The `create_dyn_any()` operation creates a new `DynAny` object from an any value. Not only the proper any value, but also its type, i.e., the `TypeCode` associated with it, is assigned to the resulting `DynAny` object. The run-time type of the result returned depends on that `TypeCode`'s value. If the type of the value in the any is neither a structure, exception, sequence, array, union, enumeration, fixed, or value type, then a `DynAny` is returned from the invocation; otherwise, the dynamic type of the object reference is a subtype of type `DynAny`. Corresponding to the value embedded in the any, a `DynSequence`, `DynStruct`, etc., might, for example, be returned. If necessary, the reference may be cast to this dynamic type with an invocation of `narrow()`. In the Java mapping, a simple Java downcast is to be used. If not sure about the actual dynamic type of a `DynAny`, we can extract its `TypeCode`, inspect the `TCKind` value, and then cast to the proper subtype.

The second factory operation, `create_dyn_any_from_type_code()`, may be invoked to create `DynAny` objects with a default initialization when the type inside the `DynAny` is already known but the value is still unknown. The respective `TypeCode` must be passed to the invocation. The default values for initialization of `DynAny` objects are

- values of type `boolean` are initialized to `FALSE`,
- values of numeric types and of type `octet`, `char`, or `wchar` are initialized to 0 or 0.0, respectively,
- the empty string is used for types `string` and `wstring`,
- object references are initialized to `null`,
- for `TypeCode` instances, the `TCKind` value of `tk_null` is used, and
- any instances are initialized such that they contain a `TypeCode` with a `TCKind` value of `tk_null` and no value.

For complex types, the following rules apply:

- sequences are initialized to an empty sequence,
- for fixed-point types, the default value is zero,
- for enumerations, the value of the enumerator is the first enumerator value indicated by the `TypeCode`,

- the members of a structure, an exception, or an array are (recursively) initialized to their default values, and
- value type values are initialized to a null value.

Creation of DynAnys with a TCKind of tk_null or tk_void is legal and results in the creation of a DynAny object without a value and with zero components. If, during creation, an invalid or obsolete TypeCode is used, the factory operations raise an exception of type InconsistentTypeCode.

Note that the TypeCode copied implicitly or explicitly into a DynAny object during its creation remains the same during the entire lifetime of that object and cannot be changed later.

13.2.2   DynAny Interface

After having discussed how DynAny objects are created, we can now turn to the contents of the actual DynAny interface. The following excerpt of the IDL specification shows the most relevant elements:

```
module DynamicAny
{
   ...
   local interface DynAny
   {
      exception InvalidValue { };
      exception TypeMismatch { };

      CORBA::TypeCode type();

      void assign(in DynAny dyn_any) raises(TypeMismatch);
      void from_any(in any value)
         raises(TypeMismatch, InvalidValue);
      any to_any();

      boolean equal(in DynAny dyn_any);

      void destroy();
      DynAny copy();

      void insert_any(in any value)
         raises(TypeMismatch, InvalidValue);
      void insert_dyn_any(in DynAny value)
         raises(TypeMismatch, InvalidValue);
      void insert_<type>(in <type> value)
         raises(TypeMismatch, InvalidValue);
      <type> get_<type>()
         raises(TypeMismatch, InvalidValue);

      boolean seek(in long index);
      void rewind();
      boolean next();
      unsigned long component_count();
```

```
DynAny current_component() raises(TypeMismatch);

    void insert_<type>_seq(in CORBA::<type>Seq value)
        raises(TypeMismatch, InvalidValue);
    CORBA::<type>Seq get_<type>_seq()
        raises(TypeMismatch, InvalidValue);
    ...
    };
};
```

The life cycle operation copy() creates a deep copy of the DynAny object on which it is invoked; similarly, a destroy() invocation destroys a DynAny object and frees the resources used to represent its data value, including any DynAny objects of which it is composed. In order to prevent memory leaks, for each DynAny that was created with a factory operation or by a copy() invocation, destroy() should be invoked explicitly before it is no longer referenced. In practice, most ORB products simply ignore the invocation but the standard requires this procedure and we keep to it for reasons of portability. Invoking copy() or destroy() on an already destroyed object results in an exception of type OB-JECT_NOT_EXIST.

The assign() operation initializes the value associated with the DynAny object to the value of the argument. Note that such an assignment is only admissible if source and target have the same TypeCode; this can be verified by means of operation TypeCode::equivalent(). If the types are not equivalent, the assignment raises a TypeMismatch.

With the help of operation equal(), two DynAny objects are compared for equality. The result is TRUE if the TypeCodes are equivalent and, recursively, all component DynAnys are equal.

The operations from_any() and to_any() provide functionality for conversions between the types any and DynAny. The from_any() operation initializes the value associated with a DynAny object with the value contained in an any; both TypeCodes must be equivalent. Vice versa, the to_any() operation creates an any value from a DynAny object.

The type() operation returns the TypeCode value associated with a DynAny instance. This operation is typically invoked when, locally, a DynAny of a complex type was obtained, which now has to be narrowed to the correct dynamic subtype of DynAny, for example, DynStruct.

The DynAny interface provides an insert operation for each basic type. For reasons of simplicity, we summarized these operations in the above IDL specification in the form insert_<type>(), where, in a concrete application, <type> has to be replaced by boolean, octet, char, wchar, etc. The target DynAny object must have a TypeCode equivalent to that of the value to be inserted so that the insertion can be carried out successfully without raising an exception. The various insert_<type>_seq operations insert sequences with elements of type <type>; the operations insert_any() and insert_dyn_any() allow us to nest any and DynAny values arbitrarily.

The extract counterparts of the insert operations, namely `get_<type>()` and `get_<type>_seq()`, extract values from `DynAny` objects. Again, the `TypeCodes` must be equivalent.

For constructed `DynAnys` consisting of several components, e.g., `DynStruct`, `DynSequence`, `DynArray`, `DynUnion`, `DynAny`, and `DynValue` objects, the `DynAny` interface provides operations to iterate through the components. Such a `DynAny` object consists of a `TypeCode` and an ordered collection of embedded `DynAnys`, which can be inspected one after the other with the iterator operations. For example, a `DynAny` for our `Time` structure would hold a collection of three `DynAny` values, one for each member, `hours`, `minutes`, and `seconds`.

An important aspect of iterator functionality is that, besides its components and `TypeCode`, each `DynAny` object maintains the notion of a "current position" pointing into its list of components. Position 0 points to the first component. A `DynAny` object for our `Time` structure would, therefore, address its components by index values between 0 and 2. The specific index value -1 indicates a position that currently points nowhere. For values that cannot have a current position, such as `DynAny` objects for basic types, the index value is fixed at -1. If a `DynAny` is initialized with a value that has components, the index is initialized to 0. In our `Time` structure example, the initial current position would point to the `hours` element.

We now turn to the `DynAny` operations relevant for component iteration. The operation `component_count()` returns the number of components of a `DynAny` on the top level. For `DynAnys` without components, which encapsulate basic types, fixed types, or enumerated types, this number is always zero. For sequences, arrays, structures, exceptions, and value types, the number of elements or members is returned.

The `current_component()` operation returns the `DynAny` object for the component at the current position. Calling the operation for a `DynAny` that cannot have components raises a `TypeMismatch` exception. In the case of a `DynAny` with components whose current position is -1, a null reference is returned. Invoking `current_component()` does not change the current position; the same holds for all the `insert...()` or the `get...()` operations discussed above.

The `next()` operation advances the current position to the next component. The operation returns `TRUE` while the resulting current position indicates an existing component and `FALSE` otherwise. In the latter case, the current position is set to -1. Invoking `next()` on a `DynAny` without components has the same effect. This object's position is always -1 anyhow.

Operation `seek()` sets the current position to the value passed as the `index` argument. The invocation returns `TRUE` if the resulting current position indicates a component of the `DynAny` and `FALSE` if `index` indicates a position that does not correspond to a component. In the latter case, the current position is set to -1. `FALSE` is also returned when `seek()` is invoked on a `DynAny` object without components.

The `rewind()` operation is equivalent to calling `seek(0)`.

13.2.3   DynFixed Interface

DynFixed is the first subinterface of DynAny that we examine. Its purpose is to dynamically manipulate any values containing fixed-point decimals. The IDL definition only consists of two operations:

```
module DynamicAny
{
  ...
  local interface DynFixed : DynAny
  {
    string get_value();
    boolean set_value(in string val)
      raises(TypeMismatch, InvalidValue);
  };
};
```

The get_value() operation returns the value of a DynFixed instance as a string. The
operation uses the IDL string type since IDL does not have a generic type that can represent fixed types with arbitrary number of digits and arbitrary scale.

With operation set_value() one can set the value of the DynFixed target object. The
val argument must contain a fixed string in the same format as used for IDL fixed-point
literals; however, the trailing d or D may be omitted (see Section 4.3.1.3). If val has more
fractional digits than specified by the scale of the DynFixed object, the extra digits are
truncated. If the truncated value has more digits than expected, an InvalidValue exception is raised. If the value is not too large, the operation returns TRUE if no truncation was
required, FALSE otherwise. If val does not contain a valid fixed-point literal, the operation
raises a TypeMismatch exception.

13.2.4   DynEnum Interface

The interface DynEnum is also subinterface of interface DynAny. It is used to manipulate
values of enumerated types dynamically. The IDL specification is as follows:

```
module DynamicAny
{
  ...
  local interface DynEnum : DynAny
  {
    string get_as_string();
    void set_as_string(in string value)
      raises(InvalidValue);
    unsigned long get_as_ulong();
    void set_as_ulong(in unsigned long value)
      raises(InvalidValue);
  };
};
```

The get_as_string() operation returns the value of the DynEnum as an IDL identifier;
set_as_string() sets the value whose identifier is passed in the value parameter. For
example, using the enumeration

```
enum Author { ALEKSY, KORTHAUS, SCHADER };
```

we could set the value of a DynEnum by invoking set_as_string("ALEKSY"). If the value argument contains a string that is not a valid IDL identifier for the corresponding enumerated type, the operation raises an InvalidValue exception. This is also the case if the operation is invoked on a DynEnum created from an any with a different enumeration; in that situation, get_as_string() returns an empty string.

The other two operations get_as_ulong() and set_as_ulong() access the values of a DynEnum on the basis of the value's ordinal value. Recall that enumerators have ordinal values 0, 1, 2..., as they appear from left to right in the corresponding IDL definition. If a value that is outside the range of ordinal values for the enumerated type is passed to set_as_ulong(), the operation raises InvalidValue.

Finally, recall that the current iterator position of a DynEnum is always -1.

13.2.5 DynStruct Interface

DynStruct is also a subinterface of DynAny. It may be used to dynamically manipulate structures as well as exceptions. The following parts of module DynamicAny's IDL specification are needed:

```
typedef string FieldName;
struct NameValuePair
{
  FieldName id;
  any value;
};
typedef sequence<NameValuePair> NameValuePairSeq;
struct NameDynAnyPair
{
  FieldName id;
  DynAny value;
};
typedef sequence<NameDynAnyPair> NameDynAnyPairSeq;

local interface DynStruct : DynAny
{
  FieldName current_member_name()
    raises(TypeMismatch, InvalidValue);
  CORBA::TCKind current_member_kind()
    raises(TypeMismatch, InvalidValue);
  NameValuePairSeq get_members();
  void set_members(in NameValuePairSeq value)
    raises(TypeMismatch, InvalidValue);
  NameDynAnyPairSeq get_members_as_dyn_any();
  void set_members_as_dyn_any(in NameDynAnyPairSeq value)
    raises(TypeMismatch, InvalidValue);
};
```

set_members() and get_members() are the central operations that allow us to set or extract the members in a structure or an exception in the form of a sequence of name/value pairs. Each member of the structure or the exception is represented by one name/value pair that describes the name of the member by a `string` and the value of the member by an any. For example, our `Time` structure would be passed and returned as a sequence of three name/value pairs. The invocation of `set_members()` raises an exception of type `Type-Mismatch` if the passed sequence does not provide a name/value pair for each member of the structure or the exception or if these pairs do not appear in the order required by the IDL specification of the structure or the exception. In addition, each sequence element must have a type equivalent to the `TypeCode` of the corresponding member; otherwise `Invalid-Value` is raised. The operations `set_members_as_dyn_any()` and `get_members_as_dyn_any()` have the same semantics as their any counterparts but accept and return sequences where the values are of type `DynAny` instead of any.

The `current_member_name()` operation returns the name of the member at the current position in the target `DynStruct` object. This result may be an empty string since element names are optional in `TypeCodes`. If the `DynStruct` represents an empty exception, the operation raises a `TypeMismatch`. If the current position is -1, an `InvalidValue` exception is raised.

Finally, operation `current_member_kind()` returns the `TCKind` value of the `Type-Code` of the member at the current position. The rules for the exceptions that may be raised are identical to those discussed above for `current_member_name()` invocations.

13.2.6   DynUnion Interface

The interface `DynUnion` is a subinterface of `DynAny`. It is provided for dynamic manipulation of `union`-based types. Since we question the usefulness of these types, we do not discuss this interface here. The methods provided by the interface can be seen in Figure 20. Readers interested in further information are referred to the CORBA specification.

13.2.7   DynSequence Interface

The interface `DynSequence` is subinterface of the `DynAny` interface. `DynSequence` objects are associated with sequences. Below, the necessary clipping from module `Dynamic-Any`'s IDL code is given:

```
typedef sequence<any> AnySeq;
typedef sequence<DynAny> DynAnySeq;

local interface DynSequence : DynAny
{
  unsigned long get_length();
  void set_length(in unsigned long len)
    raises(InvalidValue);
  AnySeq get_elements();
  void set_elements(in AnySeq value)
    raises(TypeMismatch, InvalidValue);
  DynAnySeq get_elements_as_dyn_any();
  void set_elements_as_dyn_any(in DynAnySeq value)
    raises(TypeMismatch, InvalidValue);
};
```

The get_length() operation returns the current length of the sequence. Correspondingly, set_length() sets the length of the sequence. Increasing the length of a bounded sequence to a value larger than the bound raises an InvalidValue exception. Increasing the length of a sequence adds new elements at the tail without affecting the values of already existing elements. Newly added elements are default-initialized. The current position is set to the first newly added element if the previous current position was -1; otherwise, if the current position was not -1, this position is not affected. Decreasing the length of a sequence removes elements from the tail. The new current position is always set to -1 except in one case: if the current position indicates a valid element and that element is not removed when the length is decreased, then the current position remains unaffected.

The operations get_elements() and get_elements_as_dyn_any() return the elements of the sequence as a sequence of any and DynAny objects, respectively. Their counterparts are operations set_elements() and set_elements_as_dyn_any(), which set the elements of a sequence based on the value argument, which is a sequence of anys and DynAnys, respectively. Existing elements in the DynSequence are removed and replaced by the elements passed in value. Accordingly, the length of the DynSequence is set to the length of value. The current position is set to 0 if value has non-zero length and to -1, otherwise. The operation raises TypeMismatch if value contains one or more elements whose TypeCode is not equivalent to that of the elements in the DynSequence. If the length of value exceeds the bounds of a bounded sequence, an exception of type InvalidValue is raised.

13.2.8 DynArray Interface

As to be expected, the DynArray interface, which is also a subinterface of interface DynAny, provides functionality very similar to DynSequences. The IDL definition has the following form:

```
module DynamicAny
{
  ...
  local interface DynArray : DynAny
  {
    AnySeq get_elements();
    void set_elements(in AnySeq value)
      raises(TypeMismatch, InvalidValue);
    DynAnySeq get_elements_as_dyn_any();
    void set_elements_as_dyn_any(in DynAnySeq value)
      raises(TypeMismatch, InvalidValue);
  };
};
```

The get...() and set...() operations return or set the elements of the DynArray. One difference with regard to DynSequences is that arrays always have a fixed number of elements, determined by the array dimension. This implies that the any or DynAny sequences passed to the set...() operations must contain the same number of elements as defined in the array dimension; otherwise, an InvalidValue exception is raised. If desired, the array dimension can be obtained by calling the component_count() operation, which is provided by the supertype DynAny. The new current iterator position after setting array elements is always zero. If one or more elements in the value have a type that is not equivalent to the DynArray's TypeCode, then a set...() invocation raises an exception of type TypeMismatch.

13.2.9 DynValueCommon Interface

DynValueCommon, a subinterface of DynAny, provides operations supported by both the DynValue and DynValueBox interfaces. Therefore, it also serves as superinterface for these two value type-related interfaces. The definition is as follows:

```
module DynamicAny
{
    ...
    local interface DynValueCommon : DynAny
    {
        boolean is_null();
        void set_to_null();
        void set_to_value();
    };
};
```

The operation is_null() returns TRUE if the DynValueCommon object represents a null value type. The set_to_null() operation changes the representation of a DynValue-Common object to a null value type. If the DynValueCommon represents that null value, then operation set_to_value() replaces it with a newly constructed value, with its components initialized to default values; otherwise, the invocation of this operation has no effect.

13.2.10 DynValue Interface

DynValue is the first of the two interfaces that are not direct subinterfaces of DynAny but that have DynValueCommon as a direct superinterface. DynValue objects are associated with non-boxed value types. Here is the relevant part of module DynAny:

```
local interface DynValue : DynValueCommon
{
    FieldName current_member_name()
        raises(TypeMismatch, InvalidValue);
    CORBA::TCKind current_member_kind()
        raises(TypeMismatch, InvalidValue);
    NameValuePairSeq get_members() raises(InvalidValue);
    void set_members(in NameValuePairSeq value)
        raises(TypeMismatch, InvalidValue);
    NameDynAnyPairSeq get_members_as_dyn_any()
        raises(InvalidValue);
    void set_members_as_dyn_any(in NameDynAnyPairSeq value)
        raises(TypeMismatch, InvalidValue);
};
```

The DynValue interface can represent both null and non-null value types. A DynValue object representing a null value type has no components and a current position of -1. For a DynValue object representing a non-null value type, the DynValue's components comprise the `public` and `private` members of the value type, including those inherited from concrete supertype value types, in the order of definition.

The operations on the `DynValue` interface generally have semantics equivalent to the same operations on `DynStruct` (see Section 13.2.5). When invoking `get_members()` or `get_members_as_dyn_any()` on a `DynValue` object representing a null value type, an `InvalidValue` exception is raised. When invoked on such a "null" `DynValue` object, `set_members()` and `set_members_as_dyn_any()` convert the `DynValue` to the corresponding non-null value type.

13.2.11 `DynValueBox` Interface

The second subinterface of `DynValueCommon` is `DynValueBox`; its purpose is to manipulate boxed value types dynamically:

```
local interface DynValueBox : DynValueCommon
{
  any get_boxed_value() raises(InvalidValue);
  void set_boxed_value(in any boxed)
    raises(TypeMismatch, InvalidValue);
  DynAny get_boxed_value_as_dyn_any()
    raises(InvalidValue);
  void set_boxed_value_as_dyn_any(in DynAny boxed)
    raises(TypeMismatch);
};
```

Similar to the `DynValue` interface discussed above, the `DynValueBox` interface can represent both null and non-null value types. A `DynValueBox` object representing a null value type has no components and a current position of -1. For a `DynValueBox` object representing a non-null value type, the `DynValueBox` has a single component of the boxed type.

The `get_boxed_value()` and the `get_boxed_value_as_dyn_any()` operations return the boxed value as an `any` and a `DynAny`, respectively. An `InvalidValue` exception is raised if the `DynValueBox` object represents a null value type. The `set_boxed_value()` and `set_boxed_value_as_dyn_any()` operations replace the boxed value with the specified argument value. If the type of the passed `any` or `DynAny` argument is not equivalent to the `DynValueBox` type, the operation raises `TypeMismatch`. In addition, if the argument does not contain a legal value, an `InvalidValue` exception is raised. When invoked on a "null" `DynValueBox` object, the `set...()` operations convert the `DynValueBox` to a non-null value type.

13.3   Usage of the `DynamicAny` API in Java

The Java mapping of the `DynamicAny` API does not show any specific characteristics that would need detailed discussion. We, instead, use an expandable example to demonstrate how this API can be practically employed in a distributed Java application. To that purpose, we implement a server that can accept arbitrary `Any` values, extract their components dynamically by means of the `DynamicAny` interfaces, and display the results on the server console.

To complete the application, we develop a client that also manages without the static IDL definition of a complex type, is able to define it dynamically, builds and assembles its value with the help of the DynamicAny API, converts it to an Any value, and sends it to the server for server-side processing.

13.3.1   Implementing Servant and Server Application

We base this example on the introductory example at the beginning of this chapter. The IDL definition we use is identical to the one in Section 13.1; the only difference is that, now, we do not provide the static definition of the Time structure. Hence, we start from the following IDL file:

```
// AnyServer.idl

module AnyTest
{
  interface AnyServer
  {
    void display_any(in any a);
  };
};
```

One should store this simplified version AnyServer.idl in the \Examples\DynAny directory on one's server and client hosts and compile it as usual from the respective Server and Client subdirectories.

Our server application, which we, again, store in a file AServer.java, is almost identical to the server in the previous example; therefore, one can first copy the original server to the directory \Examples\DynAny*YourORB*\Server on the server host. The only code modification necessary concerns the construction of the AnyServerImpl object, which is carried out immediately after the ORB initialization. For reasons to be discussed below, it is favorable to provide the variable orb as an argument to the servant constructor:

```
AnyServerImpl a_impl = new AnyServerImpl(orb);
```

We now turn to the implementation of the servant, which is named as usual and should be stored as file AnyServerImpl.java in directory \Examples\DynAny*Your-ORB*\Server\AnyTest. Since we have no static information on the type in the Any object passed to the display method, the TypeCode must be extracted and analyzed:

```
// AnyServerImpl.java

package AnyTest;

import org.omg.CORBA.*;
import org.omg.DynamicAny.*;
import static java.lang.System.*;

public class AnyServerImpl extends AnyServerPOA {
  private DynAnyFactory dynFactory;
  public AnyServerImpl(ORB orb) {
```

```
      try {
        dynFactory = DynAnyFactoryHelper.narrow(
          orb.resolve_initial_references("DynAnyFactory"));
      } catch (Exception ex) {
          out.println("Exception: " +
            ex.getMessage());
          exit(1);
      }
    }
  public void display_any(Any any) {
    try {
      TypeCode tc = any.type();
      while (tc.kind() == TCKind.tk_alias)
        tc = tc.content_type();
      TCKind kind = tc.kind();
      if (kind == TCKind.tk_short)
        out.println(any.extract_short());
      else if (kind == TCKind.tk_long)
        out.println(any.extract_long());
      else if (kind == TCKind.tk_ulong)
        out.println(any.extract_ulong());
      else if (kind == TCKind.tk_string)
        out.println("\""
          + any.extract_string() + "\"");
      // ... rest of basic types here
      else if (kind == TCKind.tk_except
          || kind == TCKind.tk_struct) {
        org.omg.DynamicAny.DynStruct dynStruct =
        (org.omg.DynamicAny.DynStruct)
          dynFactory.create_dyn_any(any);
        if (dynStruct.component_count() != 0)
          do {
            out.print(
              dynStruct.current_member_name() + " = ");
            display_any(
              dynStruct.current_component().to_any());
          } while (dynStruct.next());
      }
      // ... rest of complex types here
    } catch (Exception ex) {
      out.println("Exception: " + ex.getMessage());
      exit(1);
    }
  }
}
```

This servant has no static type information concerning the values that are passed to its method display_any() at run-time. The argument any might contain a value of an arbitrarily complex user-defined type. Therefore, to decompose that unknown value, usage of the DynamicAny API is inevitable. Recall that DynAny objects can only be used locally and that it is not possible to pass them directly from a client to a remote server. Thus, in the body of method display_any(), we first of all have to create a DynAny object from the received Any object; subsequently that DynAny's components can then be extracted and displayed. In order to generate the local DynAny, we need a DynAnyFactory object. The standard procedure to obtain such a factory is to invoke the ORB method `resolve_init-ial_references()` with the string `"DynAnyFactory"` as the argument. The necessity of calling a method on the ORB is the reason for the change in the server application mentioned above.

The servant's true functionality is encapsulated in method `display_any()`. In principle, we have to test for all existing IDL types. For reasons of clarity, however, we only deal with several basic types and, as an example for complex types, show the way to extract a `struct` or an `exception`.

In the first step, we proceed as in Section 13.1 and extract the any's TypeCode with the invocation `any.type()`. Then, recursively, by invoking `content_type()` in the while statement, we inspect this TypeCode, which could be an alias for some user-defined type, until we have reached the basic types, which may no longer be decomposed.

The names and values of these bottom level components shall now be displayed. We implement an `if` statement analogous to the simple `AnyServerImpl` in Section 13.1 and compare the `tc.kind()` value to `TCKind.tk_short` for a `short`, to `TCKind.tk_long` for a `long`, etc. If we find the component's type and if this type is a basic type, we print the corresponding value, which we obtain by calling the respective extract method, e.g., `any.extract_short()`. For reasons of brevity, we do without any type-specific formatting for that value.

The task to decompose a complex type is more interesting. In the example, we demonstrate how that step may be implemented for a structure. As already mentioned above, we first have to create a `DynStruct` object from the received Any. At this point, we know from our type inspection that we have to decompose a structure. Therefore, we call the factory method `create_dyn_any()` to create a new DynAny object, which is initialized with the names and values of the structure embedded in the any variable. Immediately following construction, we cast the dynamic type of the result to `DynStruct`. We can now determine the number of members in the structure by invoking `component_count()` and, if it is not empty, iterate through the different positions of the structure by repeatedly invoking `next()` on the DynStruct object. The name of the member at the current position is available through a call of `current_member_name()` and the component at the current position is returned as a DynAny if we invoke `current_component()`. In order to print the component's value, we simply invoke `display_any()` recursively after having converted the DynAny to an Any with a preceding call of `to_any()`.

This completes the discussion of the server-side implementation. One can now compile and start the server application as usual and copy the IOR string to the `Client` directory on the client hosts.

13.3.2   Implementing the Client Application

We finally turn to the client side of our application, which is here somewhat more complex. The file `AClient.java` should be stored on one's client hosts in directory `\Examples\DynAny\`*YourORB*`\Client`.

```java
// AClient.java

import AnyTest.*;
import java.io.*;
import java.util.*;
import org.omg.CORBA.*;
import org.omg.DynamicAny.*;
import static java.lang.System.*;

public class AClient {
  private ORB orb;
  private void initializeORB(String[] args) {
    ... as above in Section 8.3
  }
  private org.omg.CORBA.Object getRef(String refFile) {
    ... as above in Section 8.3
  }
  public AClient(String[] args, String refFile) {
    try {
      initializeORB(args);
      org.omg.CORBA.Object obj = getRef(refFile);
      AnyServer as = AnyServerHelper.narrow(obj);
      DynAnyFactory dynFactory =
        DynAnyFactoryHelper.narrow(
          orb.resolve_initial_references(
            "DynAnyFactory"));
      TypeCode time_tc =
        orb.create_struct_tc(
          "IDL:AnyTest/AnyServer/Time:1.0", "Time",
          new StructMember[] {
            new StructMember("hours",
              orb.get_primitive_tc(TCKind.tk_ulong),
              null),
            new StructMember("minutes",
              orb.get_primitive_tc(TCKind.tk_ulong),
              null),
            new StructMember("seconds",
              orb.get_primitive_tc(TCKind.tk_ulong),
              null)
          });
      org.omg.DynamicAny.DynStruct dynStruct =
        (org.omg.DynamicAny.DynStruct)
          dynFactory.create_dyn_any_from_type_code(
            time_tc);
      org.omg.DynamicAny.DynAny hours =
        dynFactory.create_dyn_any_from_type_code(
          orb.get_primitive_tc(TCKind.tk_ulong));
      hours.insert_ulong(12);
      org.omg.DynamicAny.DynAny minutes =
        dynFactory.create_dyn_any_from_type_code(
          orb.get_primitive_tc(TCKind.tk_ulong));
      minutes.insert_ulong(0);
      org.omg.DynamicAny.DynAny seconds =
        dynFactory.create_dyn_any_from_type_code(
          orb.get_primitive_tc(TCKind.tk_ulong));
```

```
        seconds.insert_ulong(0);
        NameDynAnyPair[] members = new NameDynAnyPair[] {
          new NameDynAnyPair("hours", hours),
          new NameDynAnyPair("minutes", minutes),
          new NameDynAnyPair("seconds", seconds),
        };
        dynStruct.set_members_as_dyn_any(members);
        Any a = dynStruct.to_any();
        as.display_any(a);
        hours.destroy();
        minutes.destroy();
        seconds.destroy();
        dynStruct.destroy();
      } catch (BAD_PARAM ex) {
        out.println("Narrowing failed");
        exit(3);
      } catch (Exception ex) {
        out.println("Exception: " + ex.getMessage());
        exit(1);
      }
    }
  public static void main(String[] args) {
    String refFile = "AnyServer.ref";
    new AClient(args, refFile);
  }
}
```

Known elements already discussed in the servant implementation, for example, how to obtain a reference to a DynAnyFactory object, are not repeated in the following.

A new aspect is the dynamic generation of a user-defined TypeCode and the creation of a default-initialized DynStruct for that type, which is demonstrated at the beginning of the application. This way of proceeding is followed in subsequent chapters when we use the Dynamic Invocation Interface. We now compose the Time structure dynamically at run-time without having provided an IDL definition for it. Several ORB methods that all follow a similar pattern are available to create a new TypeCode. Here, we invoke the method create_struct_tc(), which returns the TypeCode for an IDL struct. This method has three in parameters.

- The first parameter is a RepositoryId, which specifies the new type's unique identifier for the Interface Repository. The standard naming schema is "IDL:modulename/ interfacename/typename:1.0"; for our example, we use "IDL:AnyTest /AnyServer/Time:1.0".

- The second parameter is the unqualified name of the type that is equal to the last part of the RepositoryId preceding the version number. In our example, that name is "Time".

- The third parameter is a sequence of name/type/type triples, which define the elements of the structure. In Java, these triples are represented through objects of class StructMember, having the declaration

```
package org.omg.CORBA;

public final class StructMember
    implements org.omg.CORBA.portable.IDLEntity {
    public java.lang.String name;
    public org.omg.CORBA.TypeCode type;
    public org.omg.CORBA.IDLType type_def;
}
```

In the Java ORB interface, method create_struct_tc() is specified in this way:

```
public abstract TypeCode create_struct_tc(
    String id, String name, StructMember[] members);
```

With the help of these elements, we create time_tc, a new TypeCode representing the Time structure with its three components hours, minutes, and seconds, each of type unsigned long. A call of orb.get_primitive_tc(TCKind.tk_ulong) provides the corresponding TypeCode, needed when we construct the StructMember objects.

Now, the next step is to create a DynStruct object for that new type. Here, we simply invoke the factory method create_dyn_any_from_type_code() and immediately cast the resulting DynAny's dynamic type to DynStruct. The object dynStruct is at this point default-initialized. In order to insert the desired Time value, we first create a DynAny object for each of the three structure members by, again, invoking the factory method create_dyn_any_from_type_code(). This time, the correct type for the argument is TCKind.tk_ulong since all members are of IDL type unsigned long. After having created them, we call insert_ulong() to insert the correct values into the DynAny objects hours, minutes, and seconds. These objects still have to be inserted into the object dynStruct in order to replace its default values.

In Section 13.2.5, we saw that one way to set values in a DynStruct object is the invocation of method set_members_as_dyn_any(). The method expects an array with elements of type NameDynAnyPair, which provides the names and the values for the members of the object. In the example, we create the NameDynAnyPairs with the obvious names and the DynAny objects we just constructed. After having called set_members_as_dyn_any(), the DynStruct's construction is completed. It has the correct type, provided by time_tc, and the correct value, provided by members.

The object dynStruct can now fulfill its central purpose, namely, to transmit its content to the server during an invocation of the remote method display_any(). Since dynStruct is locality-constrained to the client side, we convert it to an Any with a call of to_any() and then invoke the server method with this Any object as an argument. To ensure standard conformity, we finally destroy all newly created DynAny objects via destroy().

After having compiled the clients, each execution should produce the following output on the server console:

```
hours = 12
minutes = 0
seconds = 0
```

In subsequent chapters, we go into more depth in order to understand the advantages of the DynAny concept, especially when invoking operations dynamically through the DII.

13.4 Exercises

1. Enhance the implementation of the servant class `AnyServerImpl` so that several additional IDL types (sequences, enumerations, arrays, etc.) can be recognized and displayed.

2. Write a simple but complete implementation in order to test the possibilities offered by the new servant.

14 Dynamic Invocation Interface

In Section 3.4.5, we briefly covered CORBA's Dynamic Invocation Interface, which was then discussed in more detail in Section 6.6. The DII enables CORBA clients to invoke operations dynamically without knowing the IDL type of the server operations at compile-time. Clients using the DII, therefore, do not rely on the stub code generated by the IDL compiler. In the context of the DynAny examples of the last chapter, it was already mentioned that it is thus possible to develop very generic and flexible applications without the restrictions of compile-time conditions. As an example, it might be necessary to build a client application even before the corresponding server interfaces are defined, requiring that the invocations of server-side operations be constructed dynamically at run-time. Typical scenarios for such procedures might be generic bridges, object browsers, or interpreters for script languages.

In these cases, the client normally obtains knowledge on the interface names and operation descriptions, needed to execute a dynamic invocation by consulting the Interface Repository. This kind of type information can be registered in the IR with the help of a command-line tool. Accessing the information in the IR, the construction of a user-defined type can be discovered dynamically. Since no stub code is available, user-defined types have to be represented and manipulated dynamically in the clients; TypeCodes and DynAnys provide the means to do so. The information and the details for the operation are assembled with the help of a local Request object. Then, in the standard case, method invoke() is called on that object, triggering the actual dynamic invocation. In principle, the following scheme is applied:

- creating a Request object;
- setting the in, inout, and out parameters;
- setting the return type;
- setting a list of user exception TypeCodes (optional);
- executing the dynamic invocation;
- testing for exceptions (optional); and
- extracting the return value and values of the inout and out parameters.

In this chapter, practical application of dynamic invocations is explained with the aid of several simple examples. Usage of the Interface Repository is not included explicitly, nor is dynamic exception handling demonstrated. The first example is based on the introductory Counter application, developed in Chapter 7. Differing from the static approach followed there, it is now shown how a client can dynamically generate and invoke server methods. CORBA's standard communication model (synchronous and blocking) is followed. For additional explanations, the well-known TimeServer examples are re-implemented dynamically; in this context, the DynAny objects introduced in the preceding chapter are employed. Finally, an example for deferred synchronous CORBA communication is presented.

14.1   Dynamic `Counter` Client

In the first DII example, we go back to the `Counter` application discussed in Chapter 7.
The IDL interface of the `Counter` object was presented in the file `Counter.idl` in Section 7.15 and is not modified. We also reuse the servant implementation `Counter-Impl.java` from Sections 7.5 and 7.15. One should, now, create a directory `\Examples\DIICounter` on the server and client hosts, copy `Counter.idl` to the server host,
and create the usual directory structure (see Sections 7.4 and 7.8). According to our assumption, the `Counter`'s IDL definition is not available on the clients. After setting the necessary environment variables, the IDL file can be translated; one should also copy the servant implementation `CounterImpl.java` presented in Section 7.5 to the directory `\Examples\DIICounter\`*YourORB*`\Server\Count`. The server application itself is also organized completely analogous to our earlier examples. Store it in directory `\Examples\DIICounter\`*YourORB*`\Server` and compile it as usual.

```
// Server.java

import Count.*;
import java.io.*;
import java.util.Properties;
import org.omg.CORBA.*;
import org.omg.PortableServer.*;
import static java.lang.System.*;

public class Server {
   private ORB orb;
   private POA rootPOA;
   private void initializeORB(String[] args) {
      ... as above in Section 8.2
   }
   private void putRef(org.omg.CORBA.Object obj,
         String refFile) {
      ... as above in Section 8.2
   }
   public Server(String[] args, String refFile) {
      try {
         initializeORB(args);
         CounterImpl c_impl = new CounterImpl();
         Counter c = c_impl._this(orb);
         putRef(c, refFile);
         rootPOA.the_POAManager().activate();
         orb.run();
      } catch (Exception ex) {
         out.println("Exception: " + ex.getMessage());
         exit(1);
      }
   }
   public static void main(String[] args) {
      String refFile = "Counter.ref";
      new Server(args, refFile);
   }
}
```

Of real interest is only the client application, which uses dynamic invocations and does not have access to the Counter's stub code generated by the IDL compiler. To that purpose, one should create the file DIIClient.java below and store it in directory \Examples\DIICounter*YourORB*\Client on the client hosts.

```java
// DIIClient.java

import java.awt.GridLayout;
import java.awt.event.*;
import java.io.*;
import java.util.*;
import javax.swing.*;
import org.omg.CORBA.*;
import static java.lang.System.*;

public class DIIClient extends JPanel {
  private ORB orb;
  private org.omg.CORBA.Object obj;
  private void initializeORB(String[] args) {
  ... as above in Section 7.13
  private org.omg.CORBA.Object getRef(String refFile) {
  ... as above in Section 7.13
  }
  private int value() {
    Request req = obj._request("_get_value");
    req.set_return_type(
      orb.get_primitive_tc(TCKind.tk_long));
    req.invoke();
    Any any = req.return_value();
    return any.extract_long();
  }
  private void createGUI() {
    setLayout(new GridLayout(2, 1));
    JPanel p = new JPanel();
    final JLabel value;
    p.add(new JLabel("Counter value: ", JLabel.RIGHT));
    p.add(value = new JLabel(String.valueOf(value())));
    add(p);
    p = new JPanel();
    JButton inc, dec;
    p.add(inc = new JButton("Increment"));
    p.add(dec = new JButton("Decrement"));
    add(p);
    inc.addActionListener(new ActionListener() {
      public void actionPerformed(ActionEvent e) {
        Request req = obj._request("inc");
        req.invoke();
        value.setText(String.valueOf(value()));
      }
    });
    dec.addActionListener(new ActionListener() {
      public void actionPerformed(ActionEvent e) {
        Request req = obj._request("dec");
        req.invoke();
        value.setText(String.valueOf(value()));
```

```
      }
    });
  }
  public DIIClient(String[] args, String refFile) {
    initializeORB(args);
    obj = getRef(refFile);
    createGUI();
  }
  public static void main(String[] args) {
    try {
      String refFile = "Counter.ref";
      JFrame f = new JFrame("DII Counter Client");
      f.getContentPane().add(new DIIClient(args,
        refFile));
      f.pack();
      f.setDefaultCloseOperation(JFrame.DISPOSE_ON_CLOSE);
      f.setVisible(true);
    } catch (Exception ex) {
      out.println("Exception: " + ex.getMessage());
      exit(1);
    }
  }
}
```

The method `main()` is declared analogous to the example GUI client in Section 7.13; methods `initializeORB()` and `getRef()` are unmodified. The `createGUI()` method, again, creates the user interface; but, it also contains the dynamic invocations in which we are especially interested. As above in 7.13, two buttons for incrementing and decrementing the current `Counter` value are created, together with the corresponding `Action-Listeners` that initiate the invocation of the remote methods `inc()` and `dec()`.

The essential difference to the client implementation in Section 7.13 lies in the remote increment and decrement operation invocations. To access the current `Counter` value, its own method `value()` is declared since, in the dynamic case, this determination is more complex than in the case of a static invocation. We now turn to the implementation of the methods `inc()`, `dec()`, and `value()`.

First, the `org.omg.CORBA.Object` method `_request()` described in Section 6.6.6 is invoked to create a pre-initialized `Request` object. Using this method, dynamic invocations of operations without arguments can be prepared by simply passing the name of the operation to invoke as a `String`. If arguments have to be passed during a dynamic invocation, one of the two `_create_request()` methods must be used (see Section 6.6.6).

The reference to the new `Request` object is stored in the variable `req`. We strongly recommend using such a `Request` object only for one single invocation since, for several ORB implementations (e.g., JacORB and OpenORB), repeated usage results in a run-time error. In our example, the statements preparing the `inc()` and `dec()` invocations are therefore

```
    Request req = obj._request("inc");
```

and

```
Request req = obj._request("dec");
```

Since both methods do not return a result value, nothing else needs to be done and the invocation can be initiated by means of a

```
req.invoke();
```

statement. As a result, the client blocks until the respective invocation is completed. Following the `inc()` and `dec()` invocations, the display of the `Counter` value in the GUI's `JLabel` (also named `value`) needs to be updated. The necessary access to the `Counter`'s `readonly` attribute `value` is more complex and is therefore incorporated into a separate method `value()`, whose body is declared as follows:

```
Request req = obj._request("_get_value");
req.set_return_type(
   orb.get_primitive_tc(TCKind.tk_long));
req.invoke();
Any any = req.return_value();
return any.extract_long();
```

On the IDL level, `readonly` attributes are equivalent to get operations, whose names are composed of the prefix `_get_` followed by the attribute's name. (For attributes, which are not specified `readonly` and may therefore also be set, a set method, whose name is prefixed by `_set_`, is generated as well.) Thus, the string `"_get_value"` is passed when the `Request` object for dynamically getting the attribute `value` is created. This process contains a potential source of error because the IDL compiler maps the `readonly` attribute `value` to the Java method `value()`, as seen on inspection of the operations interface `CounterOperations.java`; the string argument `"_get_value"` therefore might not meet one's expectations.

Since the get operation returns a value, the type of that return value must be set for the `Request` object. This is achieved by invoking method `set_return_type()` with an `org.omg.CORBA.TypeCode` argument (see Section 6.5). Here, we expect a return value of IDL type `long`. We therefore pass the `TypeCode`, which is created with an invocation of the ORB operation `get_primitive_tc()`, called with the constant `TCKind.tk_long` as an argument.

Subsequently, the `Counter` servant's method `value()` is invoked dynamically with the statement `req.invoke()`. For retrieving the return value of an invocation, the `Request` operation `return_value()` is available; it returns an `Any` result. We extract the value stored in the `Any` instance by using the method `extract_long()`, which returns a value of Java type `int`. (This is also the return type of method `value()`.)

14.2   Dynamic `TimeServer` Clients

To further deepen understanding of dynamic operation invocations following the synchronous and blocking communication model, we, again, address the different versions of the `TimeServer` example introduced in Chapter 9. We reuse the server implementations but modify the clients such that they use the DII in order to invoke the server-side methods dynamically.

14.2.1 `TimeServer` Version 1

The first variant of the `TimeServer`, presented in Section 9.1, is characterized by an IDL definition that manages information on hours, minutes, and seconds in three `readonly` attributes, each of type `unsigned long`. On the server side, we can reuse this IDL file, `TimeServer.idl`, without any modification. The `TimeServer`'s implementation, `TimeServerImpl.java`, as well as the implementation of the server application, `TimeServer.java`, can also be adapted identically to Section 9.1. One should follow the standard naming pattern for directories on the server and client hosts and start with a base directory `\Examples\DIITimeServer\1`. For the `TimeServer` examples in the following Subsections 14.2.2 – 14.2.5, the names of the base directories are `\Examples\DIITime-Server\2` through `\Examples\DIITimeServer\5`, accordingly.

With the exception of the dynamic invocations, the implementation of the client application is identical to the `TClient` discussed in Section 9.1. The only difference pertains to the constructor, which now has to have a declaration analogous to the following:

```
public TClient(String[] args, String refFile) {
  try {
    initializeORB(args);
    org.omg.CORBA.Object obj = getRef(refFile);
    Request req = obj._request("_get_hours");
    req.set_return_type(
      orb.get_primitive_tc(TCKind.tk_ulong));
    req.invoke();
    int h = req.return_value().extract_ulong();
    req = obj._request("_get_minutes");
    req.set_return_type(
      orb.get_primitive_tc(TCKind.tk_ulong));
    req.invoke();
    int m = req.return_value().extract_ulong();
    req = obj._request("_get_seconds");
    req.set_return_type(
      orb.get_primitive_tc(TCKind.tk_ulong));
    req.invoke();
    int s = req.return_value().extract_ulong();
    out.println("Time on Server: " + h
      + ((m < 10)? ":0": ":") + m
      + ((s < 10)? ":0": ":") + s);
  } catch (Exception ex) {
    out.println("Exception: " + ex.getMessage());
    exit(1);
  }
}
```

In the client application, the values of the three `readonly` attributes `hours`, `minutes`, and `seconds` of the server application's `TimeServer` object have to be determined through dynamic invocations. During discussion of the `value()` method in Section 14.1, we saw how read access to `readonly` attributes may be handled dynamically. The following four statements for getting the hours value repeat that procedure; they can be directly applied to the case of the two other attributes.

```
Request req = obj._request("_get_hours");
req.set_return_type(orb.get_primitive_tc(TCKind.tk_ulong));
req.invoke();
int h = req.return_value().extract_ulong();
```

First, a Request object is created through an invocation of _request() on the server object. The name of the operation to be invoked dynamically has to be passed as an argument. According to the rules discussed above, this name is simply _get_hours (although the attribute hours is mapped to a Java method hours() in the operations interface generated by the IDL compiler). In the next step, the return type of the operation must be set. Then, the dynamic invocation occurs when

```
req.invoke();
```

is executed. The return result is obtained as an Any by calling return_value() on the Request object req. Finally, the desired int value is extracted from the Any instance by an invocation of extract_ulong(). Recall that the IDL type unsigned long is mapped to the Java type int.

14.2.2 TimeServer Version 2

The second variant of the TimeServer, which was analyzed in Section 9.1, differs from variant one only in that the readonly attributes hours, minutes, and seconds are replaced by three operations hours(), minutes(), and seconds(), returning a value of type unsigned long. Since the Java mapping of the IDL definition of this second variant is exactly identical to the mapping for variant one, the servant implementation, TimeServerImpl.java, as well as the server application, TServer.java, can be reused directly and copied from variant one or from Section 9.1.

Now, one could expect that the dynamic client can also be copied from the example just treated above in Section 14.2.1. However, a slight adaptation is needed since the strings passed to the _request() operations are no longer built according to the rules for attribute access. They simply correspond to the names of the IDL operations. In the constructor of the client application the lines

```
Request req = obj._request("_get_hours");
...
req = obj._request("_get_minutes");
...
req = obj._request("_get_seconds");
```

therefore have to be replaced by

```
Request req = obj._request("hours");
...
req = obj._request("minutes");
...
req = obj._request("seconds");
```

No further adjustments are necessary. While the Java clients for variants one and two were identical in the static case, some differences are to be noted in the dynamic case.

14.2.3 **TimeServer** Version 3

The third variant of the TimeServer and the corresponding implementation was introduced in Section 9.2. For our next example of a client dynamically invoking server methods, the IDL definition TimeServer.idl and the servant implementation TimeServer-Impl.java can be retained unchanged. The server application TServer.java can also be reused as it was discussed in Section 9.1. One should copy these three files from \Examples\TimeServer\3 and the respective subdirectories.

The first variant of the TimeServer example used readonly attributes; in the second variant, three operations with empty parameter lists were used. Now, one single operation get_time() with a void return type and three out parameters, hours, minutes, and seconds, each of type unsigned long, is defined. The parameters transmit the time data from the server object back to the invoking client.

There are various ways to invoke an operation dynamically and to return its results in the out parameters. In the following, we discuss three alternative ways, all of which are modifications of the client application TClient.java presented in Section 9.1. These modifications only affect the TClient constructor. Here is the first alternative:

```
public TClient(String[] args, String refFile) {
  try {
    initializeORB(args);
    org.omg.CORBA.Object obj = getRef(refFile);
    // Start: Alternative 1
      Request req = obj._request("get_time");
      Any hany = req.add_out_arg(),
        many = req.add_out_arg(),
        sany = req.add_out_arg();
      hany.type(orb.get_primitive_tc(TCKind.tk_ulong));
      many.type(orb.get_primitive_tc(TCKind.tk_ulong));
      sany.type(orb.get_primitive_tc(TCKind.tk_ulong));
      req.set_return_type(
        orb.get_primitive_tc(TCKind.tk_void));
    // End: Alternative 1
    req.invoke();
    int hours = hany.extract_ulong(),
      minutes = many.extract_ulong(),
      seconds = sany.extract_ulong();
    out.println("Time on Server: " + hours
      + ((minutes < 10)? ":0": ":") + minutes
      + ((seconds < 10)? ":0": ":") + seconds);
  } catch (Exception ex) {
    out.println("Exception: " + ex.getMessage());
    exit(1);
  }
}
```

After initializing the ORB and getting the reference to the server object, we next create a new Request object. As before, the Object method _request() is called and the name of the operation to be invoked dynamically, here `"get_time"`, is passed. The operation `get_time()` has three `out` parameters. By default, the parameter list of a `Request` object created by means of `_request()` is empty. Therefore, the necessary arguments have to be subsequently provided with the `add_out_arg()` invocations. A side effect of these invocations is that three `Any` instances containing the results of the dynamic invocation are created. By calling `type()`, we set the type information for the `Any` objects appropriately so that they each can store time values of IDL type `unsigned long`. Since operation `get_time()` has a `void` return type, we still have to set that type in the familiar way, by calling `set_return_type(orb.get_primitive_tc(TCKind.tk_void))`, before we are, finally, able to call `invoke()` on the `Request` object. To access the values of the `out` parameters after the dynamic invocation is complete, we simply issue a call of `extract_ulong()` on the `Any` instances that we earlier obtained from the three invocations of `add_out_arg()`. As before, we must bear in mind that these operations return the respective value as a Java `int`. (To complement the above explanations one can also consult the description of the pseudo interface `Request` given in Section 6.6.3.)

Now, we turn to alternative two for implementing the `TClient` constructor. It is only necessary to replace the part between the two line comments `// Start: Alternative 1` and `// End: Alternative 1` by the following piece of code.

```
// Start: Alternative 2
Any hany = orb.create_any(),
  many = orb.create_any(),
  sany = orb.create_any();
hany.type(orb.get_primitive_tc(TCKind.tk_ulong));
many.type(orb.get_primitive_tc(TCKind.tk_ulong));
sany.type(orb.get_primitive_tc(TCKind.tk_ulong));
Request req = obj._request("get_time");
NVList arglist = req.arguments();
arglist.add_value("", hany, ARG_OUT.value);
arglist.add_value("", many, ARG_OUT.value);
arglist.add_value("", sany, ARG_OUT.value);
req.set_return_type(orb.get_primitive_tc(
  TCKind.tk_void));
// End: Alternative 2
```

Differing from the last alternative, we now do not use the `add_out_arg()` operations to provide arguments for the parameter list of the `Request` object. Instead, we directly manipulate that list. Recall that, in the `Request` interface, the parameter list is defined as a `readonly` attribute of type `NVList`, which is named `arguments`, and that this attribute is mapped in Java to a method `arguments()` (see Sections 6.6.2 and 6.6.3). Therefore, we invoke `arguments()` on the `Request` object to obtain a reference to the `NVList` and later we populate that parameter list with `NamedValues`, which represent the arguments to the operation to be invoked dynamically.

Creation of the actual arguments is started by calling the ORB method `create_any()`, which, again, provides three `Any` instances. The type information for these `Anys` is then set as before. Afterwards, actual arguments are inserted into the argument list in the order that corresponds to the parameter declarations in the IDL specification of the operation. To that purpose, the method `add_value()` is called with three arguments that entirely describe an operation's parameter (see Section 6.6.2). The first argument specifies the parameter name, which is insignificant here, so we left it empty. For reasons of clarity, one could use the parameter names of the IDL definition, namely `hours`, `minutes`, and `seconds`. However, the client has no knowledge of the IDL definition and its names. The second argument is the `Any`, which shall contain the returned parameter value. The third argument is the directional flag for the parameter value (see Section 6.6.1). On the Java level, these constants are named `org.omg.CORBA.ARG_IN.value`, `org.omg.CORBA.ARG_INOUT.value`, or, as in this case, `org.omg.CORBA.ARG_OUT.value`. Afterwards, the return type is set as before.

To complete this example, we describe a third alternative for the third `TimeServer` variant.

```
// Start: Alternative 3
Any hany = orb.create_any(),
  many = orb.create_any(),
  sany = orb.create_any(),
  rany = orb.create_any();
hany.type(orb.get_primitive_tc(TCKind.tk_ulong));
many.type(orb.get_primitive_tc(TCKind.tk_ulong));
sany.type(orb.get_primitive_tc(TCKind.tk_ulong));
rany.type(orb.get_primitive_tc(TCKind.tk_void));
NamedValue res = orb.create_named_value("", rany,
  ARG_OUT.value);
NVList arglist = orb.create_list(3);
arglist.add_value("", hany, ARG_OUT.value);
arglist.add_value("", many, ARG_OUT.value);
arglist.add_value("", sany, ARG_OUT.value);
Request req = obj._create_request(null, "get_time",
  arglist, res);
// End: Alternative 3
```

In this variant, we do not create the `Request` object with the easy to use `_request()` method, which only needs minimal information, specifically the name of the operation to be invoked. Instead, we use the more complex `_create_request()` method (see Section 6.6.6). One advantage of this method is that the queries that, depending on the ORB's implementation, `_request()` might automatically execute on the Interface Repository and that might negatively influence performance are avoided. For developers, the construction of the `Request` object turns out to be more complex. The `_create_request()` method that we invoke here expects four arguments that first have to be suitably prepared. Argument one specifies an invocation context, a possibility we do not utilize; therefore, that value is set to `null`. Argument two provides the name of the operation to be invoked as a string. The third argument is an `NVList` specifying the actual arguments. We create that `NVList` object with the ORB operation `create_list()`, whose argument is the number of arguments in the list; in our example, that number is 3. As above, we insert appropriately initialized `Any`s into the `NVList` object. The fourth argument is a `NamedValue` object serving as a container for the return value. We create this argument with the ORB method `create_named_value()`. The necessary arguments are a name (not needed here), an `Any` instance to be used as a container (here the additionally created object `rany`), and a directional flag (here `ARG_OUT.value`). Once the `Request` object is created, we can continue with the invocation, the extraction, and the display of the results as in the previous alternatives.

14.2.4 TimeServer Version 4

The fourth TimeServer example demonstrates how TypeCodes and DynAnys are employed when a dynamic client requires user-defined types. One should prepare the implementation by first copying version four of the TimeServer.idl definition and the corresponding servant implementation, TimeServerImpl.java, from Section 9.2 as well as the file TServer.java from Section 9.1 into the respective subdirectories of \Examples\DIITimeServer\4. Recall that, in this version of the TimeServer interface, a parameter-free operation get_time() is declared, using a structure Time as its return type. That structure is defined in the same interface; its definition simply consists of three unsigned long elements hours, minutes, and seconds. Again, only the constructor of the class TClient needs to be adapted; the rest of the implementation can be reused from the client in Section 9.2.

```
public TClient(String[] args, String refFile) {
   try {
      initializeORB(args);
      org.omg.CORBA.Object obj = getRef(refFile);
      Request req = obj._request("get_time");
      DynAnyFactory dynFactory =
      DynAnyFactoryHelper.narrow(
         orb.resolve_initial_references("DynAnyFactory"));
      TypeCode time_tc = orb.create_struct_tc(
         "IDL:Timer/TimeServer/Time:1.0", "Time",
            new StructMember[] {
               new StructMember("hours",
                  orb.get_primitive_tc(TCKind.tk_ulong),
                     null),
               new StructMember("minutes",
                  orb.get_primitive_tc(TCKind.tk_ulong),
                     null),
               new StructMember("seconds",
                  orb.get_primitive_tc(TCKind.tk_ulong),
                     null)
      });
      req.set_return_type(time_tc);
      req.invoke();
      Any res = req.return_value();
      org.omg.DynamicAny.DynStruct dynStruct =
         (org.omg.DynamicAny.DynStruct)
            dynFactory.create_dyn_any(res);
      org.omg.DynamicAny.NameValuePair[] members =
         dynStruct.get_members();
      int hours = members[0].value.extract_ulong(),
         minutes = members[1].value.extract_ulong(),
         seconds = members[2].value.extract_ulong();
      out.println("Time on Server: " + hours
         + ((minutes < 10)? ":0": ":") + minutes
         + ((seconds < 10)? ":0": ":") + seconds);
   } catch (Exception ex) {
```

```
        out.println("Exception: " + ex.getMessage());
        exit(1);
    }
}
```

Apart from the general steps when preparing and invoking an operation dynamically, we recognize numerous code elements that we discussed in Chapter 13 in connection with Dyn-Anys and TypeCodes. For example, we find determination of an initial reference to a Dyn-AnyFactory, exactly as it was described in Section 13.3.1. Following, a TypeCode named time_tc is constructed for the Time structure; again, the procedure is completely analogous to 13.3.2. This TypeCode is then used to set the return type for the Request object before dynamically invoking the requested operation. The client blocks until the result is available in the form of a Time instance embedded in an Any, which may be obtained as usual through a call of return_value() on the Request object. In order to read the elements of that Time structure, we have to create a DynAny, more precisely a Dyn-Struct, from the returned Any instance. Here, we follow the approach discussed in Section 13.3.1 exactly. Once the DynStruct instance is available, we can access its members with the help of method get_members(), which returns an array of NameValuePairs (see Section 13.2.5). In the example, we are only interested in the values. These are available as Anys via the value element. The rest of the code should be familiar by now.

14.2.5 **TimeServer** Version 5

In version five of the TimeServer, discussed in Section 9.2, the Time structure is used again. This time, however, it is not returned as the result of operation get_time(); instead, it is passed as an out parameter. For the server side, we can therefore reuse the files TimeServer.idl and TimeServerImpl.java directly from Section 9.2. The server implementation, TServer.java, still corresponds to the implementation discussed in Section 9.1; and, in the client application, TClient.java, only minor modifications are needed. The three code lines

```
    req.set_return_type(time_tc);
    req.invoke();
    Any res = req.return_value();
```

of the version presented above in Section 14.2.4 now become

```
    Any any = req.add_out_arg();
    any.type(time_tc);
    req.invoke();
```

Instead of setting the operation's return type by means of set_return_type() and, subsequently, accessing that value by invoking return_value(), we now prepare a new out parameter via add_out_arg() and then set its type to the new TypeCode before initiating the dynamic invocation.

The last adjustment necessary in the client code pertains to the creation of the DynStruct object in the next step. So far, we used the identifier res for the Any object. Now, we denote the parameter by any. The statement

```
org.omg.DynamicAny.DynStruct dynStruct =
  (org.omg.DynamicAny.DynStruct)
    dynFactory.create_dyn_any(res);
```

therefore is changed to

```
org.omg.DynamicAny.DynStruct dynStruct =
  (org.omg.DynamicAny.DynStruct)
    dynFactory.create_dyn_any(any);
```

14.3   Deferred Synchronous Invocations

At the end of this chapter, we discuss a last example that, deviating from all the other examples above, is not based on CORBA's "synchronous" and "blocking" standard communication model. Recall that, here, synchronous means a client invokes a server operation and the server executes the operation and, following, notifies the client that execution has terminated. This notification is also sent in the case of an operation with a `void` return type. While the server processes the request, the client blocks, i.e., no further action is performed on the client side. Blocking the client might be very inconvenient in the case of complex, time-consuming calculations of the server. In these cases, the client unnecessarily wastes computation time if the result of an invocation is not needed immediately and the client could, in the meantime, perform its own computations.

The Dynamic Invocation Interface also provides operations that allow initiating deferred synchronous dynamic invocations that circumvent the described blocking problems. These operations, `send_deferred()`, `get_response()`, and `poll_response()`, are all declared in the interface `Request`. In Sections 3.4.5, 6.6.3, and 6.6.6, we discussed their fundamental possibilities. `send_deferred()` is called instead of `invoke()`, whereupon the specified request is sent to the server; `send_deferred()`, however, returns immediately so that the client is able to proceed without having to wait for the completion of the server's work. At a later time, the client may invoke `get_response()` in order to determine the result of the request. If the request is completed, `get_response()` returns immediately and the result can be retrieved from the `Request` object. Otherwise, the client blocks until the result of the request is available. Blocking can be completely avoided through invocations of `poll_response()`. This operation determines whether execution of the request is complete. Return is immediate whether the response is completed or not. A `TRUE` return value indicates that it is; `FALSE` indicates it is not.

The example we use to demonstrate this approach is based on the IDL specification below:

```
// Compute.idl

module Compute
{
  interface ComputeServer
  {
    unsigned long binom(in unsigned long n,
      in unsigned long k);
  };
};
```

The interface `ComputeServer` represents an application that is executed on a powerful compute server and has to carry out complex calculations. For reasons of simplicity, only one single operation, `binom()`, is declared, determining the binomial coefficient $\dfrac{n!}{(n-k)!k!}$ of the two argument values n and k, each of type `unsigned long`. This example operation only replaces a pure *"Do Nothing"* or *"Sleep"* example and is intended to create an application where communication overhead plus remote computation time is significantly lower in comparison to local execution time on the client host.

One should store the specification `Compute.idl` in directory `\Examples\DIIAsynch` on the server host, compile it, and create the usual directories and subdirectories on the server and client hosts.

To implement the `ComputeServer` interface, we employ the well-known recurrence relation for binomial coefficients. One should store the implementation, `ComputeServer-Impl.java`, in directory `\Examples\DIIAsynch\`*YourORB*`\Server\Compute`.

```
// ComputeServerImpl.java

package Compute;

public class ComputeServerImpl extends ComputeServerPOA {
   public int binom(int n, int k) {
      if (n < 0 || k < 0 || n < k)
         return 0;
      if (k == 0 || k == n)
         return 1;
      else {
         return binom(n - 1, k) + binom(n - 1, k - 1);
      }
   }
}
```

The class `ComputeServerImpl` is implemented according to the inheritance approach.

The server application itself needs no additional comments. One could copy the file `Server.java` from the `DIICounter` example in Section 14.1 and then make the small changes that are necessary to adapt it to this example (e.g., import package `Compute`, instantiate and activate the correct type, `ComputeServerImpl`, change the file name for the object reference, etc.)

Since we implement a DII example, the more interesting aspects that deserve closer inspection concern, once again, the client application. One should store this file in directory `\Examples\DIIAsynch\`*YourORB*`\Client` on the client hosts.

```
// Client.java

import java.io.*;
import java.util.*;
import org.omg.CORBA.*;
import static java.lang.System.*;
```

```java
public class Client {
  private ORB orb;
  private void initializeORB(String[] args) {
    ... as above in Section 7.13
  private org.omg.CORBA.Object getRef(String refFile) {
    ... as above in Section 7.13
  }
  public Client(String[] args, String refFile) {
    try {
      initializeORB(args);
      org.omg.CORBA.Object obj = getRef(refFile);
      class NR {
        NR(String name, Request req) {
          this.name = name;
          this.req = req;
        }
        String name;
        Request req;
      }
      Collection<NR> nrColl = new HashSet<NR>();
      Scanner reader = new Scanner(in);
      for (;;) {
        out.print("End (0), New Computation (1), "
          + "Check Status (2)? ");
        out.flush();
        int action = reader.nextInt();
        if (action == 0)
          break;
        else if (action == 1) {
          out.print("n = ");
          out.flush();
          int n = reader.nextInt();
          out.print("k = ");
          out.flush();
          int k = reader.nextInt();
          Request req = obj._request("binom");
          req.add_in_arg().insert_ulong(n);
          req.add_in_arg().insert_ulong(k);
          req.set_return_type(
            orb.get_primitive_tc(TCKind.tk_ulong));
          req.send_deferred();
          nrColl.add(new NR("Binom(" + n + ", " + k + ")",
            req));
        }
        else if (action == 2) {
          for (NR nameReq: nrColl) {
            out.print(nameReq.name);
            Request req = nameReq.req;
            if (req.poll_response()) {
              try {
                req.get_response();
              } catch (WrongTransaction ex) { }
              out.println(" = "
                + req.return_value().extract_ulong());
            }
```

```
            else
               out.println(" n.a.");
         }
      }
   }
   } catch (Exception ex) {
      out.println("Exception: " + ex.getMessage());
      exit(1);
   }
}
public static void main(String[] args) {
   String refFile = "ComputeServer.ref";
   new Client(args, refFile);
}
}
```

In this implementation, the main work of the client is embedded in the for statement in the Client constructor. If a user enters a 1 to start a new computation, the two int values n and k have to be provided. Then, as usual, the Object method _request() is called in order to create a new Request object for the desired operation named "binom". After that, method add_in_arg() is called to create the in parameters of type Any, to add them to the Request object, and to enable insertion of the user-provided values for n and k. Next, the return type of the remote operation is specified. The respective statements are:

```
Request req = obj._request("binom");
req.add_in_arg().insert_ulong(n);
req.add_in_arg().insert_ulong(k);
req.set_return_type(
   orb.get_primitive_tc(TCKind.tk_ulong));
```

Now, the dynamic invocation is initiated. This time, we do not call invoke() but, instead, use the method send_deferred(), which returns immediately, irrespective of the time the server object needs to complete the call. To be able to find that request and to check its status and result, we store the values for n and k (in the form of a name string) as well as the reference to the Request object in a set of simple objects of type NR. Here, NR stands for Name/Request. The corresponding class is declared locally in the Client constructor.

Since the server-side computation may take a certain length of time, the client can, in the meantime, execute other statements. In this example, we let users start another computation by, again, entering a 1; or, they can check the status of their previous invocations by entering a 2. In the latter case, the elements in the set of NR objects are inspected. For each of the embedded Requests, method poll_response() is called to find out whether the result of the invocation is already available. In that case, we can access the result by invoking the Request method return_value(), which again returns an Any instance. By means of extract_ulong(), we now extract and print the value of the binomial coefficient; provided as a Java int value.

Even if the call of method poll_response() indicates that the result of the dynamic invocation is retrievable, OpenORB needs a further call of get_response() to enable access to the return value. In the case of JDK or JacORB, this is not necessary. Since this get statement does not affect the performance of the latter ORB products negatively, it should always be included for reasons of portability. As discussed in Section 6.6.6, `get_re-sponse()` may throw a `WrongTransaction` exception, hence the `try` block:

```
if (req.poll_response()) {
  try {
    req.get_response();
  } catch (WrongTransaction ex) { }
  out.println(" = "
    + req.return_value().extract_ulong());
} else
  out.println(" n.a.");
```

14.4 Exercises

1. Re-inspect the dynamic `TimeServer` example in alternative 3. Assume that creation of the `Request` object was outsourced into its own method `createRequest()`, e.g.,

```
private Request createRequest(org.omg.CORBA.Object obj) {
  Any hany = orb.create_any(),
  ...
  arglist.add_value("", sany, ARG_OUT.value);
  return obj._create_request(null, "get_time", arglist,
    res);
}
```

Now, after invocation of `createRequest()` and `invoke()`, the references to the Any instances in the parameter list of the invoked method are no longer accessible. Find out how the following construction works.

```
Request req = createRequest(obj);
req.invoke();
int hours =
  req.arguments().item(0).value().extract_ulong(),
  minutes =
    req.arguments().item(0).value().extract_ulong(),
  seconds =
    req.arguments().item(0).value().extract_ulong();
```

2. Implement a `TimeServer` with a dynamic client for the following IDL definition:

```
// TimeServer.idl
// Version 6

module Timer
{
  interface TimeServer
  {
    typedef sequence<unsigned long, 3> Time;
    Time get_time();
  };
};
```

3. Implement a `TimeServer` with a dynamic client for the following **IDL** definition:

```
// TimeServer.idl
// Version 7

module Timer
{
  interface TimeServer
  {
    typedef unsigned long Time[3];
    Time get_time();
  };
};
```

4. Implement a simple dynamic client application for the following `ComputeServer`:

```
// Compute.idl

module Compute
{
  interface ComputeServer
  {
    exception NotDefined { };
    unsigned long binom(in unsigned long n,
      in unsigned long k) raises (NotDefined);
  };
};
```

The exception should be raised when n $<$ 0 or k $<$ 0. Some useful hints might be:

- the fully qualified Java identifier of the exception is `Compute.Compute-ServerPackage.NotDefined`;
- the `Request` method `exceptions()` returns an `ExceptionList` to describe the exceptions an operation can raise;
- the `ExceptionList` method `add()` adds the `TypeCode` of a specific exception to the list;
- the `Request` method `env()` returns the `Environment` the DII uses to make exception information available; and
- the `Environment` method `exception()` returns the exception raised by an invocation, if any.

5. Specifying an operation to be invoked statically as oneway is an alternative to a dynamic invocation via `send_deferred()` as in the above `ComputeServer` example. Recall that CORBA's standard communication model refers to synchronous, blocking invocations but that oneway operations are by their very nature asynchronous in that no reply is ever received from a oneway operation and no synchrony can be assumed between the caller and the target. That is why, for oneway operations, only in parameters are admissible, the result type must be void, and there must be no list of exceptions to be raised (see Section 4.5.2). If clients are interested in the result of a oneway operation,

a callback pattern similar to the CBCount example of Chapter 11 must hence be followed.

Re-implement the ComputeServer example with a oneway operation binom(). The following IDL specification might be used:

```
//  Compute.idl

module Compute
{
  interface ComputeClient
  {
    void result(in unsigned long n,
       in unsigned long k, in unsigned long res);
  };
  interface ComputeServer
  {
    oneway void binom(in unsigned long n,
       in unsigned long k, in ComputeClient cc);
  };
};
```

Compare ease of implementation and user-friendliness of both approaches: static stub/skeleton-based oneway invocation versus DII-based deferred invocation.

15 Dynamic Skeleton Interface

The DSI, the basics of which were already covered in Section 6.7, is the server-side analog of the DII. While the DII provides a mechanism to invoke operations from the client without knowledge about the IDL definition of the server's operations, the DSI provides a similar mechanism for the server. With the help of the DSI, it is possible to implement CORBA objects whose interfaces are unknown at the server compile-time. To be able to execute the correct method for a client request, the server needs precise information on the operation's name, the parameters and the return value, and the exceptions it may raise. Normally, this information is embedded in the skeleton code that the IDL compiler generates from the IDL file and that is linked to the server application. For the remainder of this chapter, however, we assume that the operation's IDL specification is not available on the server side.

The DSI provides a unique general operation as an entry point that enables the ORB to pass arbitrary messages to the server, irrespective of their target object. For each of these messages, the ORB calls that dedicated operation and passes it the message. In the operation's body, the message is dynamically evaluated; the type information of the target object is decoded and the actual arguments of the server operation to be invoked are determined.

Potentially useful applications for the DSI might, again, be generic implementations of bridges or adapters. A distributed debugger might be an interesting example for the combined usage of DSI and DII. At run-time, the debugger receives an object reference from a client and, afterwards, poses as the proper object implementation towards that client. If, at this point of the scenario, the client invokes an operation using that reference, the debugger receives the request, protocols it suitably, and redirects the invocation to the respective object implementation. In the last step, the DII is used since no stub code for the target interface is known.

In the following, we demonstrate the DSI's usage by means of an example that concentrates on the computational details and is, therefore, kept very simple.

15.1 Defining IDL Module `Bank`

For the DSI example, we define a CORBA module `Bank` with an interface `Account`, specifying two operations `credit()` and `debit()` as well as an attribute of type `float`, which stores the account balance. The IDL file `Account.idl` is defined as follows:

```
// Account.idl

module Bank
{
  interface Account
  {
    readonly attribute float balance;
    void credit(in float amount);
```

```
        void debit(in float amount);
    };
};
```

Since it is assumed that the server has no compile-time knowledge on the client's interface definitions, one should store this file in the directory \Examples\DSIBank on the client hosts. The IDL file should then be compiled as usual.

15.2   Implementing the Servant

Analogous to the servants we discussed so far, DSI servants also receive operation requests via a POA object; their implementation, however, differs considerably from the standard approach. The typical way to realize a DSI servant can be understood through analysis of the example implementation DSIAccountImpl.java, which should be stored in directory \Examples\DSIBank*YourORB*\Server on the server host.

```
// DSIAccountImpl.java

import org.omg.CORBA.*;
import org.omg.PortableServer.*;

class DSIAccountImpl extends
     org.omg.PortableServer.DynamicImplementation {
  private ORB orb;
  private float balance;
  DSIAccountImpl(ORB orb) {
    this.orb = orb;
    balance = 0.0f;
  }
  public void invoke(ServerRequest req) {
    String op = req.operation();
    if (op.equals("_get_balance")) {
      NVList args = orb.create_list(0);
      req.arguments(args);
      Any result = orb.create_any();
      result.insert_float(balance);
      req.set_result(result);
    } else if (op.equals("credit")) {
      NVList args = orb.create_list(1);
      Any arg = orb.create_any();
      arg.type(orb.get_primitive_tc(TCKind.tk_float));
      args.add_value("", arg, ARG_IN.value);
      req.arguments(args);
      float value = arg.extract_float();
      balance += value;
    } else if (op.equals("debit")) {
      NVList args = orb.create_list(1);
      Any arg = orb.create_any();
      arg.type(orb.get_primitive_tc(TCKind.tk_float));
      args.add_value("", arg, ARG_IN.value);
      req.arguments(args);
      float value = arg.extract_float();
```

```
      balance -= value;
    }
  }
  public String[] _all_interfaces(POA poa, byte[] oid) {
    return new String[] { "IDL:Bank/Account:1.0" };
  }
}
```

The first obvious difference compared with our previous examples concerns the servant's superclass. Following the inheritance approach, and having access to the IDL specification of the `Account`, we would normally derive from the class `AccountPOA` generated by the IDL compiler. For the DSI implementation, class `DynamicImplementation` is the superclass to employ. This class is a subclass of the `Servant` class provided by the CORBA runtime library (see Sections 6.7.2 and 6.8). As indicated in the introduction above, the DSI's functionality is essentially based on a central entry point for operation invocations. In the Java mapping, this entry point is represented by method `invoke()`, which is inherited from the abstract class `DynamicImplementation` and must be suitably overridden in the servant, in order to provide the program logic for processing of DSI-based invocations.

Once the POA receives the request of a client to execute an operation invocation, it calls method `invoke()` and passes it a reference to a `ServerRequest` object (see Sections 6.7.1 and 6.7.2). The object contains all the information relevant for the request: the name of the operation, the list of arguments, etc. The name of the operation is obtained as a string through the `ServerRequest` method `operation()`. In the cases `"credit"` and `"debit"`, this result is intuitively clear; with respect to the `readonly` attribute `balance`, the pattern explained in the chapter on DII is followed. Here, the respective IDL name is returned; in the example, that name is `"_get_balance"`.

It should be noted here that in this example, somewhat unrealistically for a practical DSI application, we do not support different interfaces and we do not want to access an Interface Repository to obtain type information dynamically. For that reason, we also refrain from determining the POA and the `ObjectId` of the object first and then getting the `RepositoryId` of the object, which would be necessary steps before accessing the IR. (Also see the discussion of method `_all_interfaces()` below.) Instead, analogous to the DII examples, for reasons of simplicity, we assume that certain basic facts are known about the operations, e.g., concerning the number and types of the operation parameters. In an entirely generic application, that knowledge would not be available and it would have to be acquired dynamically from the IR.

In the `if` statement in the body of our `invoke()` implementation, the name of the actual operation is compared to the names of the three operations we support due to our above-mentioned basic knowledge. For the dynamic invocation of these operations, the values of the `in` parameters of the invocation have to be determined, values for `inout` and `out` parameters must be set, if needed, and a return value must be provided, if needed. For these activities, the `ServerRequest` object plays a role comparable to that of the `Request` object in the DII context. It is recommended that the structure of a `Request` be recalled, explained in Sections 6.7.1 and 6.7.2. There, we saw that the methods `arguments()` and `set_result()` are important. Here, method `arguments()` is called with an `NVList` argument containing entries for all `in`, `inout`, and `out` parameters. The ORB automatically enters the values passed by the client into that NVList instance. Therefore, after the invocation of arguments(), those elements of the NVList standing for in and inout parameters are supplied with the values provided by the client. These may subsequently be processed with the functionality available in the DynamicAny module. A second purpose of the NVList is to accept result values calculated for the operation's inout and out parameters; these are, again, constructed with the help of module DynamicAny. Finally, if applicable, the return result of the operation is set by calling set_result(). The value is passed inside an Any object.

Let us first analyze the operation corresponding to the name "_get_balance":

```
NVList args = orb.create_list(0);
req.arguments(args);
Any result = orb.create_any();
result.insert_float(balance);
req.set_result(result);
```

As discussed in Section 6.6.4, the necessary NVList object is created with the ORB method create_list(). Since the invoked operation is a simple read operation, we create a list with 0 parameters and directly pass it to the call of arguments(). This procedure seems to be a bit tedious and one might be tempted to call arguments(null) or simply skip list creation and the call entirely. However, of the three ORBs we use, only JacORB tolerated this shortcut and for reasons of portability, it is recommended to always proceed as in the code example above. Following the NVList creation and the invocation of arguments(), the current value of the instance variable balance has to be set as the return value. The create_any() and insert_float() invocations are familiar; the method set_result() is called to pass the return value to the ServerRequest object.

The process to handle an invocation of operation "credit" is slightly different because the operation is specified with an in parameter of type float and a void return type:

```
NVList args = orb.create_list(1);
Any arg = orb.create_any();
arg.type(orb.get_primitive_tc(TCKind.tk_float));
args.add_value("", arg, ARG_IN.value);
req.arguments(args);
float value = arg.extract_float();
balance += value;
```

As the operation has one parameter, we create the NVList by means of calling create_list(1). Before invoking arguments() on the ServerRequest object, the empty NVList must be populated with a suitable entry for the float parameter. To that end, an Any container with the necessary type information is created. In the next step, this Any instance is added to the argument list through an invocation of method add_value(). The name of the parameter (here, simply " ") and its directional attribute (here, ARG_IN.value) also have to be provided. The parameter list is now totally specified and can be passed as an argument to the arguments() method. When that call is completed, the argument passed by the client application is available in the Any instance and its value can be obtained by an appropriate extraction method. In the example, this is method extract_float(). Processing of the extracted value or values would now follow. Here, we just have to add the value to the attribute balance. The DSI implementation for the operation "debit" is defined analogous to the just described "credit" implementation.

To complete the discussion, we finally have to mention method _all_interfaces(). It is declared abstract in the Servant superclass and needs to be overridden in the concrete implementation of a DSI servant. In the case of static invocations, that method is part of the automatically generated skeleton code. Since it is occasionally called by the ORB, developers have to provide an implementation for the DSI approach. The method takes a POA instance and an ObjectId as arguments and returns a string array containing a sequence of RepositoryIds representing the type information of the target object. The first array element contains the most derived interface; additional elements stand for its supertypes. In the example, the array length is 1 and the single identifier is "IDL:Bank/Account:1.0". It might be interesting to inspect the body of the IDL compiler-generated method _all_interfaces() in our inheritance example. There, the String array {"IDL:Timer/DateTimeServer:1.0", "IDL:Timer/TimeServer:1.0"} is returned; see the class declaration DateTimeServerPOA.java.

15.3   Implementing the Server Application

The DSI server application presents only minor characteristic differences in comparison to our previous server implementations. One should store the following file DSIServer.java in directory \Examples\DSIBank\YourORB\Server on the server host. The server can be translated and started without further preparations; note that the IDL specification Account.idl is not available on the server side.

```
// DSIServer.java

import java.io.*;
import java.util.Properties;
import org.omg.CORBA.*;
import org.omg.PortableServer.*;
import static java.lang.System.*;

public class DSIServer {
  private ORB orb;
  private POA rootPOA;
  private void initializeORB(String[] args) {
    ... as above in Section 8.2
  }
  private void putRef(org.omg.CORBA.Object obj,
      String refFile) {
    ... as above in Section 8.2
  }
  public DSIServer(String[] args, String refFile) {
    try {
      initializeORB(args);
      DSIAccountImpl a_impl = new DSIAccountImpl(orb);
      org.omg.CORBA.Object a =
        rootPOA.servant_to_reference(a_impl);
      putRef(a, refFile);
```

```
        rootPOA.the_POAManager().activate();
        orb.run();
    } catch (Exception ex) {
        out.println("Exception: " + ex.getMessage());
        exit(1);
    }
}
public static void main(String[] args) {
    String refFile = "Account.ref";
    new DSIServer(args, refFile);
}
}
```

The only remarkable detail in the server application differing from earlier program code is the way in which the object reference to the newly created server object is obtained before it is written to the reference file. When we implement the static approach, we typically rely on the available skeleton code and use a statement of this kind:

```
CounterFactory cf = cf_impl._this(orb);
```

Now, a more generic procedure is needed. Different than a normal servant, a DSI servant has no type-specific _this() method. We therefore call servant_to_reference() on the root POA to obtain a generic object reference of type org.omg.CORBA.Object (see Section 6.3.2):

```
org.omg.CORBA.Object a =
    rootPOA.servant_to_reference(a_impl);
```

The remaining code corresponds to the familiar server implementations discussed in earlier examples.

15.4   Implementing the Client Application

To complete the DSI example and to obtain a runnable distributed application, the client remains to be implemented.

```
// DSIClient.java

import Bank.*;
import java.io.*;
import java.util.Properties;
import org.omg.CORBA.*;
import static java.lang.System.*;

public class DSIClient {
    private ORB orb;
    private void initializeORB(String[] args) {
        ... as above in Section 8.3
    }
    private org.omg.CORBA.Object getRef(String refFile) {
        ... as above in Section 8.3
    }
```

```
public DSIClient(String[] args, String refFile) {
  try {
    initializeORB(args);
    org.omg.CORBA.Object obj = getRef(refFile);
    Account a = AccountHelper.narrow(obj);
    a.credit(28231.15f);
    a.debit(100.9f);
    out.println("Account balance: " + a.balance());
  } catch (BAD_PARAM ex) {
    out.println("Narrowing failed");
    exit(3);
  } catch (Exception ex) {
    out.println("Exception: " + ex.getMessage());
    exit(1);
  }
}
public static void main(String[] args) {
  String refFile = "Account.ref";
  new DSIClient(args, refFile);
}
}
```

It can easily be seen that this client has no specific characteristic features differentiating it from earlier example clients. In particular, on the basis of the client's program code, it is impossible to recognize whether requests are processed dynamically or statically on the server side. In our example scenario, each client host has the IDL file and the generated stub code at its disposal so that the object reference read from "Account.ref" can be cast to its correct type as usual with the respective helper class:

```
Account a = AccountHelper.narrow(obj);
```

Also, the remote invocations of methods debit() and credit() give no indication whatsoever that the server handles the invocations dynamically with the help of the DSI.

One should store the file DSIClient.java in the directory \Examples\DSI-Bank\YourORB\Client on the client hosts, translate it, and run the completed application as usual. Again, one notices that the correct Java method name for accessing the balance attribute is balance(), as opposed to the IDL operation name inspected in the body of the DSI servant's invoke() method.

15.5 Exercises

1. Implement a DSI version of the Counter example.

2. Write a DII-DSI version of the Bank example with a DSI server and a DII client.

16 Implementing Different POAs

In Section 6.3, we introduced OMG's Portable Object Adapter, which functions like an "electrical outlet", connecting CORBA objects to the network and making them accessible to clients. More precisely, on the server side, the POA is responsible for localization of servant objects suited to process incoming client requests and for invocation of the corresponding operations on these servants. When designing the POA, the OMG found it especially important to specify a highly flexible and scalable architecture. For that reason, the possibility to determine various aspects of a POA's behavior during its creation by setting a number of policies was provided. Thus, many different types of object adapters may be generated. A detailed discussion of the various combinations of POA policies is beyond the scope of this book. And, in practice, it is rarely the case that more than two or three different POA types are used in the same application. Therefore, in this chapter, we limit our explanations to the discussion of one single example that demonstrates how a dedicated POA may be configured and employed.

Before we turn our attention to the example, it is potentially useful to review the typical sequence of operation invocations in a CORBA system and the POA's role in that scenario. The necessary basic condition is that a CORBA object be generated on the server host through the instantiation of a corresponding servant object and its subsequent activation. Normally, activation is carried out through entering the servant in the POA's Active Object Map. Recall that this map contains an ObjectId and a reference to the servant. Now, if a client request is sent to the server, it is first passed through a POAManager object, which directs the incoming messages to the POA object or one of the POA objects it controls. The POA manager can be in one of the four processing states, *holding*, *active*, *discarding*, or *inactive*. To enable its POA objects to process requests, the POAManager object must be in the active state (see Section 6.3.1). Depending on the POA's configuration, there are different strategies followed when the ObjectId contained in the client request is mapped to the corresponding servant object. By default, the 1-to-1 and the n-to-1 mapping of ObjectIds to servant objects based on an Active Object Map is supported. The n-to-1 mapping is of special interest in the case of stateless servants that need not store any object-specific attribute values. Besides the static approach based on the Active Object Map, the dynamic assignment of ObjectIds to servants is a further possibility, which we explain in the example discussed below.

All the examples presented so far managed with the root POA, which is automatically created when a CORBA server is started. This dedicated POA is configured with an immutable set of standard policies and may serve as the basis of a hierarchy of additionally created and specially configured child POAs (see Section 6.3.1). In previous examples, we see time and again how a reference to the root POA can be obtained. A child POA whose policies can be set as required is created with the help of operation create_POA(), which is invoked on an existing POA object. Depending on the type of the CORBA objects to be supported by the POA, e.g., transient objects, persistent objects, or factory objects, and depending on their desired attributes, a suitable combination of policy values must be selected.

In the following example, a child POA is created that, differing from the root POA, supports the *request processing policy* USE_SERVANT_MANAGER as well as the *servant retention policy* NON_RETAIN, i.e., it does without an Active Object Map. USE_SERVANT_MANA-GER indicates that the POA uses a ServantManager object instead, which is normally done to improve scalability of the server by influencing the life cycles and activation of the servants. Design patterns, such as the "Evictor" pattern [KJ04], may be implemented here to optimize resource consumption. In Sections 6.3.4 and 6.3.5, we noted that two types of ServantManager objects exist: ServantActivators and ServantLocators. ServantActivators rely on the existence of an Active Object Map and incarnate (create and activate) a suitable servant object in the case that the request's ObjectId is not found. On the other hand, ServantLocators are used by POAs that do not manage an Active Object Map (NON_RETAIN) so that the ServantLocator object has to dynamically map ObjectIds to servant objects when its operation preinvoke() is invoked. Since we decided to set the servant retention policy to NON_RETAIN, the concrete ServantManager in the example must inevitably be a ServantLocator.

Usage of a ServantLocator allows a CORBA programmer to implement almost any life cycle managing model for servants. As described in Section 6.3.5, to that purpose, the ServantLocator interface specifies two operations, preinvoke() and postinvoke(), which programmers may implement appropriately; these operations are automatically invoked by the POA for every request it receives. The preinvoke() implementation has to return a suitable servant object and must provide a cookie as an out parameter. The cookie should identify the invocation so that it may be used later in the operation's postinvoke() implementation, for example, to free resources of the then completed request. Between these two calls, the POA invokes the requested operation on the servant returned by preinvoke(). The original client request is then processed.

16.1 Counter **Example**

Once again, we fall back to the well-known Counter interface, discussed above in Sections 7.13–7.15. One should copy the IDL file Counter.idl from \Examples\ModCounter to directories \Examples\POA created on the server and client hosts and compile it as usual.

The servant implementation, CounterImpl.java, can be reused entirely unrevised; one should copy this file from \Examples\ModCounter*YourORB*\Server\Count to the directory \Examples\POA*YourORB*\Server\Count on the server host. The GUIClient can be copied as well. This file can be found in the directory \Examples\ModCounter*YourORB*\Client; it should be copied to directory \Examples\POA*YourORB*\Client on the client hosts. The client application is in no way affected by the server-side processing models.

All changes relevant for this chapter only touch upon the implementation of the ServantLocator, which is necessitated for the first time, and on the proper server application. Both are presented in the next sections.

16.2   Implementing `ServantLocator`

We first implement the `ServantLocator` and create a Java file `ServantLocator-Impl`, as usual to be stored in directory `\Examples\POA\`*`YourORB`*`\Server` on the server host. Since we have to provide our own implementation of the operations `preinvoke()` and `postinvoke()`, we use the opportunity to integrate a simple kind of logging functionality that is completely transparent to programmers of client or server applications. For each request that the POA directs to a servant object via the `ServantLocator`, the `ServantLocator` object in the context of its `preinvoke()` and `postinvoke()` methods writes the current date and time, an index counting how many times a `Counter` operation was invoked, and the name of the respective operation into a log file. The corresponding Java code is:

```java
// ServantLocatorImpl.java

import Count.*;
import java.io.*;
import java.text.*;
import java.util.*;
import org.omg.CORBA.*;
import org.omg.PortableServer.*;
import org.omg.PortableServer.ServantLocatorPackage.*;

class ServantLocatorImpl
    extends LocalObject implements ServantLocator {
  private CounterImpl c_impl;
  private PrintWriter writer;
  private DateFormat form;
  private Long invCount = new Long(0);
  ServantLocatorImpl() {
    c_impl = new CounterImpl();
    try {
      writer = new PrintWriter(
        new FileOutputStream("Log.txt"));
    } catch (IOException ex) { }
    form = DateFormat.getDateTimeInstance();
  }
  public synchronized Servant preinvoke(byte[] oid,
      POA adapter, String op, CookieHolder cookie) {
    writer.println(form.format(new Date())
      + " [operation(" + invCount + "): " + op + ">");
    writer.flush();
    cookie.value = invCount++;
    return c_impl;
  }
  public synchronized void postinvoke(byte[] oid,
      POA adapter, String op, java.lang.Object cookie,
      Servant servant) {
    writer.println(form.format(new Date())
      + " <operation(" + (Long)cookie + "): " + op + "]");
    writer.flush();
  }
}
```

Since the `ServantLocator` is a local IDL interface, the class `ServantLocatorImpl` inherits from class `org.omg.CORBA.LocalObject` and at the same time implements the Java interface `org.omg.PortableServer.ServantLocator`. In the constructor, an instance of the servant implementation, `CounterImpl`, is created and the log file `Log.txt` is generated as well. In the method `preinvoke()`, which is invoked by the POA each time an operation has to be executed, first the date/time, then the invocation counter, and, finally, the operation name information is written to the log. Subsequently, the cookie's value, i.e., the invocation counter, is incremented and stored. The last statement returns the reference to the servant.

`Cookie` is an *opaque* type in IDL, meaning that its representation is specified by the language mapping. In the Java mapping, the type `PortableServer::ServantLocator::Cookie` is mapped to the class `java.lang.Object`. In addition, a `CookieHolder` class is provided for passing the `Cookie` type as an `in` or an `out` parameter. The `CookieHolder` class follows exactly the same pattern as the other holder classes for basic types (see Section 5.4).

```
final public class CookieHolder implements
     org.omg.CORBA.portable.Streamable {
  public java.lang.Object value;
  public CookieHolder() { }
  public CookieHolder(java.lang.Object o) { value = o; }
  ...
}
```

For the Java mapping of the `preinvoke()` operation, a `CookieHolder` object is passed in with its value set to `null`. Developers may then set the value to any Java object. The same `Cookie` object is passed to the `postinvoke()` operation.

In the above example, the method `postinvoke()` simply writes the date/time, the invocation counter, and the operation name to the log file. This method is called after the POA initiated execution of the proper increment, decrement, or get method via the servant reference obtained from `preinvoke()`.

16.3   Implementing the Server Application

Creation of a dedicated child POA with specific policy properties has to be taken care of in the server application. For our simple example, the following implementation is able to perform that task:

```
// Server.java

import Count.*;
import java.io.*;
import java.util.Properties;
import org.omg.CORBA.*;
import org.omg.PortableServer.*;
import org.omg.PortableServer.POAPackage.*;
import static java.lang.System.*;
```

```
public class Server {
  private ORB orb;
  private POA rootPOA, locatorPOA;
  private void initializeORB(String[] args) {
    ... as above in Section 8.2
  }
  private void putRef(org.omg.CORBA.Object obj,
      String refFile) {
    ... as above in Section 8.2
  }
  private void createPOA() {
    try {
      Policy[] policies = {
        rootPOA.create_servant_retention_policy(
        ServantRetentionPolicyValue.NON_RETAIN),
        rootPOA.create_request_processing_policy(
        RequestProcessingPolicyValue.USE_SERVANT_MANAGER)
      };
      locatorPOA = rootPOA.create_POA("ServantLocatorPOA",
        rootPOA.the_POAManager(), policies);
    } catch (InvalidPolicy ex) {
    } catch (AdapterAlreadyExists ex) {
    }
  }
  public Server(String[] args, String refFile) {
    try {
      initializeORB(args);
      createPOA();
      ServantManager locator = new ServantLocatorImpl();
      locatorPOA.set_servant_manager(locator);
      org.omg.CORBA.Object counter =
        locatorPOA.create_reference(
          "IDL:Count:Counter:1.0");
      putRef(counter, refFile);
      rootPOA.the_POAManager().activate();
      orb.run();
    } catch(Exception ex) {
      out.println("Exception: " + ex.getMessage());
      exit(1);
    }
  }
  public static void main(String args[]) {
    String refFile = "Counter.ref";
    new Server(args, refFile);
  }
}
```

The fundamental design of the server application remains as it was. But, since we now intend to create a new object adapter besides the root POA, we declare the variable locatorPOA, also of type POA. In the method createPOA(), the desired policies of the new POA are set and this new POA is created as a child of the root POA. We declare a Policy array, policies, the Java equivalent of the IDL type CORBA::PolicyList. This array has to be passed when the locatorPOA is created; it specifies the new POA's properties for its whole life cycle. At this point, it should be noted that all policies not explicitly set obtain default values corresponding to the root POA configuration. There is one exception, however. The `ImplicitActivationPolicy`, which in the root POA has the value `IMPLICIT_ACTIVATION`, is set to `NO_IMPLICIT_ACTIVATION` in the default configuration of a child POA. In addition to the `policies`, the name of the new POA as well as a `POAManager` object, which manages the new POA, have to be passed to the `create_POA()` method. Two exceptions may be thrown and have to be handled when `create_POA()` is called.

To enable the newly created POA to employ a `ServantLocator` instance in order to locate servant objects, that instance needs to be generated and registered with the new POA in the next step. Registration is carried out through the invocation of method `set_servant_manager()`. All preparations are completed through a call of method `create_reference()` on the new object adapter. In that way, a reference to a `Counter` object is created that can later be stringified and written to a reference file. The `RepositoryId` of the `Counter` object, in our example `"IDL:Count:Counter:1.0"`, is passed as an argument here. The rest of the server application corresponds to the pattern known from earlier examples.

One should now store the file `Server.java` in directory `\Examples\POA\Your-ORB\Server` on the server host. After translating the server and the client applications, starting the server, and copying its reference file, `Counter.ref`, to the client hosts, the clients may be started and the complete application should be running. The log file `Log.txt` is written to the `Server` directory. It has the following structure:

```
...
Oct 10, 2005 8:36:05 AM [operation(1218): inc>
Oct 10, 2005 8:36:06 AM <operation(1218): inc]
Oct 10, 2005 8:36:06 AM [operation(1219): inc>
Oct 10, 2005 8:36:06 AM [operation(1220): _get_value>
Oct 10, 2005 8:36:06 AM <operation(1220): _get_value]
Oct 10, 2005 8:36:06 AM <operation(1219): inc]
Oct 10, 2005 8:36:06 AM [operation(1221): _get_value>
...
```

16.4   Exercise

Rewrite the `ComputeServer` example from Section 14.3 such that, for each invocation of method `binom()`, the necessary computation time in milliseconds is written to a log file. After several invocations, the log might look like this:

```
Invocation 1 took 20 msec to complete.
Invocation 2 took 3 msec to complete.
Invocation 3 took 3775 msec to complete.
...
```

Take the unmodified client implementation directly from Section 14.3 and write a servant locator analogous to the code in Section 16.2. Reuse as much as possible from the above discussed server application.

17 CORBA's Naming Service

A typical problem that needs to be solved when developing distributed object-oriented applications with clients and servers residing on different hosts on a network is how a client application can obtain a reference to the server objects with which it wants to communicate. Only by means of these references is it possible to invoke the desired remote operations on the server objects. This problem is often called a "bootstrapping problem". Its solution is complicated by the fact that utilization of CORBA object references is rather unwieldy for human users. In addition to the internal CORBA representation for IORs, which is inaccessible anyhow, we have the string representation. This, however, is only a long sequence of digits without direct meaning.

In our previous examples, we used the tedious approach of stringifying the IOR of the newly created server objects in the server application, writing it to a file residing on the server host, and transmitting it somehow manually to the client hosts. In the client application, that IOR string was then read and converted back to a valid IOR. Possible alternatives to that procedure might be the following approaches:

- the bootstrap file that stores the object reference is jointly used by applications on server host and client hosts, for example, through an NFS-based file system;
- information on the object reference is reachable via a URL—that is, there is an FTP or HTTP server in the network domain appropriately configured to allow read access to the bootstrap file; or
- users enter the IOR string themselves.

All these alternatives are at best inconvenient to use and often require additional expenditure. They are especially impractical when clients want to invoke server operations for a longer period of time during which the object references might change, e.g., when a server needs to be restarted. In such a case, all clients would have to obtain the new server reference in the same laborious way as before.

A solution to those problems is the usage of a central localizer component, or of a corresponding service, which provides an entry point known to all parts of the distributed application (also see Section 17.3) and which introduces a new level of abstraction for identification of objects. The latter goal may be reached by associating meaningful human-readable name strings with object references. With its Naming Service [OMG04a], the OMG specified a simple but interoperable CORBAservice that lets users name objects and, in reverse, find objects by name. In newer versions of the specification, that service is also denoted the *Interoperable Naming Service* (INS).

17.1   Basics

With its ability to find distributed objects by name, the Naming Service is the most fundamental CORBAservice. It is the first service specified by the OMG and it is, meanwhile, implemented by virtually any ORB vendor. The NS is like the telephone white pages. It manages associations of freely eligible names to object references and enables clients to locate object references by using the name as a search string. As a bootstrap service, executed independently of client and server applications, the NS considerably simplifies the establishment of initial connections between clients and servers.

Typically, a server application determines name-to-object associations for the objects, which are used as initial service providers for clients. These *name bindings* are then registered with the Naming Service. Each client knowing the name of a server object can then query the NS in order to obtain this object's reference. In addition to simplifying administration and transmission of speaking object names, the NS also decouples service providers and service users in that the concrete object implementation associated with a name may be exchanged although the name is maintained. In this way, also the problems of server restarts, mentioned above, are reduced since a client always receives a valid object reference bound or rebound to the originally assigned name.

In order not to be restricted to a single flat name space, the Naming Service specification lets one create naming hierarchies through the usage of *naming contexts*. Strictly speaking, two types of NS bindings must be distinguished. On the one hand, we have the object bindings mentioned above, which associate a name to an object reference and which are always valid in a specific naming context. On the other hand, we may create context bindings, which associate a name to a naming context. The name hierarchy created in this way resembles the concept of a file system consisting of named directories (analogous to naming contexts), which, again, may consist of named files (analogous to object references) or of named subdirectories (analogous to further naming contexts). Thus, a context is a set of object or context bindings. Each name is unique in its context and identifies another context or an object reference.

Before we turn to the first example demonstrating bindings for naming contexts and object references, it may be potentially useful to have a look at the IDL definition that the NS specification provides for names and naming contexts:

```
module CosNaming
{
  typedef string Istring;
  struct NameComponent {
    Istring id;
    Istring kind;
  };
  typedef sequence<NameComponent> Name;
  ...
};
```

Note that Istring was a placeholder for an IDL "internationalized string" data type in earlier versions of the specification, maintained for compatibility reasons. In principle, a Name that can be handled by the NS consists of a sequence of NameComponents. Each name component has two members, the `id` member and the `kind` member, both of which may hold a string. While it is customary to use the `id` part to store the proper identifier for the name component, the `kind` part is available for application-specific purposes. Note, however, that both parts together are considered when name components are compared for identity. A name with a single component is called a *simple name*; a name with multiple components is called a *compound name*. Each component of a compound name, except the last, is used to name a context; the last component denotes the object reference.

In addition to the just described IDL-based representation of names, the current NS specification also provides a standardized string-based name representation. We discuss this form in more detail in Section 17.7. At the moment, it should suffice to know that, in the string representation, name components are separated by a slash '`/`' whereas the `id` and the `kind` members are separated by a dot '`.`'.

Figure 21 shows an example of an NS hierarchy; this example is reused in Exercise 3 at the end of this chapter. The point on top symbolizes the unnamed *initial* naming context, which represents the entry point to the name hierarchy. In the example, it contains two naming contexts, bound to the names `"Europe.Continent"` and `"America.Continent"`. Below these, additional levels of naming contexts may be seen. The naming context named `"Europe.Continent/France.Country/Ile de France.Region/Paris.City"` contains no further naming contexts; however, two object bindings named `"Arc de Triomphe.Attraction"` and `"La Tour Eiffel.Attraction"` are defined here. An example of a compound name is `"Europe.Continent/France.Country/Ile de France.Region/Paris.City/Arc de Triomphe.Attraction"`. It consists

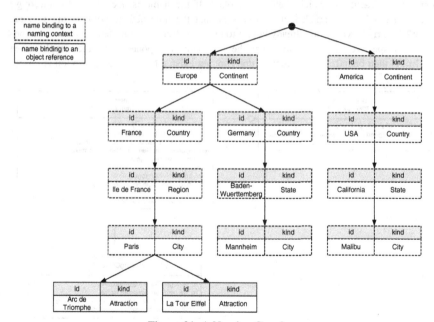

Figure 21: A Naming Graph

of the four context names, `"Europe.Continent"`, `"France.Country"`, `"Ile de France.Region"`, and `"Paris.City"`, followed by the simple name `"Arc de Triomphe.Attraction"`.

So far, the NS description may give the impression that a naming graph always has a tree-like hierarchical structure. That may be customary in practice; however, it is in no way mandatory. The NS specification even allows defining name graphs containing cycles, requiring special attention when code iterating through the naming contexts is written.

17.2   IDL Definition of the Naming Service

Three interfaces, the `NamingContext`, the `BindingIterator`, and the `NamingContextExt` interfaces, together define the Naming Service. Figure 22 shows an overview of their operations and dependencies in the form of a UML class diagram. The exceptions that may be raised are not displayed, here. At the end of the book, the complete specification of the NS is appended (Appendix C).

The fundamental interface `NamingContext` provides a number of operations for creating or removing name bindings as well as for retrieving an object bound to a name. The `NamingContext` interface further provides the means to create a new or to delete an existing `NamingContext` in a given `NamingContext`.

The operations `bind()` and `rebind()` create a name binding for a CORBA object in the `NamingContext` for which they are invoked. If the name is a compound name, e.g., `i1.k1/i2.k2/.../in.kn`, it is necessary that the intermediate components `i1.k1`, `i2.k2`,..., `in-1.kn-1` are already bound to create a structure of nested context names below the respective `NamingContext`; the last name component, i.e., the simple name `in.kn`, is then bound. If that structure does not yet exist, a `NotFound` exception is raised.

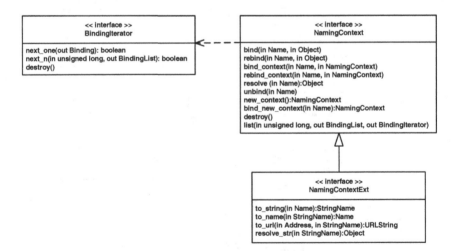

Figure 22: Dependencies Between NS Interfaces

The difference between the two operations is that bind() only creates a name binding when the name passed is not yet bound in the context. Otherwise, an AlreadyBound exception is raised. The rebind() operation creates a name binding in the naming context even if the name is already bound; in that case, the existing binding is simply overwritten. Since in most cases this is the desired behavior, programmers often prefer the rebind() to the bind() operation. In addition to the AlreadyBound exception, which may be raised by the bind() operation, and to the NotFound exception, which may be raised both by bind() and rebind(), further exceptions are possible. An InvalidName exception is raised when a syntactically incorrect name (for example, an empty name without components) is passed or a CannotProceed exception is raised whenever the NS is not able to complete the invocation (for example, due to security requirements). The IDL specification given in Appendix B shows the structure of the exceptions; this information may be useful when a caller needs to handle these exceptions.

bind_context() and rebind_context() operate with similar semantics and have a comparable list of exceptions. They create a new NamingContext in the context for which they are invoked. Both operations assume that the passed NamingContext object was already created by a new_context() invocation. Invoking operation bind_new_context() allows creating and binding such a context object at once. With these three operations, new context bindings may be generated, which expand the hierarchy of names existing so far. Again, it must be noted that the direct parent naming context of the new context must already exist because, otherwise, the NotFound exception is raised. For example, the context "Europe.Continent/France.Country/Ile de France.Region" can only be created when the parent context "Europe.Continent/France.Country" exists. As the examples below demonstrate, this means that multi-level hierarchies of naming contexts may not be created simply in one single step.

The unbind() operation removes a name binding from a context. It may be invoked to remove name bindings for objects and naming contexts as well. The exceptions NotFound, CannotProceed, and InvalidName may be raised.

To finally delete a naming context that is no longer needed, the operation destroy() is invoked. Precondition for its successful deletion is that no more bindings for objects or contexts exist in it; otherwise, a NotEmpty exception is raised.

Any named object or context object can be found using the resolve() operation. It is passed a Name and, if the corresponding object is found, returns the object's reference. Each component of the given name and each id and kind member must exactly match the bound name. The operation's return type is Object and, therefore, it has to be narrowed appropriately before it can be further used. The NamingContextExt interface, discussed in Section 17.7, provides an additional operation for retrieving objects. Exceptions of types NotFound, CannotProceed, and InvalidName may be raised.

The list() operation lets clients iterate through the name bindings contained in a naming context. It returns a BindingIterator object. Navigation is carried out by invoking operations next_one() and next_n() on the returned BindingIterator; we give an example for this procedure in Section 17.6.

Finally, the interface `NamingContextExt` has to be mentioned. It is a subinterface of interface `NamingContext` and was not yet defined in the original version of the NS specification. Besides the string format for names, which we already mentioned, a URL format for names and corresponding conversion operations are specified. Section 17.7 is dedicated to discussing the new options provided by this extension.

There are no specifics that would have to be observed with regard to the NS's Java mapping; the usual rules apply.

17.3   Bootstrapping Problem

At the beginning of the chapter, we explained that the Naming Service plays the role of a central locator for objects and that it is suited to solving the bootstrapping problem of obtaining initial object references. Usage of the NS does not solve that problem entirely because, now, the server and client applications need to obtain a reference to the Naming Service in order to bind and resolve names with it. But this problem is far easier to solve. The only prerequisites are that the NS is running on a host whose DNS-style name or IP address is known and that a specific port number is used. The next two subsections show how clients and servers can access an NS based on this minimal information. For that purpose, CORBA provides two standardized command-line options, used during server and client start-up.

17.3.1   URL Schemes

Since its version 3.0, the CORBA specification defines a number of URL-based addressing schemes, the so-called "CORBA URLs", which follow the WWW addressing schemes and may be used to localize CORBA objects and to represent object references. By means of the ORB operation `string_to_object()`, such a URL string can be converted into a true object reference. These URL schemes allow us to identify an initial reference to the NS simply on the basis of its network address and port number.

Table 12 lists the different CORBA URL formats. The column "Status" indicates whether the respective format is required or optional for a CORBA 3.0 ORB implementation.

Table 12: CORBA URL Addressing Schemes

Scheme	Description	Status
`IOR:`	Standard stringified IOR format	Required
`corbaloc:rir:`	Simple object reference; implicitly resolved via `resolve_initial_references()`	Required
`corbaloc::` or `corbaloc:iiop:`	IIOP-specific stringified IOR format	Required
`corbaname:rir:`	Name to be resolved relative to the initial naming context	Required
`corbaname::` or `corbaname:iiop:`	Name to be resolved relative to the initial naming context	Required

`file://`	Specifies a file containing the desired URL/IOR	Optional
`ftp://`	Specifies a file containing a URL/IOR that is accessible via the FTP protocol	Optional
`http://`	Specifies an HTTP URL that returns the desired URL/IOR	Optional

The `corbaloc` URL scheme as well as the `corbaname` scheme support different protocols; the composition of the URL is protocol-dependent. Currently, two standard protocols, `iiop` and `rir`, are supported.

A `corbaloc` URL for the IIOP consist of:

- the identifier `corbaloc`,
- a protocol identifier (`iiop` is the default protocol so this detail is optional),
- the protocol version information (also optional; the default value is `1.0`),
- the host name or the host's IP address,
- the port number (optional; the default value is 2089), and
- an optional object key.

The general syntax of a `corbaloc` URL scheme is therefore:

```
corbaloc:[iiop]:[version@]host[:port][/object_key]
```

A comma-separated list of protocol, host, and port information may be specified. In that case, the ORB in turn tries to find the object reference on these locations.

The `rir` protocol may be used as an abbreviation for the ORB operation `resolve_initial_references()`, hence its name. The general syntax of a `corbaloc:rir` URL is:

```
corbaloc:rir:[/key_string]
```

The optional `key_string` identifies an initial reference type; a list of admissible values is supplied in Table 11. The `key_string` is used as the argument to `resolve_initial_references()`. An empty `key_string` is interpreted as the default argument `"NameService"`.

The `corbaname` URL scheme extends the capabilities of the `corbaloc` scheme to allow URLs to denote `NamingContext` entries in an NS. This feature is not yet implemented by any of the ORBs we used; we do not discuss its syntax and semantics in this book. Also, the optional URL formats `file://`, `ftp://`, and `http://` are not treated here.

17.3.2 Standard Command-Line Options

It was previously discussed that CORBA client or server applications can gain access to basic object references such as a reference to the NS through invocations of the ORB operation `resolve_initial_references()`. This works in any case for the ORB's own root

POA; however, it is not yet clear how the ORB shall determine the references for other objects specified as an argument (again, see Table 11). In the context of the INS specification, several command-line options were standardized that provide a common bootstrap mechanism and make proprietary solutions obsolete.

The most important command-line argument is -ORBInitRef. With its help, one can overwrite the pre-configured default values of an ORB. The general syntax is:

```
-ORBInitRef <ObjectID>=<ObjectURL>
```

The ObjectID corresponds to the name of the service that would be passed to an invocation of resolve_initial_references(). The ObjectURL is any of the CORBA URLs just discussed in Section 17.3.1.

Some examples of use are:

```
-ORBInitRef NameService=IOR:00230021AB...
-ORBInitRef NameService=corbaloc::corbaserver.wifo.uni-
    mannheim.de:777/NameService
```

In addition, the command-line argument -ORBDefaultInitRef is admissible. Here, a service name ObjectID is not specified. The option may be used to determine an initial reference not known at start-up of the application. For example:

```
-ORBDefaultInitRef corbaloc::134.155.53.1:777
```

We now have the know-how necessary to discuss a first example. We provide detailed information on how the NS, the server, and the client applications have to be started for any of the three ORBs that we use.

17.4   Binding and Resolving a Name with the Naming Service

Our first example demonstrates how a server application can register the objects it manages with the NS. Since the server's business logic is of no significance here, the simple Counter example from Sections 7.13–7.15 is perfectly sufficient. One should copy the IDL file Counter.idl from \Examples\ModCounter to the directories \Examples\ NSCounter, which have to be created on the server and the client hosts. The IDL specification should then be compiled as usual.

The servant implementation, CounterImpl.java, is again reused unchanged and should be copied from \Examples\ModCounter\YourORB\Server\Count to the directory \Examples\NSCounter\YourORB\Server\Count on the server host.

Changes are necessary in the server application where the server object is named and in the GUIClient application where that name is resolved.

17.4.1 Implementing the Server Application

The server application, Server.java, should be stored in directory \Examples\NS-Counter\YourORB\Server on the server host where it should be compiled as usual.

```
// Server.java

import Count.*;
import java.util.Properties;
import org.omg.CORBA.*;
import org.omg.PortableServer.*;
import org.omg.CosNaming.*;
import org.omg.CosNaming.NamingContextPackage.*;
import static java.lang.System.*;

public class Server {
  private ORB orb;
  private POA rootPOA;
  private void initializeORB(String[] args) {
    ... as above in Section 8.2
  }
  public Server(String[] args) {
    try {
      initializeORB(args);
      NamingContext nc = NamingContextHelper.narrow(
        orb.resolve_initial_references("NameService"));
      CounterImpl c_impl = new CounterImpl();
      Counter c = c_impl._this(orb);
      NameComponent[] name = new NameComponent[1];
      name[0] = new NameComponent();
      name[0].id = "Counter";
      name[0].kind = "IIOP";
      nc.rebind(name, c);
      out.println("Server started. Stop: Ctrl-C");
      rootPOA.the_POAManager().activate();
      orb.run();
    } catch(Exception ex) {
      out.println("Exception: " + ex.getMessage());
      exit(1);
    }
  }
  public static void main(String args[]) {
    new Server(args);
  }
}
```

Following the normal ORB initialization routine, the application calls the method resolve_initial_references() with the argument "NameService" in order to obtain a reference to the NS. The result is of type org.omg.CORBA.Object and has to be narrowed to the actual type of the returned object, which is org.omg.CosNaming.NamingContext. The NamingContextHelper's method narrow() performs that cast.

In the next step, the usual Counter object c is created. The name "Counter.IIOP" is then bound to that object. To that end, a NameComponent array name with one single component is defined. According to the rules of the IDL to Java language mapping discussed previously, the IDL sequence Name is mapped to the type NameComponent[]. The single array component is a NameComponent object with variables id and kind, which have to be provided with values. Subsequently, with a call of method rebind(), the name is bound to the reference to the Counter object in the NS's initial naming context nc.

Instead of writing the five statements above in full detail, we might, alternatively, abbreviate the naming procedure by simply encoding one statement:

```
nc.rebind(new NameComponent[] {
  new NameComponent("Counter", "IIOP") }, c);
```

As discussed in Section 17.2, a call of method rebind() can throw several exceptions (InvalidName, CannotProceed, and NotFound). These exceptions are "handled" in a very superficial way in the example by simply printing the exception message and exiting the application.

17.4.2 Implementing GUIClient

We reuse the original client application, GUIClient.java, and copy it from its directory \Examples\Counter\YourORB\Client to the directories \Examples\NSCounter\YourORB\Client on the client hosts. The method getRef(), which reads the serialized object reference of the server object, is no longer needed since we use the NS to obtain that reference:

```
// GUIClient.java

import Count.*;
import java.awt.GridLayout;
import java.awt.event.*;
import java.util.Properties;
import javax.swing.*;
import org.omg.CORBA.*;
import org.omg.CosNaming.*;
import org.omg.CosNaming.NamingContextPackage.*;
import static java.lang.System.*;

public class GUIClient extends JPanel {
  private Counter c;
  private ORB orb;
  private void initializeORB(String[] args) {
    ... as above in Section 7.13
  }
  private void createGUI() {
    ... as above in Section 7.13
  }
  public GUIClient(String[] args) {
    try {
      initializeORB(args);
      NamingContext nc = NamingContextHelper.narrow(
        orb.resolve_initial_references("NameService"));
      NameComponent[] name = new NameComponent[1];
```

```
         name[0] = new NameComponent();
         name[0].id = "Counter";
         name[0].kind = "IIOP";
         org.omg.CORBA.Object obj = nc.resolve(name);
         c = CounterHelper.narrow(obj);
         createGUI();
      } catch (BAD_PARAM ex) {
         out.println("Narrowing failed");
         exit(3);
      } catch(Exception ex) {
         out.println("Exception: " + ex.getMessage());
         exit(1);
      }
   }
   public static void main(String[] args) {
      JFrame f = new JFrame("Counter Client");
      f.getContentPane().add(new GUIClient(args));
      f.pack();
      f.setDefaultCloseOperation(JFrame.DISPOSE_ON_CLOSE);
      f.setVisible(true);
   }
}
```

The statements concerning the NS are completely analogous to the server application. The only difference is that, now, we invoke the method `resolve()` in order to retrieve the server object in the initial naming context. If successful, the `NamingContext` method `resolve()` returns a reference of type `org.omg.CORBA.Object`, which in this example has to be cast to the correct type `Counter`. The `narrow()` method of class `Counter-Helper` is able to perform that cast.

Analogous to the server application, here, the five statements retrieving the server object may be abbreviated by simply writing:

```
org.omg.CORBA.Object obj = nc.resolve(
   new NameComponent[] {
      new NameComponent("Counter", "IIOP") });
```

The distributed application is now complete. In the following sections, we describe how the Naming Service, the server, and the clients are started in order to enable experimenting with the running system.

17.4.3   Starting Naming Service, Server, and Client Applications

To execute the distributed `NSCounter` application, the different components have to be started in the correct order. First, the NS is started as a separate process. Ideally, a dedicated host on the network is available so that realistic conditions of a complex application system can be simulated. As soon as the NS is running, the server application can be started on the server host. The server creates a `Counter` object and registers it with the NS under the name `"Counter.IIOP"`. Then, one or more client applications may be started on their client hosts. They first contact the NS to obtain a reference to the server object named `"Counter.IIOP"` and then invoke server operations as requested by their users.

The way the NS and the other parts of the application are started is product-specific. In the next subsections, we therefore give some short instructions describing the necessary steps on how to proceed for the three ORBs treated in this book. We decided to use the port number 777 for all examples concerning the NS since a uniform port number is helpful when different ORB products are to be tested for interoperability on the NS, server, and client hosts.

17.4.3.1   Using the JDK

The JDK comes with a tool named orbd. This *Object Request Broker Daemon* provides a "persistent" Naming Service, whose name graph is stored in a database with all the context and object bindings it contains so that they survive terminating or restarting the NS. Invoking orbd with the -ORBInitialPort or -port options allows specification the port the NS uses. Normally, it is sufficient to enter the command

```
orbd -ORBInitialPort 777
```

in a command window when the NS shall be started and directed to port number 777. If no port number is specified, orbd uses 1049 as the default value. If it is not possible to run the NS on a separate host, orbd should at least be started in its own command window.

To enable the server and client applications to find the NS, they have to be informed on the NS's CORBA URL (see Section 17.3). Assuming that orbd was started on a host with the DNS address corbaserver.wifo.uni-mannheim.de and that port number 777 was specified, then the correct commands to start the server and the clients are

```
java Server -ORBInitRef NameService=
   corbaloc::corbaserver.wifo.uni-mannheim.de:777/
     NameService
```

and

```
java GUIClient -ORBInitRef NameService=
   corbaloc::corbaserver.wifo.uni-mannheim.de:777/
     NameService
```

respectively. These commands have to be entered on a single line without any line feeds. In this way, the ORBs of the server and client applications are informed of the URL of the NS. Instead of corbaserver.wifo.uni-mannheim.de, we could also enter the IP address of the NS host, e.g., in our case 134.155.53.1. Should one test the application on a single host, one may use the name localhost or the corresponding address 127.0.0.1.

17.4.3.2   Using JacORB

JacORB's NS is implemented entirely in Java. If the JacORB ORB is installed properly according to the descriptions given in Appendix E, then a batch file, ns.bat, and a shell script, ns, which start the NS, are contained in the bin directory of the JacORB installation. It is possible to specify a port number with the -DOAPort option. The invocation for port 777 then reads:

```
ns -DOAPort=777
```

After the NS is started, the server and the clients can be started in turn. The CORBA URLs are provided in their standardized way. The only difference to the above JDK-related invocations is that, now, the Java interpreter is not invoked directly but, rather, through the batch file or script jrun that we generated in Section 7.2. Server and clients are, therefore, run with the commands

```
jrun Server -ORBInitRef NameService=
    corbaloc::corbaserver.wifo.uni-mannheim.de:777/
    NameService
```

for the server side and

```
jrun GUIClient -ORBInitRef NameService=
    corbaloc::corbaserver.wifo.uni-mannheim.de:777/
    NameService
```

for the client side, respectively. These commands have to be entered on a single line without any line feeds.

17.4.3.3 Using OpenORB

Like JacORB's Naming Service, the OpenORB Naming Service is implemented entirely in Java. The OpenORB installation, however, does not come with a batch or script file that could be used for NS start-up. It is recommended that one build one's own batch file or script. In the case of Windows NT/2000/XP, we could name that file nameserv.bat and store it in the bin directory of the OpenORB installation. Assume, again, that *OpenORB_DIR* and *JDK_DIR* denote the OpenORB and JDK installation directories. Then, this batch file contains one single long line (without line breaks) that has to look like this:

```
java -cp "%OpenORB_DIR%\lib\openorb_tools-1.3.1.jar;
    %OpenORB_DIR%\lib\xerces.jar;
    %OpenORB_DIR%\lib\openorb-1.3.1.jar;
    %OpenORB_DIR%\lib\logkit.jar;
    %OpenORB_DIR%\lib\avalon-framework.jar;
    %OpenORB_DIR%\lib\openorb_ins-1.3.1.jar;
    %OpenORB_DIR%\lib\openorb_ins_plugins-1.3.1.jar;
    %OpenORB_DIR%\lib\openorb_tns-1.3.1.jar;
    %OpenORB_DIR%\lib\openorb_pss-1.3.0.jar;
    %JDK_DIR%\jre\lib\rt.jar"
    -Xbootclasspath:
    "%OpenORB_DIR%\lib\openorb_tools-1.3.1.jar;
    %OpenORB_DIR%\lib\xerces.jar;
    %OpenORB_DIR%\lib\openorb-1.3.1.jar;
    %OpenORB_DIR%\lib\logkit.jar;
    %OpenORB_DIR%\lib\avalon-framework.jar;
    %OpenORB_DIR%\lib\openorb_ins-1.3.1.jar;
    %OpenORB_DIR%\lib\openorb_ins_plugins-1.3.1.jar;
    %OpenORB_DIR%\lib\openorb_tns-1.3.1.jar;
    %OpenORB_DIR%\lib\openorb_pss-1.3.0.jar;
    %JDK_DIR%\jre\lib\rt.jar" org.openorb.ins.Server %*
```

Under Windows 95/98/ME, the above %* syntax is not yet supported and must be replaced
by a %1 %2 %3 ending. On Unix systems, the paths have to be adjusted and %* must be replaced by a "$@".

After these preparations, the OpenORB Naming Service is started through the command

```
nameserv -ORBPort=777
```

The option -ORBPort=777 causes the NS to use port number 777. If omitted, OpenORB
uses port 2001 by default.

The commands for starting the server and the clients, again, have to provide CORBA URLs
that direct the applications to the NS. As before, they are the one-liners

```
jrun Server -ORBInitRef NameService=
    corbaloc::corbaserver.wifo.uni-mannheim.de:777/
      NameService
```

and

```
jrun GUIClient -ORBInitRef NameService=
    corbaloc::corbaserver.wifo.uni-mannheim.de:777/
      NameService
```

respectively. This time, jrun is the batch or script file presented in Section 7.3.

If using OpenORB, note that, depending on one's system, one should be prepared for the NS
to need a significant time for its initialization. It is recommendable to wait several seconds
before server or clients are started. Otherwise, although their implementation is correct and
ready to run, they might terminate with an error message because they could not yet connect
to the NS.

We were able to successfully run all 27 combinations of JDK, JacORB, and OpenORB NS,
server, and client applications following the above suggestions.

17.5   Utilizing Naming Contexts

In a distributed system, a large number of applications may take advantage of the functionality of the NS concurrently. That is why, to avoid name clashes, the NS supports the concept
of NamingContexts, which enable the creation and utilization of hierarchical structures in
the NS's name space. These naming contexts are built by operations such as bind_con-
text() or rebind_context(), the utilization of which is covered in the following example.

We start from the NSCounter application presented in Section 17.4. Since we develop two
versions of the example, we create two analogous file structures on the server and client
hosts. We begin with the two directories, \Examples\NameContext\1 and \Examp-
les\NameContext\2, and copy the files Counter.idl and CounterImpl.java to
the usual subdirectories below 1 and 2. The changes affect the Server and the GUICli-

ent applications where communication with the NS is laid out. In this example, the object reference to the `Counter` object is associated with the compound name `"Examp-les.Category/NameContext.Topic/Counter.Object"`, consisting of the two context names `"Examples.Category"` and `"NameContext.Topic"` as well as the simple name `"Counter.Object"`.

17.5.1 *Server* Implementation Version 1

To adapt the server application, we first copy file `Server.java` from `\Examples\NS-Counter\`*YourORB*`\Server` to the directory `\Examples\NameContext\1\`*Your-ORB*`\Server`, modify it, and compile it as usual. Only the code in the `Server` constructor needs to be changed and should become:

```
public Server(String[] args) {
  try {
    initializeORB(args);
    CounterImpl c_impl = new CounterImpl();
    Counter c = c_impl._this(orb);
    NamingContext nc1 = null, nc2 = null,
      root = NamingContextHelper.narrow(
        orb.resolve_initial_references("NameService"));
    try {
      nc1 = root.bind_new_context(new NameComponent[] {
        new NameComponent("Examples", "Category")
      });
    } catch (AlreadyBound ign) { }
    try {
      nc2 = nc1.bind_new_context(new NameComponent[] {
        new NameComponent("NameContext", "Topic")
      });
    } catch (AlreadyBound ign) { }
    nc2.rebind(new NameComponent[] {
      new NameComponent("Counter", "Object")
    }, c);
    out.println("Server started. Stop: Ctrl-C");
    rootPOA.the_POAManager().activate();
    orb.run();
  } catch(Exception ex) {
    out.println("Exception: " + ex.getMessage());
    exit(1);
  }
}
```

The listing shows how the naming graph is constructed below the initial naming context in three steps. After obtaining the reference to the initial naming context, a new context binding is created and its reference is returned from method `bind_new_context()`. The name for that new context is provided through a `NameComponent[]` object with one single `NameComponent` instance, which is created with the values `"Examples"` and `"Categ-ory"` for its `id` and `kind` variables. Should this context binding already exist, an `Alrea-dyBound` exception is thrown, which can safely be ignored. The procedure for creating the second context binding is completely analogous to the first, this time, however, on the level

of the first context. Finally, on this second hierarchy level, we bind the object name "Coun-
ter.Object" to the Counter object.

Once the server is running and the names are bound, one can test the content of the name hierarchy with JacORB's lsns utility. It lists the contents of the NS that is referenced via a
CORBA URL. In our system the invocation is

```
lsns -ORBInitRef NameService=
   corbaloc::corbaserver.wifo.uni-mannheim.de:777/
      NameService
```

Usage of lsns is not restricted to the JacORB Naming Service; it is possible to use it together with orbd or with OpenORB's NS.

It is obvious that building a name hierarchy in the above way is relatively tedious and involves lots of code duplication because no complex operations exist for that purpose. For a
compound name, each hierarchy level must be created separately if it does not yet exist. In
the server version 2, below, we provide a reusable method that can simplify creation of name
hierarchies by automatically calling method bind_new_context() for us.

17.5.2   *Server* Implementation Version 2

The second version of the server application defines a method bindName(), which eases
binding of compound names considerably. Let us first inspect this method:

```
private void bindName(NameComponent[] name,
   org.omg.CORBA.Object obj) throws CannotProceed,
      InvalidName, NotFound,
         org.omg.CORBA.ORBPackage.InvalidName {
         NamingContext nc = NamingContextHelper.narrow(
            orb.resolve_initial_references("NameService"));
         NameComponent[] nctx = null;
         for (int i = 0; i < name.length - 1; i++)
            try {
               nctx = new NameComponent[] { name[i] };
               nc = nc.bind_new_context(nctx);
            } catch (AlreadyBound ex) {
               nc = (NamingContext)nc.resolve(nctx);
            }
         nc.rebind(new NameComponent[] {
            name[name.length - 1] }, obj);
         out.println("Server started. Stop: Ctrl-C");
   }
```

It is assumed that the passed compound name is to be interpreted relative to the initial naming context. Therefore, at first, a reference to the initial naming context is determined. The
for statement then creates the context names top-down if they are not yet bound. If a name
is already bound, then, in the AlreadyBound handler, we simply proceed to the next hierarchy level by invoking resolve(). After the for statement is executed, the necessary hierarchy of context names is constructed and the object name can be bound.

With this method, the constructor of the Server class is significantly simplified:

```
public Server(String[] args) {
  try {
    initializeORB(args);
    CounterImpl c_impl = new CounterImpl();
    Counter c = c_impl._this(orb);
    NameComponent[] name = new NameComponent[] {
      new NameComponent("Examples", "Category"),
      new NameComponent("NameContext", "Topic"),
      new NameComponent("Counter", "Object")
    };
    bindName(name, c);
    rootPOA.the_POAManager().activate();
    orb.run();
  } catch(Exception ex) {
    out.println("Exception: " + ex.getMessage());
    exit(1);
  }
}
```

Now, a compound name can be created in a corresponding NameComponent array and one invocation of bindName() binds all context names as well as the object name.

One should store this version of file Server.java in the directory \Examples\Name-Context\2\YourORB\Server on the server host and compile it as usual.

17.5.3   Implementing GUIClient

The GUIClient application has no knowledge on the way the name of the Counter object is bound. We create GUIClient.java once for both versions and store it in the directories \Examples\NameContext\1\YourORB\Client and \Examples\Name-Context\2\YourORB\Client. Here is the code:

```
// GUIClient.java

import Count.*;
import java.awt.GridLayout;
import java.awt.event.*;
import java.util.Properties;
import javax.swing.*;
import org.omg.CORBA.*;
import org.omg.CosNaming.*;
import org.omg.CosNaming.NamingContextPackage.*;
import static java.lang.System.*;

public class GUIClient extends JPanel {
  private Counter c;
  private ORB orb;
  private void initializeORB(String[] args) {
    ... as above in Section 7.13
  }
  private org.omg.CORBA.Object resolveName(
      NameComponent[] name) {
    org.omg.CORBA.Object obj = null;
```

```
    try {
      NamingContext nc = NamingContextHelper.narrow(
        orb.resolve_initial_references("NameService"));
      obj = nc.resolve(name);
    } catch(Exception ex) {
      out.println("Exception: " + ex.getMessage());
      exit(1);
    }
    return obj;
  }
  private void createGUI() {
    ... as above in Section 7.13
  }
  public GUIClient(String[] args) {
    try {
      initializeORB(args);
      org.omg.CORBA.Object obj = resolveName(
        new NameComponent[] {
          new NameComponent("Examples", "Category"),
          new NameComponent("NameContext", "Topic"),
          new NameComponent("Counter", "Object")
        });
      c = CounterHelper.narrow(obj);
      createGUI();
    } catch (BAD_PARAM ex) {
      out.println("Narrowing failed");
      exit(3);
    } catch(Exception ex) {
      out.println("Exception: " + ex.getMessage());
      exit(1);
    }
  }
  public static void main(String[] args) {
    JFrame f = new JFrame("Counter Client");
    f.getContentPane().add(new GUIClient(args));
    f.pack();
    f.setDefaultCloseOperation(JFrame.DISPOSE_ON_CLOSE);
    f.setVisible(true);
  }
}
```

Name resolution for the compound name of the server object is moved to its own method resolveName(). It has an argument of type NameComponent[] and returns the reference to the object associated to that name. In the body of resolveName(), the NamingContext method resolve() is called for the initial naming context. Note that this method needs only one invocation; the problem of iterating through the compound name step by step is solved in resolve()'s implementation.

17.5.4   Running the Application

Both variants of the example are run in the same way described for the first example in this chapter. The distributed parts of the application have to be started in that order: Naming Service, server application, and client applications. Depending on the ORB products to be employed, the hints given in Sections 17.4.3.1-17.4.3.3 should be followed.

17.6   BindingIterators

In Section 17.2, we saw that the NamingContext interface provides an operation list(), which clients can invoke to iterate through a set of bindings in a naming context. The operation's IDL definition is:

```
void list(in unsigned long how_many,
    out BindingList bl, out BindingIterator bi);
```

The out parameter bl's semantics should be directly clear. The BindingList is a sequence where each element is a Binding containing a Name of length 1 representing a single NameComponent. Additionally, a Binding contains type information—nobject in case of an object binding and ncontext for context bindings. The IDL type definitions below are copied from module CosNaming:

```
enum BindingType { nobject, ncontext };

struct Binding
{
  Name binding_name;
  BindingType binding_type;
};
// Note: In struct Binding, binding_name is incorrectly
// defined as a Name instead of a NameComponent. This
// definition is unchanged for compatibility reasons.

typedef sequence <Binding> BindingList;
```

The comment indicates that, since a Binding always contains a name with only one component, the type NameComponent would have been more appropriate here than the type Name.

At first sight, the meaning of the list() parameters how_many and bi might be less obvious. They were introduced because, in practice, it might happen that the number of bindings in a context is huge. Returning the complete sequence of bindings in parameter bl in one go might then be hardly practicable. Instead, it is possible to return only a subset of the bindings together with an iterator that allows iterating through the complete set. The parameter how_many determines the maximum number of bindings to return in bl, with any remaining bindings accessed through the returned BindingIterator bi. If bi returns the value OBJECT_NIL, this indicates that bl contains all of the bindings in the context. A non-zero value of how_many guarantees that bl contains at most how_many elements. The implementation is free to return fewer than the number of bindings requested. The returned bi value should therefore always be examined. If how_many is set to zero, it is requested to use only the BindingIterator bi to access the bindings and the returned sequence bl is empty.

The BindingIterator's specification shows that this interface defines three operations:

```
interface BindingIterator
{
  boolean next_one(out Binding b);
  boolean next_n(in unsigned long how_many,
    out BindingList bl);
  void destroy();
};
```

If the context contains more than how_many parameters, the operation list() returns a BindingIterator object. This iterator's operation next_one() returns TRUE if at least one more binding is available; that binding is returned in the out parameter b. It returns FALSE if there are no more bindings to retrieve; the value of b then is indeterminate. Operation next_n() returns, in the out parameter bl, at most how_many elements not yet retrieved with list() or previous invocations of next_n() or next_one(). Operation next_n() returns FALSE with an empty list bl once all bindings have been retrieved. Finally, the destroy() operation destroys the iterator and releases its resources.

To understand the realization of these concepts in Java, we inspect the following client application. It uses a BindingList as well as a BindingIterator to list all top-level object and context bindings in the initial naming context of the NS. One should store and compile this example in directory \Examples\NSBinding\YourORB\Client on a client host. When the ListClient is run, the hints given in Sections 17.4.3.1-17.4.3.3 should be heeded. Also, one of the previous examples should be adapted such that the initial naming context contains several context and object bindings. The ListClient then generates some output and the BindingIterator performs some work.

```java
// ListClient.java

import java.util.Properties;
import org.omg.CORBA.*;
import org.omg.CosNaming.*;
import static java.lang.System.*;

public class ListClient {
  private ORB orb;
  private void initializeORB(String[] args) {
    Properties props = getProperties();
    orb = ORB.init(args, props);
  }
  private static void printBinding(Binding b) {
    out.print(b.binding_name[0].id + "." +
      b.binding_name[0].kind);
    switch (b.binding_type.value()) {
      case BindingType._nobject:
        out.println(" [an object]");
        break;
      case BindingType._ncontext:
        out.println(" [a context]");
        break;
    }
  }
}
```

```
public ListClient(String[] args) {
  try {
    initializeORB(args);
    NamingContext nc = null;
    nc = NamingContextHelper.narrow(
      orb.resolve_initial_references("NameService"));
    BindingListHolder blh = new BindingListHolder();
    BindingIteratorHolder bih =
      new BindingIteratorHolder();
    nc.list(2, blh, bih);
    for (Binding b: blh.value)
      printBinding(b);
    BindingIterator bit = bih.value;
    if (bit != null) {
      BindingHolder bh = new BindingHolder();
      while (bit.next_one(bh))
        printBinding(bh.value);
      bit.destroy();
    }
  } catch(Exception ex) {
    out.println("Exception: " + ex.getMessage());
    exit(1);
  }
}
public static void main(String[] args) {
  new ListClient(args);
}
}
```

After obtaining a reference to the initial naming context in the ListClient constructor, we prepare the call to list() by creating a BindingListHolder and a BindingIteratorHolder instance. Both holders are passed to list() together with the value 2, rather arbitrarily chosen here, for the parameter how_many. Following the list() invocation, we call printBinding() for each binding in the BindingList. Recall that we might find only one single list element although additional bindings are available. We, therefore, test whether the returned BindingIterator is a non-null reference and, in that case, call next_one() as long as this method returns true. In order to obtain each next binding, a BindingHolder instance must be created and passed to method next_one().

17.7   NamingContextExt Interface

As indicated above, an Interoperable Naming Service was introduced in CORBA 3.0, which replaced the earlier NS version. This specification defines the syntax for stringified names and provides operations to convert a name in stringified form to its equivalent sequence form and vice versa. It is made considerably easier for applications to conveniently deal with names.

A name consists of components that each have an id and a kind element. In the stringified name representation, the dot '.' separates the id and kind elements of a single name component. Different name components of a name are separated by a '/' character. The backslash '\' escapes the reserved meaning of '/', '.', and '\' in a stringified name. Table 13 summarizes the use of escaped characters:

Table 13: Reserved Uses of Characters in Stringified Names

Characters	Meaning
.	Separates the id and kind elements
/	Separates different name components
\.	Escape sequence for the '.' character
\/	Escape sequence for the '/' character
\\	Escape sequence for the '\' character

When composing stringified names, it is admissible to leave any of the two elements of a name component but not both empty.

- If a name component in a stringified name does not contain a '.' character, the entire component is interpreted as the id and the kind element is empty. A trailing '.' character is not permitted.
- If a name component in a stringified name starts with a '.' character, the entire component is interpreted as the kind and the id element is empty.
- The single '.' character is the only representation of a name component with empty id and the kind elements. In our view, it hardly ever makes sense to use such an empty name in practical applications.

The string "What/.a/nice/.name" therefore represents a valid name. The Naming-ContextExt interface, subinterface of NamingContext, provides the operations required to use such stringified names.

```
interface NamingContextExt: NamingContext
{
  typedef string StringName;
  typedef string Address;
  typedef string URLString;

  StringName to_string(in Name n) raises(InvalidName);
  Name to_name(in StringName sn) raises(InvalidName);

  exception InvalidAddress {};

  URLString to_url(in Address addr, in StringName sn)
    raises(InvalidAddress, InvalidName);
  Object resolve_str(in StringName sn)
    raises( NotFound, CannotProceed, InvalidName,);
};
```

The operations `to_string()` and `to_name()` convert a Name to a stringified name and vice versa. Operation `to_name()` is especially useful, as we see in the example below since it may be invoked whenever developers need the internal name format but want to use the string representation for reasons of simplicity. This holds as well for operation `resolve_str()`, which performs a resolve in the same manner as the NamingContext interface's operation `resolve()`. It accepts a stringified name as an argument instead of a Name. The last operation, `to_url()`, takes a CORBA URL and a stringified name as parameters and converts them to the URL format discussed briefly in Section 17.3.1.

17.7.1   An Example Using the `NamingContextExt` Interface

We, once again, take up the NamingContext example of Section 17.5. As before, only the Server and the GUIClient applications need to be modified. And, we, again, write two versions of the example. The preparatory steps are the same as described in Section 17.5; as base directories, one could use \Examples\NSExt\1 and \Examples\NSExt\2.

17.7.2   `Server` Implementation Version 1

Here is the first version of the file Server.java. It should be stored in directory \Examples\NSExt\1*YourORB*\Server and compiled there. Compared with the previous version, only the Server's constructor was modified:

```
// Server.java

import Count.*;
import java.util.*;
import org.omg.CORBA.*;
import org.omg.PortableServer.*;
import org.omg.CosNaming.*;
import org.omg.CosNaming.NamingContextPackage.*;
import static java.lang.System.*;

public class Server {
  private ORB orb;
  private POA rootPOA;
  private void initializeORB(String[] args) {
    ... as above in Section 8.2
  }
  public Server(String[] args) {
    try {
      initializeORB(args);
      CounterImpl c_impl = new CounterImpl();
      Counter c = c_impl._this(orb);
      NamingContextExt root =
        NamingContextExtHelper.narrow(
          orb.resolve_initial_references("NameService"));
      NamingContext nc1 = null, nc2 = null;
      try {
        nc1 = root.bind_new_context(
          root.to_name("Examples.Category"));
      } catch (AlreadyBound ign) { }
```

```
          try {
            nc2 = nc1.bind_new_context(
              root.to_name("NameContext.Topic"));
          } catch (AlreadyBound ign) { }
          nc2.rebind(root.to_name("Counter.Object"), c);
          out.println("Server started. Stop: Ctrl-C");
          rootPOA.the_POAManager().activate();
          orb.run();
        } catch(Exception ex) {
          out.println("Exception: " + ex.getMessage());
          exit(1);
        }
      }
    public static void main(String args[]) {
      new Server(args);
    }
  }
```

The first obvious difference is that the initial reference to the NS, obtained by invoking method `resolve_initial_references()`, is now converted into the type `Naming-ContextExt` instead of type `NamingContext`.

In the next statements, the `NamingContextExt` method `to_name()` is invoked in order to be able to call `bind_new_context()` and `rebind()` with the stringified name representations. For example, we now simply invoke

```
  nc2.rebind(root.to_name("Counter.Object"), c);
```

where, before, we had to construct a `NameComponent` array:

```
  nc2.rebind(new NameComponent[] {
    new NameComponent("Counter", "Object") }, c);
```

This abbreviation is even more helpful if compound names containing many context names have to be created. Nevertheless, we encounter the same problem as in version one of the server application presented in Section 17.5.1; the context names of a new not yet bound compound name have to be bound step by step. Analogous to the second version of the `Server` in Section 17.5.2, we now describe a more comfortable version declaring a method that simplifies this task.

17.7.3   `Server` Implementation Version 2

The second version of our application, `Server.java`, includes a new method, `bindNameStr()`, with a functionality adapting itself exactly to that of the method `bindName()` described in Section 17.5.2. Different than method `bindName()`, however, `bindNameStr()` expects a stringified name as its first argument instead of a `NameComponent[]`. As before, the second argument is the object reference to be associated with the name. This method can be implemented as follows:

```
  private void bindNameStr(String namestr,
    org.omg.CORBA.Object obj)
      throws CannotProceed, InvalidName, NotFound,
```

```
          org.omg.CORBA.ORBPackage.InvalidName {
    NamingContextExt ncext = NamingContextExtHelper.narrow(
      orb.resolve_initial_references("NameService"));
    NamingContext nc = ncext;
    StringTokenizer parser = new StringTokenizer(
      namestr, "/");
    int num = parser.countTokens();
    String name ="";
    for (int i = 0; i < num - 1; i++)
      try {
        name = parser.nextToken();
        nc = nc.bind_new_context(ncext.to_name(name));
      } catch (AlreadyBound ex) {
        nc = (NamingContext)nc.resolve(ncext.to_name(name));
      }
    nc.rebind(ncext.to_name(parser.nextToken()), obj);
    out.println("Server started. Stop: Ctrl-C");
  }
```

One may recognize that the stepwise top-down construction of naming contexts occurs following the same principle applied before. The sole difference is that, now, the respective parts of the name are determined with the help of a `StringTokenizer`, which separates the string argument using the '/' character as a delimiter. Invoking this method reduces the code of the server constructor to

```
public Server(String[] args) {
  try {
    initializeORB(args);
    CounterImpl c_impl = new CounterImpl();
    Counter c = c_impl._this(orb);
    bindNameStr("Examples.Category/NameContext.Topic/"
      + "Counter.Object", c);
    rootPOA.the_POAManager().activate();
    orb.run();
  } catch(Exception ex) {
    out.println("Exception: " + ex.getMessage());
    exit(1);
  }
}
```

One should store the modified server application in the directory \Examples\NS-Ext\2*YourORB*\Server on the server host and compile it as usual.

17.7.4   Implementing GUIClient

The client application presented in Section 17.5.3 may be directly used to communicate successfully with both versions of the new server application. For the sake of completeness, we show how the GUIClient can profit from invoking NamingContextExt's method resolve_str() anyhow. At this point, it should be sufficient to present the new constructor since the rest of the implementation is still copied from the original version:

```
public GUIClient(String[] args) {
  try {
    initializeORB(args);
    NamingContextExt ncext =
      NamingContextExtHelper.narrow(
        orb.resolve_initial_references("NameService"));
    c = CounterHelper.narrow(ncext.resolve_str(
      "Examples.Category/NameContext.Topic/"
      + "Counter.Object"));
    createGUI();
  } catch (BAD_PARAM ex) {
    out.println("Narrowing failed");
    exit(3);
  } catch(Exception ex) {
    out.println("Exception: " + ex.getMessage());
    exit(1);
  }
}
```

One should store the modified `GUIClient` in directories `\Examples\NSExt\1\`*Your-*
ORB`\Client` or `\Examples\NSExt\2\`*YourORB*`\Client` on the client hosts and
compile them. The examples may then be run with the ORB-specific commands explained at
the beginning of this chapter.

17.8   Concluding Remarks

In this chapter, we have seen how the Naming Service may be used to solve the bootstrapping problem of establishing initial connections between clients and servers. The Naming
Service is not only the most important CORBAservice but it is, as well, the first external
component discussed in this book that runs independently of the CORBA runtime. Once the
underlying principle is understood, readers should be able to familiarize themselves rapidly
with other CORBAservices relying on the respective OMG and vendor documentation. The
Event Service described in the next chapter is a further example for such a CORBAservice.

17.9   Exercises

1. Implement a Naming Service-based version of the `Bank` example (`\Examples\DSI-`
    `Bank`). Use server-side skeletons, not the DSI.

2. Implement a Naming Service-based version of the `Compute` example (`\Examples\`
    `DIIAsynch`). Use client-side stubs, not the DII.

3. Write a simple application that constructs a hierarchy of context names as shown below
    (output was created by JacORB's `lsns` utility).

    You might pass the names in the `args` array of method `main()`.

```
Europe.Continent/
     France.Country/
              Ile de France.Region/
                       Paris.City/
     Germany.Country/
              Baden-Wuerttemberg.State/
                       Mannheim.City/
America.Continent/
     USA.Country/
              California.State/
                       Malibu.City/
```

4. Write an UnbindClient application, which unbinds object and context names provided in args[0]. Remove some of the bindings constructed with the application developed in Exercise 3 and control the results with the lsns utility.

18 CORBA's Event Service

In the previous examples of this book, synchronous, invocation-based client/server communication between the objects in a distributed system was the focus of our attention. Typical for this type of communication, the sender of a message is connected to exactly one receiver via an object reference and the ORB. Also, normally, after sending the message, the sender blocks until the receiver handles the message content and completed the invocation or, otherwise, an exception is raised. To enable this direct way of communication, the sender must know the IDL interface of the receiver.

Although this is the most commonly used communication paradigm, there are other types of communication. For example, we saw above that CORBA makes it possible that remote operations are invoked asynchronously. A further useful communication model besides the synchronous invocation-based communication model is *event-based communication*. It differs from the standard approach in that sender and receiver of event messages are decoupled from each other, communicate only indirectly, and are not synchronized. Moreover, it is possible that one or more senders direct event notifications to an arbitrary number of receivers. The senders and receivers do not have to know where the other communication partners are located or what their IDL interface is. This concept is realized by introducing a *mediator*, a special object that functions as an *event channel*, which is positioned between the senders and the receivers. The architecture is described in the well-known "Mediator" design pattern (see, e.g., [GHJV95]). Senders as well as receivers communicate with the event channel exclusively and, therefore, only have to know the event channel interface; or, they implement their own interfaces for communication with it. They do not have to know each other's identity or characteristics. Through the mediator, communication between the cooperating objects is decoupled in such a way that it occurs indirectly, asynchronously, and anonymously.

It should be taken into consideration that, due to its indirection, event-based communication is substantially less efficient than the traditional client/server model. By involving an event channel, not only the number of invocations processed over the network is typically doubled, but also the receiver of an event notification has to interpret the transmitted event information to then execute suitable operations. Possibly, the problem arises that a multitude of various event types is produced, not all of which are of equal importance to the event receiver. As a consequence, events might unnecessarily be communicated via the network or objects receive events in which they are not interested and which they cannot interpret. An event channel has no filtering capability in the sense discussed above in Chapter 12.

Nevertheless, there are a number of reasons favorable to the event-based communication model. The mediator architecture realizes the often intended "loose coupling" of indirectly communicating objects, which might be useful if these objects do not know each other, if sender objects cannot wait for processing of their messages, or if a larger number of receivers should be reached, e.g., in an application implementing the "Publish-Subscribe" pattern. Due to its loose coupling, it is a lot easier to change or extend an event-based system than a conventional client/server system. Typical application scenarios may be found, for example, in the field of Enterprise Application Integration, where existing legacy systems need to be integrated with newly developed system components.

With its *Event Service* (ES) [OMG01], the OMG specified a basic CORBAservice, which supports event-based communication. The ES lays the foundation for the new, considerably more complex *Notification Service* [OMG04b], which remedies some of the ES's shortcomings through new and additional characteristics and functionalities and which is completely downward compatible to the ES. Two examples of these shortcomings are that no filtering mechanism for events exists or that no quality-of-service attributes, such as reliability of event notification or number of events to be queued internally, may be specified. To understand the basic concepts, however, it is fully sufficient to take a closer look at the ES and experiment with examples employing it.

In the following, we describe the untyped event model, where any event information is inserted into an `any`. It should be noted here that, in addition to untyped events, the Event Service specification also provides a typed event model, which might be advantageous in certain application contexts. However, implementation and usage of that model is more complicated and also, only very few ORB vendors, none of the ORBs we use in this book, today support typed events; therefore, we do not discuss this event model, here.

18.1   Event Service Basics

The ES specification distinguishes *event consumers* and *event suppliers*. They communicate with each other indirectly via the event channel, which is the central element of the ES and plays the role of the mediator between suppliers and consumers. In principle, event information flows from suppliers to consumers. However, that flow can be realized through various communication models, which differ in the way the involved objects invoke operations in order to pass on or to collect information. Figure 23 illustrates the different communication styles. The first fact to note is that suppliers and consumers never interact directly: suppliers communicate with proxy consumers created on their "end" of the event channel (more precisely, on the supplier host) and consumers communicate with proxy suppliers created on the consumer "end" of the event channel (more precisely, on the consumer host). The way the event channel internally directs events from proxy consumers to proxy suppliers is completely transparent to ES users. The following four styles of communication may be differentiated:

- the pure *push model*,
- the pure *pull model*,
- the hybrid *pull/push model*, and
- the hybrid *push/pull model*.

In the pure push model, a supplier operates as a push supplier, connecting to the event channel through a proxy push consumer and actively "pushing" event data to the proxy consumer. In this pure push model, the consumer operates as a push consumer, connects to the event channel through a proxy push supplier, and passively waits until the proxy supplier delivers (pushes) event data to it. The notification path is from the actual push supplier, through its proxy push consumer, through the event channel, to the proxy push supplier, and finally to the push consumer itself. With the exception of the push() invocation on the proxy push consumer in the supplier application, all other invocations on that path are automatically managed by the ES.

In the pure pull model, the roles of active and passive objects are inverted. Here, it is the consumer that drives the delivery of events. A consumer operates as a pull consumer, connecting to the event channel through a proxy pull supplier and actively "pulling" event data from the proxy supplier. The supplier operates as a pull supplier, connects to the event channel through a proxy pull consumer, and passively waits until the proxy consumer requests (pulls) event data from it. The notification path is now from the pull consumer, through the proxy pull supplier and the event channel, to the proxy pull consumer, to the pull supplier. There are two ways a pull consumer can obtain new event information. It can invoke an operation, pull(), on its pull supplier, letting it block until the next event is available in the event channel. The second option is to invoke an operation, try_pull(), also provided by the proxy pull supplier, which returns immediately with the event information if available. If no event is available, this second operation does not block but simply signals that the event channel is empty. With the exception of the pull() or try_pull() invocation on the proxy pull supplier in the consumer application, all other invocations on that path are automatically managed by the ES.

Figure 23 also demonstrates that communication does not need to be either entirely push model or pull model. To a supplier it is completely irrelevant whether the events it creates are pulled from the event channel by a pull consumer, more precisely, its proxy pull supplier, or whether the event channel pushes them to a push consumer, more precisely, its proxy push

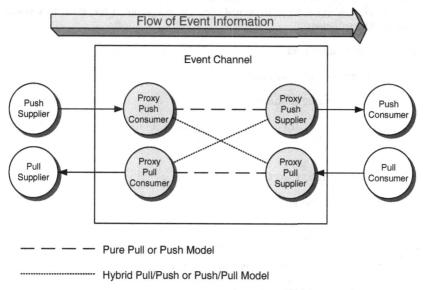

— — — — Pure Pull or Push Model

·························· Hybrid Pull/Push or Push/Pull Model

Figure 23: Different Communication Models Supported by the Event Service

supplier. And, to a consumer, it is equally irrelevant whether the events it receives are pushed to the event channel by a push supplier, or, more precisely, its proxy push consumer, or whether the event channel pulls them from a pull supplier, or, more precisely, its proxy pull consumer. In the hybrid push/pull model, a push supplier indirectly connects to a pull consumer. Vice versa, in the hybrid pull/push model, a pull supplier indirectly connects to a push consumer. An event channel can also provide many-to-many communication. The channel consumes events from one or more suppliers and supplies events to one or more consumers. An event channel also supports mixed style communication by connecting to consumers and suppliers using different communication models. It is the event channel's responsibility to allow such complicated interrelationships. CORBA application programmers do not have to concern themselves with any internal details of the respective ES implementation.

18.2   IDL Specification of the Event Service

In the following, we examine the separate parts of the ES's IDL specification more closely to work out the foundations for the example application of this chapter. The complete IDL specification of the Event Service can be found in Appendix D of this book.

18.2.1   Supplier and Consumer Interfaces

The interfaces of the four types of event suppliers and event consumers are defined in module CosEventComm. They are designed in such a way that they may be connected immediately, without explicitly taking into consideration that an event channel serves as the mediator. Nevertheless, it is helpful to know that, as to be expected, the types of the proxy objects mentioned above are subtypes of the interfaces discussed here. Thus, to their communication partners, the proxies appear to be the actual suppliers or consumers for which they stand. Here are the IDL definitions:

```
module CosEventComm
{
  exception Disconnected{};

  interface PushConsumer
  {
    void push(in any data) raises(Disconnected);
    void disconnect_push_consumer();
  };

  interface PushSupplier
  {
    void disconnect_push_supplier();
  };

  interface PullSupplier
  {
    any pull() raises(Disconnected);
    any try_pull(out boolean has_event)
      raises(Disconnected);
    void disconnect_pull_supplier();
  };
```

```
  interface PullConsumer
  {
    void disconnect_pull_consumer();
  };
};
```

Exceptions of type `Disconnected` are raised if an event supplier or consumer receives a callback invocation by its corresponding proxy although it has already disconnected because it no longer wants to supply or consume events.

A push-style consumer implements the `PushConsumer` interface to receive event data. A supplier, more precisely, the ES's proxy push supplier, communicates event data by invoking the `push()` operation on the consumer and passing the event data in the `any` parameter. The `disconnect_push_consumer()` operation is invoked by a supplier, the proxy push supplier, to terminate the event communication and release resources used at the consumer side.

The interface `PushSupplier` is the `PushConsumer`'s counterpart. Its sole operation, `disconnect_push_supplier()`, is invoked by a consumer, the ES's proxy push consumer, to terminate the event communication and release resources used at the supplier side. Further operations are not needed since the `PushSupplier` itself is the active part, invoking operations on the proxy push consumer in order to deliver event data.

A pull-style supplier implements the `PullSupplier` interface to transmit event data. A consumer, or, more precisely, the ES's proxy pull consumer, requests event data from the supplier by invoking either the `pull()` or the `try_pull()` operation on the supplier. These two operations for actively requesting events were already mentioned in Section 18.1. The `pull()` operation blocks until the event data is available or an exception is raised. It returns the event data to the consumer in the `any` return result. The `try_pull()` operation does not block: if the event data is available, it returns the event data and sets the `has_event` parameter to `true`; if the event data is not available, it sets the `has_event` parameter to `false` and the return value is undefined. The `disconnect_pull_supplier()` operation terminates the event communication and releases resources used at the supplier side.

Analogous to the `PushSupplier` in the push model, the `PullConsumer` is the active part in the pull-style communication model; the interface, therefore, defines only one operation. The operation `disconnect_pull_consumer()` terminates the event communication and releases resources used at the consumer side.

18.2.2 The Event Channel's Administration Interface

The event channel is the heart of the event service. In the module `CosEventChannelAdmin`, the ES specification defines the three interfaces `ConsumerAdmin`, `SupplierAdmin`, and `EventChannel`, providing operations that include bootstrap abilities to obtain initial access to an ES implementation.

```
  module CosEventChannelAdmin
  {
    ...
```

```
    interface ConsumerAdmin
    {
      ProxyPushSupplier obtain_push_supplier();
      ProxyPullSupplier obtain_pull_supplier();
    };

    interface SupplierAdmin
    {
      ProxyPushConsumer obtain_push_consumer();
      ProxyPullConsumer obtain_pull_consumer();
    };

    interface EventChannel
    {
      ConsumerAdmin for_consumers();
      SupplierAdmin for_suppliers();
      void destroy();
    };
};
```

Regardless of the relationship among suppliers and consumers, to establish a connection and deliver events through the event channel, five steps must be taken.

- An object of type EventChannel must be created and provided. Creation is vendor-specific, see the example program below for OpenORB's way of proceeding. No suppliers or consumers are connected to the event channel upon creation.

- The supplier must get a SupplierAdmin object from the event channel; this is obtained by invoking the event channel's for_suppliers() operation. In the same way, the consumer invokes the event channel's operation for_consumers() to get a ConsumerAdmin object.

- Suppliers and consumers must obtain their proxy objects from the admin object. Depending on the selected push or pull communication model, a supplier invokes operation obtain_push_consumer() or operation obtain_pull_consumer() on the SupplierAdmin object to get a ProxyPushConsumer or a ProxyPullConsumer object, respectively. Analogously, a consumer invokes operation obtain_push_supplier() or obtain_pull_supplier() on the ConsumerAdmin object to get the ProxyPushSupplier or the ProxyPullSupplier object it needs.

- The supplier and consumer must be added to the event channel, more precisely, to their proxy consumer and to their proxy supplier, respectively, via a connect call. The connect operations are specified in the proxy interfaces discussed next.

- Event data may now be transferred via invocations of push(), try_pull(), or pull() on the respective proxy objects.

To complete discussion of the EventChannel interface, it should be mentioned here that the destroy() operation destroys an EventChannel object when it is no longer needed. Destroying an event channel destroys all ConsumerAdmin and SupplierAdmin objects created via that channel.

18.2.3 Proxy Interfaces

Together with two exceptions, AlreadyConnected and TypeError, the different proxy interfaces are also part of the definition of module CosEventChannelAdmin:

```
module CosEventChannelAdmin
{
    exception AlreadyConnected {};
    exception TypeError {};

    interface ProxyPushConsumer: CosEventComm::PushConsumer
    {
        void connect_push_supplier(
            in CosEventComm::PushSupplier push_supplier)
            raises(AlreadyConnected);
    };

    interface ProxyPullSupplier: CosEventComm::PullSupplier
    {
        void connect_pull_consumer(
            in CosEventComm::PullConsumer pull_consumer)
            raises(AlreadyConnected);
    };

    interface ProxyPullConsumer: CosEventComm::PullConsumer
    {
        void connect_pull_supplier(
            in CosEventComm::PullSupplier pull_supplier)
            raises(AlreadyConnected,TypeError);
    };

    interface ProxyPushSupplier: CosEventComm::PushSupplier
    {
        void connect_push_consumer(
            in CosEventComm::PushConsumer push_consumer)
            raises(AlreadyConnected, TypeError);
    };
    ...
};
```

An AlreadyConnected exception is raised whenever a proxy object is already connected but a supplier or consumer, again, attempts to connect to it. The TypeError exception is only relevant in applications using typed events.

The IDL specification of the proxy interfaces shows that these are defined as subtypes of the supplier and consumer interfaces defined in module CosEventComm. Therefore, as intended, objects implementing the proxy interfaces can be used as proxies for the event suppliers or consumers and accept pull(), try_pull(), or push() invocations for them on the event channel's "other" side. The only new element in the proxy definitions is the connect operation, which is invoked in step four of the five steps mentioned above. The connect_push_supplier() operation connects a PushSupplier to a Proxy-PushConsumer, which is in turn automatically connected to the event channel. The other connect methods have corresponding semantics.

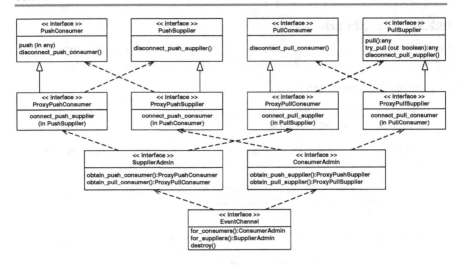

Figure 24: Interfaces of the Event Service

Figure 24 gives a UML-based overview on all the interfaces discussed so far and demonstrates their inheritance and usage dependencies.

18.3   Using OpenORB's Event Service

Before we turn our attention to a practical example, we have to discuss some technical details on system setup. Since the JDK does not provide its own Event Service and since the Event Service coming with JacORB's current release (Version 2.2.1) caused several problems, we test the following example application exclusively with the OpenORB Event Service. CORBA's interoperability, nevertheless, allows us to translate and run all the other components of the application with any of the three ORBs we used. Several additional preparatory steps are required here. We explain them below for advanced readers; it is, however, easiest to test the complete example with the OpenORB implementation.

The ES implementation of JacORB comes with a Unix start script, evc; whereas, a corresponding batch file for Windows users is missing. It is relatively simple to write this batch file using the Unix script as a basis. In addition to an ES, the JacORB implementation also contains a Notification Service, which the OMG specified as a downward compatible successor of the ES. Readers interested in experimenting with this implementation are referred to the JacORB documentation.

18.3.1   Setup and Start of OpenORB's Event Service

Like the Naming Service, the Event Service coming with OpenORB is implemented entirely in Java. Since the OpenORB installation does not supply any batch or script file starting the service, such a file should be built and stored in the installation's bin directory (see Section

7.3). This file could be named `eventserv.bat`; it should contain the following long line
without line breaks (Windows NT/2000/XP):

```
java -cp "%OpenORB_DIR%\lib\openorb_tools-1.3.1.jar;
  %OpenORB_DIR%\lib\xerces.jar;
  %OpenORB_DIR%\lib\openorb-1.3.1.jar;
  %OpenORB_DIR%\lib\logkit.jar;
  %OpenORB_DIR%\lib\avalon-framework.jar;
  %OpenORB_DIR%\lib\openorb_event-1.3.0.jar;
  %OpenORB_DIR%\lib\openorb_pss-1.3.0.jar;
  %JDK_DIR%\jre\lib\rt.jar"
  -Xbootclasspath:
  "%OpenORB_DIR%\lib\openorb_tools-1.3.1.jar;
  %OpenORB_DIR%\lib\xerces.jar;
  %OpenORB_DIR%\lib\openorb-1.3.1.jar;
  %OpenORB_DIR%\lib\logkit.jar;
  %OpenORB_DIR%\lib\avalon-framework.jar;
  %OpenORB_DIR%\lib\openorb_event-1.3.0.jar;
  %OpenORB_DIR%\lib\openorb_pss-1.3.0.jar;
  %JDK_DIR%\jre\lib\rt.jar" org.openorb.event.Server %*
```

As above, *OpenORB_DIR* and *JDK_DIR* denote the installation directories of OpenORB
and the JDK, respectively.

An application that needs to use the ES determines an initial reference to an event channel
through an inquiry with the Naming Service. Therefore, a Naming Service must be running
before OpenORB's ES may be started because the ES has to register with the NS. The Open-
ORB ES communicates with the JDK NS or the JacORB NS without any problems.

If we use the OpenORB implementation, the command line to start the NS is

```
nameserv -ORBPort=777
```

Then, the ES may be started with the usual reference to the NS's host name and port number,
e.g.,

```
eventserv -ORBInitRef NameService=
  corbaloc::corbaserver.wifo.uni-mannheim.de:777/
  NameService
```

(one line, no line breaks). One has to replace the name `corbaserver.wifo.uni-
mannheim.de` by the name of the host the NS is running on; in the simplest scenario this
might be `localhost` or `127.0.0.1`. As always, the NS can be directed to another port
number; then, 777 must be replaced as appropriate.

18.3.2   Using OpenORB's ES with JDK's ORB

It is possible to work primarily with the JDK but, nevertheless, to run the following example
with OpenORB's ES. In order to do so, one has to download the necessary archives—the
`jar` files listed in the above batch file `eventserv.bat`—from the OpenORB web site
(see Appendix E) and write the batch file `eventserv.bat`. Since stubs and skeletons of
the ES are not bundled with the JDK, one also needs the files `CosEventComm.idl` and

CosEventChannelAdmin.idl. One might copy these from this book (Appendix D); or, if JacORB has been installed, one finds them in the installation's subdirectory idl\omg. Then, the stubs and skeletons can be generated with JDK's IDL compiler. This step is only necessary once and need not be repeated for each application using the ES; one might carry it out in the \Examples\ESPush\JDK directory. The JDK IDL compiler does not treat the #pragma prefix directives contained in the two IDL files correctly and does not support the newer typeprefix at all. Therefore, the two IDL compiler options -pkgPrefix and -pkgTranslate must be specified so that both invocations read (one line, no line breaks)

```
idlj -fall -pkgPrefix CosEventComm org.omg
  -pkgTranslate CosEventComm org.omg.CosEventComm
    CosEventComm.idl

idlj -fall -pkgPrefix CosEventChannelAdmin org.omg
  -pkgTranslate CosEventComm org.omg.CosEventComm
    CosEventChannelAdmin.idl
```

The resulting Java files are stored in a newly created directory, org.omg, and its subdirectories. They should now be compiled to class files with the invocations

```
javac org\omg\CosEventComm\*.java
javac org\omg\CosEventChannelAdmin\*.java
```

The content of org.omg should be packaged into a Java archive, ES.jar, with the command

```
jar -cvf ES.jar org
```

Since the java sources are not needed in the archive, one might delete them following the javac commands and preceding the jar command. The archive then has to be specified in the class path whenever javac or java are invoked. To that end, one should copy ES.jar into the Publisher and Subscriber subdirectories. Alternatively, one might want to store the archive in the JDK's extensions directory JDK_DIR\jre\lib\ext; in that case, no class path needs to be specified.

18.3.3   Using OpenORB's ES with JacORB

If the JacORB implementation shall be used together with the OpenORB ES, then, as above, the Java archives of the OpenORB implementation have to be obtained and the batch file eventserv.bat must be written. But, in contrast to the JDK environment, it is now not necessary to first translate the IDL specifications CosEventComm.idl and CosEvent-ChannelAdmin.idl because the respective stubs and skeletons are already part of the archive jacorb.jar, which is included in the class paths of batch files jmake.bat and jrun.bat.

The preparatory explanations are now complete and we can start with developing the example application. As usual, we give hints referring to the specifics of the three ORBs that need to be considered when translating and running the application.

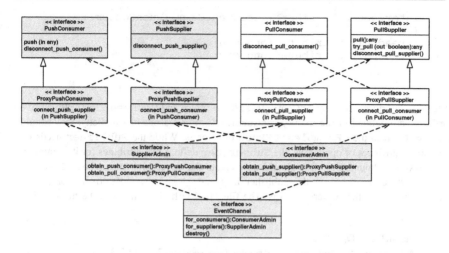

**Figure 25: Interfaces of the Event Service
Needed in a Pure Push Model Implementation**

18.4 Push-Style Publish-Subscribe Example

Since the pure push model seems to be the model most often come across in practice, in the following, we implement an example application communicating in push-style. As we are going to implement push communication on both sides of the event channel, only the ES interfaces shaded in grey in Figure 25 are of significance, here.

The example realizes a simple Publish-Subscribe scenario similar to the one developed in Chapter 12. A publisher application continually creates event objects by randomly generating integer numbers between 0 and 1000, inserting them into an Any object, and pushing them to the event channel. On the other side, one or more subscriber applications can connect to the event channel to receive event objects from it. During start-up of the subscriber, a minimum and maximum value can be specified, indicating the range of events in which the subscriber is interested. In addition, the number of seconds the subscriber wants to be connected is provided as a third command-line argument.

18.4.1 IDL Interfaces for the Example

One should now write the IDL file Publish.idl and store it on the publisher (supplier) and subscriber (consumer) hosts. Suitable directories would be \Examples\ESPush:

```
// Publish.idl

#include "\Examples\ESPush\CosEventComm.idl"

module PublishSubscribe
{
    interface Publisher : CosEventComm::PushSupplier{ };
```

```
    interface Subscriber : CosEventComm::PushConsumer
    {
      readonly attribute long min;
      readonly attribute long max;
    };
};
```

The superinterfaces CosEventCom::PushConsumer and CosEventCom::PushSu-
pplier are defined in file CosEventComm.idl. For reasons of simplicity, they should
also be stored in the \Examples\ESPush directories. While the Publisher needs no
additional attributes or operations, the Subscriber defines two attributes for its minimum
and maximum boundaries. One should now create the directory \Examples\ESPush\
YourORB\Publisher on the publisher host and \Examples\ESPush\YourORB\
Subscriber on the subscriber hosts. The file Publish.idl may then be translated as
follows:

- JacORB and OpenORB
  After setting the environment variables (see Sections 7.2 and 7.3), change the directory to the Publisher and Subscriber, respectively, and enter the commands

  ```
  idl ..\..\Publish.idl              for JacORB
  idl -d . ..\..\Publish.idl         for OpenORB
  ```

- JDK
  The command to be entered in the respective Publisher or Subscriber directory is (in one line, without line breaks)

  ```
  idlj -fall -pkgTranslate CosEventComm
      org.omg.CosEventComm ..\..\Publish.idl
  ```

18.4.2   Implementing the Event Supplier

We first implement the PublisherImpl servant and store it in the directory \Examp-
les\ESPush\YourORB\Publisher\PublishSubscribe on the publisher host.

```
// PublisherImpl.java

package PublishSubscribe;

import static java.lang.System.*;
import org.omg.CORBA.*;
import org.omg.CosEventComm.*;
import org.omg.CosEventChannelAdmin.*;

public class PublisherImpl extends PublisherPOA {
  private ORB orb;
  private ProxyPushConsumer ppc;
  private boolean disconn = false;
  public PublisherImpl(ORB orb, ProxyPushConsumer ppc) {
    this.orb = orb;
```

```
      this.ppc = ppc;
   }
   public void publish(int value) {
      Any message = orb.create_any();
      message.insert_long(value);
      try {
         ppc.push(message);
      } catch (Disconnected ex) {
         out.println("ProxyPushConsumer is disconnected"
            + " from ES");
         exit(0);
      }
   }
   public void disconnect_push_supplier() {
      if (disconn)
         throw new OBJECT_NOT_EXIST();
      disconn = true;
      ppc.disconnect_push_consumer();
      out.println("Disconnected Publisher");
   }
}
```

The only method that needs to be implemented due to the fact that we defined the IDL interface `Publisher` as an IDL subinterface of `CosEventComm::PushSupplier` is the
method `disconnect_push_supplier()`. More precisely, we implement the inheritance approach and declare class `PublisherImpl` to be a subclass of `PublisherPOA`.
The class `PublisherPOA` implements the Java interface `PublisherOperations`,
which in turn extends the Java interface `org.omg.CosEventComm.PushSupplier-
Operations`, and the disconnect method is declared in that interface.

In our example, calling `disconnect_push_supplier()` causes the implementation to
call the `disconnect_push_consumer()` operation on the corresponding `ProxyPu-
shConsumer` to release resources symmetrically. With the `disconn` variable, we avoid
infinite recursive calls to these disconnect operations. The most interesting part of the servant, however, is the local method `publish()`. The publisher (supplier) communicates
event data by invoking this method and passing event data as an `int` value. In the body of
method `publish()`, the `push()` method is invoked on the `ProxyPushConsumer`; before the `int` value can be passed, it has to be inserted into an `Any` instance. The `Discon-
nected` exception, which may be thrown when calling `push()`, is handled in a very simple
manner.

18.4.3   Implementing the `Publisher` Application

The publisher application of our example, `PublisherApp`, is responsible for establishing a
connection and creating and delivering events through the event channel corresponding to the
five customary steps discussed in Section 18.2.2. One should store the file `Publisher-
App.java` on the publisher host in directory `\Examples\ESPush\`YourORB`\Pub-
lisher` and translate it as usual.

```java
// PublisherApp.java

import PublishSubscribe.*;
import java.util.Properties;
import org.omg.CORBA.*;
import org.omg.PortableServer.*;
import org.omg.CosNaming.*;
import org.omg.CosEventComm.*;
import org.omg.CosEventChannelAdmin.*;
import static java.lang.System.*;

public class PublisherApp {
  private ORB orb;
  private POA rootPOA;
  private void initializeORB(String[] args) {
    ... as above in Section 8.2
  }
  private void businessLogic(final PublisherImpl p_impl) {
    new Thread(new Runnable() {
      public void run() {
        for (;;) {
          int message = (int) (1000*Math.random());
          out.println("Pushing message: " + message);
          p_impl.publish(message);
          try {
            Thread.sleep(1000);
          } catch (InterruptedException ign) { }
        }
      }
    }).start();
  }
  public PublisherApp(String[] args) {
    try {
      initializeORB(args);
      new Thread(new Runnable() {
        public void run() {
          orb.run();
        }
      }).start();
      NamingContextExt nc = NamingContextExtHelper.narrow(
        orb.resolve_initial_references("NameService"));
      EventChannel ec = EventChannelHelper.narrow(
        nc.resolve_str(
          "COS/EventService/DefaultEventChannel"));
      SupplierAdmin sa = ec.for_suppliers();
      ProxyPushConsumer ppc = sa.obtain_push_consumer();
      PublisherImpl p_impl = new PublisherImpl(orb, ppc);
      Publisher p = p_impl._this(orb);
      try {
        ppc.connect_push_supplier(
          PushSupplierHelper.narrow(p));
      } catch(AlreadyConnected ex) { }
      out.println("Publisher started. Stop: Ctrl-C");
      rootPOA.the_POAManager().activate();
      businessLogic(p_impl);
```

```
      } catch (BAD_PARAM ex) {
        out.println("Narrowing failed");
        exit(3);
      } catch (Exception ex) {
        out.println("Exception: " + ex.getMessage());
        exit(1);
      }
    }
  }
  public static void main(String[] args) {
    new PublisherApp(args);
  }
}
```

When working with the JDK, the archive created according to the outline presented in Section 18.3.2 must be added to the class path; therefore, the Java compiler is invoked with the command

```
javac -classpath .;ES.jar PublisherApp.java
```

unless the archive was copied to the extensions directory.

It can be seen that the publisher application in turn executes the five steps mentioned above. Before we can begin this sequence of steps, a reference to the NS is obtained because the initial reference to the ES is looked up with the NS. CORBA does not define a standard name for the ES so step one is vendor-specific, restricting portability of the application. Open-ORB's ES provides a default EventChannel object, which can be obtained by resolving the stringified name "COS/EventService/DefaultEventChannel" with the NS.

From the event channel object, one can request a SupplierAdmin object (step two); from this, a ProxyPushConsumer object is obtained (step three). An instance of the publisher servant and the corresponding Publisher object are created. This object plays the role of a PushSupplier and is connected to the ProxyPushConsumer (step four).

A notable difference to previous examples is that the orb.run() statement is executed in its own thread; it appears earlier in the code and directly follows the ORB's initialization. The intention is, first, to prevent the publisher from trying to push events to the event channel immediately after being connected to it, possibly before the ORB is running. Second, an orb.run() statement blocks its caller, waiting for incoming requests, so there is no other way to reach the statements following it (see Section 6.2.4).

In method businessLogic(), in the for statement, each second, a new publication event is generated and published. Invoking publish() on the PublisherImpl, finally, results in an invocation of method push() on the ProxyPushConsumer (step five).

Figure 26 illustrates important method invocations of the above-described sequence of steps in the form of a UML sequence diagram. Determination of the initial references was omitted here.

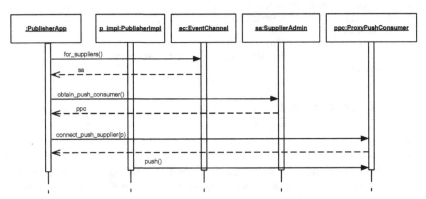

**Figure 26: UML Sequence Diagram Presenting the Steps Required in the
Publisher Application to Initiate Event Communication with the Event Channel**

18.4.4   Implementing the Event Consumer

On the consumer side of the event channel, the `Subscriber` objects wait for publication events being pushed to them. One should store the subscriber servant class, `Subscriber-Impl.java`, in directory `\Examples\ESPush\`*YourORB*`\Subscriber\Publish-Subscribe` on the subscriber hosts.

```java
// SubscriberImpl.java

package PublishSubscribe;

import static java.lang.System.*;
import org.omg.CORBA.*;
import org.omg.CosEventChannelAdmin.*;

public class SubscriberImpl extends SubscriberPOA {
  private ProxyPushSupplier pps;
  private int min, max;
  private boolean disconn = false;
  public int min() {
    return min;
  }
  public int max() {
    return max;
  }
  public SubscriberImpl(ProxyPushSupplier pps,
      int min, int max) {
    this.pps = pps;
    this.min = min;
    this.max = max;
  }
  public void push(Any message) {
    int value = message.extract_long();
    if (min > value || value > max)
      return;
```

```
      out.println("Received message: " + value);
    }
    public void disconnect_push_consumer() {
      if (disconn)
        throw new OBJECT_NOT_EXIST();
      disconn = true;
      pps.disconnect_push_supplier();
      out.println("Disconnected Subscriber");
    }
  }
```

The only remarkable feature of this implementation is that we defined the IDL interface Publisher as an IDL subinterface of CosEventComm::PushConsumer; therefore, bodies for the two methods push() and disconnect_push_consumer() have to be implemented. Note that both methods are declared in the Java interface org.omg.CosEventComm.PushConsumerOperations. The push() method is called by the event channel if new events are available. Here, we simply extract the published int value and print it if it lies in the interval [min, max] in which the subscriber is interested. Equivalent to the procedure on the supplier side of the event channel, calling disconnect_push_consumer() causes the implementation to call the disconnect_push_supplier() operation on the corresponding ProxyPushSupplier to release resources.

18.4.5 Implementing the Subscriber Application

Finally, the subscriber application remains to be implemented. It is responsible for establishing the connection on the subscriber side and for receiving events from the channel. Similar to Exercise 3 in Chapter 12, we introduce a third command-line argument that specifies the duration (in seconds) of a subscription; the time a subscriber is interested in receiving publication events.

Again, we follow the five customary steps discussed in Section 18.2.2. One should store the file SubscriberApp.java on the subscriber hosts in the directories \Examples\ES-Push\YourORB\Subscriber and translate it as usual.

```
// SubscriberApp.java

import PublishSubscribe.*;
import java.util.Properties;
import org.omg.CORBA.*;
import org.omg.PortableServer.*;
import org.omg.CosNaming.*;
import org.omg.CosEventChannelAdmin.*;
import static java.lang.System.*;
import static java.lang.Math.*;

public class SubscriberApp {
  private ORB orb;
  private POA rootPOA;
  private void initializeORB(String[] args) {
    ... as above in Section 8.2
  }
```

```java
    public SubscriberApp(String[] args) {
      try {
        int lo = Integer.valueOf(args[0]),
          hi = Integer.valueOf(args[1]);
        final int min = min(max(lo, 0), min(hi, 1000)),
          max = max(max(lo, 0), min(hi, 1000));
        initializeORB(args);
        new Thread(new Runnable() {
          public void run() {
            orb.run();
          }
        }).start();
        NamingContextExt nc = NamingContextExtHelper.narrow(
          orb.resolve_initial_references("NameService"));
        EventChannel ec = EventChannelHelper.narrow(
          nc.resolve_str(
            "COS/EventService/DefaultEventChannel"));
        ConsumerAdmin ca = ec.for_consumers();
        ProxyPushSupplier pps = ca.obtain_push_supplier();
        SubscriberImpl s_impl =
          new SubscriberImpl(pps, min, max);
        Subscriber s = s_impl._this(orb);
        try {
          pps.connect_push_consumer(s);
        }
        catch(AlreadyConnected ex) { }
        out.println("Activating Subscriber filtering with "
          + min + " and " + max);
        rootPOA.the_POAManager().activate();
        try {
          Thread.sleep(1000*Integer.valueOf(args[2]));
        } catch(InterruptedException ign) { }
        pps.disconnect_push_supplier();
        orb.shutdown(true);
      } catch(BAD_PARAM ex) {
        out.println("Narrowing failed");
        exit(3);
      } catch(Exception ex) {
        out.println("Exception: " + ex.getMessage());
        exit(1);
      }
    }
    public static void main(String[] args) {
      if (args.length < 3) {
        out.println("Start with"
          + "\n\tjrun SubscriberApp <min> <max>"
          + " <subscriptiontime> -ORBInitRef...,"
          + " 0 <= min < max <= 1000");
        return;
      }
      new SubscriberApp(args);
    }
  }
```

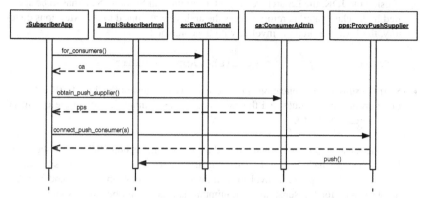

Figure 27: UML Sequence Diagram Presenting the Steps Required in the Subscriber Application to Initiate Event Communication with the Event Channel

When working with the JDK, the archive created according to the outline presented in Section 18.3.2 must be added to the class path; therefore, the Java compiler is invoked with the command

```
javac -classpath .;ES.jar SubscriberApp.java
```

unless the archive was copied to the extensions directory.

To a large extent, the structure of the application is symmetrical to the publisher application. Again, the thread construction starting `orb.run()` might deserve some explanation. Similar to the publisher application, we now want to prevent the event channel from pushing events to the subscriber before the ORB is running. Once the ORB is running, and all connections are set up, we wait until the specified subscription time expires, disconnect supplier from consumer, and terminate the application.

Figure 27 illustrates important method invocations between the objects involved on the subscriber side in the form of a UML sequence diagram (also see Figure 26).

18.4.6 Running the Application

To run and test the complete application, the different components have to be started in this order:

- Start a Naming Service. Sections 17.4.3.1–17.4.3.3 give details on how to do this for JDK, JacORB, and OpenORB.
- Start OpenORB's Event Service and direct it to the running Naming Service with the `-ORBInitRef` command-line argument as described in Section 18.3.1.
- Start the publisher application in the usual way with any of the three ORBs. Provide the reference to the Naming Service with an `-ORBInitRef` command-line argument.

If using the JDK, the ES archive created as outlined in Section 18.3.2 has to be specified in the class path; therefore, unless the archive was copied to the extensions directory, the Java interpreter is invoked with the command

```
javac -cp .;ES.jar PublisherApp -ORBInitRef...
```

- Start the subscriber applications in the usual way with any of the three ORBs. Provide
  the min and max values and the reference to the Naming Service in the command
  line (-ORBInitRef).

  If using the JDK, the ES archive created as outlined in Section 18.3.2 has to be specified in the class path; therefore, unless the archive was copied to the extensions directory, the Java interpreter is invoked with the following command (0, 99, and 5 are example values for the subscriber's minimum and maximum boundaries and the subscription time)

  ```
  javac -cp .;ES.jar SubscriberApp 0 99 5 -ORBInitRef...
  ```

All four components of the application can run on different hosts on the network. The object
references are determined and provided by the NS as needed. For our applications, we normally use one dedicated host that runs all CORBAservices.

18.5   Exercises

1. Once the ES is running, use JacORB's lsns utility to see which ES-related objects are
   provided and how they are named (see Section 17.5.1).

2. Experiment with the push-style Publish-Subscribe example. What happens if the subscriber needs some time to digest the events it receives? You might, for example, include
   a Thread.sleep(1500) or a Thread.sleep(2500) statement in the SubscriberImpl's push() method.

3. Write a new version of the Publish-Subscribe example implementing a pure pull model.
   Now, only the ES interfaces shaded in grey in Figure 28 are of significance.

   In the SubscriberImpl, declare a method receive() that pulls an Any from the
   ProxyPullSupplier and prints the received event value. In the Subscriber-
   App's businessLogic(), actively call receive() continually, for example, once
   per second.

   In the PublisherImpl, one has to provide implementations for the methods pull()
   and try_pull() that the event channel needs to call. Similar to the push example, one
   might return a random int value from pull(). And, for the try_pull() method,
   we suggest an implementation that simply sets the holder.value to true and returns the result of a pull() invocation. In the PublisherApp, it is sufficient to connect the publisher to the proxy pull consumer.

4. Experiment with the pull-style Publish-Subscribe example. What happens if the publisher needs some time to prepare the events it publishes? You might, for example, include a `Thread.sleep(500)` or a `Thread.sleep(1500)` statement in the `Publisher-Impl`'s `pull()` method.

5. Write a new version of the Publish-Subscribe example implementing a hybrid pull/push model. In this version, the `Publisher` acts as a `PullSupplier` while `Subscribers` act as a `PushConsumers`. Recycle as much as possible from earlier implementations.

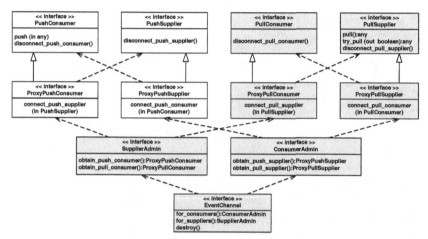

**Figure 28: Interfaces of the Event Service
Needed in a Pure Pull Model Implementation**

Appendix A – IDL Grammar

(1) <specification> ::= <import>* <definition>+
(2) <definition> ::= <type_dcl> ";"
             | <const_dcl> ";"
             | <except_dcl> ";"
             | <interface> ";"
             | <module> ";"
             | <value> ";"
             | <type_id_dcl> ";"
             | <type_prefix_dcl> ";"
             | <event> ";"
             | <component> ";"
             | <home_dcl> ";"
(3) <module> ::= "module" <identifier> "{" <definition>+ "}"
(4) <interface> ::= <interface_dcl>
             | <forward_dcl>
(5) <interface_dcl> ::= <interface_header> "{" <interface_body> "}"
(6) <forward_dcl> ::= ["abstract" | "local"] "interface" <identifier>
(7) <interface_header> ::= ["abstract" | "local"] "interface" <identifier>
     [<interface_inheritance_spec>]
(8) <interface_body> ::= <export>*
(9) <export> ::= <type_dcl> ";"
           | <const_dcl> ";"
           | <except_dcl> ";"
           | <attr_dcl> ";"
           | <op_dcl> ";"
           | <type_id_dcl> ";"
           | <type_prefix_dcl> ";"
(10) <interface_inheritance_spec> ::= ":" <interface_name>
            { "," <interface_name> }*
(11) <interface_name> ::= <scoped_name>
(12) <scoped_name> ::= <identifier>
            | "::" <identifier>
            | <scoped_name> "::" <identifier>
(13) <value> ::= (<value_dcl> | <value_abs_dcl>
       | <value_box_dcl> | <value_forward_dcl>)
(14) <value_forward_dcl> ::= ["abstract"] "valuetype" <identifier>
(15) <value_box_dcl> ::= "valuetype" <identifier> <type_spec>
(16) <value_abs_dcl> ::= "abstract" "valuetype" <identifier>
            [<value_inheritance_spec>]
            "{" <export>* "}"
(17) <value_dcl> ::= <value_header> "{" <value_element>* "}"
(18) <value_header> ::= ["custom"] "valuetype" <identifier>
            [<value_inheritance_spec>]
(19) <value_inheritance_spec> ::= [":" ["truncatable"] <value_name>
            { "," <value_name> }*]

```
                                   [ "supports" <interface_name>
                                   { "," <interface_name> }* ]
(20) <value_name> ::= <scoped_name>
(21) <value_element> ::= <export> | < state_member> | <init_dcl>
(22) <state_member> ::= ( "public" | "private" )
                        <type_spec> <declarators> ";"
(23) <init_dcl> ::= "factory" <identifier>
                    "(" [ <init_param_decls> ] ")"
                    [ <raises_expr> ] ";"
(24) <init_param_decls> ::= <init_param_decl> { "," <init_param_decl> }*
(25) <init_param_decl> ::= <init_param_attribute> <param_type_spec>
                          <simple_declarator>
(26) <init_param_attribute> ::= "in"
(27) <const_dcl> ::= "const" <const_type>
                     <identifier> "=" <const_exp>
(28) <const_type> ::= <integer_type>
                    | <char_type>
                    | <wide_char_type>
                    | <boolean_type>
                    | <floating_pt_type>
                    | <string_type>
                    | <wide_string_type>
                    | <fixed_pt_const_type>
                    | <scoped_name>
                    | <octet_type>
(29) <const_exp> ::= <or_expr>
(30) <or_expr> ::= <xor_expr>
                 | <or_expr> "|" <xor_expr>
(31) <xor_expr> ::= <and_expr>
                  | <xor_expr> "^" <and_expr>
(32) <and_expr> ::= <shift_expr>
                  | <and_expr> "&" <shift_expr>
(33) <shift_expr> ::= <add_expr>
                    | <shift_expr> ">>" <add_expr>
                    | <shift_expr> "<<" <add_expr>
(34) <add_expr> ::= <mult_expr>
                  | <add_expr> "+" <mult_expr>
                  | <add_expr> "-" <mult_expr>
(35) <mult_expr> ::= <unary_expr>
                   | <mult_expr> "*" <unary_expr>
                   | <mult_expr> "/" <unary_expr>
                   | <mult_expr> "%" <unary_expr>
(36) <unary_expr> ::= <unary_operator> <primary_expr>
                    | <primary_expr>
(37) <unary_operator> ::= "-"
                        | "+"
                        | "~"
(38) <primary_expr> ::= <scoped_name>
                      | <literal>
                      | "(" <const_exp> ")"
(39) <literal> ::= <integer_literal>
                 | <string_literal>
```

```
                 | <wide_string_literal>
                 | <character_literal>
                 | <wide_character_literal>
                 | <fixed_pt_literal>
                 | <floating_pt_literal>
                 | <boolean_literal>
(40) <boolean_literal> ::= "TRUE"
                 | "FALSE"
(41) <positive_int_const> ::= <const_exp>
(42) <type_dcl> ::= "typedef" <type_declarator>
                       | <struct_type>
                       | <union_type>
                       | <enum_type>
                       | "native" <simple_declarator>
                       | <constr_forward_decl>
(43) <type_declarator> ::= <type_spec> <declarators>
(44) <type_spec> ::= <simple_type_spec>
                         | <constr_type_spec>
(45) <simple_type_spec> ::= <base_type_spec>
                                 | <template_type_spec>
                                 | <scoped_name>
(46) <base_type_spec> ::= <floating_pt_type>
                               | <integer_type>
                               | <char_type>
                               | <wide_char_type>
                               | <boolean_type>
                               | <octet_type>
                               | <any_type>
                               | <object_type>
                               | <value_base_type>
(47) <template_type_spec> ::= <sequence_type>
                                   | <string_type>
                                   | <wide_string_type>
                                   | <fixed_pt_type>
(48) <constr_type_spec> ::= <struct_type>
                                 | <union_type>
                                 | <enum_type>
(49) <declarators> ::= <declarator> { "," <declarator> }*
(50) <declarator> ::= <simple_declarator>
                       | <complex_declarator>
(51) <simple_declarator> ::= <identifier>
(52) <complex_declarator> ::= <array_declarator>
(53) <floating_pt_type> ::= "float"
                               | "double"
                               | "long" "double"
(54) <integer_type> ::= <signed_int>
                            | <unsigned_int>
(55) <signed_int> ::= <signed_short_int>
                         | <signed_long_int>
                         | <signed_longlong_int>
(56) <signed_short_int> ::= "short"
(57) <signed_long_int> ::= "long"
```

(58) <signed_longlong_int> ::= "long" "long"
(59) <unsigned_int> ::= <unsigned_short_int>
                      | <unsigned_long_int>
                      | <unsigned_longlong_int>
(60) <unsigned_short_int> ::= "unsigned" "short"
(61) <unsigned_long_int> ::= "unsigned" "long"
(62) <unsigned_longlong_int> ::= "unsigned" "long" "long"
(63) <char_type> ::= "char"
(64) <wide_char_type> ::= "wchar"
(65) <boolean_type> ::= "boolean"
(66) <octet_type> ::= "octet"
(67) <any_type> ::= "any"
(68) <object_type> ::= "Object"
(69) <struct_type> ::= "struct" <identifier> "{" <member_list> "}"
(70) <member_list> ::= <member>+
(71) <member> ::= <type_spec> <declarators> ";"
(72) <union_type> ::= "union" <identifier> "switch"
                      ("" <switch_type_spec> ")"
                      "{" <switch_body> "}"
(73) <switch_type_spec> ::= <integer_type>
                          | <char_type>
                          | <boolean_type>
                          | <enum_type>
                          | <scoped_name>
(74) <switch_body> ::= <case>+
(75) <case> ::= <case_label>+ <element_spec> ";"
(76) <case_label> ::= "case" <const_exp> ":"
                    | "default" ":"
(77) <element_spec> ::= <type_spec> <declarator>
(78) <enum_type> ::= "enum" <identifier>
                     "{" <enumerator> { "," <enumerator> }* "}"
(79) <enumerator> ::= <identifier>
(80) <sequence_type> ::= "sequence" "<" <simple_type_spec> ","
                         <positive_int_const> ">"
                       | "sequence" "<" <simple_type_spec> ">"
(81) <string_type> ::= "string" "<" <positive_int_const> ">"
                     | "string"
(82) <wide_string_type> ::= "wstring" "<" <positive_int_const> ">"
                          | "wstring"
(83) <array_declarator> ::= <identifier> <fixed_array_size>+
(84) <fixed_array_size> ::= "[" <positive_int_const> "]"
(85) <attr_dcl> ::= <readonly_attr_spec>
                  | <attr_spec>
(86) <except_dcl> ::= "exception" <identifier> "{" <member>* "}"
(87) <op_dcl> ::= [<op_attribute>] <op_type_spec>
                  <identifier> <parameter_dcls>
                  [<raises_expr>] [<context_expr>]
(88) <op_attribute> ::= "oneway"
(89) <op_type_spec> ::= <param_type_spec>
                      | "void"
(90) <parameter_dcls> ::= "(" <param_dcl> { "," <param_dcl> }* ")"
                        | "(" ")"

(91) <param_dcl> ::= <param_attribute> <param_type_spec>
                          <simple_declarator>
(92) <param_attribute> ::= "in"
                          | "out"
                          | "inout"
(93) <raises_expr> ::= "raises" "(" <scoped_name>
                          { "," <scoped_name> }* ")"
(94) <context_expr> ::= "context" "(" <string_literal>
                          { "," <string_literal> }* ")"
(95) <param_type_spec> ::= <base_type_spec>
                          | <string_type>
                          | <wide_string_type>
                          | <scoped_name>
(96) <fixed_pt_type> ::= "fixed" "<" <positive_int_const> ","
                          <positive_int_const> ">"
(97) <fixed_pt_const_type> ::= "fixed"
(98) <value_base_type> ::= "ValueBase"
(99) <constr_forward_decl> ::= "struct" <identifier>
                          | "union" <identifier>
(100) <import> ::= "import" <imported_scope> ";"
(101) <imported_scope> ::= <scoped_name> | <string_literal>
(102) <type_id_dcl> ::= "typeid" <scoped_name> <string_literal>
(103) <type_prefix_dcl> ::= "typeprefix" <scoped_name>
                          <string_literal>
(104) <readonly_attr_spec> ::= "readonly" "attribute" <param_type_spec>
                          <readonly_attr_declarator>
(105) <readonly_attr_declarator > ::= <simple_declarator> <raises_expr>
                          | <simple_declarator>
                          { "," <simple_declarator> }*
(106) <attr_spec> ::= "attribute" <param_type_spec>
                          <attr_declarator>
(107) <attr_declarator> ::= <simple_declarator> <attr_raises_expr>
                          | <simple_declarator>
                          { "," <simple_declarator> }*
(108) <attr_raises_expr> ::= <get_excep_expr> [<set_excep_expr>]
                          | <set_excep_expr>
(109) <get_excep_expr> ::= "getraises" <exception_list>
(110) <set_excep_expr> ::= "setraises" <exception_list>
(111) <exception_list> ::= "(" <scoped_name>
                          { "," <scoped_name> }* ")"

Note – Grammar rules 1 through 111 with the exception of the last three lines
of rule 2 constitutes the portion of IDL that is not related to components.

(112) <component> ::= <component_dcl>
                          | <component_forward_dcl>
(113) <component_forward_dcl> ::= "component" <identifier>
(114) <component_dcl> ::= <component_header>
                          "{" <component_body> "}"

(115) <component_header> ::= "component" <identifier>
                            [<component_inheritance_spec>]
                            [<supported_interface_spec>]
(116) <supported_interface_spec> ::= "supports" <scoped_name>
                            { "," <scoped_name> }*
(117) <component_inheritance_spec> ::= ":" <scoped_name>
(118) <component_body> ::= <component_export>*
(119) <component_export> ::= <provides_dcl> ";"
                            | <uses_dcl> ";"
                            | <emits_dcl> ";"
                            | <publishes_dcl> ";"
                            | <consumes_dcl> ";"
                            | <attr_dcl> ";"
(120) <provides_dcl> ::= "provides" <interface_type> <identifier>
(121) <interface_type> ::= <scoped_name>
                            | "Object"
(122) <uses_dcl> ::= "uses" ["multiple"]
                            <interface_type> <identifier>
(123) <emits_dcl> ::= "emits" <scoped_name> <identifier>
(124) <publishes_dcl> ::= "publishes" <scoped_name> <identifier>
(125) <consumes_dcl> ::= "consumes" <scoped_name> <identifier>
(126) <home_dcl> ::= <home_header> <home_body>
(127) <home_header> ::= "home" <identifier>
        [<home_inheritance_spec>]
        [<supported_interface_spec>]
        "manages" <scoped_name>
        [<primary_key_spec>]
(128) <home_inheritance_spec> ::= ":" <scoped_name>
(129) <primary_key_spec> ::= "primarykey" <scoped_name>
(130) <home_body> ::= "{" <home_export>* "}"
(131) <home_export ::= <export>
                            | <factory_dcl> ";"
                            | <finder_dcl> ";"
(132) <factory_dcl> ::= "factory" <identifier>
                            "(" [<init_param_decls>] ")"
                            [<raises_expr>]
(133) <finder_dcl> ::= "finder" <identifier>
                            "(" [<init_param_decls>] ")"
                            [<raises_expr>]
(134) <event> ::= (<event_dcl> | <event_abs_dcl> |
                            <event_forward_dcl>)
(135) <event_forward_dcl> ::= ["abstract"] "eventtype" <identifier>
(136) <event_abs_dcl> ::= "abstract" "eventtype" <identifier>
                            [<value_inheritance_spec>]
                            "{" <export>* "}"
(137) <event_dcl> ::= <event_header> "{" <value_element>* "}"
(138) <event_header> ::= ["custom"] "eventtype"
                            <identifier> [<value_inheritance_spec>]

Appendix B – IDL to Java: Mapping of IDL Standard Exceptions

IDL Exception	Java Class Name
CORBA::UNKNOWN	org.omg.CORBA.UNKNOWN
CORBA::BAD_PARAM	org.omg.CORBA.BAD_PARAM
CORBA::NO_MEMORY	org.omg.CORBA.NO_MEMORY
CORBA::IMP_LIMIT	org.omg.CORBA.IMP_LIMIT
CORBA::COMM_FAILURE	org.omg.CORBA.COMM_FAILURE
CORBA::INV_OBJREF	org.omg.CORBA.INV_OBJREF
CORBA::NO_PERMISSION	org.omg.CORBA.NO_PERMISSION
CORBA::INTERNAL	org.omg.CORBA.INTERNAL
CORBA::MARSHAL	org.omg.CORBA.MARSHAL
CORBA::INITIALIZE	org.omg.CORBA.INITIALIZE
CORBA::NO_IMPLEMENT	org.omg.CORBA.NO_IMPLEMENT
CORBA::BAD_TYPECODE	org.omg.CORBA.BAD_TYPECODE
CORBA::BAD_OPERATION	org.omg.CORBA.BAD_OPERATION
CORBA::NO_RESOURCES	org.omg.CORBA.NO_RESOURCES
CORBA::NO_RESPONSE	org.omg.CORBA.NO_RESPONSE
CORBA::PERSIST_STORE	org.omg.CORBA.PERSIST_STORE
CORBA::BAD_INV_ORDER	org.omg.CORBA.BAD_INV_ORDER
CORBA::TRANSIENT	org.omg.CORBA.TRANSIENT
CORBA::FREE_MEM	org.omg.CORBA.FREE_MEM
CORBA::INV_IDENT	org.omg.CORBA.INV_IDENT
CORBA::INV_FLAG	org.omg.CORBA.INV_FLAG
CORBA::INTF_REPOS	org.omg.CORBA.INTF_REPOS
CORBA::BAD_CONTEXT	org.omg.CORBA.BAD_CONTEXT
CORBA::OBJ_ADAPTER	org.omg.CORBA.OBJ_ADAPTER
CORBA::DATA_CONVERSION	org.omg.CORBA.DATA_CONVERSION
CORBA::OBJECT_NOT_EXIST	org.omg.CORBA.OBJECT_NOT_EXIST
CORBA::TRANSACTION_REQUIRED	org.omg.CORBA.TRANSACTION_REQUIRED
CORBA::TRANSACTION_ROLLEDBACK	org.omg.CORBA.TRANSACTION_ROLLEDBACK
CORBA::INVALID_TRANSACTION	org.omg.CORBA.INVALID_TRANSACTION
CORBA::INV_POLICY	org.omg.CORBA.INV_POLICY
CORBA::CODESET_INCOMPATIBLE	org.omg.CORBA.CODESET_INCOMPATIBLE
CORBA::TRANSACTION_MODE	org.omg.CORBA.TRANSACTION_MODE
CORBA::TRANSACTION_UNAVAILABLE	org.omg.CORBA.TRANSACTION_UNAVAILABLE
CORBA::REBIND	org.omg.CORBA.REBIND
CORBA::TIMEOUT	org.omg.CORBA.TIMEOUT
CORBA::BAD_QOS	org.omg.CORBA.BAD_QOS

Appendix C – Naming Service IDL

```
// CosNaming.idl
#ifndef _COSNAMING_IDL_
#define _COSNAMING_IDL_
#pragma prefix "omg.org"
module CosNaming
{
  typedef string Istring;
  struct NameComponent
  {
    Istring id;
    Istring kind;
  };
  typedef sequence<NameComponent> Name;

  enum BindingType { nobject, ncontext };

  struct Binding
  {
    Name binding_name;
    BindingType binding_type;
  };
  // Note: In struct Binding, binding_name is incorrectly
  // defined as a Name instead of a NameComponent. This
  // definition is unchanged for compatibility reasons.
  typedef sequence <Binding> BindingList;

  interface BindingIterator;
  interface NamingContext
  {
    enum NotFoundReason
    {
      missing_node, not_context, not_object
    };
    exception NotFound
    {
      NotFoundReason why;
      Name rest_of_name;
    };
    exception CannotProceed
    {
      NamingContext cxt;
      Name rest_of_name;
    };
    exception InvalidName{};
    exception AlreadyBound {};

    exception NotEmpty{};

    void bind(in Name n, in Object obj)
```

```
        raises(NotFound, CannotProceed,
        InvalidName, AlreadyBound);
      void rebind(in Name n, in Object obj)
        raises(NotFound, CannotProceed, InvalidName);
      void bind_context(in Name n, in NamingContext nc)
        raises(NotFound, CannotProceed,
        InvalidName, AlreadyBound);
      void rebind_context(in Name n, in NamingContext nc)
        raises(NotFound, CannotProceed, InvalidName);
       Object resolve(in Name n)
        raises(NotFound, CannotProceed, InvalidName);
      void unbind(in Name n)
        raises(NotFound, CannotProceed, InvalidName);
      NamingContext new_context();
      NamingContext bind_new_context(in Name n)
        raises(NotFound, AlreadyBound,
        CannotProceed, InvalidName);
      void destroy() raises(NotEmpty);
      void list(in unsigned long how_many,
        out BindingList bl, out BindingIterator bi);
    };
    interface BindingIterator
    {
      boolean next_one(out Binding b);
      boolean next_n(in unsigned long how_many,
        out BindingList bl);
      void destroy();
    };
    interface NamingContextExt: NamingContext
    {
      typedef string StringName;
      typedef string Address;
      typedef string URLString;
      StringName to_string(in Name n) raises(InvalidName);
      Name to_name(in StringName sn) raises(InvalidName);
      exception InvalidAddress {};
      URLString to_url(in Address addr, in StringName sn)
        raises(InvalidAddress, InvalidName);
      Object resolve_str(in StringName n)
        raises(NotFound, CannotProceed, InvalidName);
    };
};
#endif // _COSNAMING_IDL_
```

Appendix D – Event Service IDL

```
// CosEventComm.idl
#ifndef _COS_EVENT_COMM_IDL_
#define _COS_EVENT_COMM_IDL_
#pragma prefix "omg.org"
module CosEventComm
{
  exception Disconnected{};
  interface PushConsumer
  {
    void push(in any data) raises(Disconnected);
    void disconnect_push_consumer();
  };
  interface PushSupplier
  {
    void disconnect_push_supplier();
  };
  interface PullSupplier
  {
    any pull() raises(Disconnected);
    any try_pull(out boolean has_event)
      raises(Disconnected);
    void disconnect_pull_supplier();
  };
  interface PullConsumer
  {
    void disconnect_pull_consumer();
  };
};
#endif


// CosEventChannelAdmin.idl
#ifndef _COS_EVENT_CHANNEL_ADMIN_IDL_
#define _COS_EVENT_CHANNEL_ADMIN_IDL_
#include <CosEventComm.idl>
#pragma prefix "omg.org"
module CosEventChannelAdmin
{
  exception AlreadyConnected {};
  exception TypeError {};
  interface ProxyPushConsumer: CosEventComm::PushConsumer
  {
    void connect_push_supplier(
      in CosEventComm::PushSupplier push_supplier)
      raises(AlreadyConnected);
  };
  interface ProxyPullSupplier: CosEventComm::PullSupplier
  {
    void connect_pull_consumer(
```

```
          in CosEventComm::PullConsumer pull_consumer)
          raises(AlreadyConnected);
  };
  interface ProxyPullConsumer: CosEventComm::PullConsumer
  {
     void connect_pull_supplier(
        in CosEventComm::PullSupplier pull_supplier)
        raises(AlreadyConnected,TypeError);
     };
  interface ProxyPushSupplier: CosEventComm::PushSupplier
  {
     void connect_push_consumer(
        in CosEventComm::PushConsumer push_consumer)
        raises(AlreadyConnected, TypeError);
  };
  interface ConsumerAdmin
  {
     ProxyPushSupplier obtain_push_supplier();
     ProxyPullSupplier obtain_pull_supplier();
  };
  interface SupplierAdmin
  {
     ProxyPushConsumer obtain_push_consumer();
     ProxyPullConsumer obtain_pull_consumer();
  };
  interface EventChannel
  {
     ConsumerAdmin for_consumers();
     SupplierAdmin for_suppliers();
     void destroy();
  };
};
#endif
```

Appendix E – ORB Product Installation

We assume in the following that the Java 2 Platform Standard Edition 5.0 (J2SE 5.0) is installed on the system. Since the JDK ORB is part of the J2SE distribution, it is automatically installed and ready if the J2SE is properly installed. Should assistance be needed with this, please refer to Sun's Website with the URL http://java.sun.com/j2se/1.5.0/.

How to Install and Configure OpenORB-1.3.1 on Windows

Download:

- URL: http://openorb.sourceforge.net/downloads.html

- Click on "Download" for OpenORB "Release 1.3.1".

- Download the following files:

    o OpenORB-1.3.1.zip (in section "OpenORB")
    o NamingService-1.3.1.zip (in section "NamingService")
    o PersistantStateService-1.3.0.zip (in section "PersistentStateService")
    o EventService-1.3.0.zip (in section "EventService")

Installation:

- Unpack OpenORB-1.3.1.zip. It creates a directory OpenORB-1.3.1.

- Unpack the remaining files to OpenORB-1.3.1, automatically creating subdirectories.

- Create a new folder bin in directory OpenORB-1.3.1, which is needed later for several startup scripts when we implement and test our examples throughout the book. The resulting folder structure should look as follows:

        OpenORB-1.3.1
        ➤ bin
        ➤ config
        ➤ doc
        ➤ EventService-1.3.0
        ➤ examples
        ➤ idl
        ➤ lib
        ➤ NamingService-1.3.1
        ➤ PersistantStateService-1.3.0
        ➤ test

- Preparing the ORB batch file:

    o Create a new file idl.bat in folder OpenORB-1-3-1/bin containing the
      following line of code (Attention: it must be just one single line!):

```
java -cp
 "%OPENORB_DIR%\lib\openorb_tools-1.3.1.jar;
%OPENORB_DIR%\lib\xerces.jar;
%OPENORB_DIR%\lib\openorb-1.3.1.jar;
%OPENORB_DIR%\lib\junit.jar;
%OPENORB_DIR%\lib\logkit.jar;
%OPENORB_DIR%\lib\excalibur-configuration.jar;
%OPENORB_DIR%\lib\avalon-framework.jar;."
 org.openorb.compiler.IdlCompiler %*
```

- Preparing the Naming Service:

    o Copy all .jar archives from directories

```
OpenORB-1.3.1/NamingService-1.3.1/lib and
OpenORB-1.3.1/PersistantStateService-1.3.0/lib
```

    to directory

```
OpenORB-1.3.1/lib
```

    o Create a new file nameserv.bat in folder OpenORB-1-3-1/bin containing
      the following line of code (Attention: it must be just one single line!):

```
java -cp
 "%OPENORB_DIR%\lib\openorb_tools-1.3.1.jar;
%OPENORB_DIR%\lib\xerces.jar;
%OPENORB_DIR%\lib\openorb-1.3.1.jar;
%OPENORB_DIR%\lib\logkit.jar;
%OPENORB_DIR%\lib\avalon-framework.jar;
%OPENORB_DIR%\lib\openorb_ins-1.3.1.jar;
%OPENORB_DIR%\lib\openorb_ins_plugins-1.3.1.jar;
%OPENORB_DIR%\lib\openorb_tns-1.3.1.jar;
%OPENORB_DIR%\lib\openorb_pss-1.3.0.jar;
%JDK_DIR%\jre\lib\rt.jar"
 -Xbootclasspath:
"%OPENORB_DIR%\lib\openorb_tools-1.3.1.jar;
%OPENORB_DIR%\lib\xerces.jar;
%OPENORB_DIR%\lib\openorb-1.3.1.jar;
%OPENORB_DIR%\lib\logkit.jar;
%OPENORB_DIR%\lib\avalon-framework.jar;
%OPENORB_DIR%\lib\openorb_ins-1.3.1.jar;
%OPENORB_DIR%\lib\openorb_ins_plugins-1.3.1.jar;
%OPENORB_DIR%\lib\openorb_tns-1.3.1.jar;
%OPENORB_DIR%\lib\openorb_pss-1.3.0.jar;
%JDK_DIR%\jre\lib\rt.jar"
 org.openorb.ins.Server %*
```

- Preparing the Event Service:

  o Copy all .jar archives from directory

    `OpenORB-1.3.1/EventService-1.3.0/lib`

  to directory

    `OpenORB-1.3.1/lib`

  o Create a new file `eventserv.bat` in folder `OpenORB-1-3-1/bin` containing the following line of code (Attention: it must be just one single line!):

```
java -cp
  "%OPENORB_DIR%\lib\openorb_tools-1.3.1.jar;
%OPENORB_DIR%\lib\xerces.jar;
%OPENORB_DIR%\lib\openorb-1.3.1.jar;
%OPENORB_DIR%\lib\logkit.jar;
%OPENORB_DIR%\lib\avalon-framework.jar;
%OPENORB_DIR%\lib\openorb_event-1.3.0.jar;
%OPENORB_DIR%\lib\openorb_pss-1.3.0.jar;
%JDK_DIR%\jre\lib\rt.jar"
  -Xbootclasspath:
  "%OPENORB_DIR%\lib\openorb_tools-1.3.1.jar;
%OPENORB_DIR%\lib\xerces.jar;
%OPENORB_DIR%\lib\openorb-1.3.1.jar;
%OPENORB_DIR%\lib\logkit.jar;
%OPENORB_DIR%\lib\avalon-framework.jar;
%OPENORB_DIR%\lib\openorb_event-1.3.0.jar;
%OPENORB_DIR%\lib\openorb_pss-1.3.0.jar;
%JDK_DIR%\jre\lib\rt.jar"
  org.openorb.event.Server %*
```

How to Install and Configure JacORB_2_2_1 on Windows

Download:

- If not installed already, download Ant:

  o `http://ant.apache.org/bindownload.cgi`
  o Download file `apache-ant-1.6.2-bin.zip`.
  o Unpack the file. It creates a subdirectory `apache-ant-1.6.2`.

- URL: `http://www.jacorb.org/download.html`

- Click "Full version with source code (Zip format)" .

  o Download file `JacORB_2_2_1-full.zip`.
  o Create a directory `JacORB_2_2_1`.
  o Unpack the downloaded file to the new directory.

Installation:

- Setting environment variables for Ant:

  - o Open a command line window and set the following environment variables (At-
    tention: Modify the paths in the first and second command according to your spe-
    cific system environment!):

    ```
    set ANT_HOME=C:\apache-ant-1.6.2
    set JAVA_HOME=C:\jdk1.5.0_01
    set PATH=%PATH%;%ANT_HOME%\bin
    ```

- Go to directory JacORB_2_2_1

- Execute Ant by typing ant in the command line window at hitting enter. The required
  JacORB files are now automatically built.

Acronyms

API	Application Programming Interface
BOA	Basic Object Adapter
CCM	CORBA Component Model
CDR	Common Data Representation
COM+	Component Object Model Plus
CORBA	Common Object Request Broker Architecture
DCE	Distributed Computing Environment
DCOM	Distributed Component Object Model
DII	CORBA Dynamic Invocation Interface
DSI	Dynamic Skeleton Interface
EBNF	Extended Backus Naur Format
ES	Event Service
ESIOP	Environment-Specific Inter-ORB Protocol
FTP	File Transfer Protocol
GIOP	General Inter-ORB Protocol
HTTP	Hypertext Transfer Protocol
IDL	Interface Definition Language
IEEE	Institute of Electrical and Electronics Engineers
IIOP	Internet Inter-ORB Protocol
INS	Interoperable Naming Service
IOR	Interoperable Object Reference
IP	Internet Protocol
IR	Interface Repository
ISO	International Standards Organization
J2EE	Java 2 Platform, Enterprise Edition
JDK	Java Development Kit
MOM	Message-Oriented Middleware
NS	Naming Service
OMA	Object Management Architecture
OMG	Object Management Group
ORB	Object Request Broker
OSF	Open Software Foundation
PIDL	Pseudo-IDL
POA	Portable Object Adapter
RMI	Remote Method Invocation
RPC	Remote Procedure Call
TCP/IP	Transmission Control Protocol/Internet Protocol
UDP	User Datagram Protocol
UML	Unified Modeling Language
URL	Universal Resource Locator
WWW	World Wide Web

References

[BMRS96]   Buschmann, F., Meunier, R., Rohnert, H., Sommerlad, P., Stal, M. (1996): Pattern-Oriented Software Architecture—A System of Patterns. John Wiley & Sons, Chichester

[Bolt02]   Bolton, F. (2002): Pure CORBA—A Code-Intensive Premium Reference. SAMS Publishing, USA

[Emme00]   Emmerich, W. (2000): Engineering Distributed Objects. John Wiley & Sons, Chichester

[GHJV95]   Gamma, E., Helm, R., Johnson, R., Vlissides, J. (1995): Design Patterns: Elements of Reusable Object-Oriented Software. Addison-Wesley Longman

[GJS96]   Gosling, J., Joy, B., Steele, G. (1996): The Java Language Specification, First Edition. Addison-Wesley, Online-Version: http://java.sun.com/docs/books/jls/index.html

[KJ04]   Kircher, M., Jain, P. (2004): Pattern-Oriented Software Architecture, Vol.3 : Patterns for Resource Management. John Wiley & Sons, Chichester

[Linn98]   Linnhoff-Popien, C. (1998): CORBA – Kommunikation und Management. Springer-Verlag, Berlin

[MM97]   Mowbray, T. und R. Malveau (1997): CORBA Desing Patterns. In: John Wiley & Sons, Chichester

[OMG01]   Object Management Group (2001): Event Service Specification. OMG Technical Document Number formal/01-03-01, URL: ftp://ftp.omg.org/pub/docs/formal/01-03-01.pdf

[OMG02]   Object Management Group (2002): IDL to Java Language Mapping Specification. Version 1.2, OMG Technical Document formal/02-08-05

[OMG03a]   Object Management Group (2003): Object Transaction Service Specification. Version 1.4, OMG Technical Document Number formal/03-09-02, URL: http://www.omg.org/cgi-bin/doc?formal/03-09-02

[OMG03b]   Object Management Group (2003): OMG Unified Modeling Language Specification. Version 1.5, OMG Technical Document Number formal/03-03-01, URL: http://www.omg.org/cgi-bin/doc?formal/03-03-01

[OMG04a]   Object Management Group (2004): Naming Service Specification. Version 1.3, OMG Technical Document Number formal/04-10-03, URL: http://www.omg.org/cgi-bin/doc?formal/04-10-03

[OMG04b]   Object Management Group (2004): Notification Service Specification. Version 1.1, OMG Technical Document Number formal/04-10-13, URL: http://www.omg.org/cgi-bin/doc?formal/04-10-13

[OMG04c]   Object Management Group (2004): The Common Object Request Broker: Architecture and Specification. Version 3.0.3, OMG Technical Document Number formal/04-03-12, URL: ftp://ftp.omg.org/pub/docs/formal/04-03-12.pdf

[OMG98]   Object Management Group (1998): OMG IDL Style Guide. OMG Technical Document Number ab/98-06-03

Index